THE GUINNESS
EUROPEAN
DATA BOOK

GUINNESS PUBLISHING

Editor: Clive Carpenter
Systems support: Kathy Milligan
Layout: Robert and Rhoda Burns
Cover Design: Ad Vantage Studios/Robert and Rhoda Burns
Artwork, maps and diagrams: Robert and Rhoda Burns, Eddie
Botchway
Contributors: Clive Carpenter; Dr David Dyker, University of
Sussex; Garth Owen Hughes, The University College of Wales
Aberystwyth; Dr Christopher Pass, University of Bradford;
Frank Riess

1st Edition
First published 1994
Reprint 10 9 8 7 6 5 4 3 2 1 0

Published in Great Britain by Guinness Publishing Ltd.,
33 London Road, Enfield, Middlesex

Colour origination by Master Images Pte Ltd., Singapore
Printed and bound in Italy by New Interlitho SpA, Milan

British Library Cataloguing in Publication Data
The Guinness European Data Book
1. World Statistics
910.21

ISBN 085112-523-9

CONTENTS

CENTRAL AND EASTERN EUROPE

EUROPE

THE CONTINENT OF EUROPE

Area: 10 505 000 km² (4 056 000 sq mi).
Greatest extent: 4340 km (2700 mi).

Russia, which straddles the divide between Europe and Asia, does not recognize a dividing line between the two continents. However, a boundary running along the eastern foot of the Ural Mountains and following the boundary of Kazakhstan to the Caspian Sea is generally recognized as Europe's eastern limit.

The boundary between Europe and Asia in the Caucasus is disputed. Some authorities recognize the crest of the Caucasus Mountains – which is for the most part the southern boundary of Russia – as the dividing line, while others prefer a boundary following the valley of the River Manych to the estuary of the River Don. For convenience, the political boundary between Russia to the north and Georgia and Azerbaijan to the south is often used as the southern limit of Europe in the Caucasus.

Physically, Europe excludes Asiatic Turkey, thus dividing the city of Istanbul between two continents. However, the entire country of Turkey is usually regarded as part of Europe for social, economic and political purposes, and Turkey enjoys membership of various European organizations including the Council of Europe (see p. 17). Cyprus, which strictly speaking is an attendant island to Asia, is also generally included in Europe.

The islands of Madeira, the Azores and the Canary Islands – although strictly attendant islands to Africa – are almost always included in Europe.

MOUNTAIN RANGES OF EUROPE

Mountain range and its length	Countries	Highest point
Ural Mountains 2000 km (1250 mi)	Russia	Gora Narodnaya 1894 m (6214 ft)
Scandinavian Range 1530 km (950 mi)	Norway/Sweden	Galdhoppigen 2469 m (8098 ft)
Carpathian Mountains 1450 km (900 mi)	Czech Republic/ Poland/Slovakia/ Ukraine/Romania	Gerlachovka 2655 m (8711 ft)
Caucasus 1200 km (750 mi)	Russia/Georgia/ Azerbaijan	El'brus West Peak 5642 m (18 510 ft)
Appennines 1130 km (700 mi)	Italy	Corno Grande 2931 m (9617 ft)
Alps 1050 km (650 mi)	France/Italy/ Switzerland/ Germany/Austria/ Slovenia	Mont Blanc 4807 m (15 771 ft)

HIGHEST MOUNTAINS OF THE ALPS

Subsidiary peaks or tops on the same massif have been omitted except in the case of Mont Blanc and Monte Rosa, where they are shown in italics

Name	Height	Country
Mont Blanc	4807 m (15 771 ft)	France
Monte Bianco di Courmayeur	*4748 m (15 577 ft)*	*Italy[1]-France*
Le Mont Maudit	*4465 m (14 649 ft)*	*Italy-France*
Picco Luigi Amedeo	*4460 m (14 632 ft)*	*Italy*
Dôme du Goûter	*4304 m (14 120 ft)*	*France*
Monte Rosa		
Dufourspitze	4634 m (15 203 ft)	Switzerland
Nordend	4609 m (15 121 ft)	Swiss-Italian border
Ostspitze	*4596 m (15 078 ft)*	*Swiss-Italian border*
Zumstein Spitze	*4563 m (14 970 ft)*	*Swiss-Italian border*
Signal Kuppe	*4556 m (14 947 ft)*	*Swiss-Italian border*
Dom	4545 m (14 911 ft)	Switzerland
Lyskamm (Liskamm)	4527 m (14 853 ft)	Swiss-Italian border
Weisshorn	4506 m (14 780 ft)	Switzerland
Täschhorn	4491 m (14 733 ft)	Switzerland
Matterhorn	4476 m (14 683 ft)	Swiss-Italian border

[1] The highest point on Italian territory is a shoulder on the main summit of Mont Blanc (Monte Bianco) through which a 4760 m (15 616 ft) contour passes.

HIGHEST MOUNTAINS OF CAUCASIA

One of the two traditional boundaries of Europe – see above – runs along the spine of the Caucasus Mountains, which include 15 peaks higher than Mont Blanc

Name	Height metres	Height feet
Elbrus, West Peak	5642 m	18 510 ft
Elbrus, East Peak	*5595 m*	*18 356 ft*
Dykh Tau	5203 m	17 070 ft
Shkhara	5201 m	17 063 ft
Pik Shota Rustaveli	5190 m	17 028 ft
Koshtantau	5144 m	16 876 ft
Pik Pushkin	5100 m	16 732 ft
Jangi Tau, West Peak	5051 m	16 572 ft
Jangi Tau, East Peak	*5038 m*	*16 529 ft*
Dzhangi Tau	5049 m	16 565 ft
Kazbek	5047 m	16 558 ft
Katyn Tau (Adishi)	*4985 m*	*16 355 ft*
Pik Rustaveli	4960 m	16 272 ft
Mishirgi, West Peak	4922 m	16 148 ft
Mishirgi, East Peak	*4917 m*	*16 035 ft*
Kunjum Mishirgi	4880 m	16 011 ft
Gestola	4860 m	15 944 ft
Tetnuld	4853 m	15 921 ft

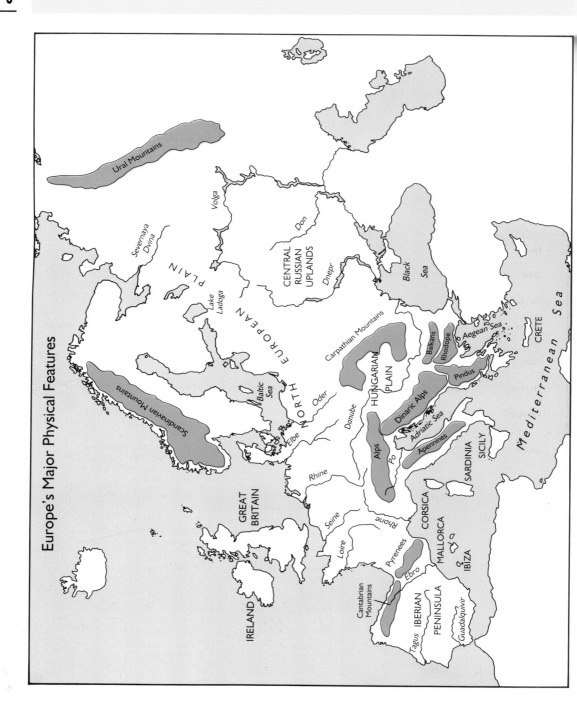

Europe's Major Physical Features

Ural Mountains

Severnaya Dvina

Volga

Don

Dnepr

CENTRAL RUSSIAN UPLANDS

Black Sea

Lake Ladoga

NORTH EUROPEAN PLAIN

Carpathian Mountains

Balkans

Rhodope

Aegean Sea

CRETE

Mediterranean Sea

Scandinavian Mountains

Baltic Sea

Oder

Elbe

HUNGARIAN PLAIN

Dinaric Alps

Pindus

Danube

Adriatic Sea

Apennines

SICILY

Rhine

Alps

Po

SARDINIA

GREAT BRITAIN

Seine

Rhone

CORSICA

MALLORCA

IBIZA

Loire

Pyrenees

Ebro

Cantabrian Mountains

IBERIAN PENINSULA

Tagus

Guadalquivir

IRELAND

EUROPE'S PRINCIPAL RIVERS

River	Length (km)	Length (mi)	Source	Course and outflow
Volga	3530 km	2193 mi	Nameless headwaters of 160 km (99 mi) flowing into Rybinskoye reservoir in Valdai Hills north of Moscow, Russia	Flows east and south in a great curve and empties in a delta into the Caspian Sea
Danube	2850 km	1770 mi	Rises as the rivers Breg and Brisach in the Black Forest in SW Germany	Flows east through Germany, Austria, Slovakia, Hungary, Yugoslavia, Bulgaria, Romania and Ukraine and empties in a delta in the Black Sea
Ural	2540 km	1575 mi	Rises in the south central Ural Mountains, Moscow	The Ural is sometimes quoted as the third longest river in Europe but part of its path to the Caspian Sea runs through the Asian republic of Kazakhstan
Dnepr	2285 km	1420 mi	Rises west of Moscow, Russia	Flows south through Russia, Belarus and Ukraine to the Black Sea
Don	1969 km	1224 mi	Rises in southwest Russia	Flows south through Russia to the Sea of Azov
Pechora	1809 km	1124 mi	Rises in the Ural Mountains, Russia	Flows north through Russia to the Barents Sea
Kama	1805 km	1122 mi	Rises north of Perm in Russia	Flows south through Russia to join the River Volga through the Kuybyshevskoye reservoir
Oka	1500 km	930 mi	Rises southwest of Moscow, Russia	Flows east through Russia to join the River Volga near Nizhny Novgorod
Belaya	1430 km	889 mi	Rises in the south of the Ural Mountains, Russia	Flows north through Russia to join the River Kama
Dnestr	1352 km	840 mi	Rises near the Polish border in western Ukraine	Flows south and east through Ukraine and Moldova to the Black Sea
Rhine	1320 km	820 mi	Rises in the Swiss Alps	Flows east then north through Switzerland, Liechtenstein, Austria, Germany and the Netherlands to the North Sea
Severnaya Dvina (Northern Dvina)	1320 km	820 mi	Rises in northern Russia as the River Sukhona	Flows north to the White Sea
Elbe	1165 km	724 mi	Rises in south Bohemia in the Czech Republic	Flows north through the Czech Republic and Germany to the North Sea
Vistula	1069 km	664 mi	Rises near the Polish-Slovak border	Flows north through Poland to the Baltic Sea
Loire	1020 km	634 mi	Rises in the Massif Central of France	Flows north then west through France to the Atlantic Ocean
Dvina	1018 km	632 mi	Rises in the Valdai Hills in central Russia	Flows south and west through Russia, Belarus and Latvia to the Baltic Sea
Tagus	1007 km	626 mi	Rises on the border of Aragon and Castile, Spain	Flows west through Spain and Portugal to the Atlantic Ocean

THE MAKING OF MODERN EUROPE

1870
Spanish Bourbon monarchy overthrown; liberal monarchy established.
Italian troops occupied Rome effectively ending the Papal States.

1871
France defeated in Franco-Prussian War; Second French Empire replaced by Third French Republic; Alsace-Lorraine ceded to Germany; German unification under Prussia – Wilhelm I of Prussia became German emperor (Kaiser), Bismarck became federal Chancellor.

1873
Liberal Spanish monarchy overthrown; First Spanish Republic established.

1874
Carlist insurrection in Spain; Bourbon monarchy restored.

1875
Carlists expelled from Catalonia and Valencia; liberal Spanish constitution.

1876
The Bulgarian Massacre – Turkey savagely repressed revolt in Bulgaria.
End of Spanish Carlist Wars.

1877
Russo-Turkish War liberated Bulgaria from Turkish rule.

1878
Congress of Berlin – the independence of Romania, Serbia and Montenegro and the autonomy of Bulgaria from Turkey recognized.

1879
Irish Land League formed under Parnell.
Bismarck abandoned free trade in Germany.

1880
Anticlericalism in France – Benedictines, Carmelites and Jesuits expelled.
Church-state conflict ended in Germany with repeal of May Laws.

1882
Germany, Austria and Italy formed the Triple Alliance.
Phoenix Park murders sparked an Anglo-Irish crisis.

1886
First Irish Home Rule Bill failed.

1888
Wilhelm II became emperor (Kaiser) of Germany.

1890
Bismarck dropped as German Chancellor.

1891
Launch of reformist Young Turk Movement.

1893
Second Irish Home Rule Bill failed.

1894
Start of the Dreyfus Affair in France.
Franco-Russian alliance formed.

1897
First Zionist Congress met in Basel.

1900
Assassination of King Umberto I of Italy.

1901
Death of Queen Victoria.

1903
Obrenovic dynasty massacred in Serbian coup.
Bolshevik-Menshevik split in Russian Communist Party.

1904
Entente Cordiale between UK and France.

1905
'Bloody Sunday' revolt in Russia; Duma (parliament) with limited powers established.
Norway gained independence from Sweden.

1906
End of Dreyfus Affair in France.

1907
Anglo-Russian entente.
Germany opposed arms limitations at the Hague Peace Conference.

1908
Bulgarian independence from Turkey.
Austria annexed Bosnia-Herzegovina.
Assassinaton of King Carlos of Portugal.

1910
Monarchy overthrown in Portugal; republic established.

1912
First Balkan War – Balkan states defeated Turkey, which lost most of its European territory; Albania independent.
Italy seized the Dodecanese from Turkey.

1913
Second Balkan War – Balkan states and Turkey defeated Bulgaria.
Third Irish Home Rule failed.

1914
Assassination of Austrian heir Franz Ferdinand led to Austrian declaration of war against Serbia; general mobilization; Germany declared war on Russia and France; outbreak of World War I; trench warfare began; first Battle of Ypres; Turkey entered war allied to Central Powers; Germany defeated Russia at Tannenberg.

1915
Second Battle of Ypres; Italy joined war against Central Powers; abortive allied campaign at Gallipoli.

1916
Battle of Verdun; naval Battle of Jutland; Battle of the Somme; failure of Russian offensive.
Abortive Easter Rising in Dublin.

1917
Battle of Passchendaele; Italy defeated at Caporetto.
February Revolution in Russia – abdication of Tsar and formation of provisional government; October Revolution – Bolsheviks under Lenin seized power.
Finland, the Baltic states and other nationalities within the Russian Empire seceded.
Icelandic independence.

1918
Russia withdrew from war; Russian Imperial family massacred; seizure of industry by the state; start of Russian civil war.
German defeat in the Second Battle of the Marne; revolution in Germany – Kaiser abdicated; German surrender.
Austria-Hungary surrendered; Habsburgs deposed.

1919
Czechoslovakia, Hungary, Poland and Yugoslavia established as independent states.
Versailles Peace Settlement began – France regained Alsace-Lorraine; Rhineland demilitarized.

1920
Independence of Estonia, Latvia and Lithuania recognized. Ukraine reconquered by Russia.

1921
Partition of Ireland; Irish Free State established.

1922
Establishment of USSR.
Fascists under Mussolini seized power in Italy.

1923
Franco-Belgian occupation of the Ruhr when Germany defaulted on reparations.

1924
Death of Lenin; Stalin became Soviet leader.

1925
Rampant German inflation.

1926
General Strike in UK.

1927
German economy collapsed on Black Friday.

1929
Salazar came to power in Portugal.
Lateran Treaty recognized sovereignty of the Vatican.

1930
French forces left the Rhineland.
Height of the seizure of land from peasants in USSR to create collectives; destruction of the kulak class.

Collapse of German monetary system.

1931
Abdication of Alfonso XIII of Spain; Second Spanish Republic established.

1932
Great Hunger March in UK.

1933
Nazi Party came to power in Germany – Hitler became Chancellor; start of anti-Semitic legislation.

1934
Night of the Long Knives in Germany.
Start of Stalinist purges in USSR.

1935
Restoration of the Greek monarchy.
Treason trials in USSR.

1936
Start of Spanish Civil War – Republicans and Communists confronted by Franco's Falangists.
Rome-Berlin axis formed.

1937
Sudetenland Crisis – Munich Pact allowed Germany to annex German-speaking areas of Bohemia.
Irish Free State became Republic of Eire.

1938
Anschluss – Germany annexed Austria.

1939
Germany signed non-aggression pact with USSR, invaded Czechoslovakia and Poland; outbreak of World War II.

1940
German invasion of Denmark, Norway and the Low Countries; British evacuation of Dunkirk; Italy entered war as ally of Germany; fall of France; Churchill became British PM; aerial Battle of Britain; USSR invaded Baltic states.

1941
Extermination of Jews began in German concentration camps; German invasion of Greece, Yugoslavia and USSR – siege of Leningrad; Romania and Bulgaria joined Axis Powers.

1942
Start of massive Allied air raids on Germany; USSR defeated Germany at Stalingrad.

1943
Mussolini overthrown; Allied invasion of Italy; German retreat from USSR began; German surrender at Stalingrad; German extermination of Jews intensified.

1944
Germans expelled from north Italy; D-Day Allied landings in Normandy; Paris and Brussels liberated; failure of Allied Arnhem campaign; final German offensive – Battle of the Bulge; Allies entered Germany; Yugoslavia liberated; Soviet offensive in Eastern Europe; Germans pulled back in Poland, Hungary and the Balkans.

1945

Mussolini killed by partisans; Yalta Conference – Allied leaders decided future division of Europe; Berlin surrendered to Soviet forces; German defeat; Hitler committed suicide.
Start of Cold War – Soviet-inspired Communist regimes established in Eastern Europe.

1946

Greek civil war.

1948

Communist takeover in Czechoslovakia.
Berlin airlift to West Berlin.

1949

Foundation of NATO – Western military alliance.
Foundation of Federal Republic of (West) Germany and (East) German Democratic Republic.
Ireland left Commonwealth.

1952

Start of campaign by Greek Cypriots to end British rule.
End of Allied occupation of West Germany.

1953

Death of Stalin; Khruschev came to power in USSR.
East German uprising against Soviet rule.

1955

Warsaw Pact formed.

1956

Hungarian Uprising against Soviet rule put down by Soviet forces.

1957

Treaty of Rome established Common Market (EEC).

1958

Fifth French Republic established by de Gaulle.

1959

EFTA launched.

1960

Cyprus independent.

1961

Berlin Wall constructed.

1963

France vetoed UK's application to join EEC.

1964

Clashes between Greeks and Turks in Cyprus.
Brezhnev came to power in USSR – claimed right of USSR to intervene in the affairs of Communist states.
Malta independent.

1965

Ceausescu came to power in Romania.

1967

Military junta seized power in Greece.

1968

Dubcek's attempt to reform Communism in Czechoslovakia crushed by Soviet forces.
Student unrest in much of Western Europe.

1969

British troops sent to Northern Ireland to restore order.
Resignation of de Gaulle in France.

1970

Unrest in Poland; Gdansk riots.

1971

Women gained the vote in Switzerland.

1972

Direct rule introduced in Northern Ireland.

1973

UK, Denmark and Ireland joined EC.
East and West Germany established diplomatic relations.

1974

Turkish invasion and partition of Cyprus.
Portuguese revolution – authoritarian regime deposed.
Democracy restored in Greece.

1975

Death of Franco; Spanish democracy restored.

1980

Solidarity – free trade union – suppressed in Poland.

1981

Greece joined EC.

1985

Gorbachov came to power in USSR and began reforms.
Anglo-Irish Accord on Northern Ireland.

1986

Spain and Portugal joined EC.

1989

Beginning of the collapse of Communism in Eastern Europe; Berlin Wall reopened; former Soviet satellites became multi-party democracies and moved towards market economies; Romanian revolution.

1990

German reunification.

1991

Attempted coup by Communist hardliners in Moscow; Estonia, Latvia and Lithuania regained independence; break-up of USSR – Ukraine, Belarus and Moldova independent; Yeltsin came to power in Russia.
Civil war led to break-up of Yugoslavia.

1992

Single European Market established.
Independence of Croatia, Slovenia and Bosnia recognized.

1993

Break-up of Czechoslovakia into Czech Republic and Slovakia.
Serbia overran much of Bosnia and Croatia.
Attempted hardline coup in Moscow.

THE EUROPEAN UNION

A new European body – the European Union (EU) – came into being on 1 November 1993 following the ratification of the Maastricht Treaty (see p. 19) by Germany, the last EC member to ratify the document. However, the term European Union – and what membership of that Union implies – have received relatively little publicity and, it has been suggested, are surrounded by general public confusion.

Many citizens of member-states of the Common Market seem to be unsure whether their countries belong to the Common Market, the European Community, the European Economic Community or the European Union – or, indeed, to all four of those organizations. It has even been suggested that the European Community no longer exists and that it has been replaced by the new European Union.

EC, EEC or EU?

The term 'Common Market' is a long-established popular name for the European Community (EC). The European Economic Community (EEC) – which with the European Coal and Steel Community (ECSC) and Euratom was one of the elements of the European Community – officially disappeared on 1 November 1993 when it was subsumed into the European Community, although, in popular usage, the initials EC had long joined if not completely replaced EEC. Also from 1 November 1993 the European Community was officially absorbed into the European Union but – unlike the European Economic Community – the European Community did not cease to exist. The EC, its bodies and structure now form one of the three 'pillars' that comprise the European Union (see below).

The European Union, as defined in the opening clause of the Maastricht Treaty, is an expression of 'an ever-closer union among the peoples of Europe'. The governments of the 12 member-states that ratified the Maastricht Treaty agreed a series of objectives that include (eventually) a single currency and a commitment that the European Union should 'assert its identity on the international scene'.

WHAT IS THE EU?

The Union implies no additional obligations upon members or their citizens. It does, however, mean some additional rights for citizens of EC countries.

Every citizen of the 12 states is, now, also a citizen of the European Union. Every EU citizen has the right to vote and to stand for election in elections for local and regional government authorities in any country of the Union. Also every EU citizen may vote or stand for election in elections for the European Parliament in any EC state.

Any EU citizen who finds him- or herself in difficulty in any country which is outside the EC may apply to the embassy or consulate of any EC state for assistance.

Those who are opposed to the idea of a European federation or the emergence of EC authorities with near-federal powers argue that the establishment of citizenship of the European Union is the first step towards a gradual diminution of the rights and obligations of citizenship of individual countries and an increase of the powers of Brussels. However, a majority of EC members – and all of the countries whose candidature for EC membership is being negotiated (Austria, Finland, Norway and Sweden) – are currently opposed to any such reduction of the powers of national governments.

SCHENGEN

The Treaty of Schengen – originally signed in the small Luxembourg town of Schengen by France, Germany, Italy and the Benelux countries – allows for the free movement of individuals between signatories of the Treaty without border controls such as passport checks. This right of free movement is implicit within the terms of the European Union and, by the time the EU came into being on 1 November 1993, the following countries had adhered to the Treaty of Schengen: Belgium, France, Germany, Greece, Italy, Luxembourg, the Netherlands, Portugal, and Spain. The UK, Denmark and Ireland have retained certain border formalities for security reasons.

THE 'PILLARS'

The EC is one of the three pillars of the EU, but even here there is some confusion. In most of its dealings the European Commission acts as the Commission of the EC. However, there are circumstances in which the Commissioners may be called upon to act for the EU rather than the EC. Under the terms of the Maastricht Treaty the EC assumes additional monetary responsibilities, in particular the establishment of a central European bank and the adoption of a single European currency. Agreement was reached in October 1993 to establish a European monetary institute. The institute – which will become the European Central Bank – is to be based in Frankfurt, Germany. However, progress towards a single European currency was effectively halted by the virtual collapse of the ERM system in the summer of the same year. Nevertheless, Maastricht and the European Union imply a two-stage timetable to a single currency which is, in theory, to be introduced in 1999 for those EC states that meet certain strict economic conditions of 'convergence'.

The second 'pillar' of the European Union is concerned with foreign and security matters which will be the realm of intergovernmental bodies representing the 12 EC members rather than the concern of the European Commission.

The third 'pillar' of the European Union encompasses cooperation in a wide variety of fields such as immigration, asylum and law enforcement. This 'pillar' is also the concern of intergovernmental bodies established by the 12 EC states rather than the responsibility of the EC Commission.

Europe: Main Economic Groupings

ICELAND

European Community (EC)

European Free Trade
Area (EFTA)

NORWAY

SWEDEN

FINLAND

RUSSIA

ESTONIA

LATVIA

DENMARK

RUSSIA

LITHUANIA

THE
NETHERLANDS

BELARUS

IRELAND

POLAND

UK

UKRAINE

GERMANY

MOLDOVA

SLOVAKIA

BELGIUM
LUXEMBOURG

CZECH R

FRANCE

AUSTRIA

HUNGARY

ROMANIA

SWITZER-
LAND

ITALY

YUGOSLAVIA

SLOVENIA

BULGARIA

PORTUGAL

CROATIA

SPAIN

GREECE

TURKEY

BOSNIA-HERZEGOVINA

ALBANIA

MACEDONIA

THE EUROPEAN COMMUNITY

In 1950 the governments of Belgium, France, the Federal Republic of Germany (West Germany), Italy, Luxembourg and the Netherlands began negotiations to integrate their interests in specific fields. The result was the Treaty of Paris (1951) under which the European Coal and Steel Community was created. Attempts to establish a community concerned with cooperation in foreign affairs and defence proved abortive, but in 1957 the European Economic Community (the EEC) and the European Atomic Energy Community (Euratom) – with memberships identical to the European Coal and Steel Community – came into being under the terms of the Treaty of Rome.

The three Communities were distinct entities until 1967 when – for all practical purposes – they merged their executives and decision-making bodies into a single European Community (the EC). The Community has been enlarged through the accession of Denmark, Greece, Ireland, Portugal, Spain and the UK.

Membership

Country	Year of accession to the EC
Belgium	founder member
Denmark	1973
France	founder member
Germany	founder member
Greece	1981
Ireland	1973
Italy	founder member
Luxembourg	founder member
Netherlands	founder member
Portugal	1986
Spain	1986
UK	1973

Austria, Finland, Norway and Sweden are beginning negotiations for EC membership and are expected to become full EC members in 1996 (see p. 20). Turkey, Cyprus, Malta and Switzerland have also applied for membership. An application from Morocco was rejected. Associate agreements have been concluded with Poland, Hungary, the Czech Republic and Slovakia (see p. 21).

In 1992 the EC achieved a Single European Market (see pp. 17–18) in which all duties, tariffs and quotas have been removed on trade between member states and many obstacles to the free movement of people, money and goods have been abolished within the Community.

Finance

EC plans for economic and monetary union (see p. 19) have been discussed, and there has been increased coordination in many other fields. Since 1975 the EC has had its own revenue independent of national contributions. The general budget of the EC covers all the expenditure of the Community. Member states are required to supply funds appropriate to these needs. Each EC institution draws up an estimate of its expenditure for the following financial year (January-December) by 1 July in the previous year. The Commission (see below) consolidates these estimates and sends them to the Council (see below) by 1 September for approval. The budget is, in turn, submitted to the European Parliament (see below) by 5 October.

Budget expenditure

Purpose	Appropriations for 1992 commitments (ECUs)
Administration	1 871 734 000
Agricultural guidance and guarantees	36 039 000 000
Structural operations/ fisheries	19 393 171 000
Training, youth, culture, information, social	443 895 000
Energy, Euratom, environment	288 944 000
Consumer protection, internal market, industry, technology	270 071 000
Research and development	2 233 047 000
Developing and Third World countries	2 897 101 000
Other	1 078 853 000
Total	64 515 816 000

EC revenue

Source of revenue	1992 estimate (ECUs)
Agricultural levies	1 216 200 000
Sugar amd related levies	1 112 400 000
Customs duties	11 599 900 000
VAT own resources	34 232 400 000
GNP-based own resources based on levy of each member's GNP	14 079 500 000
Other revenue	378 000 000
Total	62 618 400 000

EC member's contributions

Country	% of total revenue contributed (1991)
Belgium	4.2%
Denmark	2.0%
France	20.2%
Germany	28.3%
Greece	1.4%
Ireland	0.9%
Italy	15.9%
Luxembourg	0.2%
Netherlands	6.1%
Portugal	1.3%
Spain	8.2%
UK	11.3%

EC INSTITUTIONS

The Commission of the European Community

The European Commission consists of 17 members appointed by their national governments for a term of four years. The Commissioners elect from their number a President and six Vice-Presidents. The Commission – which acts independently of national governments – makes proposals to the Council of Ministers (see below) and executes the decisions of the Council.

Headquarters: The Commission is based in Brussels, Belgium.

Composition of the European Commission: Belgium is represented by 1 Commissioner, Denmark 1, France 2, Germany 2, Greece 1, Ireland 1, Italy 2, Luxembourg 1, the Netherlands 1, Portugal 1, Spain 2, and the UK 2.

Members of the Commission: (who took office in January 1993 for a four-year term)
President of the European Commission: Jacques Delors (*France*) – also responsible for the Legal Service, monetary affairs, interpreting and conference services, the Forward Studies Unit and security;
Commissioner for economic and financial affairs: Henning Christophersen (*Denmark*) – also responsible for credit and investments, and the Statistical Office;
Commissioner for cooperation and development: Manuel Marin (*Spain*) – responsible for cooperation with Mediterranean, Middle East, Asian and Latin American states and the countries of the Lomé Convention (see below); also responsible for humanitarian aid;
Commissioner for industrial affairs: Martin Bangemann (*Germany*) – also responsible for information and telecommunications technology;
Commissioner for external economic affairs and trade: Sir Leon Brittan (*UK*) – responsible for cooperation with the USA and Canada, Central and Eastern Europe, China, Japan and the countries of the former Soviet Union; also responsible for commercial policy;
Commissioner for energy and transport: Abel Matutes (*Spain*) – also responsible for the Euratom Supply Agency;
Commissioner for budgets and fraud prevention: Peter Schmidhüber (*Germany*) – also responsible for financial control, the Cohesion Fund, and coordination and management;
Commissioner for customs, taxation and consumer policy: Christiane Scrivener (*France*);
Commissioner for regional policy: Bruce Millan (*UK*);
Commissioner for competition and personnel: Karel van Miert (*Belgium*) – also responsible for administration policy, translation and information;
Commissioner for external political relations and enlargement negotiations: Hans van den Broek (*The Netherlands*) – also responsible for common foreign and security policies;
Commissioner for communications and information, and Commissioner for culture: João de Deus Pinheiro (*Portugal*) – responsible for internal relations with member states; also responsible for publications;
Commissioner for social affairs, employment, immigration and judicial affairs: Padraig Flynn (*Ireland*);
Commissioner for science, research and development: Antonio Ruberti (*Italy*) – also responsible for education and training, human resources and youth;
Commissioner for agriculture: René Steichen (*Luxembourg*) – also responsible for rural development;
Commissioner for the environment and fisheries: Ioannis Paleokrassas (*Greece*) – also responsible for nuclear safety and civil protection;
Commissioner for the international market and financial institutions: Raniero Vanni d'Archirafi – also responsible for enterprise policy, small and medium-sized businesses, trade and crafts.

The Commission's work is administered through 31 main bodies: the Secretariat-General of the Commission, the Legal Service, the Spokesman's Service, the Joint Interpreting and Conference Service, the Statistical Office, the Euratom Supply Agency, the Security Office and 23 Directorates-General – numbered from I (External Relations) to XXIII (Enterprise Policy, Distributive Trades, Tourism and Cooperation).

The Council of Ministers
The Council of Ministers is the main decision-making body of the EC. The Council consists of the foreign ministers of each of the 12 member states. Specialist councils – for example, of the 12 ministers of agriculture – also meet, while heads of government meet three times a year as the *European Council*.

Ministers represent national interests. The decisions of the Council are normally unanimous although there is provision for majority voting in certain areas. The *Presidency of the Council of Ministers* rotates, with each member state taking the chair for a period of six months (see below). Council meetings are normally held in the country that currently holds the Presidency, but are also held in Brussels, Belgium.

Country	Next period as President of the Council of Ministers*
Belgium	July-December 1999
Denmark	January-June 1999
France	January-June 1995
Germany	July-December 1994
Greece	January-June 1994
Ireland	July-December 1996
Italy	January-July 1996
Luxembourg	July-December 1997
Netherlands	January-July 1997
Portugal	July-December 1998
Spain	July-December 1995
UK	January-June 1998

* The current sequence of rotation of the Presidency will be interrupted by the admission of Austria, Norway, Sweden and Finland to membership, probably in 1996. The current sequence is in alphabetical order in the principal language of each member country, with each 'pair' of countries alphabetically reversed: Danmark (Denmark), België/Belgique (Belgium), Ellas (Greece), Deutschland (Germany), France, España (Spain), Italia (Italy), Ireland, Nederland (The Netherlands), Luxembourg, United Kingdom, Portugal.

The European Parliament
The European Parliament consists of 567 members directly elected for five years by universal adult suffrage according to the local practice of each member state. Members (MEPs) have the right to be consulted on legislative proposals submitted by the Council of Ministers or the Commission and the power to reject or amend the budget of the EC. The Parliament also has the power to dismiss the Commission in a vote of censure.

Headquarters: The Parliament meets in Strasbourg (France), its committees meet in Brussels (Belgium) and its Secretariat is based in Luxembourg City.

Composition of the European Parliament: Elections for the European Parliament are held every five years. At the elections scheduled for June 1994 the composition of the Parliament will be:

Country	Number of MEPs
Belgium	25
Denmark	16
France	87
Germany	99
Greece	25
Ireland	15
Italy	87
Luxembourg	6
Netherlands	31
Portugal	25
Spain	64
UK	87

Political groupings: The European Parliament elected in June 1989 – and supplemented in October 1990 by 18 members from the former East Germany – comprised:

Political grouping	No. of seats
Socialist Group	179
European People's Party (Christian Democrats)	161
Liberal and Democratic Reformist Group	45
Group of the European Unitarian Left	29
The Green Group	27
Group of the European Democratic Alliance	21
Rainbow Group	16
Technical Group of the European Right	14
Left Unity	14
Unattached	13
Group representing the former East Germany	18
Total	*536*

Beginning each March, the European Parliament has an annual session which comprises about 12 one-week sessions. There are 19 parliamentary Standing Committees specializing in matters ranging from foreign affairs and security to womens' rights, and from transport and tourism to budgetary control. Parliament is run by a bureau consisting of a President and 14 Vice-Presidents elected by MEPs from among their number.

President of the European Parliament: Egon Klepsch (*Germany*).

The European Court of Justice

The European Court of Justice consists of 13 judges and six advocates-general appointed for six years by the governments of member states acting in concert. At least one representative is appointed from each state. The Court is responsible for deciding upon the legality of the decisions of the Council of Ministers and the Commission and for adjudicating between states in the event of disputes.

Headquarters: Luxembourg City.

Court of Auditors of the European Community

The Court – established in 1977 – is responsible for the external audit of the resources managed by the EC. It consists of 12 members elected for six years by the Council of Ministers.

President: Aldo Angioi (*Italy*).

Headquarters: Luxembourg City.

European Investment Bank

The Bank – which works on a non-profit basis – makes or guarantees loans for investment projects in member states. Priority is given to regional development. The capital is subscribed by EC members and in 1991 this sum stood at 57 600 000 000 ECUs.

Country	% of capital supplied (1991)	% of capital received (1990)
Belgium	5.3%	1.6%
Denmark	2.7%	4.5%
France	19.1%	13.3%
Germany	19.1%	6.8%
Greece	1.4%	1.4%
Ireland	0.7%	1.7%
Italy	19.1%	30.4%
Luxembourg	0.1%	0.1%
Netherlands	5.3%	1.9%
Portugal	0.9%	6.3%
Spain	7.0%	15.3%
UK	19.1%	14.9%
Other*		1.8%

* Supranational rather than an individual country.

CONSULTATIVE BODIES

Economic and Social Committee

The Committee is an advisory body consulted by the Commission and the Council of Ministers on issues such as free movement of workers, agriculture, transport and harmonization of laws. It has 189 members – one-third representing employers, one-third representing employees and one-third representing special interest groups (e.g. agriculture). Members are nominated by individual EC governments and appointed by the Council of Ministers for four years. Belgium is represented by 12 members, Denmark 9, France 24, Germany 24, Greece 12, Ireland 9, Italy 24, Luxembourg 6, Netherlands 12, Portugal 12, Spain 21 and the UK 24. The Committee is based in Brussels, Belgium.

European Coal and Steel Community Consultative Committee

The Committee – which advises the Commission – is appointed by the Council of Ministers for two years. It comprises 84 members – 21 representing coal and steel producers, and 21 each representing workers, consumers and dealers in these fields.

Agricultural Advisory Committees

There are four agricultural committees – one dealing with the organization of the market, one dealing with structures and two concerned with social matters in agriculture.

Committee of the Regions

The Maastricht Treaty (see p. 19) provided for a new Committee of the Regions, an advisory body that would represent local and regional governments within member states. The Committee is expected to be formed in 1994 and will comprise members elected by regional and local government bodies from their own number. Details concerning the method of election and the number of representatives are not yet available.

COMMUNITY ACTIVITIES

Agriculture
EC cooperation in agriculture is highly developed. Expenditure on agriculture (through the European Agricultural Guidance and Guarantee Fund/EAGGF) is the EC's single largest item of expenditure. The operation and objectives of the Common Agricultural Policy (CAP) are described on p. 96.

Consumer Policy
The EC has implemented two Consumer Protection Programmes which have standardized health and safety measures, and introduced rules on food additives, packaging, machines and equipment, measures for monitoring the quality and durability of products, the improvement of after-sales service and legal redress concerning faulty goods. Consumer associations have also been encouraged.

Economic and Monetary Union
The aim of monetary union and the adoption of a single common currency throughout the Community (the ECU) was detailed in the Maastricht Treaty (see p. 19), but these goals have now been postponed following the collapse of the ERM; see pp. 104–05.

Education
Education was excluded from the Treaty of Rome but recent efforts at harmonization have been taken, in particular moves to define equivalent standards in professional qualifications. Other initiatives have included:
- the establishment of a postgraduate European University in Florence, Italy;
- the foundation of *Eurydice*, an educational information network, based in London;
- ERASMUS (the European Action Scheme for Mobility of University Students), which supports university cooperation schemes and enables students to spend time in other EC countries. (See also pp. 86–90.)

Energy
The EC has developed overall energy policies within the EEC, Euratom and the ECSC; see p. 110.

Environment
The EC's environmental action programmes have laid down various principles for action concerning pollution and environmental protection; see p. 136.

Financial Services
Various directives on banking, insurance and capital movement have been implemented; see p. 104.

Fisheries
The Common Fisheries Policy (CFP) came into force in 1983; see p. 102.

Industry
Industrial cooperation between members began with the establishment of the ECSC; see p. 106.

Overseas Aid – the Lomé Convention
The principal channel for EC aid to developing countries is the Lomé Convention. (Technical and financial aid is also given through the agency of the Mediterranean Financial Protocols and directly to over 30 Asian and Latin American states.)

The Lomé Convention – which came into force in 1975 and has been renewed three times – provides a framework for cooperation with developing countries in Africa, the Caribbean and the Pacific (the so-called ACP countries). Seventy states are party to the current Fourth Lomé Convention as recipients and various AC-EC institutions have been established to enable the provisions of the Convention to be enacted. They include:
- *The ACP-EC Council of Ministers*, which includes one minister from each of the 82 countries (the 12 EC members and the 70 ACP states). The Council meets annually.
- *The ACP-EC Committee of Ambassadors*, which comprises 82 ambassadors, one from each signatory. The Committee meets at least once every six months.
- *The ACP-EC Joint Assembly*, which comprises equal numbers of MEPs (Members of the European Parliament) and delegates from ACP countries. The Assembly meets twice a year.
- *The ACP Council of Ministers*, which comprises one representative from the government of each ACP country.
- *The ACP Secretariat*, which is based in Brussels, Belgium.

Social Policy
In 1987 measures were added to the Treaty of Rome to emphasize the need for 'economic and social cohesion' in particular the need to reduce the disparities between regions (see p. 94). In 1989 the Commission produced a Charter of Fundamental Social Rights of Workers – now better known as the Social Chapter (see p. 93).

Transport
The establishment of a Community transport policy – to allow the free movement of traffic throughout the EC – is one of the objectives of the Treaty of Rome; see p. 118.

EC STRUCTURAL FUNDS

The EC's structural funds are:

European Agricultural Guidance and Guarantee Fund (EAGGF)
The European Agricultural Guidance and Guarantee Fund – Guidance section – was created in 1962 and is administered by the European Commission (see above). It covers EC aid for projects to improve farming conditions in member states and is currently the largest single item of Community expenditure; see above and p. 96.

European Regional Development Fund (ERDF)
The ERDF began making grants towards regional development projects in 1975. Payments are made to finance projects in 'problem regions'. Up to 15% of the Fund may be spent on supra-national projects.

European Social Fund
The Social Fund makes payments to improve training and workers' mobility and to aid job creation. In recent years the main beneficiaries of the Fund have been Spain and the UK, which have both received over 20% of total payments.

OTHER EUROPEAN ORGANIZATIONS

EEA see p. 21, **EFTA** p. 21, **NATO** and **WEU** p. 102

CEFTA

The Central European Free Trade Agreement (see p. 142) aims to establish a free trade area between the Czech Republic, Hungary, Poland and Slovakia by 2001.

CIS

The Commonwealth of Independent States (founded 1991; HQ: Minsk, Belarus) maintains some of the economic, political and military cooperation that existed in the USSR. *Members*: Armenia, Azerbaijan, Belarus, Georgia, Kazakhstan, Kyrgyzstan, Moldova, Russia, Tajikistan, Turkmenistan, Ukraine, Uzbekistan.

COUNCIL OF EUROPE

The Council of Europe (founded 1949) aims to achieve a greater European unity, to safeguard members' common European heritage and to facilitate economic and social progress. Membership is restricted to European democracies. The *Council of Ministers*, comprising the foreign ministers of member states, meets twice a year. Agreements by members are either formalized as *European Conventions* or recommendations to governments. The *Parliamentary Assembly of the Council* – which meets three times a year – comprises parliamentary delegates from member states. Delegations range in size from France, Germany, Italy and the UK with 18 members to Liechtenstein and San Marino with two. The Council (based in Strasbourg, France) has achieved over 140 conventions and agreements including the European Convention for the Protection of Human Rights (1950). *Members*: Austria, Belgium, Bulgaria, Cyprus, Czech Republic, Denmark, Estonia, Finland, France, Germany, Greece, Hungary, Iceland, Ireland, Italy, Liechtenstein, Lithuania, Luxembourg, Malta, Netherlands, Norway, Poland, Portugal, San Marino, Slovakia, Slovenia, Spain, Sweden, Switzerland, Turkey, UK.

CSCE

Members of the Conference on Security and Cooperation in Europe (CSCE; founded 1975; reformed 1990) affirm a 'commitment to settle disputes by peaceful means' and a 'common adherence to democratic values and to human rights and fundamental freedoms'. CSCE foreign ministers meet at least once a year. Its institutions are the *CSCE Secretariat* (in Prague, Czech Republic), a small secretariat, the *CSCE Conflict Prevention Centre* (in Vienna, Austria), which is charged with reducing the risk of conflict in Europe, and the *CSCE Office of Free Elections* (in Warsaw, Poland), which monitors the conduct of elections in Europe. *Members:* all European countries plus the Asian former Soviet republics. Yugoslavia was suspended in 1992.

NORDIC COUNCIL

The Council (based in Stockholm) was founded in 1950 to promote cooperation between Denmark, Finland, Sweden and Norway.

THE SINGLE EUROPEAN MARKET

A key objective of the European Community (EC) is to secure the economic benefits of free trade through the creation of a 'common market' providing for the unrestricted movement of goods, services, capital and labour. Under the founding legislation of the EC – the Treaty of Rome (1957) – attention centred on the elimination of various visible restrictions on inter-state trade such as tariffs, quotas and cartels. More recently, under the Single European Act, 1986, and the Maastricht Treaty, 1991, the intent has been to create a more unified EC bloc providing not only greater trading opportunities but also paving the way for a deeper integration of the member states of the EC both in the economic and monetary fields and also politically and socially.

The Single European Act itself is concerned specifically with sweeping away a large number of less visible obstacles to trade arising from historical differences in the policies and practices of individual EC states. The general intention is to end the fragmentation of the EC into 'national' markets and to create a 'level playing field' so that businesses can produce and sell their products throughout the EC bloc of some 350 million people without discrimination. (This free trade area is to be extended to the European Free Trade Association bloc – see the European Economic Area, p. 22.)

The Single European Act committed the 12 EC States to remove various impediments to the movement of goods, services, capital and people through the progressive introduction of various practices and regulations aimed at creating a single, unified market by 31 December 1992. In practice the time-scale for implementing some of the more complex measures involved has inevitably extended beyond this date. Hitherto, trade has been obstructed and costs and prices increased in many ways: by different national bureaucratic requirements and technical standards, different national taxation structures, and restrictive government procurement practices and subsidies given to local firms.

The Act was introduced at a time when intra-Community trade already accounted for over 50% of members' total external trade and it helped boost that total to over 60% in the immediate run-up to 1992 (see table, below). Significant increases in intra-Community trade have occurred (as expected) in the case of the EC's newest members, Greece, Spain and Portugal, but sizeable increases have also been recorded by France, Italy, Denmark and the UK.

THE NUTS AND BOLTS OF THE SINGLE EUROPEAN ACT

Under the Act a large number of 'directives' – designed to harmonize members' practices on an EC-wide basis – have been agreed. They include:

Removal of frontier controls on goods Goods are now free to move routinely from one EC state to another without any systematic customs intervention. This eliminates the need for elaborate documentation of goods in transit. Certain frontier checks have been retained on a discretionary basis to combat the smuggling of illicit goods such as drugs, weapons and pornography.

Movement of people Cross border visits by tourists have been freed from passport checks and customs limitations on goods purchased for personal use. However, to safeguard against illegal entry by non-EC residents and terrorists, some formalities have been retained (e.g. screening luggage at airports). Nationals of EC states have the right to go to another member state to take up employment and receive the same rights as domestic workers. However, various practical barriers remain to full labour mobility, for example, qualifications obtained in one member state may not be acceptable in another, and it may not be possible to transfer pension entitlements. Harmonization in these areas can only be resolved on a longer-term basis.

Value added tax (VAT) The minimum standard of VAT applicable in all member states has been set at 15%. The UK, however, has been allowed for the time being to continue with its zero-rating of certain goods such as children's clothing and food. For VAT registered businesses, the 'destination system' applies to goods sold in another member state – exported goods are zero-rated, with the tax being paid in the country where the product is actually purchased.

Transport services Liberalized transport services have a central place in the single market because the transport industry (road, rail, sea and air) plays a crucial role in moving goods between member states. In the case of road haulage, for example, all permits and quotas that had previously restricted the movement of goods by road have been abolished.

Public purchasing The bias favouring domestic firms in the award of contracts for government projects and supplies has been attacked by the implementation of various regulations taken to promote 'open' tendering, thereby facilitating 'fair' competition for contracts between suppliers irrespective of their national identity.

Technical standards National technical barriers to trade have been progressively replaced by common EC standards so that products can be freely marketed throughout the EC unimpeded by different national rules, standards or testing and certification practices.

Food law harmonization Common standards have been introduced with regard to the use of food additives and flavourings, food labelling and food packaging materials, both to promote product safety and hygiene and to enable food products to be sold across the market without discrimination.

Capital movements The UK abolished all foreign exchange controls on capital movements in 1979, but many other EC members continued to operate restrictions until the late 1980s. A directive removing exchange controls on capital movements within the EC was adopted in 1988.

Financial services A bank or insurance company which has obtained a licence to operate in one member state is now able to supply its services and products across the market without restriction, either directly or

by setting up a branch network in other member states.

THE BENEFITS OF A SINGLE EC MARKET

The immediate benefits of the single market initiative are primarily economic. Consumers benefit from a wider choice of goods and services, and from lower prices resulting from greater economies of scale and increased competition. For businesses, the single market has reduced costly paperwork and administration in respect of exporting and has provided greater opportunities to sell their products throughout the EC.

The authoritative Cecchini report estimates the combined cost savings emanating from the single market programme at around 4.3 – 6.4% of 1988 EC gross domestic product (see table, below). These estimates, of course, are subject to wide margins of error, but nevertheless suggest that even limited economic integration can improve economic welfare. Fuller integration of the kind proposed by the Maastricht Treaty (e.g. a common currency) would be likely to result in even more significant gains.

Intra-Community Trade as a Percentage of Member States' Foreign Trade 1980, 1985 and 1991

	1980	1985	1991
Total EC	50%	52%	60%
Denmark	49%	46%	54%
Belgium–Luxembourg	66%	68%	73%
Germany	47%	49%	54%
Greece	–	49%	61%
Spain	–	43%	62%
France	49%	52%	64%
Ireland	74%	69%	72%
Italy	45%	46%	59%
Netherlands	62%	64%	67%
Portugal	–	47%	73%
UK	40%	45%	53%

Source: European Commission

Potential Gains in Economic Welfare for the EC Resulting from Completion of the Internal Market

	% GDP
1. Gains from the removal of barriers affecting trade, mainly customs formalities (paperwork etc.)	0.2% – 0.3%
2. Gains from the removal of barriers affecting production (divergent national product specifications and standards, regulations, testing and certification procedures)	2.0% – 2.4%
3. Gains from exploiting economies of scale more fully	2.1%
4. Gains from intensified competition, lower costs resulting from the removal of business inefficiencies	1.6%
Total Gains : at 1988 prices	4.3% – 6.4%

Source: European Commission, Cecchini Report, 1988

THE MAASTRICHT TREATY

The Maastricht Treaty was drawn up by the 12 members of the European Community in 1991. A target date of 1 January 1993 was set for its entry into force. However this deadline was not met as all 12 member states did not ratify the Treaty on time. On 2 June 1992 the Danish electorate voted against the Treaty in a referendum. The electorates of Ireland and France approved the Treaty in June and September 1992 respectively. Meanwhile other members ratified the Treaty in parliament without calling referenda. In May 1993 a second Danish referendum approved Maastricht (following clarification of issues such as subsidiarity). The UK has negotiated a separate 'protocol', reserving its position on the third stage of European Monetary Union (EMU), and an agreement to opt out of the Social Chapter (see p. 93). The UK ratified the Treaty in August 1993.

Looked at in the context of the evolution of the EC the Treaty marks the decisive step from 'common market' status (with its emphasis on the promotion of free trade) to a much closer and deeper unification of the economic, political and social systems of member countries.

THE ECONOMIC DIMENSION

A central feature of the Treaty is the proposal to establish monetary union. It was hoped that this could be achieved in a three-stage plan for the irrevocable change to a single currency, the European Currency Unit (ECU). In the first stage all countries were expected to participate in the 'Exchange Rate Mechanism' (ERM) of the European Monetary System, which requires members to keep the exchange value of their currency at a 'fixed' rate against other members' currencies. Keeping exchange rates fixed, however, can be difficult as evidenced by the withdrawal of the UK and Italy from the ERM in 1992 following speculative pressures on their currencies. In August 1993 pressure on the French franc and other currencies by speculators, coupled with high German interest rates, forced the D-mark artificially high against the French franc, the Spanish peseta and Portuguese escudo. EC governments were forced to effectively suspend the ERM by allowing member currencies to move by 15% on either side of their central rate. This enabled member states to pursue their own exchange policies but at the cost of at least postponing the goal of economic union and single currency. However, other measures of value within the Treaty can still be implemented as planned.

SUBSIDIARITY

The main authorities of the EC (the European Council in particular) have only limited powers to formulate and implement common policies across the whole of the Community. Some EC countries hoped that Maastricht would help establish a 'federalist' EC with strong central direction involving the ceding of policy-making from national governments to the EC authorities. This has been resisted for the time being. The Treaty affirms that, wherever possible, decisions should be 'taken as closely as possible to the citizens'. This principle, referred to as subsidiarity (Article 3b of the Treaty) requires that the Community confines itself to doing what cannot be sufficiently achieved by member states acting alone and can therefore be better achieved at Community level. This opens up the problem, of course, as to where the dividing line is between issues that can be resolved at the individual state level and those that can only be tackled at the Community-wide level.

The subsidiarity clause has yet to be tested to the full, but a pointer to the general principle underlying it is provided by, for example, established EC procedures for controlling mergers between firms. The EC's Merger Regulation is designed to maintain effective competition across the EC market. Under the Regulation, a merger with an EC dimension, that is a merger where the aggregate Community-wide sales of the firms concerned is more than ECU 250 million and where over one-third of those sales accrue in two or more member states, can be investigated by the European Commission and vetoed if found to be against the interests of competition. Mergers that do not meet the above criteria are left to be investigated (if at all) under individual members' own competition law. Thus, for example, a merger between two UK companies with little business in the EC can be investigated under UK merger law without interference from the EC authorities.

PILLARS

Under Maastricht, cooperation in certain fields is to be channelled through new inter-governmental bodies rather than through existing institutions of the EC. In some areas, most notably in foreign policy and defence, the Treaty provides for greater 'inter-governmental cooperation' with a view to establishing a common approach to matters of mutual concern. Points emphasized by the Treaty include a stronger commitment to joint actions where all members agree and a stronger EC voice in defence through NATO. Maastricht defined a European Union resting upon three 'pillars'. The first pillar is the EC, which was to have assumed additional monetary responsibilities (see above). The second pillar, concerning foreign and security matters, and the third pillar, concerning cooperation in a wide variety of areas such as immigration, political asylum and law enforcement, were defined as inter-governmental bodies representing the 12 states. With the postponement of monetary union, the Treaty represents a major widening of cooperation between the EC states without adding substantially to the powers of the EC itself.

To sum up, a union of countries such as the EC obviously needs some common policies if it is to function effectively. A customs union built on 'free trade' can produce economic benefits but these can be considerably enhanced by a deeper integration of members' economies. The EC, of course, is more than just a matter of economics; it represents a social and political movement aimed at creating something resembling new 'superstate'. There are those in the European movement who would like to see the EC itself assuming the role of the nation state. The Maastricht Treaty is a further, albeit very limited, move in this direction.

WIDENING THE EC

Where are the limits on ultimate membership of the EC to be drawn? Twenty members, 30 members? The Treaty of Rome states that 'any European state may apply to become a member of the Community', so, in theory, the EC could extend to the entire continent. However, the enlargement of the EC raises many imponderables including the problem of absorbing new members with relatively backward economies. The larger original members would also have to face being outvoted by an ever increasing number of smaller member states on qualified-majority decisions, that is those matters that require roughly 70% of votes to enact a European law.

The first major enlargement of the EC occurred in 1973 when the UK, Denmark and Ireland joined the Community. Greece joined the EC in 1981 and Spain and Portugal in 1986 increasing the total membership of the EC to 12 countries.

EFTA ABSORBED BY THE EC?

Although distinct alliances, the EC and the EFTA (see p. 21) have maintained close trading relations. In 1972 and 1973, the EC and the EFTA concluded a number of free trade agreements to provide tariff-free access throughout the two blocs for a wide range of industrial goods. This has now been carried a stage further with the establishment of the European Economic Association (see p. 21).

The future of the EFTA itself, however, has been put in the melting pot by the application of five EFTA members – Austria, Sweden, Finland, Norway and Switzerland (see below) – to join the EC. Negotiations with Austria, Finland, Norway and Sweden will be conducted separately and, providing an agreement can be successfully concluded, it is expected that these four states will join the EC in 1996. In fiscal terms and their economic structures, these four countries should be admirably suited to the EC. All are relatively wealthy nations with established EC trade links, and each would be a net contributor to the EC's budget, providing more resources for the development of less developed areas of the EC – Spain, Portugal, Ireland and Greece. However, some 'problem' areas in respect of their applications and their adjustment to the EC framework remain.

Public opinion in Norway is greatly divided concerning EC membership. A bitter campaign preceded a previous Norwegian attempt to join the Community in the early 1970s. Opinion polls suggest that there is still a majority against membership and opposition to Norwegian membership has been voiced in some EC countries because of Norway's resumption of whaling. Sweden's traditional neutrality is seen by some Swedes and EC members as a possible impediment to membership. There also seems to be a lack of public enthusiasm for EC membership in Sweden. Finnish public opinion appears to favour joining the EC, but Finland's neutrality could be an obstacle. Austria, too, is neutral, but – as may be the case of all neutral candidates for EC membership – this factor could be less of a problem in post-Cold War Europe.

Switzerland is still a candidate for EC membership even though Swiss membership of the EEA was rejected in a referendum (1992). It is, however, probably unrealistic to envisage Switzerland in the EC given the depth of opposition – particularly in German-speaking Switzerland – to joining the EEA, which would have involved fewer commitments than EC membership. Liechtenstein – an EFTA member – has indicated that it is unlikely to apply to join the EC and its very small size would make the responsibilities of full membership a problem. Iceland, the final EFTA member, might also experience difficulties in gaining EC membership on account of its small population, but a greater impediment is the country's heavy dependence upon fishing. Iceland would wish to keep control over its fisheries and not become subject to EC fishing policies (see p. 102).

ASSOCIATE AGREEMENTS

Seven countries – Turkey, Malta, Cyprus, the Czech Republic, Hungary, Poland and Slovakia – currently operate Association Agreements with the EC allowing free access to the EC for most industrial goods and tariff reductions for most foodstuffs.

Turkey applied to join the EC in 1987 but its application is perceived to be hampered by several impediments. Turkey's large population and relative lack of development would not make it an easy country to integrate into the Community. There are also worries in Western Europe about the free movement of people from Turkey that membership would imply. Turkey's Islamic tradition and Greece's long-standing antipathy to Turkey are also seen as obstacles to Turkish membership.

Cyprus and Malta have both applied to join the EC, but the division of Cyprus into Greek and Turkish sectors since 1974 and Malta's small size and population are seen as obstacles to membership.

Poland, Hungary, the Czech Repblic and Slovakia may apply for membership of the EC when full trade liberalization is due to be established in 1999. The enlargement of the EC even further is where the real problems begin, as this group of East European applicants comprises, by current EC and EFTA standards, relatively poorer countries. Their absorption would severely stretch the Community's resources. One East European state, East Germany, has already been absorbed into the EC by the 'back door' with its unification with West Germany in 1990. The strains the German economy is now under to upgrade its eastern Länder – uncompetitive and impoverished after years of neglect and stifling bureaucracy – has not only posed serious problems in Germany, but has also impaired its contribution to the functioning of the EC as a whole (see p. 23). Thus, the absorption of other similarly backward economies would raise equally thorny problems of internal resource allocation and economic harmonization as well as accentuate the political debate of 'centralization' versus 'subsidiarity'.

The road ahead for the EC is likely to be increasingly bumpy as divisions between the existing large members over the internal development of the Community as enshrined in the Maastricht Treaty become magnified by the need to accommodate the economic and political aspirations of an increasing number of smaller members.

EFTA

The European Free Trade Association (EFTA) aims to achieve free trade in industrial goods between member states, to help create a single West European market and to encourage an expansion in world trade. The first aim was met in December 1966 when nearly all internal tariffs on industrial goods were abolished. Considerable progress was made towards the second aim in April 1984 when trade agreements with the EC abolished tariffs on industrial goods between EC and EFTA countries.

Closer integration between the European Community and the EFTA is being achieved by the foundation of the European Economic Area (the EEA), a single West European trading area (see the second column of this page). The EEA will not replace the EFTA or the EC, although, as most EFTA countries have applied or are considering applying to join the EC, the long-term future of the EFTA is in some doubt.

The EFTA was founded in 1960 by a group of West European countries that felt unable to accept the political and economic consequences of joining the EC. Austria, Denmark, Norway, Portugal, Sweden, Switzerland and the UK were the original EFTA members. Iceland joined the EFTA in 1970. Denmark and the UK withdrew from the EFTA in 1972 and Portugal withdrew in 1986 to become members of the EC. Finland became an associate member of the EFTA in 1961 and a full member in 1986. Liechtenstein, which was formerly an associate member of the EFTA by virtue of its customs union with Switzerland, became a full member of the EFTA in 1991. In 1990 declarations of cooperation were signed with Poland and Hungary. In the same year, a similar declaration was signed with Czechoslovakia; this has since been replaced by separate agreements with the Czech Republic and Slovakia.

Each full EFTA member state maintains a permanent delegation in Geneva, the heads of which meet – as the EFTA Council — once a fortnight. Twice a year the EFTA Council comprises ministers of EFTA governments. Council decisions are binding on members and each state has a single vote. Decisions on existing obligations are taken by majority vote but unanimity is required where increased obligations are involved. There is a permanent Secretariat, headed by a Secretary-General, in Geneva and six standing committees:
- the Committee of Trade Experts;
- the Committee of Origin and Customs Experts;
- the Committee on Technical Barriers to Trade;
- the Economic Committee;
- the Consultative Committee; and
- the Committee of Members of Parliament of EFTA Countries.

Headquarters: Geneva, Switzerland.

Secretary-General: Georg Reisch (Austria).

Current members: Austria (*original member*), Finland (*associate member 1961, full member 1986*), Iceland (*member 1970*), Liechtenstein (*associate member 1960, full member 1991*), Norway (*original member*), Sweden (*original member*), and Switzerland (*original member*).

THE EUROPEAN ECONOMIC AREA

The European Economic Area (EEA) is a free trade alliance between the 12 member countries of the EC – Belgium, Denmark, France, Germany, Greece, Ireland, Italy, Luxembourg, Netherlands, Portugal, Spain and the United Kingdom – and six of the seven member countries of the EFTA – Austria, Finland, Iceland, Liechtenstein, Norway and Sweden. The EEA should have come into force on 1 January 1993. However, Switzerland, the seventh EFTA member, decided in a referendum in December 1992, not to participate in the EEA. As a result it has been necessary to draw up a 'protocol' to make adjustments to the Agreement to allow the EEA to proceed without Switzerland. A protocol was signed in March 1993 and the EEA is expected to commence before the end of 1993.

The EEA's main aim is to extend the EC's four 'single market freedoms' in the movement of goods, services, capital and labour to include EFTA, thus creating a unified market of nearly 375 million people. EFTA states will adopt the various harmonization measures which have been, or are being, implemented by EC countries under the Single European Act, 1986 (see p. 17). The objective of the EEA is thus to widen the gains to be achieved by the formation of a 'common market' in which goods and services are free to circulate unencumbered by differences in national product requirements, technical specifications and standards, differences in labelling and packaging stipulations, differences in taxation structures, and so on.

There are different forms of trade integration ranging from a loose association of trade partners to a fully integrated group of nation states. The EC and the EFTA are different types of trade association. The EFTA is a *free trade area*, where members eliminate trade barriers between themselves but each continues to operate its own particular barriers against non-members. The EC is a *common market*, that is, a customs union which also provides for the free movement of capital and labour across national boundaries. However, the EC is moving towards becoming an *economic union*, that is, a common market which also provides for the harmonization of national business practices and regulations (as established by the EC's Single European Act, 1986), and the harmonization and integration of monetary, fiscal and other macroeconomic policies.

The formation of the EEA and the likelihood of an eventual 'merger' of the two blocs (see p. 20) comes at a time of growing interdependency in trade between the EC and the EFTA. As the table below indicates, however, individual EFTA states export far more to the EC than they do to other EFTA countries, a development fostered by various bilateral trade preference agreements giving tariff-free access to the EC market for a wide range of goods. However, for most EC states the EFTA market currently accounts for only a small proportion of their total exports.

EC and EFTA Trade 1991

	% of total exports	
EC Members	EC	EFTA
Belgium and Luxembourg	73%	6%
Denmark	54%	24%
France	64%	7%
Germany	54%	16%
Greece	61%	6%
Ireland	72%	6%
Italy	59%	9%
Netherlands	67%	6%
Portugal	73%	10%
Spain	62%	4%
UK	53%	8%
EFTA Members		
Austria	65%	10%
Finland	47%	20%
Iceland	68%	9%
Norway	65%	16%
Sweden	54%	19%
Switzerland and Liechtenstein	58%	7%

Source: European Commission

MAIN FEATURES OF THE EEA AGREEMENT

EFTA is committed to taking on board a large volume of existing EC legislation. Provision has been made for the EFTA to influence new EC legislation in areas relevant to the EEA by participation in the legislative process. However, EFTA states cannot vote on or veto EC legislation. The EC and individual EFTA members will continue to set their own tariffs on goods coming from non-members. Border controls between the EC and EFTA states, and between the EFTA states themselves, will still remain. It may well be, however, that the EEA will cease to exist before too long since five of the EFTA countries have applied to join the EC.

The most important aspect of the Agreement is that the four EC 'freedoms', the free movement of goods, services, capital and people, will apply throughout the EEA.

Free movement of goods Before the establishment of the EEA a wide range of industrial goods and some agricultural products were already traded freely between the EC and EFTA under the EC EFTA Free Trade Agreements of 1972–73. The EEA provides for the abolition of remaining tariffs and quotas on such products as whisky, beer, confectionery, soups, sauces and processed vegetables. The Agreement does not cover unprocessed agricultural produce. EFTA will not join the Common Agricultural Policy (see p. 96) so tariff and quota restrictions will remain in place on unprocessed agricultural produce, although steps will be taken to liberalize these restrictions. The Agreement also involves the removal of an extensive range of non-tariff obstacles to trade between the two blocs involving the adoption of common technical standards and regulations, a ban on discriminatory taxation and an open public purchasing policy.

Free movement of services The Agreement provides for the liberalization of movement of services. Any business established in an EEA state will be free to provide services such as banking, insurance, commercial or professional services and transport services throughout the EEA under the same conditions that apply within the EC single market. In sectors such as financial services and telecommunications the EFTA states will adopt the relevant EC rules thus ensuring a common approach throughout the Area.

Free movement of capital The Agreement removes restrictions on capital movements. This will have a significant impact on investment flows. Until now, EFTA countries have imposed major restrictions on inward investment (direct investment in setting up businesses, share purchases and purchases of real estate). Removal of these restrictions will open up greater opportunities for cross-border takeovers, mergers and joint ventures. A common approach to the regulation of financial markets and the conduct of stock exchange dealings has also been adopted.

Free movement of people The Agreement gives all EC and EFTA nationals the right to work throughout the EEA on the same terms as local workers, without discrimination in respect of employment, pay or working conditions. There are, however, restrictions on claiming public funds: people cannot move to another state just to claim social security benefits. As the establishment of common standards in respect of professional qualifications cannot be introduced overnight, the free movement of professional personnel may be restricted for some time to come. Cultural and language differences will also tend to restrict labour mobility. Passport controls will remain at EC-EFTA border crossings, but formalities will be eased.

Other provisions The Agreement involves the introduction of common rules on competition and state aid throughout the EEA. Those EFTA states which now have rather 'lax' competition policies will adopt the much stricter competition rules of the EC in respect of cartels, monopoly abuse and anti-competitive mergers and takeovers. The EEA will also adopt the strict EC rules on state aid in order to ensure that firms based in the EFTA do not enjoy unfair competitive advantage over EC-based firms. The Agreement also provides for greater cooperation between the two blocs in a number of important areas (research and technology, social policy, the environment, etc.) and the establishment of a new fund to assist economically-backward regions.

EEA INSTITUTIONS AND DECISION-MAKING

Several new institutions have been established to administer the EEA. These include:

The EEA Council which is responsible for the strategic and political direction of the EEA at the ministerial level;

The EEA Joint Committee which is responsible for the day-to-day operation of the EEA; and

The EFTA Surveillance Authority which will ensure compliance with single market rules.

A NEW GERMANY

The social and economic cost of German unification is a major factor influencing Germany and Europe. Germany's public-sector deficit has deteriorated from near balance in the 1980s to over 6% of GNP because of the needs of the former East Germany. Although modest spending cuts and tax increases have been introduced, the German government is at present unwilling or unable to take stronger tax and spending measures to bring fiscal and monetary policies into balance. The burden of anti-inflationary policy has thus come to rest on the Bundesbank, which has responded to wage pressures and excessive money supply growth with a regime of high real interest rates. The Bundesbank's bid to squeeze out inflation has been criticized by other European governments, who have argued that by keeping interest rates high the Bundesbank has dragged Germany and the rest of Europe into recession. This led to a decline in German GDP and industrial output (even in the former West Germany), and the resulting strains saw the forced exit of Britain and Italy from the ERM system (1992), devaluations of the Spanish and Portuguese currencies and pressure on the French franc (1993) that finally obliged the EC central bank governors to widen ERM fluctuation margins to 15%. The result is now a vacuum at the heart of European monetary policy.

Many of the problems following German unification were created by the decision to convert the East German currency into Deutschmarks at a rate of 1:1 and the choice of a relatively short adjustment period during which wages in the east would rise to parity with those in the west. The cost of bringing East Germany up to Western levels with uncompetitive labour and a poor infrastructure has created the deficit in German public finances.

COSTS OF UNIFICATION

The Bundesbank has made no secret of its view that until public finances were clearly under control it would be very difficult to justify substantial cuts in interest rates. The 1994 German budget was portrayed by Bonn as paving the way to future rate cuts. The budget comprises a DM 21 billion savings package approved for 1994 and includes a cut of three percentage points in unemployment and social assistance benefits, a freeze on pay in the public sector, and a clampdown on social security and tax fraud intended to yield DM 6 billion. However, the problems of unification also need to be set in the context of the increasing uncompetitiveness of West German industry, and the debate over Bonn's spending cuts is expected to become increasingly rancorous as Germany prepares for national elections in 1994.

The problem of costs is especially acute among the small- and medium-sized companies responsible for around half of the country's industrial output. German exporters, often characterized by distinct quality and individuality, were able in the past to mask unit labour costs which were increasingly becoming out of line with those of Germany's major competitors. By the eve of unification, however unit labour costs were well over 30% and 40% above those of the UK and France respectively. The pre- and post-unification boom translated into relatively generous wage increases, especially in the east, where unions extracted the wage rates equalization agreement from employers. Initially, the impact on costs was concealed, as thousands of easterners came west, willing to work for lower wages than their fellow citizens. However, once the exodus stopped, and the remaining eastern workers received 30% wage rises, the impact on costs became visible. It was exacerbated by the slowing of economic growth and the accompanying fall in productivity.

Germany, consequently, now urgently needs to address these major structural problems, and in this respect the 'solidarity pact' on the future funding of unification is an encouraging start. The March 1993 pact between Chancellor Helmut Kohl's Christian Democrats, the opposition Social Democrats led by Bjorn Engholm and the leaders of the federal states provides the basic framework for the future funding of unification. Centrally it turns on the Länder receiving additional tax revenues in the form of a bigger share of VAT receipts to assist with their financial transfers to the eastern Länder after 1995, with the hole in central government revenue filled by a 7.5% income tax surcharge commencing that year. The deal avoids cuts in social spending, but does call for limited annual expenditure cutbacks. Despite this accord, the brutal fact remains that the cost of subsidizing the development of the east will remain immense in the foreseeable future – it is estimated at DM 110 billion in 1995 alone when the pact comes into operation. Transfers to the East have so far totalled DM 500 billion, and will reach DM 180 billion in 1993. The cost of upgrading East Germany will need to go on for several years.

GERMANY IN EUROPE

The end of the Cold War has left Germany no longer squeezed between an Atlantic alliance dominated by America and a powerful Soviet Union. The new Germany has emerged united with 17 million more citizens and, no less important, with a hinterland of countries (the Czech Republic especially, but also Poland and Hungary) which look to Germany for investment and trade. Moreover, the security problems of the future – like immigration and aid to the east – are matters on which Germany has experience and on which its voice is likely to be increasingly heard.

It is not, as it seemed at the time of unification in 1990, a matter of choosing between a Germany 'bound in' to the EC or lured towards the east. Whatever the EC does, Germany will have to look in both directions, as well as sorting out its own affairs. Since 1945, Europe has been the main international forum in which Germany has pursued its national interests. But, in its current form, the EC will be increasingly unable to persuade Germany – with its interests in Central and Eastern Europe – to keep doing this. The real Europe – stretching from the Atlantic to the Urals – is now so different from the artificial 'Europe' of the Community. (See pp. 32–35).

WESTERN EUROPE

BELGIUM

Official name: Royaume de Belgique or Koninkrijk België (Kingdom of Belgium).

Member of: UN, NATO, EC/EU, CSCE, WEU, Council of Europe, OECD.

Area: 30 519 km² (11 783 sq mi).

Population: 10 022 000 (1992 est).

Capital: Brussels (Bruxelles/Brussel) 951 000 (1992 est).

Other major cities: Antwerp (Antwerpen or Anvers) 917 000 (city 465 000), Liège (Luik) 601 000 (city 196 000), Ghent (Gent or Gand) 485 000 (city 230 000), Charleroi 429 000 (city 207 000), Malines (Mechelen) 293 000 (city 76 000), Courtrai (Kortrijk) 275 000 (city 76 000), Namur (Namen) 264 000 (city 104 000), Bruges (Brugge) 260 000 (city 117 000), Mons (Bergen) 92 000, La Louvière 77 000, Ostend (Oostende or Ostende) 69 000 (1992 est).

Languages: Flemish, French; see pp. 77–9.

Religion: Roman Catholic; see pp. 80–81.

Education: See pp. 86–90.

Defence: See pp. 122–24.

Transport: See pp. 118–22.

Media: See pp. 126–32.

GOVERNMENT

Belgium is a constitutional monarchy. The Chamber of Deputies (lower house) has 212 members elected by universal adult suffrage for four years by proportional representation. The Senate (upper house) has 182 members: 106 directly elected, 50 chosen by provincial councils, 25 co-opted, and the heir to the throne. The King appoints a Prime Minister, who commands a parliamentary majority; the PM chooses a Cabinet. The three regions have their own administrations. Political parties include the (conservative Flemish) CVP (Christelijke Volkspartei), the (conservative Francophone) Parti social chrétien (PSC), the (Socialist Flemish) Socialistische Partei (SP), the (Socialist Francophone) Parti socialiste belge (PS), the (Flemish) Liberal Freedom and Progress Party (PVV), the (Francophone) Liberal Reform Party (PRL), (Green Flemish) Agalev, (Green Francophone) Ecolo, the (Flemish nationalist) Vlaams Blok and Volksunie, and the (Francophone) Democratic Front (FDF). At the general election of 24 November 1991 these parties obtained the following number of seats in the Chamber. A coalition of CVP, SP, PSC and PS members was formed in March 1992.

Party	Seats
CVP	39
PS	35
SP	28
PVV	26
PRL	20
PSC	18
Vlaams Blok	12
Volksunie	10
Ecolo	10
Agalev	7
Van Rossem List	3
FDF	3
Front National	1
Total	*212*

King: HM Albert II, King of the Belgians (inaugurated 9 August 1993 after the death of his brother, 31 July 1993).

THE CABINET

Prime Minister: Jean-Luc Dehaene (CVP).
Deputy Prime Minister (and Minister of Communications and Public Enterprises): Guy Coëme (PS).
Deputy Prime Minister (and Minister of Foreign Affairs): Willy Claes (SP).
Deputy Prime Minister (and Minister of Justice and Minister of Economic Affairs): Melchior Wathelet (PSC).
Minister of Agriculture: André Bourgeois (CVP).
Minister for the Budget: Mieke Offeciers-Van De Wiele (CVP).
Minister of Communications and Public Enterprises: See above.
Minister of Defence: Leo Delcroix (CVP).
Minister of Employment, Labour and Equality: Miel Smet (CVP).
Minister of Finance: Philippe Maystadt (PSC).
Minister of Foreign Affairs: See above.
Minister of Foreign Trade and European Affairs: Robert Urbain (PS).
Minister of the Interior and the Civil Service: Louis Tobback (SP).
Minister of Justice: See above.
Minister of Pensions: Freddy Willockx (PS).
Minister of Science Policy: Jean-Maurice Dehousse (PS).
Minister of Social Affairs: Philippe Moureaux (PS).
Minister of Social Integration: Laurette Onkelinx (PS).

REGIONS

Brussels (Bruxelles/Brussel) *Area*: 162 km² (63 sq mi). *Population*: 951 000 (1992 est). *Centre*: Brussels.

Flanders (Vlaanderen) *Area*: 13 512 km² (5217 sq mi). *Population*: 5 725 000 (1991 census). *Centre*: Ghent.

Wallonia (Wallonie) *Area*: 16 844 km² (6503 sq mi). *Population*: 3 165 000 (1991 census). *Centre*: Namur.

GEOGRAPHY

The forested Ardennes plateau occupies the southeast. The plains of central Belgium, an important agricultural region, are covered in fertile loess. The flat, low-lying north contains the sandy Kempenland plateau in the east and the plain of Flanders in the west. Enclosed by dykes behind coastal sand dunes are polders – former marshes and lagoons reclaimed from the sea. *Principal rivers*: Scheldt (Schelde or Escaut), Meuse (Maes), Sambre. *Highest point*: Botrange 694 m (2272 ft). Belgium experiences relatively cool summers and mild winters. Summers are warmer and winters colder inland.

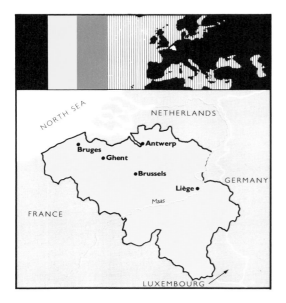

have mirrored Belgium's linguistic divide, with high unemployment concentrated in the Francophone (Walloon) south, while the industries of the Flemish north have prospered. Banking, commerce and administration employ increasing numbers, and Brussels has benefited as the unofficial 'capital' of the EC. For data on currency see pp. 104–5, GNP p. 125, imports and exports pp. 112–13 and the national budget see pp. 134–36.

Labour force (1991)

Sector	Number employed
Industry	790 000
Agriculture	99 000
Construction	225 000
Public utilities	30 000
Trade, hotels, restaurants	628 000
Transport and communications	253 000
Finance	315 000
Services and administration	1 370 000
Other (inc. unemployed)	435 000
Total	*4 145 000*

RECENT HISTORY

Belgium's neutrality was broken by the German invasion in 1914 (leading to Britain's declaration of war against Germany). The brave resistance of King Albert in 1914–18 earned international praise; the capitulation of Leopold III when Belgium was again occupied by Germany (1940–45) was criticized. The Belgian Congo (Zaïre), acquired as a personal possession by Leopold II (1879), was relinquished amidst scenes of chaos in 1960. Belgium is now the main centre of administration of the EC and of NATO, but is troubled by the acute rivalry between its Flemish and French speakers and a federal system based on linguistic regions has evolved.

ECONOMY

Belgium is a densely populated industrial country. In the centre and the north, soils are generally fertile and the climate encourages high yields of wheat, sugar beet, grass and fodder crops. Metalworking is a major industry. Textiles, chemicals, ceramics, glass and rubber are also important, but almost all industrial raw materials have to be imported. Economic problems since the 1970s

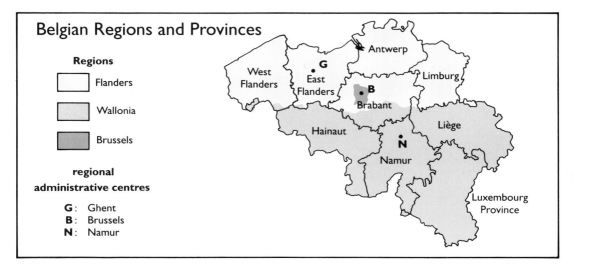

Belgian Regions and Provinces

Regions

Flanders

Wallonia

Brussels

regional administrative centres

- **G**: Ghent
- **B**: Brussels
- **N**: Namur

DENMARK

Official name: Kongeriget Danmark (Kingdom of Denmark).

Member of: UN, EC/EU, NATO, Council of Europe, CSCE, OECD, WEU (associate). (The Faeroes are not part of the European Community.)

Area: 43 092 km² (16 638 sq mi) – metropolitan Denmark, excluding the Faeroes; 44 491 km² (17 178 sq mi) including the Faeroes.

Population: 5 162 000 – metropolitan Denmark, excluding the Faeroes (1992 est); 5 211 000 including the Faeroe Islands (1992 est).

Capital: Copenhagen (København) 1 337 000 (city 465 000; Frederiksberg 86 000) (1992 est).

Other major cities: Aarhus (Århus) 268 000, Odense 179 000, Aalborg (Ålborg) 157 000, Esbjerg 82 000, Randers 61 000, Kolding 58 000, Helsingor 57 000, Horsens 55 000, Vejle 52 000, Roskilde 50 000 (all including suburbs; 1992 est).

Language: Danish; see pp. 77–9. Faeroese is – with Danish – the official language of the Faeroes.

Religion: Lutheran (89%); see pp. 80–81.

Education: See pp. 86–90.

Defence: See pp. 122–24.

Transport: See pp. 118–22.

Media: See pp. 126–32.

GOVERNMENT

Denmark is a constitutional monarchy. The 179 members of Parliament (Folketing) are elected by universal adult suffrage under a system of proportional representation for four years. Two members are elected from both of the autonomous dependencies (Greenland and the Faeroes). The autonomous dependencies also have their own governments. The Monarch appoints a Prime Minister, who commands a majority in the Folketing. The PM, in turn, appoints a State Council (Cabinet), which is responsible to the Folketing. The main political parties are the Social Democratic Party (SDP), the Conservative People's Party, the Liberal Party, the Socialist People's Party, the Progress Party, the Centre Democrats (CD), the Christian People's Party (KF), and the Radical Liberals (RV). At the general election held on 12 December 1990 these parties obtained the following number of seats and in January 1993 a new SDP, CD, KF and RV coalition was formed.

Party	Seats
Social Democratic Party	69
Conservative People's Party	30
Liberal Party	29
Socialist People's Party	15
Progress Party	12
Centre Democrats	9
Radical Liberals	7
Christian People's Party	4
Faeroese/Greenland members	4
Total	179

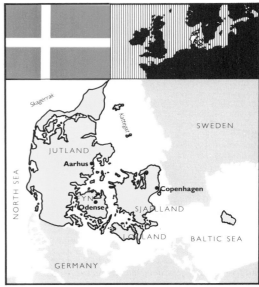

Queen: HM Queen Margrethe II (succeeded upon the death of her father, 14 January 1972).

THE CABINET

Prime Minister: Poul Nyrup Rasmussen (SDP).

Minister of Agriculture and Fisheries: Bjorn Westh (SDP).

Minister of Aid and Cooperation: Helle Degn (SDP).

Minister for Business Affairs: Mimi Stilling Jakobsen (CD).

Minister for Church Affairs: Arne Oluf Andersen (CD).

Minister for Communications and Tourism: Arne Melchior (CD).

Minister of Culture: Jytte Hilden (SDP).

Minister of Defence: Hans Haekkerup (SDP).

Minister for Economics: Marianne Jelved (RV).

Minister of Education: Ole Vig Jensen (RV).

Minister of Energy: Jann Sjursen (KF).

Minister for the Environment: Svend Auken (SDP).

Minister of Finance: Mogens Lykketoft (SDP).

Minister of Foreign Affairs: Niels Helveg Petersen (RV).

Minister of Health: Torben Lund (SDP).

Minister of Housing and Minister of Nordic and Baltic Affairs: Flemming Kofod Svendsen (KF).

Minister of Industry: Jan Trojborg (SDP).

Minister of the Interior: Birthe Weiss (SDP).

Minister of Justice: Pia Gjellerup (SDP).

Minister of Labour: Jytte Andersen (SDP).

Minister of Research: Svend Bergstein (CD).

Minister for Social Affairs: Karen Jespersen (SDP).

Minister of Taxation: Ole Stavad (SDP).

Minister of Transport: Helge Mortensen (SDP).

AUTONOMOUS DEPENDENCY

Denmark has two autonomous dependencies – the Faeroes (see below) and Greenland. The former is part of the continent of Europe; the latter is part of North America.

Faeroe Islands (Faeroerne) *Area*: 1399 km² (540 sq mi). *Population*: 48 400 (1990 est). *Capital*: Tórshavn 16 200 (1990 est).

GEOGRAPHY

Denmark is a lowland of glacial moraine – only the island of Bornholm has ancient hard surface rocks. The country comprises the Jutland peninsula – which occupies about two-thirds of the total area of Denmark – and, to the east of Jutland, a series of over 400 islands, of which 97 are inhabited. The largest islands are Zealand (Sjaelland), Fyn and Lolland. The island of Bornholm lies to the east in the Baltic Sea. *Principal river:* Gudená. *Highest point:* Yding Skovhøj 173 m (568 ft). The climate is temperate and moist with mild summers and cold winters. Bornholm is more extreme.

The Faeroes are an archipelago of 17 inhabited and numerous small uninhabited mountainous islands. They experience a wet climate which is cold and windy in the winter.

ECONOMY

Denmark has a high standard of living, but few natural resources. Danish agriculture is famous for its efficiency is organized on a cooperative basis, and produces cheese and other dairy products, bacon and beef – all mainly for export. About one fifth of the labour force is involved in manufacturing, with iron- and metal-working, food processing and brewing, engineering and chemicals as the most important industries. The high cost of imported fuel has been a problem for the economy, but this has been partly alleviated by petroleum and natural gas from the North Sea. For information on Denmark's GNP see p. 125, currency see pp. 104–5, foreign trade pp. 112–13 and national budget see pp. 134–36.

Labour force (1991)

Sector	Number employed
Industry	528 000
Agriculture	151 000
Public utilities	19 000
Construction	170 000
Trade, restaurants, hotels	331 000
Transport and communications	182 000
Finance	258 000
Services and administration	954 000
Total	*2 592 000*

The Faeroese economy depends heavily upon deep-sea fishing. Severe economic problems have been averted only through financial assistance from the central Danish government.

RECENT HISTORY

In the 20th century, Denmark's last colonial possessions were either sold (Virgin Islands) or given independence (Iceland) or autonomy (Greenland and the Faeroe Islands). In 1920 northern Schleswig – surrendered to Germany in 1864 – was returned to Denmark. The country was occupied by Nazi Germany (1940–45), and has since been a member of the Western Alliance. From the 1960s, Denmark's economic and political ties have increasingly been with Germany, the UK and the Netherlands, rather than the traditional links with the Nordic countries (Norway and Sweden). Thus, in 1973 Denmark joined the EC, but the political consequence of joining the Common Market has been a further fragmentation of the country's political parties, which has made the formation of coalition and minority governments a protracted and difficult process. The initial failure of the Danish electorate to approve the EC Maastricht Treaty (1992) temporarily halted moves towards European integration.

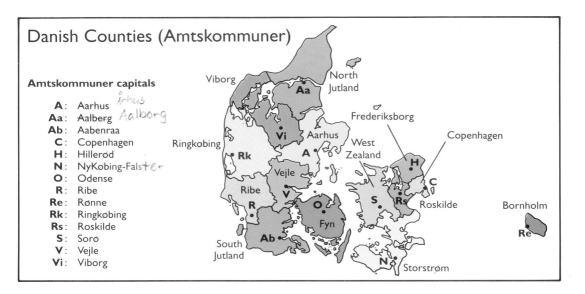

Danish Counties (Amtskommuner)

Amtskommuner capitals

A: Aarhus
Aa: Aalberg
Ab: Aabenraa
C: Copenhagen
H: Hillerød
N: NyKobing-Falster
O: Odense
R: Ribe
Re: Rønne
Rk: Ringkøbing
Rs: Roskilde
S: Sorø
V: Vejle
Vi: Viborg

FRANCE

Official name: La République Française (The French Republic).

Member of: UN, EC/EU, NATO, WEU, G7, OECD, CSCE, Council of Europe.

Area: 543 965 km² (210 026 sq mi).

Population: 57 456 000 (1992 est.).

Capital: Paris 9 063 000 (city 2 175 000).

Other major cities: Lyon 1 262 000 (city 422 000), Marseille 1 087 000 (city 808 000), Lille 950 000 (city 178 000), Bordeaux 686 000 (city 213 000), Toulouse 608 000 (city 366 000), Nantes 492 000 (city 252 000), Nice 476 000 (city 346 000), Toulon 438 000 (city 170 000), Grenoble 400 000 (city 154 000), Strasbourg 388 000 (city 256 000), Rouen 380 000 (city 105 000), Valenciennes 336 000 (town 39 000), Cannes 336 000 (city 69 000), Lens 323 000 (town 35 000), Saint-Etienne 313 000 (city 202 000), Nancy 311 000 (city 102 000), Tours 272 000 (city 133 000), Béthune 260 000 (town 26 000), Clermont-Ferrand 254 000 (city 140 000), Le Havre 254 000 (city 197 000), Rennes 245 000 (city 204 000), Orléans 243 000 (city 108 000), Montpellier 235 000 (city 211 000), Dijon 226 000 (city 152 000), Mulhouse 224 000 (city 110 000), Reims 206 000 (city 185 000), Angers 206 000 (city 146 000), Brest 201 000 (city 153 000), Douai 200 000 (city 44 000), Dunkerque 193 000 (town 71 000), Metz 193 000 (city 124 000), Le Mans 189 000 (city 148 000), Caen 189 000 (city 116 000), Mantes-la-Jolie 189 000 (town 45 000), Avignon 181 000 (city 89 000), Limoges 170 000 (city 136 000) (1990 census).

Languages: French, with Breton and Basque minorities; see pp. 77–9.

Religions: Roman Catholic (74%); see pp. 80–81.

Education: See pp. 86–90.

Defence: See pp. 122–24.

Transport: See pp. 118–22.

Media: See pp. 126–32.

GOVERNMENT

Executive power is vested in the President, who is directly elected for seven years. The President appoints a Prime Minister and a Council of Ministers – both responsible to Parliament – but it is the President, rather than the PM, who presides over the Council. The Senate (upper house) has 321 members – 296 representing individual départements and 13 representing overseas départements and territories – elected by members of local councils. The remaining 12 senators are elected by French citizens resident abroad. Senators serve for nine years, with one third of the Senate retiring every three years. The National Assembly (lower house) has 577 deputies – including 22 for overseas départements and territories – elected for five years by universal adult suffrage from constituencies, with a second ballot for the leading candidates if no candidate obtains an absolute majority in the first round. The 96 metropolitan départements are grouped into 22 regions which have increasing powers. Political parties include the (conservative Gaullist) RPR (Rally for the Republic), the (centrist) UDF (Union for French Democracy), the PS (Socialist Party), the PCF (Communist Party), and the (right-wing) FN (National Front). At the general election held on 21 and 28 March 1993 these parties obtained the following number of seats in the Assembly.

Party	Seats
RPR	247
UDF	213
PS (and allied parties)	70
PCF	23
Various right-wing parties	24
Total	277

President: François Mitterrand (elected 1981, re-elected 1988).

THE CABINET

Prime Minister: Edouard Balladur (RPR).

Minister of Agriculture and Fisheries: Jean Puech (UDF).

Minister for the Budget and Government Spokesman: Nicolas Sarkozy (RPR).

Minister of Business and Economic Development: Alain Madelin (UDF).

Minister for the Civil Service: André Rossinot (UDF).

Minister of Communications: Alain Carignon (RPR).

Minister for Co-operation: Michel Poussin (RPR).

Minister of Culture and the French Language: Jacques Toubon (RPR).

Minister of Defence: François Léotard (UDF).

Minister of the Economy: Edmond Alphandéry (UDF).

Minister of Education: François Bayrou (UDF).

Minister for the Environment: Michel Barnier (RPR).

Minister of Foreign Affairs: Alain Juppé (RPR).

Minister of Higher Education and Research: François Fillon (RPR).

Minister of Housing: Hervé de Charette (UDF).

Minister for Industry, Posts, Telecommunications and Foreign Trade: Gérard Longuet (UDF).

Minister of the Interior: Charles Pasqua (RPR).

Minister of Justice: Pierre Méhaignerie (UDF).

Minister of Labour, Employment and Professional Training: Michel Giraud (RPR).

Minister for Overseas Départements and Territories: Dominique Perben (RPR).

Minister of Public Works, Transport and Tourism: Bernard Bosson (UDF).

Minister (of State) for Social, Health and Urban Affairs: Simone Veil (UDF).

Minister for Veterans and War Victims: Philippe Mestre (UDF).

Minister for Youth and Sport: Michèle Alliot-Marie (RPR).

REGIONS

Population figures are from the 1990 census.

Alsace *Area*: 8280 km² (3197 sq mi). *Population*: 1 624 000. *Administrative centre*: Strasbourg.

Aquitaine *Area*: 41 308 km² (15 949 sq mi). *Population*: 2 796 000. *Administrative centre*: Bordeaux.

Auvergne *Area*: 26 013 km² (10 044 sq mi). *Population*: 1 321 000. *Administrative centre*: Clermont-Ferrand.

Brittany (Bretagne) *Area*: 27 208 km² (10 505 sq mi). *Population*: 2 796 000. *Administrative centre*: Rennes.

Burgundy (Bourgogne) *Area*: 31 582 km² (12 194 sq mi). *Population*: 1 609 000. *Administrative centre*: Dijon.

Centre *Area*: 39 151 km² (15 116 sq mi). *Population*: 2 371 000. *Administrative centre*: Orléans.

Champagne-Ardenne *Area*: 25 606 km² (9886 sq mi). *Population*: 1 348 000. *Administrative centre*: Reims.

Corsica (Corse) *Area*: 8680 km² (3351 sq mi). *Population*: 250 000. *Administrative centre*: Ajaccio.

Franche-Comté *Area*: 16 202 km² (6256 sq mi). *Population*: 1 097 000. *Administrative centre*: Besançon.

Ile-de-France *Area*: 12 012 km² (4638 sq mi). *Population*: 10 660 000. *Administrative centre*: Paris.

Languedoc-Roussillon *Area*: 27 376 km² (10 570 sq mi). *Population*: 2 115 000. *Administrative centre*: Montpellier.

Limousin *Area*: 16 942 km² (6541 sq mi). *Population*: 723 000. *Administrative centre*: Limoges.

Lorraine *Area*: 23 547 km² (9091 sq mi). *Population*: 2 306 000. *Administrative centre*: Nancy.

Lower Normandy (Basse Normandie) *Area*: 17 589 km² (6791 sq mi). *Population*: 1 391 000. *Administrative centre*: Caen.

Midi-Pyrénées *Area*: 45 348 km² (17 509 sq mi). *Population*: 2 431 000. *Administrative centre*: Toulouse.

Nord-Pas-de-Calais *Area*: 12 414 km² (4793 sq mi). *Population*: 3 965 000. *Administrative centre*: Lille.

Pays de la Loire *Area*: 32 082 km² (12 387 sq mi). *Population*: 3 059 000. *Administrative centre*: Nantes.

Picardy (Picardie) *Area*: 19 399 km² (7490 sq mi). *Population*: 1 811 000. *Administrative centre*: Amiens.

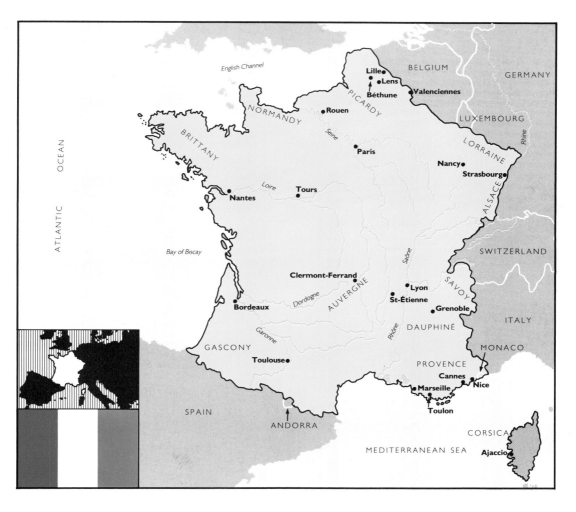

Poitou-Charentes *Area*: 25 810 km² (9965 sq mi). *Population*: 1 595 000. *Administrative centre*: Poitiers.

Provence-Côte d'Azur *Area*: 31 400 km² (12 124 sq mi). *Population*: 4 258 000. *Administrative centre*: Marseille.

Rhône-Alpes *Area*: 43 698 km² (16 872 sq mi). *Population*: 5 351 000. *Administrative centre*: Lyon.

Upper Normandy (Haute-Normandie) *Area*: 12 317 km² (4756 sq mi). *Population*: 1 737 000. *Administrative centre*: Rouen.

GEOGRAPHY
The Massif Central – a plateau of old hard rocks, rising to almost 2000 m (6500 ft) – occupies the middle of France. The Massif is surrounded by four major lowlands, which together make up almost two thirds of the total area of the country. The Paris Basin – the largest of these lowlands – is divided by low ridges and fertile plains and plateaux, but is united by the river system of the Seine and its tributaries. To the east of the Massif Central is the long narrow Rhône-Saône Valley, while to the west the Loire Valley stretches to the Atlantic. Southwest of the Massif Central lies the Aquitaine Basin, a large fertile region drained by the River Garonne and its tributaries. A discontinuous ring of highlands surrounds France. In the northwest the Armorican Massif (Brittany) rises to 411 m (1350 ft). In the southwest the Pyrenees form a high natural boundary with Spain. The Alps in the southeast divide France from Italy and contain the highest peak in Europe (outside the Caucasus). The lower Jura – in the east – form a barrier between France and Switzerland, while the Vosges Mountains separate the Paris Basin from the Rhine Valley. In the northeast, the Ardennes extend into France from Belgium. The Mediterranean island of Corsica is an ancient massif rising to 2710 m (8891 ft). *Principal rivers:* Rhine (Rhin), Loire, Rhône, Seine, Garonne, Saône. *Highest point:* Mont Blanc 4807 m (15 771 ft). The Mediterranean south has warm summers and mild winters. The rest of France has a temperate climate, although the more continental east experiences warmer summers and colder winters. Rainfall is moderate, with highest falls in the mountains and lowest falls around Paris.

ECONOMY
Over 60% of France is farmed. The principal products include cereals (wheat, maize, barley and even rice), meat and dairy products, sugar beet, and grapes for wine. France is remarkably self-sufficient in agriculture, with tropical fruit and animal feeds being the only major imports. However, the small size of land holdings remains a problem, despite consolidation and the efforts of cooperatives. Reafforestation is helping to safeguard the future of the important timber industry. Natural resources include coal, iron ore, copper, bauxite and tungsten, as well as petroleum and natural gas, and plentiful sites for hydroelectric power plants. The major French industries include: textiles, chemicals, steel, food processing, motor vehicles, aircraft, and mechanical and electrical engineering. Traditionally French firms have been small, but mergers have resulted in larger corporations able to compete internationally. France is now the world's fourth industrial power after the USA, Japan and Germany. Since the late 1980s many state-owned corporations were privatized. Over one half of the labour force is involved in service industries, in particular administration, banking, finance, and tourism. For information on the French currency see pp. 104–5, on GNP see p. 125, on imports and exports pp. 112–13 and on the national budget see pp. 134–36.

Labour force (1990–91)

Sector	Number employed
Industry	4 710 000
Agriculture	1 325 000
Construction	1 590 000
Public utilities	205 000
Trade, restaurants, hotels	3 760 000
Transport and communications	1 400 000
Finance, etc.	2 180 000
Services and administration	6 870 000
Total	*22 040 000*

RECENT HISTORY
Georges Clemenceau (1841–1929) – who had led France as prime minister during the World War I – lost power in 1919 when the French electorate perceived the harsh peace terms as being too lenient to Germany. Between 1919 and 1939 French government was characterized by instability and frequent changes of administration. In 1936 Léon Blum (1872–1950) led a Popular Front (Socialist-Communist-Radical) coalition to power and instituted many important social reforms. In World War II (1939–45), Germany rapidly defeated the French in 1940 and completely occupied the country in 1942. Marshal Philippe Pétain (1856–1951) led a collaborationist regime in the city of Vichy, while General Charles de Gaulle (1890–1970) headed the Free French in exile in London from 1940. France was liberated following the Allied landings in Normandy in 1944. After the war, the Fourth Republic (1946–58) was marked by instability and the Suez Crisis of 1956 – when France and the UK sought to prevent Egypt's nationalization of the canal. The end of the colonial era was marked by nationalist revolts in some of the colonies, notably Vietnam – where the Communists defeated French colonial forces at Dien Bien Phu in 1954 – and Algeria. The troubles in Algeria – including the revolt of the French colonists and the campaign of their terrorist organization, the OAS – led to the end of the Fourth Republic and to the accession to power of General de Gaulle in 1959.

As first president of the Fifth Republic, de Gaulle granted Algerian independence in 1962. While the French colonial empire – with a few minor exceptions – was being disbanded, France's position within Western Europe was being strengthened, especially by vigorous participation in the European Community. At the same time, de Gaulle sought to pursue a foreign policy independent of the USA, building up France's nuclear capability and withdrawing French forces from NATO's integrated command structure. Although restoring political and economic stability to France, domestic dissatisfaction – including the student revolt of May 1968 – led de Gaulle to resign in 1969. De Gaulle's policies were broadly pursued by his successors as president, Georges Pompidou (in office 1969–74) and Valéry Giscard d'Estaing (1974–81). The modernization of France continued apace under the country's first Socialist president, François Mitterrand (1916–), who was elected in 1981.

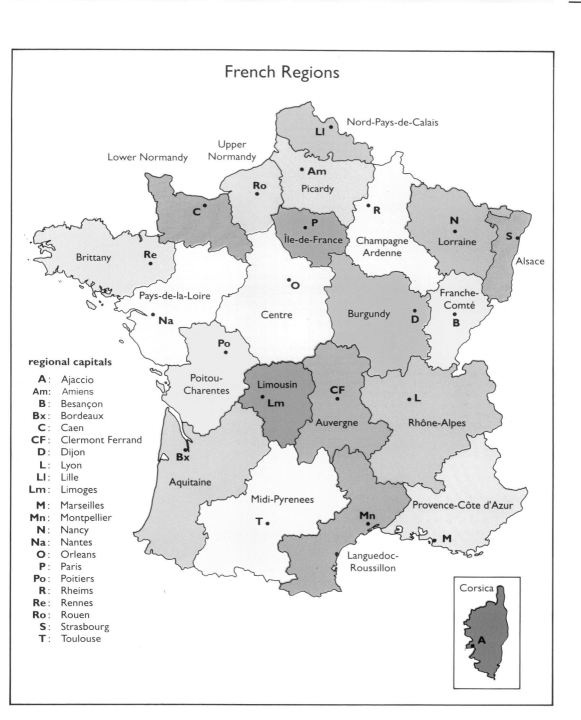

French Regions

Nord-Pays-de-Calais

Ll

Upper
Normandy

Lower Normandy

Am

Picardy

Ile-de-France

Ro

C

R

P

Champagne
Ardenne

N

Lorraine

S

Alsace

Brittany

Re

Pays-de-la-Loire

O

Franche-
Comté

Na

Centre

Burgundy

D

B

Po

regional capitals

A :	Ajaccio
Am :	Amiens
B :	Besançon
Bx :	Bordeaux
C :	Caen
CF :	Clermont Ferrand
D :	Dijon
L :	Lyon
Ll :	Lille
Lm :	Limoges
M :	Marseilles
Mn :	Montpellier
N :	Nancy
Na :	Nantes
O :	Orleans
P :	Paris
Po :	Poitiers
R :	Rheims
Re :	Rennes
Ro :	Rouen
S :	Strasbourg
T :	Toulouse

Poitou-
Charentes

Limousin

Lm

CF

Auvergne

L

Rhône-Alpes

Bx

Aquitaine

Midi-Pyrenees

T

Mn

Provence-Côte d'Azur

M

Languedoc-
Roussillon

Corsica

A

GERMANY

Official name: Bundesrepublik Deutschland (The Federal Republic of Germany).

Member of: UN, EC/EU, NATO, CSCE, WEU, G7, OECD, Council of Europe.

Area: 357 050 km² (137 857 sq mi).

Population: 79 754 000 (1991 est).

Capital: Berlin (capital in name only; the Bundestag is scheduled to move to Berlin by 2000) 3 590 000 (city 3 446 000), Bonn (capital *de facto*) 542 000 (city 296 000).

Other major cities: Essen 4 700 000 (Essen/Ruhr; city 627 000), Hamburg 1 924 000 (city 1 669 000), Munich (München) 1 465 000 (city 1 229 000), Cologne (Köln) 1 419 000 (city 960 000), Frankfurt 1 268 000 (city 654 000), Stuttgart 1 091 000 (city 592 000), Düsseldorf 913 000 (city 578 000), Hannover 680 000 (city 518 000), Bremen 622 000 (city 553 000), Nuremberg (Nürnberg) 617 000 (city 498 000), Dortmund (part of the Essen agglomeration; see above) 601 000, Dresden 580 000 (city 485 000), Mannheim 539 000 (city 315 000), Duisburg (part of the Essen agglomeration; see above) 537 000, Leipzig 532 000 (city 503 000), Wuppertal 485 000 (city 386 000), Bochum (part of the Essen/Ruhr agglomeration; see above) 399 000, Solingen 357 000 (city 166 000), Hagen 342 000 (city 216 000), Mönchengladbach 341 000 (city 263 000), Bielefeld 322 000 (city 288 000), Chemnitz 306 000 (city 288 000), Halle 303 000, Gelsenkirchen (part of the Essen agglomeration; see above) 294 000, Augsburg 281 000 (city 260 000), Karlsruhe 279 000, Magdeburg 275 000, Münster 264 000, Wiesbaden 264 000, Brunswick (Braunschweig) 259 000, Kiel 259 000 (city 247 000), Krefeld 246 000, Aachen 244 000, Rostock 244 000, Saarbrücken 236 000 (city 192 000), Lübeck 230 000 (city 216 000), Oberhausen (part of the Essen agglomeration; see above) 225 000, Erfurt 205 000, Kassel 197 000, Freiburg 194 000, Mainz 183 000, Hamm 180 000, Herne (part of the Essen agglomeration; see above) 179 000, Mülheim (part of the Essen/Ruhr agglomeration; see above) 177 000, Ludwigshafen (part of the Mannheim agglomeration; see above) 165 000, Osnabrück 165 000, Leverkusen (part of the Cologne agglomeration; see above) 161 000, Ulm 160 000 (city 112 000), Oldenburg 145 000, Darmstadt 140 000 (1990–91 est).

Language: German; see also pp. 77–79.

Religions: Lutheran and Lutheran tradition (43%), Roman Catholic (36%); see also pp. 80–81.

Education: See pp. 86–90.

Defence: See pp. 122–24.

Transport: See pp. 118–22.

Media: See pp. 126–31.

GOVERNMENT

Each of the 16 states (Länder; singular Länd) is represented in the 79-member upper house of Parliament – the Federal Council (Bundesrat) – by three, four or six members of the state government (depending on population). The lower house – the Federal Assembly (Bundestag) – has 662 members elected for four years by universal adult suffrage under a mixed system of single-member constituencies and proportional representation. Executive power rests with the Federal Government, led by the Federal Chancellor – who is elected by the Bundestag. The Federal President is elected for five years by the Bundesrat and an equal number of representatives of the states. Each state has its own government. The main political parties include the (conservative) CDU (Christian Democratic Union) and CSU (Christian Social Union, its Bavarian equivalent), the (socialist) SPD (Social Democratic Party), the (liberal) FDP (Free Democratic Party), Die Grünen (the Green Party), and the PDS (Party of Democratic Socialism; the former East German Communist Party). At the general election held on 2 December 1990 these parties obtained the following number of seats and a coalition of CDU/CSU and FDP members was formed.

Party	Seats
Christian Democrats/CSU	319
Social Democratic Party	239
Free Democrats	79
Democratic Socialists	17
Greens	8
Total	*662*

Federal President: Dr Richard von Weizsäcker (elected 1984; re-elected 1989).

THE CABINET
Federal Chancellor: Dr Helmut Kohl (CDU).
Minister at the Chancellery: Friedrich Bohl (CDU).
Minister for Construction: Irmgard Adam-Schwätzer (FDP).
Minister of Defence: Volker Rühe (CDU).
Minister of Economic Co-operation: Carl-Dieter Spranger (CSU).
Minister for the Economy: Günter Rexrodt (FDP).
Minister of Education and Science: Rainer Ortleb (FDP).
Minister for the Environment and Conservation: Klaus Töpfer (CDU).
Minister for the Family and the Elderly: Hannelore Rönsch (CDU).
Minister of Finance: Theo Waigel (CSU).
Minister of Food, Agriculture and Forestry: Jochen Borchert (CDU).
Minister of Foreign Affairs: Klaus Kinkel (ind).
Minister of Health: Horst Seehofer (CSU).
Minister of the Interior: Rudolf Seiters (CDU).
Minister of Justice: Sabine Leutheusser-Schnarrenberger (FDP).
Minister of Labour and Social Affairs: Dr Norbert Blüm (CDU).
Minister of Posts and Telecommunications: Wolfgang Bötsch (CSU).
Minister of Research and Technology: Matthias Wissman (CDU).
Minister of Transport: Günter Krause (CDU).
Minister for Women and Youth: Angela Merkel (CDU).

LANDER
Baden-Württemberg *Area*: 35 752 km^2 (13 803 sq mi). *Population*: 9 822 000 (1991 est). *Capital*: Stuttgart.

Bavaria (Bayern) *Area*: 70 546 km^2 (27 238 sq mi). *Population*: 11 449 000 (1991 est). *Capital*: Munich (München).

Berlin *Area*: 883 km^2 (341 sq mi). *Population*: 3 446 000 (1991 est). *Capital*: Berlin.

Brandenburg *Area*: 28 016 km^2 (10 817 sq mi). *Population*: 2 578 000 (1991 est). *Capital*: Potsdam.

Bremen *Area*: 404 km^2 (156 sq mi). *Population*: 682 000 (1991 est). *Capital*: Bremen.

Hamburg *Area*: 755 km^2 (292 sq mi). *Population*: 1 669 000 (1991 est). *Capital*: Hamburg.

Hesse (Hessen) *Area*: 21 114 km^2 (8152 sq mi). *Population*: 5 763 000 (1991 est). *Capital*: Wiesbaden.

Lower Saxony (Niedersachsen) *Area*: 47 431 km^2 (18 313 sq mi). *Population*: 7 387 000 (1991 est). *Capital*: Hannover.

Mecklenburg-West Pomerania (Mecklenburg-Vorpommern) *Area*: 26 694 km^2 (10 307 sq mi). *Population*: 1 924 000 (1991 est). *Capital*: Schwerin.

North Rhine-Westphalia (Nordrhein-Westfalen) *Area*: 34 066 km^2 (13 153 sq mi). *Population*: 17 350 000 (1991 est). *Capital*: Düsseldorf.

Rhineland-Palatinate (Rheinland-Pfalz) *Area*: 19 848 km^2 (7663 sq mi). *Population*: 3 764 000 (1991 est). *Capital*: Mainz.

Saarland *Area*: 2571 km^2 (993 sq mi). *Population*: 1 073 000 (1991 est). *Capital*: Saarbrücken.

Saxony (Sachsen) *Area*: 17 713 km^2 (6839 sq mi). *Population*: 4 764 000 (1991 est). *Capital*: Dresden.

Saxony-Anhalt (Sachsen-Anhalt) *Area*: 20 297 km^2 (7837 sq mi). *Population*: 2 874 000 (1991 est). *Capital*: Magdeburg.

Schleswig-Holstein *Area*: 15 720 km^2 (6069 sq mi). *Population*: 2 626 000 (1991 est). *Capital*: Kiel.

Thuringia (Thüringen) *Area*: 15 209 km^2 (5872 sq mi). *Population*: 2 611 000 (1991 est). *Capital*: Erfurt.

GEOGRAPHY
The North German Plain – a region of fertile farmlands and sandy heaths – is drained by the Rivers Elbe and Weser and their tributaries. In the west, the plain merges with the North Rhine lowlands which contain the Ruhr coalfield and over 20% of Germany's population. A belt of plateaux crosses the country from east to west and includes the Hunsrück and Eifel highlands in the Rhineland, the Taunus and Westerwald uplands in Hesse, and extends into the Harz and Erz Mountains in Thuringia. The Rhine cuts through these central plateaux in a deep gorge. In southern Germany, the Black Forest (Schwarzwald) separates the Rhine valley from the fertile valleys and scarplands of Swabia. The forested edge of the Bohemian uplands marks the Czech border, while the Bavarian Alps form the frontier with Austria. *Principal rivers:* Rhine (Rhein), Elbe, Danube (Donau), Oder, Moselle (Mosel), Neckar, Havel, Leine, Weser. *Highest point:* Zugspitze 2963 m (9721 ft). The climate of Germany is temperate, but with considerable variations between the generally mild northern coastal plain and the Bavarian Alps in the south, which have cool summers and cold winters. Local relief is also responsible for significant climatic variations. Eastern Germany has warm summers and cold winters.

ECONOMY
Germany is the world's third industrial power after the USA and Japan. The country's recovery after World War II has been called the 'German economic miracle'. The principal industries include mechanical and electrical engineering, chemicals, textiles, food processing and vehicles, with heavy industry and engineering concentrated in the Ruhr, chemicals in cities on the Rhine, and motor vehicles in large provincial centres such as Stuttgart. From the 1980s, there has been a spectacular growth in high-technology industries. Apart from coal and brown coal, and relatively small mineral deposits such as iron ore, potash and salt, Germany has relatively few natural resources and has to rely upon imports. Labour has also been in short supply, and large numbers of 'guest workers' (Gastarbeiter) – particularly from Turkey and the former Yugoslavia – have been recruited. Since 1990 the labour shortage in the western part of the country has also been met by migration from the former GDR. The service sector is well developed. Banking and finance are major foreign-currency earners, and Frankfurt is one of the world's leading financial and business centres.

The unification of Germany in October 1990 presented a major problem for the German economy (see also p. 23)

German Länder

K • Schleswig-Holstein

H

Br • Hamburg

Bremen

Lower Saxony

Sw • Mecklenburg-West Pomerania

Hv •

North Rhine-Westphalia

D •

Mg • Saxony-Anhalt

B
P • • Berlin

Brandenburg

Hesse

Saxony   Dr •

W
Mz •

E • Thuringia

Rhineland-Palatinate

Sa •
Saarland

S •

Baden-Württemberg

Bavaria

M •

Länder capitals

B :	Berlin
Br :	Bremen
D :	Düsseldorf
Dr :	Dresden
E :	Erfurt
H :	Hamburg
Hv :	Hannover
K :	Kiel
M :	Munich
Mg :	Magdeburg
Mz :	Mainz
P :	Potsdam
S :	Stuttgart
Sa :	Saarbrücken
Sw :	Schwerin
W :	Wiesbaden

and, coupled with the effects of international recession, the costs of reunification have resulted in an economic downturn in Germany. The GDR's economy had previously been the most successful in CMEA (Comecon), but, compared with West Germany, it lagged in terms of production, quality, design, profitability and standards of living. A trust – the *Treuhandanstalt* (THA) – was established to oversee the privatization of the state-run firms in eastern Germany. It inherited 270 socialist *kombinate* with 8500 state enterprises. These were broken up into firms and recast as joint-stock companies owned by the THA. By the autumn of 1993, the agency had already privatized 8224 companies and liquidated 2597. The Trabant and Wartburg car firms, for example, ceased production in 1991, and, bought by West German firms, began production of western models. By late 1992 unemployment in the former GDR stood at nearly 40%.

The main German agricultural products include hops (for beer), grapes (for wine), sugar beet, wheat, barley, and dairy products. The collectivized farms of the former GDR were privatized in 1990–91. Forests cover almost one third of the country and support a flourishing timber industry. For information on the German currency see pp. 104–5, on GNP see p. 125, on imports and exports see pp. 112–13 and on the national budget see pp. 134–36.

Labour force (1991)

Sector	Number employed
Industry	11 941 000
Mining, quarrying	250 000
Agriculture	1 963 000
Construction	2 409 000
Public utilities	320 000
Commerce and finance	3 058 000
Transport and communications	2 212 000
Services and administration	9 909 000
Other (including unemployed)	4 228 000
Total	*36 290 000*

RECENT HISTORY

Defeat in World War I led to the loss of much territory in Europe, the end of the German monarchies, the imposition of substantial reparations, and the occupation of the Rhineland by Allied forces until 1930. The liberal Weimar republic (1919–33) could not bring economic or political stability. In the early 1930s the Nazi Party grew, urging the establishment of a strong centralized government, an aggressive foreign policy, 'Germanic character' and the overturn of the postwar settlement. In 1933, the Nazi leader Adolf Hitler (1889–1945) became Chancellor and in 1934 President. His Third Reich annexed Austria (1938), dismembered Czechoslovakia (1939), and embarked on the extermination of the Jews and others that the Nazis regarded as 'inferior'. In 1939 Hitler concluded the Nazi-Soviet Non-Aggression Pact, which allowed the USSR to annex the Baltic states and agreed to divide Poland between the Soviets and the Nazis. Hitler invaded Poland on 1 September 1939. Britain and France declared war on Germany but could do nothing to help the Poles. After a pause known as the 'Phoney War', Hitler turned towards the west (1940) and invaded Denmark, Norway, the Low Countries and France. The German invasion of the USSR (1941) opened the Eastern Front. At the height of Axis power in 1942,

Germany controlled – directly or through allies – virtually the whole of Europe except the British Isles, and neutral Switzerland, Sweden, Spain and Portugal. The tide against the Axis countries turned in North Africa late in 1942. In 1943, Soviet forces started to push back the Germans. In 1944 the Allied landings in Normandy began the liberation of Western Europe. After massive Allied bombing attacks, the end came swiftly for Germany. Hitler committed suicide in April 1945 and Berlin fell to the Soviets early in May.

In 1945, Germany lost substantial territories to Poland, and was divided – as was its capital, Berlin – into four zones of occupation by the Allies (Britain, France, the USA and the USSR). Cooperation between the Allies rapidly broke down, and in 1948–49 the USSR blockaded West Berlin. The western zones of Germany were merged to form the Federal Republic of Germany and the German Democratic Republic was proclaimed in the Soviet zone (1949). The GDR's economic progress suffered by comparison with that of West Germany. Food shortages and repressive Communist rule led to an uprising in 1953. West Germany gained sovereignty – as a member of the Western alliance – in 1955. Chancellor Konrad Adenauer (1876–1967) refused to recognize East Germany as a separate state and relations with the USSR remained uncertain. Relations between the two Germanys were soured as large numbers of East Germans fled to the West, and this outflow was stemmed only when Walter Ulbricht (East German Communist Party leader 1950–71) ordered the building of the Berlin Wall (1961). Adenauer strove to gain the acceptance of West Germany back into Western Europe through reconciliation with France and participation in the EC. The economic revival of Germany begun by Adenauer continued under his Christian Democrat (conservative) successors as Chancellor – Ludwig Erhard (1963–66) and Georg Kiesinger (1966–69). Under the Social Democrat Chancellors – Willy Brandt (1969–74) and Helmut Schmidt (1974–82) – treaties were signed with the Soviet Union (1970) and Poland (recognizing the Oder-Neisse line as Poland's western frontier), and relations with the GDR were normalized (1972).

In the late 1980s, West Germany – under Helmut Kohl (Christian Democrat Chancellor from 1982) – acted as an economic and cultural magnet for much of Eastern Europe. The root causes of the GDR's problems remained, however, and resurfaced in the late 1980s. The ageing Communist leadership led by Erich Honecker proved unresponsive to the mood of greater freedom emanating from Gorbachov's USSR. In 1989 fresh floods of East Germans left the GDR for the West by way of Poland, Czechoslovakia and Hungary. Massive public demonstrations in favour of reform led to the appointment of a new East German leadership. The Berlin Wall was reopened (November 1989) allowing free movement between the two Germanys. A government including members of opposition groups was appointed. Free elections were held in East Germany in March 1990 and the Communists were reduced to a minority. When the East German economy collapsed, the call for German reunification became unstoppable and German reunification took place on 3 October 1990. Soviet troops are scheduled to withdraw from the former GDR by 1994.

GREECE

Official name: Ellenikí Dimokrátia (Hellenic Republic) or Ellás (Greece).

Member of: UN, EC/EU, NATO, Council of Europe, CSCE, OECD, WEU.

Area: 131 957 km² (50 949 sq mi).

Population: 10 269 000 (1991 census).

Capital: Athens (Athínai) 3 097 000 (including suburbs; 1991 census).

Other major cities: Thessaloníki (formerly known as Salonika) 706 000, Piraeus (Piraiévs; part of the Athens agglomeration) 196 000, Patras (Pátrai) 155 000, Volos 107 000, Lárisa 102 000, Heraklion (Iráklion, formerly known as Candia) 102 000, Kavalla 57 000, Canea (Khania) 48 000 (all including suburbs; 1991 census).

Language: Greek (official); see pp. 77–9.

Religion: Orthodox (98%; official); see pp. 80–81.

Education: See pp. 86–90.

Defence: See pp. 122–24.

Transport: See pp. 118–22.

Media: See pp. 126–32.

GOVERNMENT

The 300-member Parliament is elected for four years by universal adult suffrage under a system of proportional representation. The President – who is elected for a five-year term by Parliament – appoints a Prime Minister (who commands a majority in Parliament) and other Ministers. The main political parties include PASOK (the Pan-Hellenic Socialist Party), the (conservative) NDP (New Democracy Party), the (centre-right) Political Spring, and the (Communist-led) Left Alliance (KKE). At the general election held on 10 October 1993 these parties obtained the following number of seats and a PASOK government was formed.

Party	Seats
PASOK	171
New Democracy	111
Political Spring	10
KKE	9
Total	163

President: Konstantinos Karamanlis (elected 1990).

THE CABINET

Prime Minister: Andreas Papandreou.
Minister for the Aegean: Konstantinos Skandalides.
Minister of Agriculture: Giorgios Moraitis.
Minister of Culture: Melina Mercouri.
Minister of Defence: Gerasimos Arsenis.
Minister of Education and Religious Affairs: Dimitris Fatouros.
Minister of the Environment, Town Planning and Public Works: Costas Laliotis.
Minister of Foreign Affairs: Karolos Papoulias.
Minister of Health, Welfare and Social Services: Dimitri Kremastinos.
Minister of Industrial Energy and Technology, and of Commercial Industry: Konstantinos Simitis.
Minister of the Interior: Apostolos Tsohatzopoulos.
Minister of Justice: Giorgios Kouvelakis.
Minister of Labour: Evangelos Yiannopoulos.
Minister for Macedonia and Thrace: Konstantinos Triarides.
Minister for the Merchant Marine: Giorgios Katsifaras.
Minister of the National Economy and Finance: Giorgios Yennimatas.
Minister to the PM's Office: Anastasios Peponis.
Minister of Public Order: Stelios Papathemelis.
Minister of Transport and Communications: Ioannis Haralambous.
Deputy Minister to the PM: Antonis Livanis.

SELF-GOVERNING COMMUNITY

Mount Athos (Ayion Oros) (an autonomous monks' republic) *Area:* 336 km² (130 sq mi). *Population:* 1400 (1990 est). *Capital:* Karyai.

GEOGRAPHY

Over 80% of Greece is mountainous. The mainland is dominated by the Pindus Mountains, which extend from Albania south into the Peloponnese Peninsula. The Rhodope Mountains lie along the Bulgarian border. Greece has some 2000 islands, of which only 154 are inhabited. *Principal rivers:* Aliákmon, Piniós, Akhelóös. *Highest point:* Mount Olympus 2911 m (9550 ft). Greece has a Mediterranean climate with hot dry summers and mild wet winters. The north and the mountains are colder.

ECONOMY

Agriculture involves about one quarter of the labour

force. Much of the land is marginal – in particular the extensive sheep pastures. Greece is largely self-sufficient in wheat, barley, maize, sugar beet, fruit, vegetables and cheese, and produces enough wine, olives (and olive oil) and tobacco for export. The industrial sector is expanding rapidly and includes the processing of natural resources such as petroleum and natural gas, lignite, uranium and bauxite. Tourism, the large merchant fleet, and money sent back by Greeks working abroad are all important foreign-currency earners. Greece is burdened by a large state sector and receives special economic assistance from the EC.

Labour force (1989–90)

Sector	Number employed
Industry	730 000
Agriculture	970 000
Construction	230 000
Public utilities	35 000
Finance, etc.	160 000
Trade, restaurants and hotels	600 000
Services and administration	685 000
Other (including unemployed)	300 000
Total	*3 683 000*

For information on the Greek currency see pp. 104–5, on GNP see p. 125. on imports and exports see pp. 112–13 and on the national budget see pp. 134–36.

RECENT HISTORY

Greece in the 20th century has been marked by great instability. Eleuthérios Venizélos (1864–1936) dominated Greek politics from 1910 to 1935, a period of rivalry between republicans and royalists. An attempt by his rival King Constantine I to seize Anatolia from Turkey (1921–22) ended in military defeat and the establishment of a republic in 1924. The monarchy was restored in 1935, but it depended upon a military leader, General Ioannis Metaxas (1871–1941), who, claiming the threat from Communism as justification, ruled as virtual dictator. The nation was deeply divided. The German invasion of 1941 was met by rival resistance groups of Communists and monarchists, and the subsequent civil war between these factions lasted from 1945 to 1949, when, with British and US aid, the monarchists emerged victorious.

Continued instability in the 1960s led to a military coup in 1967. King Constantine II, who had not initially opposed the coup, unsuccessfully appealed for the overthrow of the junta and went into exile. The dictatorship of the colonels ended in 1974 when their encouragement of a Greek Cypriot coup brought Greece to the verge of war with Turkey. Civilian government was restored, and a new republican constitution was adopted in 1975. Greece has since forged closer links with Western Europe, in particular through membership of the EC (1981). Greek opposition delayed international recognition of the former Yugoslav republic of Macedonia in 1992–93.

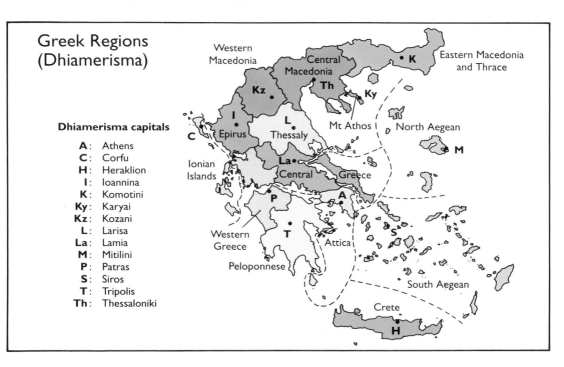

Greek Regions (Dhiamerisma)

Dhiamerisma capitals

A: Athens
C: Corfu
H: Heraklion
I: Ioannina
K: Komotini
Ky: Karyai
Kz: Kozani
L: Larisa
La: Lamia
M: Mitilini
P: Patras
S: Siros
T: Tripolis
Th: Thessaloniki

IRELAND

Official name: Poblacht na h'Éireann (Republic of Ireland).

Member of: UN, EC/EU, CSCE, Council of Europe, OECD, WEU (associate).

Area: 70 282 km² (27 136 sq mi).

Population: 3 523 000 (1991 census).

Capital: Dublin 921 000 (city 478 000; Dún Laoghaire 55 000) (1991 census).

Other major cities and towns: Cork 174 000 (city 127 000), Limerick 77 000 (city 52 000), Galway 51 000, Waterford 41 000, Dundalk 29 000 (town 27 000), Bray 25 000, Drogheda 24 000, Sligo 18 000 (1991 census).

Languages: Irish (official); English; see pp. 77–79.

Religion: Roman Catholic (93%); see pp. 80–81.

Education: See pp. 86–90.

Defence: See pp. 122–24.

Transport: See pp. 118–22.

Media: See pp. 127–32.

GOVERNMENT

The Seanad (Senate) has 60 members – 11 nominated by the Taoiseach (PM), six elected by the universities and 43 indirectly elected for a five-year term to represent vocational and special interests. The Dáil (House) comprises 166 members elected by proportional representation for five years by universal adult suffrage. The President is directly elected for seven years. The Taoiseach and a Cabinet of Ministers are appointed by the President upon the nomination of the Dáil, to whom they are responsible. The main political parties are the (centre-right) Fianna Fáil, (centre-right) Fine Gael, (left-wing) Labour Party, (centre-right) Progressive Democrats and the Democratic Left. At the general election on 25 November 1992 these parties won the following number of seats and a Fianna Fáil (FF) –Labour Party (Lab) coalition was formed.

Party	Seats
Fianna Fáil	68
Fine Gael	45
Labour Party	33
Progressive Democrats	10
Democratic Left	4
Others	6
Total	*166*

President: Mary Robinson (elected 1990).

THE CABINET

Prime Minister (Taoiseach): Albert Reynolds (FF).
Deputy Prime Minister (Tánaiste): Dick Spring (Lab).
Minister of Agriculture: Joe Walsh (FF).
Minister of Arts, Culture and the Gaeltacht: Michael Higgins (Lab).
Minister of Defence: David Andrews (FF).
Minister of Education: Niamh Bhreathnach (Lab).
Minister of Employment and Enterprise: Ruairi Quinn (Lab).
Minister for the Environment: Michael Smith (FF).
Minister for Equality and Law Reform: Mervyn Taylor (Lab).
Minister of Finance: Bertie Ahern (FF).
Minister of Foreign Affairs: see above; the Deputy Prime Minister.
Minister of Health: Brendan Howlin (Lab).
Minister of Justice: Maire Geoghegan-Quinn (FF).
Minister of Social Welfare: Michael Woods (FF).
Minister of Trade and Tourism: Charlie McCreevy (FF).
Minister of Transport, Energy and Communications: Brian Cowan (FF).

GEOGRAPHY

Central Ireland is a lowland crossed by slight ridges and broad valleys, bogs and large lakes, including Loughs Derg and Ree. Except on the east coast north of Dublin, the lowland is surrounded by coastal hills and mountains including the Wicklow Mountains, and the hills of Connemara and Donegal in the west and the Macgillicuddy's Reeks in the southwest. The rugged Atlantic Coast is highly indented. *Principal rivers:* Shannon, Suir, Boyne, Barrow. *Highest point:* Carrauntuohill 1041 m (3414 ft). Ireland has a mild temperate climate. Rainfall is high, ranging from over 2500 mm (100 in) in the west and southwest to 750 mm (30 in) in the east.

ECONOMY

Manufactured goods – in particular machinery, metals and engineering, electronics and chemical products – make a major contribution to Ireland's exports. Agriculture concentrates upon the production of livestock, meat and dairy products. Food processing and brewing are major industries. Natural resources include lead-zinc, offshore petroleum and natural gas, and hydroelectric power sites. Ireland suffers high rates of unemployment and emigration. For information on Ireland's GNP see p. 125, national budget pp. 134–36, imports and exports see pp. 112–13 and currency pp. 104–5.

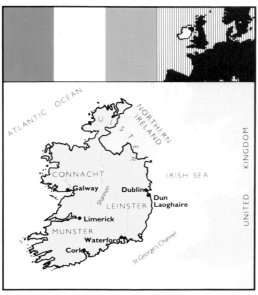

Labour force (1991)

Sector	Number employed
Industry	227 000
Agriculture/fishing	155 000
Construction	77 000
Public utilities	14 000
Commerce	230 000
Transport and communications	66 000
Services/administration	372 000
Total	1 121 000

RECENT HISTORY

In the 19th century Ireland campaigned for reform and later independence from the British Parliament. After Home Rule Bills were rejected by Parliament (1883 and 1893), more revolutionary nationalist groups gained support in Ireland. Fearing Catholic domination, Protestant Unionists in Ulster strongly opposed the Third Home Rule Bill (1912). Nationalists declared an independent Irish state in the Dublin Easter Rising of 1916, which was put down by the British. After World War I, Irish nationalist MPs formed a provisional government in Dublin led by Eamon de Valera (later PM and President; 1882–1975). Except in the northeast, British administration in Ireland crumbled. Fighting broke out between nationalists and British troops and police, and by 1919 Ireland had collapsed into violence. In response the UK offered Ireland two Parliaments – one in Protestant Ulster, another in the Catholic south. Partition was initially rejected by the south, but by the Anglo-Irish Treaty (1921) dominion status was granted, although six (mainly Protestant) counties in Ulster – Northern Ireland – opted to remain British. The Irish Free State was proclaimed in 1922 but de Valera and the Republicans refused to accept it and civil war (1922–23) broke out between the provisional government – led by Arthur Griffith and Michael Collins – and the Republicans. In 1937 the Irish Free State became the Republic of Eire. The country remained neutral in World War II and left the Commonwealth (as the Republic of Ireland) in 1949. Relations between south and north – and between the Republic and the UK – have often been tense during the 'troubles' in Northern Ireland (1968–).

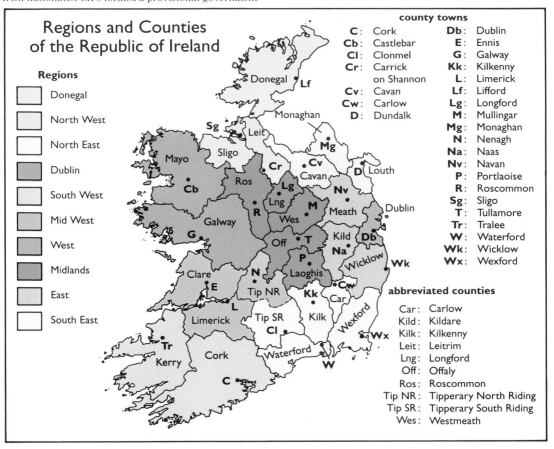

Regions and Counties of the Republic of Ireland

Regions

- Donegal
- North West
- North East
- Dublin
- South West
- Mid West
- West
- Midlands
- East
- South East

county towns

C :	Cork
Cb :	Castlebar
Cl :	Clonmel
Cr :	Carrick on Shannon
Cv :	Cavan
Cw :	Carlow
D :	Dundalk
Db :	Dublin
E :	Ennis
G :	Galway
Kk :	Kilkenny
L :	Limerick
Lf :	Lifford
Lg :	Longford
M :	Mullingar
Mg :	Monaghan
N :	Nenagh
Na :	Naas
Nv :	Navan
P :	Portlaoise
R :	Roscommon
Sg :	Sligo
T :	Tullamore
Tr :	Tralee
W :	Waterford
Wk :	Wicklow
Wx :	Wexford

abbreviated counties

Car :	Carlow
Kild :	Kildare
Kilk :	Kilkenny
Leit :	Leitrim
Lng :	Longford
Off :	Offaly
Ros :	Roscommon
Tip NR :	Tipperary North Riding
Tip SR :	Tipperary South Riding
Wes :	Westmeath

ITALY

Official name: Italia (Italy) or Repubblica Italiana (Republic of Italy).

Member of: UN, EC/EU, NATO, WEU, G7, Council of Europe, OECD, CSCE.

Area: 301 277 km² (116 324 sq mi).

Population: 57 104 000 (1991 est).

Capital: Rome (Roma) 2 985 000 (city 2 791 000; 1990 census).

Other major cities: Milan (Milano) 3 670 000 (city 1 432 000), Naples (Napoli) 2 905 000 (city 1 206 000), Turin (Torino) 1 114 000 (city 992 000), Genoa (Genova) 786 000 (city 701 000), Palermo 755 000 (city 734 000), Florence (Firenze) 433 000 (city 408 000), Bologna 412 000, Catania 384 000 (city 364 000), Bari 373 000 (city 353 000), Venice (Venezia) 318 000, Messina 275 000, Verona 257 000, Trieste 252 000 (city 230 000), Taranto 244 000, Padua (Padova) 218 000, Cagliari 212 000, Salerno 206 000 (city 151 000), Brescia 202 000 (city 196 000), Reggio di Calabria 179 000, Modena 178 000, Parma 173 000, Livorno 171 000, Prato 166 000, Foggia 159 000, Perugia 151 000, Ferrara 141 000 (1990 census).

Languages: Italian (official), with small minorities speaking German, French and Albanian; see pp. 77–9.

Religion: Roman Catholic (83%); see pp 80–81.

Education: See pp. 86–90.

Defence: See pp. 122–24.

Transport: See pp. 118–22.

Media: See pp. 126–32.

GOVERNMENT

Until 1993 the two houses of Parliament were elected for a five-year term by proportional representation. Future elections to the Senate and the Chamber of Deputies will be by first-past-the-post for the majority of seats with a minority still elected by proportional representation. The Senate has 315 members elected by citizens aged 25 and over to represent the regions, plus former Presidents and five life senators chosen by the President. The Chamber of Deputies has 630 members elected by citizens aged 18 and over. The President is elected for seven years by an electoral college comprising Parliament and 58 regional representatives. The President appoints a PM (who commands a majority in Parliament) and a Council of Ministers who are responsible to Parliament. Political parties include the (conservative) Christian Democratic Party (CD), the (former Communist) Democratic Party of the Left, the (federalist) Northern League (including the Lombard League), the (Southern-based anti-Mafia) La Rete, the (Marxist) Communist Refoundation, the Socialist Party (PSI), the Republican Party (RPI), the Radical Party, the Liberal Party (PLI), the Social Democratic Party (PDSI), the (reformist) Democratic Alliance and the (right-wing) Italian Social Movement (MSI-DN). The 20 regions of Italy have their own governments. In elections to the Chamber held on 5–6 April 1992 the parties obtained the following number of seats and a coalition of CD, PSI, RPI, PSDI and PLI members and non-party experts was formed in May 1993.

Party	Seats
Christian Democrats	206
Democratic Party of the Left	107
Socialist Party	92
Northern League	55
Refounded Communists	35
Italian Social Movement	34
Republican Party	27
Liberal Party	17
Greens	16
Social Democratic Party	16
La Rete	12
Others	13
Total	*630*

President: Oscar Luigi Scalfaro (elected May 1992).

THE CABINET

Prime Minister: Carlo Azeglio Ciampi (ind).
Minister of Agriculture: Alfredo Diana (CD).
Minister for the Budget: Prof. Luigi Spaventa (ind).
Minister of Culture: Prof. Alberto Ronchey (ind).
Minister of Defence: Fabio Fabbri (PSI).
Minister of Education: Rosa Russo Jervolino (CD).
Minister of Employment and Social Welfare: Gino Giugni (PSI).
Minister for the Environment: Valdo Spini (PSI).
Minister of Finance: Prof. Franco Gallo (ind).
Minister of Foreign Affairs: Prof. Beniamino Andreatta (CD).
Minister of Foreign Trade: Paolo Baratta (PSI).
Minister of Health: Maria Pia Garavaglia (CD).
Minister of Industry and Privatization: Prof. Paolo Savona (RPI).

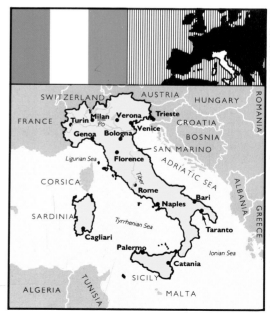

Minister of the Interior: Nicola Mancino (CD).
Minister of Justice: Prof. Giovanni Conso (ind).
Minister of Posts and Telecommunications: Maurizio Pagani (PDSI).
Minister of Public Administration: Prof. Sabino Cassese (ind).
Minister of Public Works: Francesco Merloni (CD).
Minister of Transport: Raffaele Costa (PLI).
Minister for the Treasury: Prof. Piero Barucci (CD).
Minister for Universities and Research: Prof. Umberto Colombo (ind).
Ministers without Portfolio: Prof. Paolo Barile (*responsible for relations with Parliament*; ind), Fernanda Conti (*responsble for Social Affairs*; PSI), Prof. Leopoldo Elia (*responsible for Electoral and Institutional Reform*; ind), Prof. Livio Paladin (*responsible for Community Affairs and the Regions*; ind).

REGIONS

Abruzzi *Area*: 10 794 km² (4168 sq mi). *Population*: 1 249 000 (1991 census). *Capital*: L'Aquila; Pescara shares some of the functions of capital with L'Aquila.

Basilicata *Area*: 9992 km² (3858 sq mi). *Population*: 592 000 (1991 census). *Capital*: Potenza.

Calabria *Area*: 15 080 km² (5822 sq mi). *Population*: 2 010 000 (1991 census). *Capital*: Catanzaro.

Campania *Area*: 13 595 km² (5249 sq mi). *Population*: 5 626 000 (1991 census). *Capital*: Naples.

Emilia Romagna *Area*: 22 123 km² (8542 sq mi). *Population*: 3 984 000 (1991 census). *Capital*: Bologna.

Friuli-Venezia Giulia *Area*: 7846 km² (3029 sq mi). *Population*: 1 216 000 (1991 census). *Capital*: Trieste.

Lazio *Area*: 17 203 km² (6642 sq mi). *Population*: 5 146 000

Italian Regions

regional capitals

A : Ancona
Ao : Aosta
B : Bari
Bg : Bologna
Bz : Bolzano
C : Cagliari
Cz : Catanzaro
F : Florence
G : Genoa
L'A : L'Aquila
M : Milan
N : Naples
P : Palermo
Pg : Perugia
Pt : Potenza
R : Rome
T : Turin
Tr : Trento
Ts : Trieste
V : Venice

(1991 census). *Capital*: Rome.

Liguria *Area*: 5413 km² (2090 sq mi). *Population*: 1 702 000 (1991 census). *Capital*: Genoa.

Lombardy (Lombardia) *Area*: 23 834 km² (9202 sq mi). *Population*: 8 941 000 (1991 census). *Capital*: Milan.

Marche *Area*: 9692 km² (3742 sq mi). *Population*: 1 447 000 (1991 census). *Capital*: Ancona.

Molise *Area*: 4438 km² (1714 sq mi). *Population*: 321 000 (1991 census). *Capital*: Campobasso.

Piedmont (Piemonte) *Area*: 25 399 km² (9807 sq mi). *Population*: 4 338 000 (1991 census). *Capital*: Turin.

Puglia *Area*: 19 347 km² (7470 sq mi). *Population*: 3 970 000 (1991 census). *Capital*: Bari.

Sardinia (Sardegna) *Area*: 24 090 km² (9301 sq mi). *Population*: 1 645 000 (1991 census). *Capital*: Cagliari.

Sicily (Sicilia) *Area*: 25 708 km² (9926 sq mi). *Population*: 4 990 000 (1991 census). *Capital*: Palermo.

Trentino-Alto Adige *Area*: 13 613 km² (5256 sq mi). *Population*: 935 000 (1991 census). *Capitals*: Trento and Bolzano.

Tuscany (Toscana) *Area*: 22 992 km² (8877 sq mi). *Population*: 3 599 000 (1991 census). *Capital*: Florence.

Umbria *Area*: 8456 km² (3265 sq mi). *Population*: 823 000 (1991 census). *Capital*: Perugia.

Valle d'Aosta *Area*: 3262 km² (1259 sq mi). *Population*: 117 000 (1991 census). *Capital*: Aosta.

Veneto *Area*: 18 368 km² (7092 sq mi). *Population*: 4 453 000 (1991 census). *Capital*: Venice.

GEOGRAPHY

The Alps form a natural boundary between Italy and its neighbours. A string of lakes where the mountains meet the foothills includes Lakes Maggiore, Lugano and Como. The fertile Po Valley – the great lowland of northern Italy – lies between the Alpine foothills in the north, the foothills of the Apennines in the south, the Alps in the west and the Adriatic Sea in the east. The narrow ridge of the Ligurian Alps joins the Maritime Alps to the Apennines, which form a backbone down the entire length of the Italian peninsula. Coastal lowlands are few and relatively restricted but include the Arno Basin in Tuscany, the Tiber Basin around Rome, the Campania lowlands around Naples, and plains beside the Gulf of Taranto and in Puglia (the 'heel' of Italy). The islands of Sardinia and Sicily are both largely mountainous. Much of Italy is liable to earthquakes. The country has four active volcanoes, including Etna on Sicily and Vesuvius near Naples. *Principal rivers:* Po, Tiber (Tevere), Arno, Volturno, Garigliano. *Highest point:* a point just below the summit of Monte Bianco (Mont Blanc) 4760 m (15 616 ft). Italy enjoys a Mediterranean climate with warm, dry summers and mild winters. Northern Italy is cooler and wetter. Sicily and Sardinia tend to be warmer and drier than the mainland.

ECONOMY

Northern Italy, with its easy access to the rest of Europe, is the main centre of Italian industry. The south, in contrast, remains mainly agricultural, producing grapes, sugar beet, wheat, maize, and tomatoes. Most farms are small and many southern farmers have resisted change; thus, incomes in southern Italy (the

'Mezzogiorno') are on average much lower than in the north. Agriculture in the north is more mechanized; major crops include wheat, maize, rice, grapes (for wine), fruit and fodder crops for dairy herds. Industrialization in the south has been promoted. The industries of the north are well-developed and include electrical and electronic goods, cars and bicycles, textiles, clothing, leather goods, cement, glass, china and ceramics. The north is also an important financial and banking area: Milan is the commercial capital of Italy. Apart from Alpine rivers that have been harnessed for HEP, Italy has few natural resources. Tourism and money sent back by Italians living abroad are important sources of foreign currency. Recession and a crippling public deficit have added to Italy's growing economic problems. Unemployment increased sharply in the 1990s. For information on Italy's GNP see p. 125, national budget pp. 134–36, imports and exports see pp. 112–13 and currency pp. 104–5.

Labour force (1991)

Sector	Number employed
Industry	4 757 000
Agriculture/fishing	1 895 000
Construction	1 859 000
Public utilities	229 000
Trade, restaurants, hotels	4 537 000
Finance, etc.	895 000
Transport and communications	1 146 000
Services/administration	5 986 000
Unemployed, others	2 622 000
Total	*8 872 000*

RECENT HISTORY

Italy entered World War I on the Allied side in the expectation of territorial gains from Austria. However, Italy won far less territory than anticipated in the post-war peace treaties. Fear of Communist revolution led to an upsurge of Fascism and the Fascist Benito Mussolini (1883–1945) became PM in 1922 with a programme of extensive domestic modernization and an aggressive foreign policy. In 1936 Italy allied with Germany in the Rome-Berlin Axis, and declared war on Britain and France in 1940. When Italy was invaded by Allied troops in 1943, Mussolini was dismissed by the king and Italy joined the Allies. In 1946 a republic was proclaimed. Communist influence increased and Communists gained control of the administration of many large cities. However, the dominance of the (conservative) Christian Democrat Party kept the Communists out of the succeeding coalitions that ruled Italy. Particularly in the 1970s, terrorist movements (both left- and right-wing) were active, kidnapping and assassinating politicians and industrialists, including the former PM Aldo Moro (1978). The political structure of Italy remained unstable and coalitions were often short-lived – between 1945 and 1993 over 50 governments came to and fell from power. In the 1990s, public disillusion with state institutions grew and Italy was weakened by corruption, the activities of the Mafia and the growth of regional separatism in the North. The power and influence of the traditional political parties collapsed and new movements – such as the Northen League and La Rete – appeared. In 1993 an interim government was formed to effect constitutional changes.

LUXEMBOURG

Official name: Grand-Duché de Luxembourg (Grand Duchy of Luxembourg).

Member of: UN, EC/EU, NATO, WEU, CSCE, OECD, Council of Europe.

Area: 2586 km² (999 sq mi).

Population: 390 000 (1992 est).

Capital: Luxembourg 117 000 (city 78 000; 1991 census).

Other main towns: Esch-sur-Alzette 24 000, Differdange 16 000, Dudelange 15 000, Pétange 12 000, Sanem 12 000 (1991 census).

Languages: Letzeburgish (national), French and German (both official); see pp. 77–9.

Religions: Roman Catholic (95%); see pp. 80–1-.

Education: See pp. 86–90.

Defence: See pp. 122–4.

Transport: See pp. 118–22.

Media: See pp. 127–32.

GOVERNMENT

Luxembourg is a constitutional monarchy with a Grand Duke or Duchess as sovereign. The 60-member Chamber of Deputies is elected by proportional representation by universal adult suffrage for five years. A Council of Ministers and a President of the Council (Premier) are appointed by the sovereign. The main political parties are the (centre-right) Social Christian Party (PSC), the Socialist Party (PS), the (liberal) Democratic Party, Green Alternative, Green Ecologists and the (pension rights) 5/6 Action Committee. At elections held on 18 June 1989 the parties gained the following number of seats and a PSC-PS coalition was formed.

Party	Seats
Christian Social	22
Socialist Party	18
Democrats	12
5/6 Action Committee	3
Green Alternatives	2
Green Ecologists	2
Communist	1
Total	*60*

Grand Duke: HRH Grand Duke Jean I (succeeded upon the abdication of his mother, 12 November 1964).

THE CABINET

Prime Minister: (also *Minister for the Exchequer and Minister for Cultural Affairs*) Jacques Santer (PSC).

Deputy Prime Minister, Minister for Foreign Affairs and Foreign Trade, Minister for the Armed Forces: Jacques Poos (PS).

Minister of Agriculture, Viticulture, Country Planning: René Steichen (PS).

Minister for the Economy, Minister of Public Works and Transport: Robert Goebbels (PCS).

Minister of Education, Minister of Justice, Minister for Sport: Marc Fischbach (PCS).

Minister for Family Affairs, Social Solidarity, the Middle Classes, Minister of Tourism: Fernand Boden (PCS).

Minister of Finance, Minister of Labour: Jean-Claude Juncker (PCS).

Minister of Health and Social Security, Minister of Sport: Johny Lahure (PS).

Minister of the Interior, Housing and Town Planning: Jean Spautz: (PCS).

Minister of Land Planning, the Environment, Energy and Communications: Alex Bodry (PS).

Secretaries of State: Georges Wohlfart (PS), Mady Delvaux-Stehres (PS).

GEOGRAPHY

The Oesling is a wooded plateau in the north. The Gutland in the south is a lowland region of valleys and ridges. *Principal rivers:* Moselle, Sûre, Our, Alzette. *Highest point:* Huldange 550 m (1833 ft). Luxembourg has cool summers and mild winters.

ECONOMY

The iron and steel industry – once based on local ore – is important. Luxembourg has become a major banking centre. The north grows potatoes and fodder crops; the south produces wheat and fruit, including grapes. See also p. 125, pp. 134–36, pp. 112–13 and pp. 104–5.

Labour force (1991)

Sector	Number employed
Industry	37 500
Agriculture	6 200
Construction	18 900
Finance	17 000
Trade, restaurants, hotels	68 800
Transport and communications	13 100
Services/administration	26 200
Total	*189 000*

RECENT HISTORY

From 1815 to 1890, Dutch kings were also sovereigns of Luxembourg, but in 1890 Luxembourg was inherited by a junior branch of the House of Orange. Occupied by the Germans during both World Wars, Luxembourg concluded an economic union with Belgium in 1922 and has enthusiastically supported European unity.

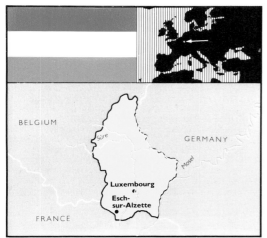

BELGIUM

Sûre

GERMANY

Mosel

Luxembourg

Esch-
sur-Alzette

FRANCE

THE NETHERLANDS

Official name: Koninkrijk der Nederlanden (The Kingdom of the Netherlands).

Member of: UN, EC/EU, NATO, CSCE, WEU, Council of Europe, OECD.

Area: 41 785 km² (16 140 sq mi).

Population: 15 129 000 (1992 est.).

Capital: Amsterdam – capital in name only – 1 080 000 (city 713 000), The Hague ('s Gravenhage) – capital *de facto*; the seat of government and administration – 693 000 (city 445 000) (1992 est.).

Other major cities: Rotterdam 1 060 000 (city 590 000), Utrecht 540 000 (city 233 000), Eindhoven 388 000 (city 194 000), Arnhem 306 000 (city 133 000), Heerlen-Kerkrade 269 000 (Heerlen city 95 000), Enschede 253 000 (city 147 000), Nijmegen 246 000 (city 146 000), Tilburg 234 000 (city 161 000), Haarlem 214 000 (city 150 000), Dordrecht 210 000 (city 112 000), Groningen 208 000 (city 169 000), 's Hertogenbosch 200 000 (city 93 000), Leiden 191 000 (city 113 000), Geleen-Sittard 183 000 (Sittard town 46 000), Maastricht 164 000 (city 118 000), Breda 163 000 (city 127 000) (all including suburbs; 1992 est.).

Language: Dutch (official); see pp. 77–9.

Religions: Roman Catholic (36%), Reformed and Calvinist (27%); see pp. 80–81.

Education: See pp. 86–90.

Defence: See pp. 122–24.

Transport: See pp. 118–22.

Media: See pp. 126–32.

GOVERNMENT

The Netherlands is a constitutional monarchy. The 75-member First Chamber of the States-General is elected for six years by the 12 provincial councils – with one half of the members retiring every three years. The 150-member Second Chamber is elected for four years by universal adult suffrage by proportional representation. The monarch appoints a Prime Minister who commands a majority in the States-General. The PM, in turn, appoints a Council of Ministers (Cabinet) who are responsible to the States-General. The main political parties include the (conservative) CDA (Christian Democratic Appeal Party), PvdA (the Labour Party), the (liberal) VVD (People's Party for Freedom and Democracy), D66 (Democracy 66), the (Calvinist) SGP (Political Reformed Party), the PPR (Reformed Political Federation), the (Calvinist) Evangelical Political Federation, the Green Left and the Centre Democrats. In the current Second Chamber these political parties have the following number of seats. (A general election is scheduled for May 1994.) A CDA–PvdA coalition was formed in November 1992.

Party	Seats
Christian Democrats	54
Labour Party	49
People's Party for Freedom/Democracy	22
Democracy 66	12
Green Left	6
Political Reformed Party	3
Evangelical Political Federation	2
Reformed Political Federation	1
Centre Democrats	1
Total	*150*

Queen: HM Queen Beatrix (succeeded on the abdication of her mother, 30 April 1980).

THE CABINET

Prime Minister: Ruud F.M. Lubbers (CDA).

Deputy Prime Minister and Minister of Finance: Wim Kok (PvdA).

Minister of Agriculture, Nature Management and Fisheries: Piet Bukman (CDA).

Minister of Defence: A.L. ter Beek (PvdA).

Minister of Development Cooperation: Jan P. Pronk (PvdA).

Minister of Economic Affairs: Dr J.E. Andriessen (CDA).

Minister of Education and Science: Dr. Jo M.M. Ritzen (PvdA).

Minister of Finance: (see above).

Minister of Foreign Affairs: Dr P.H. Kooijmans (CDA).

Minister of Foreign Trade: Y.M.C.T. van Rooy (CDA).

Minister of Home Affairs: C. Ien Dales (PvdA).

Minister of Housing, Planning and the Environment: J. (Hans) G.M. Alders (PdvA).

Minister of Justice and Minister of Netherlands Antillean and Aruban Affairs: Dr. Ernst Hirsch Ballin (CDA).

Minister for Social Affairs and Employment: Dr. Bert de Vries (CDA).

Minister of Transport and Public Works: J.R. Hanja Maij-Weggen (CDA).

Minister of Welfare, Health and Cultural Affairs: Hedy d'Ancona (PvdA).

Minister Plenipotentiary of the Netherlands Antilles: E.A.V. Jesrun.

Minister Plenipotentiary of Aruba: R.H. Laclé.

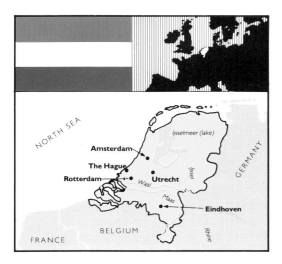

GEOGRAPHY

Over one quarter of the Netherlands – one of the world's most densely populated countries – lies below sea level. A network of canals and canalized rivers cross the west of the country where sand dunes and man-made dykes protect low-lying areas and polders (land reclaimed from the sea). The coast has been straightened by sea walls protecting Zeeland in the southwest and enclosing a freshwater lake, the IJsselmeer, in the north. The east comprises low sandy plains. *Principal rivers:* Rhine (Rijn) – dividing into branches including the Lek, Waal and Oude Rijn, Maas (Meuse). *Highest point:* Vaalserberg 321 m (1053 ft). The country has a maritime temperate climate, with cool summers and mild winters.

ECONOMY

Despite having few natural resources – except natural gas – the Netherlands has a high standard of living.

Labour force (1991)

Sector	Number employed
Industry	1 196 000
Agriculture	289 000
Construction	409 000
Public utilities	41 000
Trade	1 104 000
Finance	648 000
Transport and communications	382 000
Services and administration	2 229 000
Other	574 000
Total	*6 872 000*

Agriculture and horticulture are highly mechanized with a concentration on dairying and glasshouse crops, particularly flowers. Food processing is a major industry, and the country is a leading exporter of cheese. Manufacturing includes chemical, machinery, petroleum refining, metallurgical and electrical engineering industries. Raw materials are imported through Rotterdam, which is the largest port in the world and serves much of Western Europe. Banking and finance are well developed. For information on the Dutch currency see pp. 104–5, on GNP see p. 125, on imports and exports see pp. 112–13 and on the national budget see pp. 134–36.

RECENT HISTORY

The Dutch were neutral in World War I, but suffered occupation by the Germans 1940 to 1945. Following a bitter colonial war, the Dutch accepted that they could not reassert control over Indonesia after World War II. The Netherlands has shown enthusiasm for European unity, and, with the other Low Countries, founded Benelux, the core of the EC. Dutch politics has been characterized by a large number of small parties, some of a confessional nature, and a system of proportional representation has prevented any of these parties attaining a parliamentary majority. The formation of a new coalition government after each general election has often been difficult and time-consuming.

Provinces of the Netherlands

provincial capitals

A:	Arnhem
As:	Assen
G:	Groningen
H:	The Hague
Ha:	Haarlem
L:	Lelystad
Le:	Leeuwarden
M:	Middelburg
Ma:	Maastricht
's-H:	's-Hertogenbosch
U:	Utrecht
Z:	Zwolle

PORTUGAL

Official name: A República Portuguesa (The Portuguese Republic).

Member of: UN, EC/EU, NATO, Council of Europe, CSCE, WEU, OECD.

Area: 92 072 km² (33 549 sq mi) including Madeira and the Azores.

Population: 10 421 000 (1991 est).

Capital: Lisbon (Lisboa) 2 131 000 (city 950 000; Amadora 100 000; Barreiro 55 000; Almada 45 000; Queluz 45 000) (1990 est).

Other major cities: Oporto (Porto) 1 695 000 (city 450 000; Vila Nova de Gaia 65 000,), Setúbal 80 000, Coímbra 75 000, Braga 67 000, Funchal 47 000 (all including suburbs; 1990 est).

Language: Portuguese (official); see pp. 77–9.

Religion: Roman Catholic (94%); see pp. 80–81.

Education: See pp. 86–90.

Defence: See pp. 122–24.

Transport: See pp. 118–22.

Media: See pp. 126–32.

GOVERNMENT

An executive President is elected for five years by universal adult suffrage. The 230-member Assembly is directly elected for four years. The President appoints a Prime Minister who commands a majority in the Assembly. The PM, in turn, appoints a Council of Ministers (Cabinet), responsible to the Assembly. Madeira and the Azores have their own autonomous governments. The main political parties include PSD (the Social Democratic Party), PS (the Socialist Party), the (centre-left) Centre Democratic Party (CDS), the Communist alliance (CDU) and the (pensioners') National Solidarity Party (PSN). At the general election held on 6 October 1991 these parties obtained the following number of seats. The PSD formed a government.

Party	Seats
Social Democratic Party	135
Socialist Party	72
Communist alliance	17
Centre Democrats	5
National Solidarity Party	1
Total	230

President: Mario Alberto Soares (elected 1986 and 1991).

THE CABINET

Prime Minister: Annibal Cavaço Silva.
Deputy Prime Minister (and Minister of Defence): Fernando Nogueira.
Minister of Agriculture, Fisheries and Food: Arlindo Cunha.
Minister of Defence: See above.
Minister of Education: Antonio Couto dos Santos.

Minister for the Environment and National Resources: Carlos Borrego.
Minister of Finance: Jorge Braga de Macedo.
Minister of Foreign Affairs: Jose Durão Barroso.
Minister of Health: Arlindo Carvalho.
Minister of Industry and Energy: Luis Mira Amaral.
Minister of the Interior: Manuel Dias Loureiro.
Minister of Justice: Dr. Alvaro Laborino Lucio.
Minister of Labour and Social Security: José Silva Peneda.
Minister for Parliamentary Affairs: Luis Marques Mendes.
Minister of Planning and Territorial Administration: Luis Valente de Oliveira.
Minister of Public Works, Transport and Communications: Joaquim Ferreira do Amaral.
Minister for the Sea: Eduardo de Azevedo Soares.
Minister of Trade and Tourism: Fernando Faria de Oliveira.

AUTONOMOUS REGIONS

Azores (Açores) *Area*: 2247 km² (868 sq mi). *Population*: 253 000 (1991 est). *Capital*: Ponta Delgada 22 000 (1981).

Madeira (includes Porto Santo) *Area*: 794 km² (306 sq mi). *Population*: 273 000 (1991 est). *Capital*: Funchal 47 000 (1990 est).

GEOGRAPHY

Behind a coastal plain, Portugal north of the River Tagus is a highland region, at the centre of which is the country's principal mountain range, the Serra da Estrela. A wide plateau in the northeast is a continuation of the Spanish Meseta. Portugal south of the Tagus is mainly an undulating lowland. The Atlantic islands of Madeira and the Azores are respectively nearly 1000 km (620 mi) and 1200 km (745 mi) southwest of the mainland. *Principal rivers:* Tagus (Rio Tejo), Douro, Guadiana. *Highest point:* Pico 2315 m (7713 ft) in the Azores. Malhao de Estrela, at 1993 m (6537 ft), is the highest point on the mainland. Portugal has a mild and temperate climate which is wetter and more Atlantic in the north, and drier, hotter and more Mediterranean in the south.

The Azores comprise nine main islands and many much smaller islets. The mountainous islands, which include volcanic craters, are in three groups. The island of São Miguel contains over 50% of the population. Madeira is a

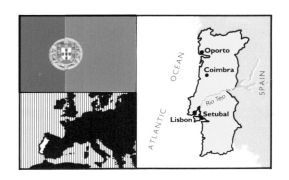

tropical island group comprising Madeira island, Porto Santo and seven other tiny uninhabited islets. Agriculture and tourism (particularly in Madeira) are important, but both the Azores and Madeira have lost population because of widescale migration to Europe and North America.

ECONOMY
Agriculture involves about 15% of the labour force, but lacks investment following land reforms in the 1970s, since when production has fallen. The principal crops include wheat and maize, as well as grapes (for wines such as port and Madeira), tomatoes, potatoes and cork trees. The country lacks natural resources. Manufacturing industry includes textiles and clothing (major exports), footwear, food processing, cork products, and, increasingly, electrical appliances and petrochemicals. Tourism and money sent back by Portuguese working abroad are major foreign-currency earners. Despite recent impressive economic development – following severe disruption during and immediately after the 1974 revolution – Portugal remains Western Europe's poorest country.

Labour force (1991 est)

Sector	Number employed
Industry	1 200 000
Agriculture	845 000
Construction	385 000
Public utilities	45 000
Trade, restaurants, hotels	725 000
Transport and communications	215 000
Finance, etc.	210 000
Services and administration	1 100 000
Other (including unemployed)	235 000
Total	*4 960 000*

For information on the Portuguese currency see pp. 104–5, on the GNP see p. 125, on imports and exports see pp. 112–13 and on the national budget see pp. 134–36.

RECENT HISTORY
Portugal experienced political instability for much of the 19th century. The monarchy was violently overthrown in 1910, but the Portuguese republic proved unstable and the military took power in 1926. From 1932 to 1968, under the dictatorship of Premier Antonio Salazar (1889–1970), stability was achieved but at great cost. Portugal became a one-party state, and expensive colonial wars dragged on as Portugal attempted to check independence movements in Angola and Mozambique. In 1974 there was a left-wing military coup whose leaders granted independence to the African colonies (1974–75), and initially attempted to impose a Marxist system on the country. However, elections in 1976 decisively rejected the far left. Civilian rule was restored as Portugal effected a transition from dictatorship to democracy, and simultaneously – through the loss of empire and membership of the EC (from 1986) – became more closely integrated with the rest of Europe.

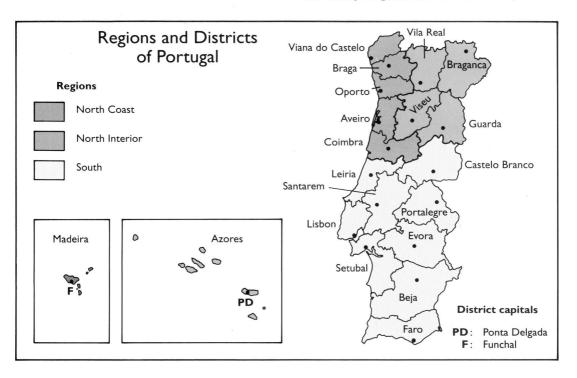

Regions and Districts of Portugal

Regions

- North Coast
- North Interior
- South

Madeira

Azores

Vila Real
Viana do Castelo
Braga
Braganca
Oporto
Viseu
Aveiro
Guarda
Coimbra
Castelo Branco
Leiria
Santarem
Portalegre
Lisbon
Evora
Setubal
Beja
Faro

F

PD

District capitals

PD: Ponta Delgada
F: Funchal

SPAIN

Official name: Reino de España (Kingdom of Spain).

Member of: UN, NATO, EC/EU, WEU, CSCE, Council of Europe, OECD.

Area: 504 782 km² (194 897 sq mi) including the Canary Islands, Ceuta and Melilla.

Population: 39 952 000 (1991 census) including the Canary Islands, Ceuta and Melilla.

Capital: Madrid 4 846 000 (city 3 121 000; Móstoles 193 000; Leganés 173 000; Alcalá de Henares 159 000; Fuenlabrada 145 000; Alcorcon 140 000; Getafe 139 000; 1991 census).

Other major cities: Barcelona 3 400 000 (city 1 707 000; L'Hospitalet 269 000; Badalona 206 000; Sabadell 184 000; Santa Coloma de Gramanet 132 000), Valencia 1 060 000 (city 777 000), Seville (Sevilla) 754 000 (city 684 000), Zaragoza 614 000, Málaga 525 000, Bilbao 477 000 (city 372 000), Las Palmas de Gran Canaria 348 000, Valladolid 345 000, Murcia 329 000, Córdoba 309 000, Palma de Mallorca 309 000, Granada 287 000, Vigo 277 000, Alicante 271 000, Gijón 260 000, La Coruña 251 000, Cádiz 240 000 (city 157 000), Vitoria 209 000, Oviedo 203 000, Santander 194 000, Santa Cruz de Tenerife 192 000, Pamplona 191 000, Salamanca 186 000, Jérez de la Frontera 184 000, Elche 181 000, Donostia-San Sebastián 174 000, Cartagena 172 000, Burgos 169 000, Salamanca 163 000, Tarrasa 154 000, Alméria 153 000, León 144 000, Huelva 141 000 (all including suburbs; 1991 census).

Languages: Spanish or Castilian (official; as a first language over 70%), Catalan (as a first language over 20%), Basque (3%), Galician (4%); see pp. 77–9.

Religion: Roman Catholic (95%); see pp. 80–81.

Education: See pp. 86–90.

Defence: See pp. 122–24.

Transport: See pp. 118–22.

Media: See pp. 126–32.

GOVERNMENT

Spain is a constitutional monarchy. The Cortes (Parliament) comprises a Senate (Upper House) and a Chamber of Deputies (Lower House). The Senate consists of 208 senators – 4 from each province, 5 from the Balearic Islands, 6 from the Canary Islands and 2 each from Ceuta and Melilla – elected by universal adult suffrage for four years, plus 49 senators indirectly elected by the autonomous communities. The Congress of Deputies has 350 members directly elected for four years under a system of proportional representation. The King appoints a Prime Minister (President of the Council) who commands a majority in the Cortes. The PM, in turn, appoints a Council of Ministers (Cabinet) responsible to the Chamber of Deputies. Each of the 17 regions has its own legislature. The main political parties include the PSOE (Socialist Workers' Party), the (conservative) PP (Partido Popular), the (left-wing coalition) Izquierda Unida (United Left, which includes the Communist Party), the (Catalan) Convergencia i Unio (CIU) and PNV (the Basque Nationalist Party). At the general election held on 6 June 1993 these parties obtained the following number of seats in the Cortes and a PSOE government was formed.

Party	Seats
PSOE	159
PP	141
United Left	18
CIU	17
PNV	5
Others	10
Total	350

King: HM King Juan Carlos I (succeeded upon the restoration of the monarchy, 22 November 1975).

THE CABINET

Prime Minister: Felipe González Marquez.
Deputy Prime Minister: Narcis Serra y Serra.
Minister of Agriculture: Vicente Albero Silla.
Minister of Commerce and Tourism: Javier Gomez-Navarro Navaretta.
Minister of Culture: Carmen Alborch Bataller.
Minister of Defence: Julián Garcia Vargas.
Minister of Economic Affairs and Finance: Pedro Solbes Mira.
Minister of Education and Science: Gustavo Suarez Pertierra.
Minister of Foreign Affairs: Javier Solana Madariaga.
Minister of Health and Consumer Affairs: Angeles Amador Millán.
Minister of Industry: Juan Eguiagaray Ucelay.
Minister of the Interior: Antonio Asunción.
Minister of Justice: Juan Belloch Julve.
Minister of Labour and Social Security: José Antonio Griñan Martinez.
Minister for Parliamentary Relations: Alfredo Pérez Rubalcaba.
Minister of Public Administration: Jerónimo Saavedra Acevedo.

Minister of Public Works, Transportation and the Environment: José Borrell Fontellas.

Minister of Social Affairs: Cristina Alberdi Alonso.

AUTONOMOUS COMMUNITIES

Andalusia (Andalucia) Area: 87 268 km² (33 694 sq mi). Population: 6 860 000 (1991 census). Capital: Seville (Sevilla).

Aragón Area: 47 669 km² (18 405 sq mi). Population: 1 179 000 (1991 census). Capital: Zaragoza.

Asturias Area: 10 565 km² (4079 sq mi). Population: 1 091 000 (1991 census). Capital: Oviedo.

Balearic Islands (Islas Baleares) Area: 5014 km² (1936 sq mi). Population: 703 000 (1991 census). Capital: Palma de Mallorca.

Basque Country (Euzkadi or Pais Vasco) Area: 7261 km² (2803 sq mi). Population: 2 093 000 (1991 census). Capital: Vitoria.

Canary Islands (Islas Canarias) Area: 7273 km² (2808 sq mi). Population: 1 456 000 (1991 census). Equal and alternative capitals: Las Palmas and Santa Cruz de Tenerife.

Cantabria Area: 5289 km² (2042 sq mi). Population: 524 000 (1991 census). Capital: Santander.

Castile-La Mancha (Castilla-La Mancha) Area: 79 226 km² (30 589 sq mi). Population: 1 650 000 (1991 census). Capital: Toledo.

Castile and León (Castilla y León) Area: 94 147 km² (36 350 sq mi). Population: 2 538 000 (1991 census). Capital: Valladolid.

Catalonia (Catalunya or Cataluña) Area: 31 930 km² (12 328 sq mi). Population: 5 960 000 (1991 census). Capital: Barcelona.

Extremadura Area: 41 602 km² (16 063 sq mi). Population: 1 050 000 (1991 census). Capital: Mérida.

Spanish Autonomous Communities

Galicia (Galiza) *Area*: 29 434 km² (11 364 sq mi). *Population*: 2 710 000 (1991 census). *Capital*: Santiago de Compostela.

Madrid *Area*: 7995 km² (3087 sq mi). *Population*: 4 846 000 (1991 census). *Capital*: Madrid.

Murcia *Area*: 11 317 km² (4369 sq mi). *Population*: 1 032 000 (1991 census). *Capital*: Murcia (although the regional parliament meets at Cartagena).

Navarre (Navarra) *Area*: 10 421 km² (4024 sq mi). *Population*: 516 000 (1991 census). *Capital*: Pamplona.

La Rioja *Area*: 5034 km² (1853 sq mi). *Population*: 262 000 (1991 census). *Capital*: Logroño.

Valencia *Area*: 23 305 km² (8998 sq mi). *Population*: 3 831 000 (1991 census). *Capital*: Valencia.

Ceuta-Melilla (North African enclaves) *Area*: Ceuta – 19 km² (7 sq mi); Melilla – 14 km² (5.5 sq mi). *Population*: 125 000 (1991 census). *Capitals*: Ceuta and Melilla.

GEOGRAPHY

In the north of Spain a mountainous region stretches from the Pyrenees – dividing Spain from France – through the Cantabrian mountains to Galicia on the Atlantic coast. Much of the country is occupied by the central plateau, the Meseta. This is around 600 m (2000 ft) high, but rises to the higher Sistema Central in Castile, and ends in the south at the Sierra Morena. The Sierra Nevada range in Andalusia in the south contains Mulhacén, mainland Spain's highest peak at 3478 m (11 411 ft). The principal lowlands include the Ebro Valley in the northeast, a coastal plain around Valencia in the east, and the valley of the Guadalquivir River in the south. The Balearic Islands in the Mediterranean comprise four main islands – Mallorca (Majorca), Menorca (Minorca), Ibiza and Formentera – with seven much smaller islands. The Canary Islands, off the coast of Morocco and the Western Sahara, comprise five large islands – Tenerife, Fuerteventura, Gran Canaria, Lanzarote and La Palma – plus two smaller islands and six islets. The cities of Ceuta and Melilla are enclaves on the north coast of Morocco. *Principal rivers:* Tagus (Tajo), Ebro, Douro (Duero), Guadiana, Guadalquivir. *Highest point:* Pico del Tiede 3716 m (12 192 ft) in the Canaries. The southeast has a Mediterranean climate with hot summers and mild winters. The dry interior is continental with hot summers and cold winters. The high Pyrenees have a cold Alpine climate, while the northwest (Galicia) has a wet Atlantic climate with cool summers.

ECONOMY

Over 10% of the labour force is involved in agriculture. The principal crops include barley, wheat, sugar beet, potatoes, citrus fruit and grapes (for wine). Pastures for livestock occupy some 20% of the land. Manufacturing developed rapidly from the 1960s, and there are now major motor-vehicle, textile, plastics, metallurgical, shipbuilding, chemical and engineering industries, as well as growing interests in telecommunications and electronics. Foreign investors have been encouraged to promote new industry, but unemployment remains high. Banking and commerce are important, and tourism is a major foreign-currency earner with around 53 000 000 foreign visitors a year, mainly staying at beach resorts

on the Mediterranean, Balearic Islands and the Canaries. After the G7 countries, Spain has the largest gross national product in the world. For information on the Spanish currency see pp. 104–5, on GNP see p. 125, on imports and exports see pp. 112–13 and on the national budget see pp. 134–36.

Labour force (1991)

Sector	Number employed
Industry	2 632 000
Mining	481 000
Agriculture	1 686 000
Construction	1 434 000
Public utilities	152 000
Trade, restauranrs, hotels	3 076 000
Transport and communications	772 000
Finance, etc.	725 000
Services and administration	2 978 000
Other	1 084 000
Total	*15 020 000*

RECENT HISTORY

When Cuba, the Philippines, Guam and Puerto Rico were lost after the Spanish-American War (1989), doubts grew as to whether Alfonso XIII's constitutional monarchy was capable of delivering the dynamic leadership that Spain was thought to require. Spain remained neutral in World War I. Social tensions increased and a growing disillusionment with parliamentary government and political parties led to a military coup (1923) led by General Miguel Primo de Rivera (1870–1930). Primo was supported by Alfonso XIII until 1930 when the King withdrew support. However, the range of forces arrayed against the monarchy and the threat of civil war led Alfonso to abdicate (1931). The peace of the succeeding republic was short-lived. Neither of the political extremes – left nor right – was prepared to tolerate the perceived inefficiency and lack of authority of the Second Spanish Republic. In 1936, nationalist army generals rose against a new republican government. Led by General Francisco Franco (1892–1975) and supported by Germany and Italy, the nationalists fought the republicans in the bitter Spanish Civil War. Franco triumphed in 1939 to become ruler – Caudillo – of the neo-Fascist Spanish State. Political expression was restricted, and from 1942 to 1967 the Cortes (Parliament) was not directly elected. Spain remained neutral in World War II, although it was beholden to Germany. After 1945, Franco emphasized Spain's anti-Communism – a policy that brought his regime some international acceptance from the West during the Cold War.

In 1969, Franco named Alfonso XIII's grandson Juan Carlos (1938–) as his successor. The monarchy was restored on Franco's death (1975) and the King eased the transition to democracy through the establishment of a new liberal constitution in 1978. In 1981 Juan Carlos played an important role in putting down an attempted army coup. In 1982 Spain joined NATO and elected a socialist government, and since 1986 the country has been a member of the EC. Despite the granting of some regional autonomy since 1978, Spain continues to be troubled by campaigns for provincial independence – for example in Catalonia – and by the violence of the Basque separatist movement ETA.

UNITED KINGDOM

Official name: The United Kingdom of Great Britain and Northern Ireland.

Member of: UN, EC/EU, NATO, Commonwealth, G7, OECD, CSCE, Council of Europe.

Area: 244 103 km² (94 249 sq mi).

Population: 57 561 000 (1992 est).

Capital: London (see below).

COUNTRIES OF THE UNITED KINGDOM
ENGLAND
Area: 130 441 km² (50 363 sq mi).

Population: 47 837 300 (1991 est.).

Capital: London 7 825 000 (London Urban Area – Greater London 6 803 100).

Other major cities: Birmingham 2 326 000 (West Midlands Urban Area; city 994 500; Dudley 305 000; Walsall 259 000; Wolverhampton 242 000; Solihull 199 000; West Bromwich 153 000), Manchester 2 281 000 (Greater Manchester Urban Area; city 432 600; Stockport 284 000; Bolton 258 000; Salford 220 000; Oldham 217 000; Rochdale 202 000), Leeds-Bradford 1 543 000 (West Yorkshire Urban Area; Leeds city 706 300, Bradford city 468 700; Huddersfield 147 000), Newcastle-upon-Tyne 761 000 (Tyneside Urban Area; city 273 300; Gateshead 199 000), Liverpool 663 000 (Urban Area; city 474 500), Sheffield 644 000 (Urban Area; city 520 300; Rotherham 122 000), Nottingham 612 000 (Urban Area; city 276 000), Bristol 547 000 (Urban Area; city 392 600), Brighton 482 000 (Brighton-Worthing Urban Area; Brighton town 153 800; Worthing 96 000), Portsmouth 461 000 (Urban Area; city 185 200; Havant 120 000; Fareham 99 000), Leicester 406 000 (Urban Area; city 280 500), Stoke-on-Trent 377 000 (The Potteries Urban Area; city 249 700; Newcastle-under-Lyme 120 000), Middlesbrough 372 000 (Teesside Urban Area; town 144 400; Stockton-on-Tees 174 000), Bournemouth 364 000 (Urban Area; town 159 100; Poole 133 000), Coventry 338 000 (Coventry-Bedworth Urban Area; city 306 300), Preston 317 000 (Urban Area; town 129 900), Hull 317 000 (Kingston-upon-Hull Urban Area; city 262 900), Southampton 311 000 (Southampton-Eastleigh Urban Area; Southampton city 204 500), Southend 292 000 (Urban Area; town 162 900), Blackpool 292 000 (Urban Area; town 151 100), Birkenhead 279 000 (Urban Area; town 93 000), Plymouth 255 000 (Urban Area; city 254 400), Rochester 243 000 (Medway Towns Urban Area; city 147 100; Gillingham 95 000), Aldershot 242 000 (Urban Area; Aldershot with Farnborough 86 000), Luton 223 000 (Luton-Dunstable Urban Area; Luton town 174 600), Derby 223 000 (Urban Area; city 222 500), Reading 212 000 (Urban Area; town 134 600), Sunderland 202 000 (Urban Area; the city has a population of 296 400 and covers a wider area than the Urban Area), Norwich 192 000 (Urban Area; city 125 300), Northampton 185 000 (Urban Area; town 184 400), Milton Keynes 179 000. (The population figures for the Urban Areas – the cities and their agglomerations are 1991 est. based on the 1991 census).

NORTHERN IRELAND
Area: 14 120 km² (5452 sq mi).

Population: 1 589 400 (1991 est).

Capital: Belfast 433 000 (Urban Area; city 287 100; Newtownabbey 74 000; Castlereagh 61 000).

Other major towns and cities: Londonderry/Derry 95 000, Craigavon-Portadown-Lurgan 74 000 (Portadown 24 000, Lurgan 22 000), Bangor 35 000, Lisburn 28 000, Ballymena 20 000 (town 17 000). (Population figures for Urban Areas – the cities and their agglomerations are 1991 est. based on the 1991 census).

SCOTLAND
Area: 78 775 km² (30 415 sq mi).

Population: 5 102 400 (1991 est.).

Capital: Edinburgh 527 000 (Urban Area; city 438 800).

Other major cities and towns: Glasgow 1 648 000 (Central Clydeside Urban Area; city 687 600; Paisley 84 000; Hamilton 52 000; Clydebank 45 000), Aberdeen 219 000 (Urban Area; city 213 900), Dundee 173 000, Greenock 93 000 (Urban Area; town 58 000), Falkirk 74 000 (Urban Area; 36 000), Ayr 62 000 (Urban Area; town 49 000), Dunfermline 58 000 (Urban Area; town 52 000), Irvine 56 000, Kilmarnock 55 000 (town 52 000), Cumbernauld 50 000. (Population figures for Urban Areas – the cities and their agglomerations are 1991 est. based on the 1991 census).

WALES
Area: 20 768 km² (8019 sq mi).

Population: 2 881 000 (1991 est).

Capital: Cardiff 320 000 (Urban Area; city 290 000).

Other major cities and towns: Swansea 287 0000 (Urban Area; city 187 600; Neath 48 000; Port Talbot 40 000), Newport 127 000, Rhondda-Pontypool 126 000 (Urban Area; Rhondda 77 000; Pontypool 36 000); Wrexham 80 000 (Urban Area; town 40 000), Merthyr Tydfil 60 000, Aberdare 55 000 (Urban Area; town 32 000), Pontypool 50 000 (Urban Area; town 36 000), Bridgend 50 000 (Urban Area; town 31 000). (Population figures for Urban Areas – the cities and their agglomerations are 1991 est. based on the 1991 census).

CROSS REFERENCES

Languages: English, Welsh, Gaelic; see pp. 77–9.

Religions: Anglican (55% nominal, 4% practising), Roman Catholic (9%), Presbyterian (3%, including Church of Scotland); see pp. 80–81.

Education: See pp. 86–90.

Defence: See pp. 122–24.

Transport: See pp. 118–22.

Media: See pp. 126–32.

GOVERNMENT
The UK is a constitutional monarchy without a written constitution. The UK comprises four countries – England, Scotland, Wales and Northern Ireland; there is (suspended) constitutional provision for devolved government for the latter. The House of Lords – the Upper (non-elected) House of Parliament – comprises over 750 hereditary peers and peeresses, over 20 Lords of Appeal (non-hereditary peers), over 370 life peers, and 2 archbishops and 24 bishops of the Church of England.

The House of Commons consists of 651 members elected for five years by universal adult suffrage. The sovereign appoints a Prime Minister who commands a majority in the Commons. The main political parties include the Conservative Party, the Labour Party, the Liberal Democrats and regional parties including the Scottish National Party, the (Welsh Nationalist) Plaid Cymru, the Ulster Unionists, the Democratic Unionist Party and the (Northern Ireland) Social Democratic and Labour Party. At the general election held on 9 April 1992 these parties obtained the following number of seats in the Commons – the following list includes changes to these totals as a result of by-elections. A Conservative government was formed.

Party	Seats
Conservative	334
Labour	270
Liberal Democrats	22
Ulster Unionist Party	9
Plaid Cymru	4
Social Democratic and Labour Party	4
Scottish National Party	3
Democratic Unionist Party	3
Ulster Popular Unionist Party	1
The Speaker	1
Total	651

Queen: HM Queen Elizabeth II (succeeded upon the death of her father, 6 February 1952).

THE CABINET
Prime Minister: John Major.
Minister of Agriculture, Fisheries and Food: Gillian Shephard.
Secretary of State for Defence: Malcolm Rifkind.
Secretary of State for Education: John Patten.
Secretary of State for Employment: David Hunt.
Secretary of State for the Environment: John Selwyn Gummer.
Chancellor of the Exchequer: Kenneth Clarke.
Foreign Secretary: Douglas Hurd.
Secretary of State for Health: Virginia Bottomley.
Home Secretary: Michael Howard.
Secretary of State for National Heritage: Peter Brooke.
Secretary of State for Northern Ireland: Sir Patrick Mayhew.
(Chancellor of the Duchy of Lancaster and) Minister of Public Service and Science: William Waldegrave.
Secretary of State for Scotland: Ian Lang.
Secretary of State for Social Security: Peter Lilley.
Secretary of State for Trade and Industry and President of the Board of Trade: Michael Heseltine.
Secretary of State for Transport: John McGregor.
Chief Secretary to the Treasury: Michael Portillo.
Secretary of State for Wales: John Redwood.
Lord Chancellor: Lord Mackay of Clashfern.

CROWN DEPENDENCIES
The Crown Dependencies are autonomous islands which are associated with but not part of the UK.

Guernsey (includes Alderney, Sark and smaller dependencies)
Area: 75 km² (29 sq mi) — Guernsey (island) 63.3 km² (24.5 sq mi); Alderney 7.9 km² (3.07 sq mi); Sark 5.1 km² (1.99 sq mi). *Population:* 57 000 (Guernsey island; 1989 est); Alderney 2000 (1986 est); Sark 600 (1986 est). *Capital:* St Peter Port 18 000 (1986 est). The capital of Alderney is St Anne's. There are no towns or villages on Sark, on which settlement is scattered.

Isle of Man
Area: 572 km² (221 sq mi). *Population:* 70 000 (1991 census). *Capital:* Douglas 22 000 (1991 census).

Jersey
Area: 116.2 km² (44.8 sq mi). *Population:* 83 000 (1989 est). *Capital:* St Helier 30 000 (1986 est).

GEOGRAPHY
The UK comprises the island of Great Britain, the northeast part of Ireland plus over 4000 other islands. Lowland Britain occupies the south, east and centre of England. Clay valleys and river basins – including those of the Thames and the Trent – separate relatively low ridges of hills, including the limestone Cotswolds and Cleveland Hills, and the chalk North and South Downs and the Yorkshire and Lincolnshire Wolds. In the east, low-lying Fenland is largely reclaimed marshland. The flat landscape of East Anglia is covered by glacial soils. The northwest coastal plain of Lancashire and Cheshire is the only other major lowland in England. A peninsula in the southwest – Devon and Cornwall – contains granitic uplands, including Dartmoor and Exmoor. The limestone Pennines form a moorland backbone running through northern England. The Lake District (Cumbria) is an isolated mountainous dome rising to Scafell Pike, the highest point in England at 978 m (3210 ft).

Wales is a highland block, formed by a series of plateaux above which rise the Brecon Beacons in the south, Cader Idris and the Berwyn range in the centre, and Snowdonia in the north, where Snowdon reaches 1085 m (3560 ft).

In Scotland, the Highlands in the north and the Southern Uplands are separated by the rift valley of the Central Lowlands, where the majority of Scotland's population, agriculture and industry are to be found. The Highlands are divided by the Great Glen in which lies Loch Ness. Although Ben Nevis is the highest point, the most prominent range of the Highlands is the Cairngorm Mountains. The Southern Uplands lie below 853 m (2800 ft). Other Scottish lowlands include Buchan in the northeast, Caithness in the north, and a coastal plain around the Moray Firth. To the west of Scotland are the many islands of the Inner and Outer Hebrides, while to the north are the Orkney and Shetland Islands.

Northern Ireland includes several hilly areas, including the Sperrin Mountains in the northwest, the uplands in County Antrim, and the Mourne Mountains rising to Slieve Donard at 852 m (2796 ft). Lough Neagh – at the centre of Northern Ireland – is the UK's largest lake.
Principal rivers: Severn, Thames (with Churn), Trent-Humber, Aire (with Ouse), (Great or Bedford) Ouse, Wye, Tay (with Tummel), Nene, Clyde. *Highest point:* Ben Nevis 1392 m (4406 ft).

The temperate climate of the UK is warmed by the North Atlantic Drift. There is considerable local variety, particularly in rainfall totals, which range from just over 500 mm (20

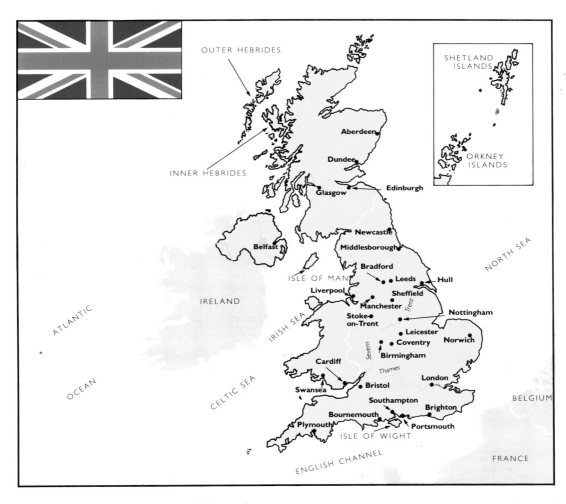

in) in the southeast to 5000 mm (200 in) in northwest Scotland.

ECONOMY

Over one sixth of the British labour force is involved in manufacturing.

Labour force (1991)

Sector	Number employed
Industry, mining, utilities	5 195 000
Agriculture	272 000
Construction	960 000
Trade	4 596 000
Finance	2 595 000
Transport and communications	1 313 000
Services and administration	6 736 000
Other	6 743 000
Total	*28 410 000*

For information on the British currency – the pound sterling – see pp. 104–5, on GNP see p. 125, on British imports and exports see pp. 112–13 and on the national budget see pp. 134–36.

The principal industries include iron and steel, motor vehicles, electronics and electrical engineering, textiles and clothing, aircraft, and consumer goods. British industry relies heavily upon imports of raw materials. The country is self-sufficient in petroleum (from the North Sea) and has important reserves of natural gas and coal – although the coal industry is declining as seams in traditional mining areas become uneconomic. As Britain is a major trading nation, London is one of the world's leading banking, financial and insurance centres, and the 'invisible earnings' from these services make an important contribution to exports. Tourism is

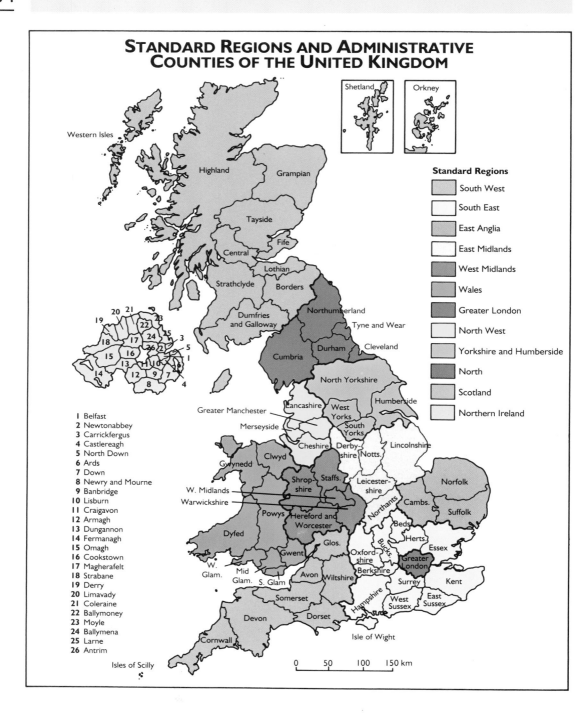

STANDARD REGIONS AND ADMINISTRATIVE COUNTIES OF THE UNITED KINGDOM

Shetland

Orkney

Western Isles

Highland

Grampian

Standard Regions

South West

South East

East Anglia

East Midlands

West Midlands

Wales

Greater London

North West

Yorkshire and Humberside

North

Scotland

Northern Ireland

Tayside

Fife

Central

Lothian

Strathclyde

Borders

Dumfries and Galloway

Northumberland

Tyne and Wear

Durham

Cleveland

Cumbria

North Yorkshire

Humberside

Lancashire

West Yorks

Greater Manchester

Merseyside

South Yorks

Cheshire

Derbyshire

Notts.

Lincolnshire

Gwynedd

Clwyd

Shropshire

Staffs.

Leicestershire

Norfolk

W. Midlands

Warwickshire

Northants

Cambs.

Suffolk

Powys

Hereford and Worcester

Beds

Dyfed

Glos.

Herts

Essex

Gwent

Oxfordshire

Bucks

W. Glam.

Mid Glam.

S. Glam

Avon

Wiltshire

Berkshire

Greater London

Surrey

Kent

Somerset

Hampshire

West Sussex

East Sussex

Devon

Dorset

Isle of Wight

Cornwall

Isles of Scilly

1 Belfast
2 Newtonabbey
3 Carrickfergus
4 Castlereagh
5 North Down
6 Ards
7 Down
8 Newry and Mourne
9 Banbridge
10 Lisburn
11 Craigavon
12 Armagh
13 Dungannon
14 Fermanagh
15 Omagh
16 Cookstown
17 Magherafelt
18 Strabane
19 Derry
20 Limavady
21 Coleraine
22 Ballymoney
23 Moyle
24 Ballymena
25 Larne
26 Antrim

0   50   100   150 km

another major foreign-currency earner. Agriculture (with forestry) involves about 1% of the labour force and is principally concerned with raising sheep and cattle. Arable farming is widespread in the east, where the main crops are barley, wheat, potatoes and sugar beet.

In the 1970s and 1980s the UK did not experience the same rate of economic growth as most other West European states. Economic problems have included repeated crises of confidence in the value of the pound, credit squeezes and high (regional) rates of unemployment. However, in 1993 the UK experienced a very tentative economic recovery while most of the rest of Western Europe remained in recession. Since 1980 most major nationalized industries have been privatized.

RECENT HISTORY

By the end of the 19th century the economic dominance Britain had enjoyed since the industrial revolution was beginning to be challenged by the USA and, more particularly, by Germany. Rivalry with Imperial Germany was but one factor contributing to the causes of World War I. PM Herbert Asquith (1852–1928) led a reforming Liberal Government from 1908 to 1916 but – after criticism of his conduct of the war – he was replaced by David Lloyd George (1863–1945), who as Chancellor of the Exchequer had introduced health and unemployment insurance.

The 'old dominions' – Canada, Australia, New Zealand and South Africa – emerged from the war as autonomous countries, and their independent status was confirmed by the Statute of Westminster (1931). The Easter Rising in Ireland (1916) led to the partition of the island in 1922. Only Northern Ireland – the area with a Protestant majority – stayed within the United Kingdom, but since the 1970s bitter conflict has resurfaced in the province as Roman Catholic republicans – seeking unity with the Republic of Ireland – clashed with Protestant Loyalists intent upon preserving the link with Britain. British troops were stationed in Northern Ireland to keep order and to defeat the terrorist violence of the IRA and (Protestant) Loyalist illegal organizations.

In World War II Britain – led by PM Sir Winston Churchill (1874–1965), who had strenuously opposed appeasement in the 1930s – played a major role in the defeat of the Axis powers, and from 1940 to 1941 the UK stood alone against an apparently invincible Germany. Following the war, the Labour government of Clement Attlee (1883–1967) established the 'welfare state'. At the same time, the British Empire began its transformation into a Commonwealth of some 50 independent states, starting with the independence of India in 1947. By the late 1980s decolonization was practically complete and Britain was no longer a world power, although a British nuclear deterrent was retained. By the 1970s the United Kingdom was involved in restructuring its domestic economy and, consequently, its welfare state – from 1979 to 1990 under the Conservative premiership of Margaret Thatcher (1925–). The country has also joined (1973) and has attempted to come to terms with the European Community. Under John Major (1943–) – Prime Minister since 1990 – the UK participated in the coalition against Iraq in the Second Gulf War (1991).

GIBRALTAR

The British possession of Gibraltar is the only remaining colonial territory in Europe.

Area: 2.5 km^2 (6.5 sq mi).

Population: 31 300 (1991 est).

Capital: Gibraltar 31 300 (1991 est).

Languages: English (official); Spanish- and Arab-speaking minorities.

Religions: Roman Catholic (75%), Sunni Islam (9%), Anglican (8%), Jewish (2%).

Education: Education is compulsory between the ages of five and 15.

Defence: There is a local voluntary defence force of about 150 personnel. British naval and air force units are based at Gibraltar.

Transport: There are 50 km (31 mi) of roads. Gibraltar is a port and has an international airport.

Media: There are five newspapers – one daily and four weekly. The Gibraltar Broadcasting Corporation is responsible for radio and TV broadcasts.

Government

Gibraltar is a British Crown Colony in which the British sovereign is represented by a Governor who is the executive authority. The Governor is adviced by the Gibraltar Council which is composed of four ex-officio members and five members elected by the House of Assembly. The House comprises the Speaker (who is appointed by the Governor), two ex-officio members and 15 members who are elected by universal suffrage for four years. Under the terms of the constitution, no party may win more than eight seats. The Gibraltarian political parties are the Gibraltar Socialist Labour Party (GSLP), the Gibraltar Social Democrats (GSD) and the Gibraltar National Party (GNP). At the general election held in January 1992 the GSLP gained eight seats and the GSD gained seven seats. A GSLP government was formed. *Chief Minister:* Joe Bossano.

Geography

Gibraltar is a rocky peninsula connected to Spain by a narrow isthmus. *Highest point:* The Rock 428 m (1396 ft). Gibraltar has a Mediterranean climate.

Economy

Gibraltar depends on tourism, ship repairing, banking and finance – the Rock has become an 'offshore' banking centre – and the re-export trade (for example, fuel for visiting ships). Owing to lack of space there is no agriculture.

Recent History

The strategic importance of Gibraltar – a British colony since 1713 – has greatly diminished with the decline of the British Empire since World War II. Spain continues to claim the Rock and blockaded Gibraltar from 1969 to 1983. Gibraltar has enjoyed self-government since 1964 and became part of the EC when the UK joined that organization in 1973.

AUSTRIA

Official name: Republik Österreich (Republic of Austria)

Member of: UN, EFTA, OECD, CSCE, Council of Europe.

Area: 83 855 km² (32 367 sq mi).

Population: 7 812 000 (1991 census).

Capital: Vienna (Wien) 2 045 000 (city 1 533 000) (1991 census).

Other major cities: Linz 434 000 (city 203 000), Graz 395 000 (city 232 000), Salzburg 267 000 (city 144 000), Innsbruck 235 000 (city 115 000), Klagenfurt 135 000 (city 90 000), Villach 55 000, Wels 53 000, Sankt Pölten 50 000, Dornbirn 41 000, Steyr 40 000, Wiener Neustadt 35 000 (1991 census).

Language: German (official; 96%); see also pp. 78–9.

Religion: Roman Catholic (84%); Lutheran (6%); see also pp. 80–1.

Education: see pp. 86–90.

Defence: see pp. 122–24.

Transport: see pp. 118–19.

Media: see pp. 126–29.

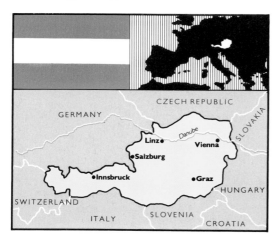

GOVERNMENT

Executive power is shared by the Federal President – who is elected by universal adult suffrage for a six-year term – and the Council of Ministers (Cabinet), led by the Federal Chancellor. The President appoints a Chancellor who commands a majority in the Federal Assembly's lower chamber, the Nationalrat, whose 183 members are elected by universal adult suffrage according to proportional representation for a term of four years. The 63 members of the upper chamber – the Bundesrat – are elected by the assemblies of the nine provinces of the Federal Republic. The main political parties are the (socialist) Social Democratic Party (SPO), (conservative) People's Party (OVP), (right-wing) Freedom Party (FPO), the Liberal Forum (LF) and the Greens (VGO). At the general election held on 7 October 1990 these parties obtained the following number of seats in the Nationalrat.

Party	Seats
Social Democratic Party	80
People's Party	60
Freedom Party*	28
Greens	10
Liberal Forum	5
Total	163

* The Liberal Forum broke away from the FPO after the election.

A coalition of SPO and OVP members was formed.

Federal President: Thomas Klestil (elected 1992).

THE CABINET

Federal Chancellor: Franz Vranitzky (SPO).

Deputy Chancellor (also Minister of Science): Dr Erhard Busek (OVP).

Minister of Agriculture and Forestry: Dr Franz Fischler (OVP).

Minister of Economic Affairs: Dr Wolfgang Schüssel (OVP).

Minister of Education and the Arts: Dr Rudolf Scholten (SPO).

Minister of Employment and Social Affairs: Dr Josef Hesoun (SPO).

Minister for the Environment and for Youth and Family Affairs: Ruth Feldgrill-Zankel (OVP).

Minister of Federal Affairs: Jürgen Weiss (OVP).

Minister of Finance: Ferdinand Lacina (SPO).

Minister of Foreign Affairs: Dr Alois Mock (OVP).

Minister of Health, Consumer Protection and Sport: Dr Michael Ausserwinkler (SPO).

Minister of the Interior: Dr Franz Löschnak (SPO).

Minister of Justice: Dr Nikolaus Michalek (ind).

Minister of National Defence: Dr Werner Fasslabend (OVP).

Minister of Public Economy and Transport: Dr Viktor Klima (SPO).

Minister of Science: Dr Erhard Busek (OVP; see above).

Minister for Women's Affairs: Johanna Dohnal (SPO).

PROVINCES (Länder)

Burgenland *Area*: 3966 km² (1531 sq mi). *Population*: 274 000 (1991 census). *Capital*: Eisenstadt.

Carinthia (Kärnten) *Area*: 9533 km² (3681 sq mi). *Population*: 552 000 (1991 census). *Capital*: Klagenfurt.

Lower Austria (Niederösterreich) *Area*: 19 171 km² (7402 sq mi). *Population*: 1 481 000 (1991 census). *Capital*: Sankt Pölten.

Salzburg *Area*: 7154 km² (2762 sq mi). *Population*: 484 000 (1991 census). *Capital*: Salzburg.

Styria (Steiermark) *Area*: 16 387 km² (6327 sq mi). *Population*: 1 185 000 (1991 census). *Capital*: Graz.

Tirol *Area*: 12 647 km² (4883 sq mi). *Population*: 630 000 (1991 census). *Capital*: Innsbruck.

Upper Austria (Oberösterreich) *Area*: 11 979 km² (4625 sq mi). *Population*: 1 340 000 (1991 census). *Capital*:

Linz.

Vienna (Wien) *Area*: 415 km² (160 sq mi). *Population*: 1 533 000 (1991 census). *Capital*: Vienna.

Vorarlberg *Area*: 2601 km² (1004 sq mi). *Population*: 333 000 (1991 census). *Capital*: Dornbirn.

GEOGRAPHY

The Alps – much of which are covered by pastures and forests – occupy nearly two thirds of Austria. Lowland Austria – in the east – consists of low hills, the Vienna Basin and a flat marshy area beside the Neusiedler See on the Hungarian border. Along the Czech border is a forested massif rising to 1200 m (4000 ft). *Principal rivers*: Danube (Donau), Inn, Mur. *Highest point*: Grossglockner 3798 m (12 462 ft).

There are many local variations in climate owing to altitude and aspect. The east is drier than the west, and is, in general, colder than the Alpine region in the winter and hotter, but more humid, in the summer. Areas over 3000 m (10 000 ft) are snow-covered all year.

ECONOMY

Although Austria produces about 90% of its own food requirements, agriculture employs only 7% of the labour force. The arable land in the east has fertile soils producing good yields of cereals, as well as grapes for wine. Dairy produce is an important export from the pasturelands in the east and in the Alps.

The mainstay of the economy is manufacturing industry, including machinery and transport equipment, iron and steel products, refined petroleum products, cement and paper. Natural resources include magnesite and iron ore, as well as hydroelectric power potential and the most considerable forests in central Europe. The Alps

attract both winter and summer visitors, making tourism a major earner of foreign currency. Austria retains economic links with countries in Central Europe that were once part of the Habsburg empire. However, Austria's main trading partners are Germany, Italy, France and Switzerland (see pp. 112–13).

Labour force (1991)

Sector	Number employed
Industry	980 000
Agriculture	259 000
Construction	313 000
Public utilities	40 000
Commerce	515 000
Transport and communications	228 000
Services	1 234 000
Other	40 000
Total	*3 609 000*

For information on the Austrian currency – the Schilling – see pp. 104–5 – and on the national budget see pp. 134–36.

RECENT HISTORY

In 1918–19, the Austro-Hungarian Habsburg empire was dismembered. An Austrian republic was established as a separate state, despite support for union with Germany. Unstable throughout the 1920s and 1930s, Austria was annexed by Germany in 1938 (the Anschluss). Austria was liberated in 1945, but Allied occupation forces remained until 1955 when the independence of a neutral Austrian republic was recognized. The upheavals in Central Europe in 1989–90 encouraged Austria to renew links with Hungary, the Czech Republic, Slovenia, Croatia and Slovakia (all once Habsburg territories). Austria is a candidate for membership of the EC.

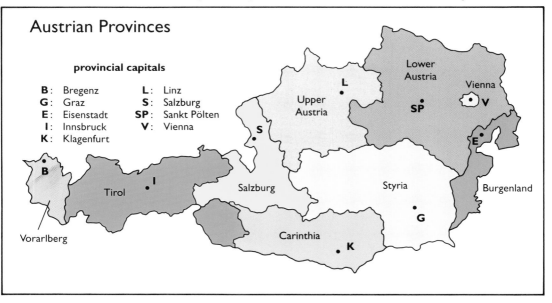

Austrian Provinces

provincial capitals

B : Bregenz
G : Graz
E : Eisenstadt
I : Innsbruck
K : Klagenfurt

L : Linz
S : Salzburg
SP : Sankt Pölten
V : Vienna

FINLAND

Official name: Suomen Tasavalta (Republic of Finland).

Member of: UN, EFTA, CSCE, Council of Europe, OECD.

Area: 338 145 km² (130 557 sq mi).

Population: 5 029 000 (1992 est).

Capital: Helsinki (Helsingfors) 1 005 000 (city 498 000; Espoo (Esbo) 176 000; Vantaa (Vanda) 157 000) (1992 est).

Other major cities: Turku (Åbo) 265 000 (city 159 000), Tampere (Tammerfors) 262 000 (city 174 000), Oulu (Uleaborg) 102 000, Lahti 93 000, Kuopio 82 000, Pori (Björneborg) 76 000, Jyväskylä 67 000, Kotka 57 000, Lappeenranta (Villmanstrand) 55 000, Vaasa (Vasa) 54 000, Joensuu 48 000, Hämeenlinna (Tavastehus) 40 000, Kajaani 37 000, Kokkola (Karleby) 35 000 (1992 est).

Languages: Finnish (94%), Swedish (6%); see pp. 77–9.

Religion: Lutheran (88%); see pp. 80–81.

Education: See pp. 86–90.

Defence: See pp. 122–24.

Transport: See pp. 118–22.

Media: See pp. 126–32.

GOVERNMENT

The 200-member Eduskunta (Parliament) is elected for four years under a system of proportional representation by universal adult suffrage. Executive power is vested in a President elected for six years by direct popular vote. The President appoints a Council of State (Cabinet) – headed by a Prime Minister – responsible to the Parliament. The Åland Islands have a considerable degree of self-government. The main political parties include the Centre Party (Kesk), the Social Democratic Party (SDP), the (conservative) National Coalition Party (Kok), the Left-Wing Alliance, the Green Union, the Swedish People's Party (SFP), the Liberal People's Party (LKP), the Rural Party (SMP), the Finnish Christian Union (SKL) and the Communist Workers' Party. At the general election held on 19 March 1991 these parties obtained the following number of seats and a coalition government of members of Kesk, Kok, SFP and SKL was was formed in March 1992.

Party	Seats
Centre Party	55
Social Democratic Party	48
National Coalition Party	40
Left-Wing Alliance	19
Swedish People's Party	12
Green Union	10
Finnish Christian Union	8
Rural Party	7
Liberal People's Party	1
Total	200

President: Mauno Koivisto (elected 1982 and 1988).

THE CABINET
Prime Minister: Esko Aho (Kesk).
Minister of Agriculture and Forestry: Martti Pura (Kesk).
Minister of Culture: Tytti Isohookana-Asunmaa (Kesk).
Minister of Defence: Elisabeth Rehn (SFP).
Minister of Development and Cooperation: Toimi Kankaanniemi (SKL).
Minister of Education: Riita Uosukainen (Kok).
Minister for the Environment: Sirpa Pietikäinen (Kok).
Minister of Finance: Iiro Viinanen (Kok).
Minister of Foreign Affairs: Paavo Väyrynen (Kesk).
Minister of Foreign Trade: Pertti Salolainen (Kok).
Minister of Justice: Hannele Pokka (Kesk).
Minister of Housing: Pirjo Rusanen (Kok).
Minister of the Interior: Mauri Pekkarinen (Kesk).
Minister of Labour: Ilkka Kanerva (Kok).
Minister of Social Affairs and Health: Jorma Huuhtanen (Kesk).
Minister of Trade and Industry: Pekka Tuomisto (Kesk).
Minister of Transport and Communications: Ole Norrback (SFP).

AUTONOMOUS COUNTY
Åland Islands (Ahvenanmaa) *Area*: 1527 km² (590 sq mi). *Population*: 24 800 (1992 est). *Capital*: Mariehamn.

GEOGRAPHY
Nearly one third of Finland lies north of the Arctic Circle and one tenth of the country is covered by lakes, some 50 000 in all. Saimaa – the largest lake – has an area of over 4400 km² (1700 sq mi). During the winter months the Gulfs of Bothnia (to the west) and of Finland (to the south) freeze, and ports have to be kept open by icebreakers. The land has been heavily glaciated, and except for mountains in the northwest most of the country is lowland. *Principal rivers:* Paatsjoki, Torniojoki, Kemijoki, Kokemäenjoki. *Highest point:* Haltiatunturi 1342 m (4344 ft). Finland's climate is characterized by warm summers and long, extremely cold winters (particularly in the north).

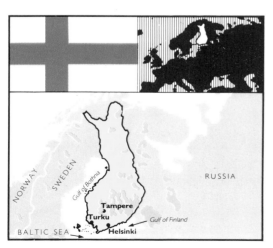

ECONOMY

Forests cover about two thirds of the country and wood products are one of the most important sources of Finland's foreign earnings. Metalworking and engineering – in particular shipbuilding – are among the most important of Finland's industries, which have a

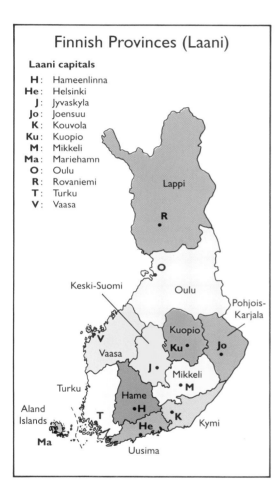

Finnish Provinces (Laani)

Laani capitals

H :	Hameenlinna
He :	Helsinki
J :	Jyvaskyla
Jo :	Joensuu
K :	Kouvola
Ku :	Kuopio
M :	Mikkeli
Ma :	Mariehamn
O :	Oulu
R :	Rovaniemi
T :	Turku
V :	Vaasa

reputation for quality and good design. Finland enjoys a high standard of living, although – apart from forests, copper and rivers suitable for hydroelectric power – the country has few natural resources. There is a large fishing industry, and the agricultural sector produces enough cereals and dairy products for export. (There is concern about the future of Finland's subsidized agriculture within an enlarged EU/EC.) The collapse of

trade with Russia – traditionally a major trading partner – brought severe economic difficulties to Finland in 1991–93.

Labour force (1991)

Sector	Number employed
Industry	539 000
Mining	4 000
Agriculture and forestry	213 000
Construction	221 000
Public utilities	28 000
Finance, etc.	205 000
Transport and communications	183 000
Trade, restaurants and hotels	402 000
Services and administration	766 000
Others	15 000
Total	*2 576 000*

For information on the Finnish currency see pp. 104–5, on GNP see p. 125, on imports and exports see pp. 112–13 and on the national budget see pp. 134–36.

RECENT HISTORY

After the Russian Revolution of 1917, civil war broke out in Russian-ruled Finland. The left-wing forces were eventually defeated at the Battle of Tampere by right-wing forces led by General Carl Gustaf Mannerheim. In 1919 Finland adopted an independent republican constitution, which is still in force today. A Russian Red Army invasion in 1920 was repulsed. The demands of the Swedish-speaking inhabitants of the Åland Islands for union with Sweden were rejected but the islands gained considerable autonomy (1921). Finland's territorial integrity lasted until 1939 when a Soviet invasion followed Finland's refusal to make territorial concessions to the USSR. Despite fierce resistance Finland was defeated (1940) and was forced to cede the Karelian isthmus, the shores of Lake Ladoga and Viipuri (Vyborg) – which was then Finland's second city – to the Soviet Union. In 1941 the transit of German troops across Finnish soil was allowed and, when Germany attacked the USSR, Finland was drawn into a second war against the Soviet Union. Finnish forces made initial advances but, upon Germany's retreat (1944), Finland had to make peace with the USSR. As well as previous territorial losses Finland had to cede her only access to the Arctic Ocean, the port of Petsamo, and was burdened with heavy reparation payments to the USSR. The Soviet Union also gained a long-term lease on the Porkkala peninsula near Helsinki.

Finland has, since 1945, retained its neutrality and independence. Despite having to resettle over 300 000 refugees from areas ceded to the USSR and repaying war reparations, Finland recovered quickly. The country has achieved some influence through the careful exercise of its neutrality, for example, hosting the initial sessions of CSCE (the 'Helsinki accords'). Government in Finland is characterized by multi-party coalitions, and since 1987 parties of the left have lost favour. Economically, Finland is integrated into Western Europe through membership of EFTA and OECD, and is a candidate for EC/EU membership.

ICELAND

Official name: Lýdveldid Island (The Republic of Iceland).

Member of: UN, NATO, EFTA, Council of Europe, CSCE, OECD.

Area: 103 001 km² (39 769 sq mi).

Population: 260 000 (1992 est.).

Capital: Reykjavik 147 000 (city 99 000; Kópavogur 16 000; Hafnarfjördhur 15 000) (1991 est.).

Other major towns: Akureyri 14 000, Keflavik 7500 (1991 est.).

Language: Icelandic (official); see pp. 77–9.

Religion: Lutheran (93%); see pp. 80–1.

Education: See pp. 86–90.

Defence: See pp. 122–4.

Transport: See pp. 118–22.

Media: See pp. 127–32.

GOVERNMENT

The 63-member Althing (Parliament) is elected by proportional representation by universal adult suffrage for a four-year term. The Althing elects 20 of its members to sit as the Upper House and the remaining 43 members to sit as the Lower House. The President – who is directly elected for four years – appoints a Prime Minister and a Cabinet who are responsible to the Althing. The main political parties include the (conservative) Independence Party (IP), the Progressive Party (PP), the Social Democratic Party (SDP), the (socialist) People's Alliance (PA), and the Women's Alliance (WA). At elections held on 20 April 1991 these parties gained the following seats and a SDP-IP coalition was formed:

Party	Seats
Independence Party	26
Progressive Party	13
Social Democratic Party	10
People's Alliance	9
Women's Alliance	5
Total	63

President: Vigdis Finnbogadottir (elected 1980, 1984, 1988 and 1992).

THE CABINET

Prime Minister: David Oddsson (IP).

Minister for the Statistical Bureau: (see above; the PM).

Minister of Agriculture and Communications: Halldór Blöndal (IP).

Minister of Commerce and Industry: Jón Sigurdsson (SDP).

Minister of Finance: Fridrik Sophusson (IP).

Minister of Education and Culture: Olafur G. Einarsson (IP).

Minister of the Environment: Eidur Gudnason (SDP).

Minister for Fisheries, Justice and Ecclesiatical Affairs: Thorsteinn Pálsson (IP).

Minister of Foreign Affairs and Foreign Trade: Jón Baldvin Hannibalsson (SDP).

Minister of Health and Social Security: Sighvatur Björnvinsson (SDP).

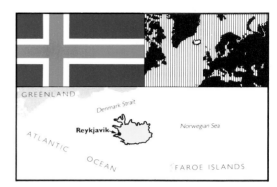

Minister of Social Affairs: Jóhanna Sigurdardóttir (SDP).

GEOGRAPHY

The greater part of Iceland has a volcanic landscape with hot springs, geysers and some 200 volcanoes – some of them active. There are several volcanic islands including Vestmannaeyjar and Surtsey. Much of the country is tundra. The south and centre are covered by glacial icefields. *Principal rivers:* Thjórsá, Skjalfanda Fljót. *Highest point:* Hvannadalshnúkur 2119 m (6952 ft). The cool temperate climate is warmed by the Gulf Stream, which keeps Iceland milder than most places at the same latitude.

ECONOMY

The fishing industry (see pp. 102–03) provides the majority of Iceland's exports (see pp. 112–13). Hydroelectric power is used in the aluminium-smelting industry, while geothermal power warms extensive greenhouses which make Iceland virtually self-sufficient in many fruits and vegetables. Ample grazing land makes the country self-sufficient in meat and dairy products (see pp. 96–100). Economic problems include high inflation and over dependence upon a single export. Details of Iceland's GNP are to be found on p. 125, currency on pp. 104–105 and national budget on pp. 134–36.

Labour force (1990)

Sector	Number employed
Industry	23 200
Agriculture/fishing	13 300
Construction	12 400
Trade, restaurants, hotels	18 100
Services	38 100
Other	19 600
Total	*124 700*

RECENT HISTORY

Icelandic nationalism grew in the 19th century, and in 1918 Iceland gained independence from Denmark. However, the two countries remained linked by their shared monarchy. In World War II the Danish link was severed and a republic was declared (1944). Disputes over fishing rights in Icelandic territorial waters led to clashes with British naval vessels in the 1950s and 1970s.

LIECHTENSTEIN

Official name: Fürstentum Liechtenstein (The Principality of Liechtenstein).
Member of: UN, Council of Europe, CSCE, EFTA.
Area: 160 km² (62 sq mi).
Population: 29 400 (1991 est).
Capital: Vaduz 4900 (1991 est).
Other major towns: Schaan 5000, Balzers 3 800, Triesen 3 600 (1991 est).
Language: German (official); see pp. 77–9.
Religion: Roman Catholic (87%); see pp. 80–81.
Education: See pp. 86–90.
Defence: See pp. 122–24.
Transport: See pp. 118–22.
Media: See pp. 126–32.

GOVERNMENT

The country is a constitutional monarchy ruled by a Prince. The 25-member Landstag (Parliament) is elected by universal adult suffrage by proportional representation for four years. The Landstag elects a 5-member National Committee (Cabinet) including a Prime Minister, who is then appointed by the Prince. The main political parties are the VU (Fatherland Union), the FBP (Progressive Citizens' Party) and the (Green) Free List. At the general election held on 24 October 1993 these parties obtained the following number of seats. At the time of going to press negotiations to form a new coalition government comprising members of the Fatherland Union and the Progressive Citizens' Party were still proceding although Mario Frick, leader of the Fatherland Union, had been appointed Prime Minister.

Party	Seats
VU	13
FBP	11
Free List	1
Total	25

Prince: HSH Prince Hans Adam II (succeeded upon the death of his father, 13 November 1989).

THE CABINET
Prime Minister: Mario Frick.

Four other Ministers (including a Deputy Prime Minister) remain to be appointed. The 13 government portfolios – Agriculture, Construction, Culture, the Economy, Education, Environmental Protection, Finance, Foreign Relations, Health and Welfare, the Interior, Justice, Sport and Transport – will be divided between the five members of the Cabinet.

GEOGRAPHY

The Alps stand in the east of the principality. The west comprises the floodplain of the River Rhine. *Principal rivers:* Rhine (Rhein), Samina. *Highest point:* Grauspitze 2599 m (8326 ft). The country has an Alpine climate.

ECONOMY

Liechtenstein has one of the highest standards of living in the world. Tourism, insurance and manufacturing (precision goods) and, in particular, banking are all important foreign-currency earners. Tourism is represented by both summer visitors on day trips to the principality and winter visitors attracted by skiing.

Labour force (1991)

Sector	Number employed
Industry	4 800
Construction	1 200
Public utilities	180
Transport and communications	450
Mining	60
Trade	1 700
Agriculture and forestry	350
Finance, etc.	1 100
Services and administration.	4 800
Total	*14 640*

Liechtenstein uses the Swiss currency see pp. 104–5. For information concerning GNP see p. 125, on imports and exports see pp. 112–13 and on the national budget see pp. 134–36.

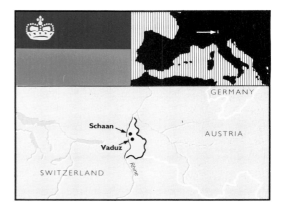

RECENT HISTORY

Liechtenstein was the only German principality not to join the German Empire in 1871. Before World War I (1914–18) the Princes of Liechtenstein – Austrian nobles with very considerable properties in Austria, Bohemia and Moravia – resided on those estates rather than within the principality. Since 1924 the country has enjoyed a customs and monetary union with Switzerland, which also represents Liechtenstein diplomatically. However, since 1989 the country has taken a more active role on the international stage, for instance, joining EFTA and the UN. Controversy concerning the principality's future relations with the EEA and EU led to unprecedented political argument and two general elections in 1993.

NORWAY

Official name: Kongeriket Norge (Kingdom of Norway).

Member of: UN, EFTA, NATO, CSCE, Council of Europe, OECD.

Area: 323 878 km² (125 050 sq mi) or 386 958 km² (149 469 sq mi) including Svalbard and Jan Mayen.

Population: 4 274 000 (1992 est) – excluding Svalbard and Jan Mayen (see below).

Capital: Oslo 467 000 (1992 est).

Other major cities: Bergen 213 000, Trondheim 138 000, Stavanger 98 000, Kristiansand 66 000, Drammen 52 000, Tromso 51 000, Skien 48 000, Sandnes 45 000, Asker 42 000, Bodo 37 000, Sandefjord 36 000, Alesund 36 000 (all including suburbs; 1990 census).

Languages: Two official forms of Norwegian – Bokmaal and Nynorsk; see pp. 77–9.

Religion: Lutheran (official; 88%); see pp. 80–81.

Education: See pp. 86–90.

Defence: See pp. 122–24.

Transport: See pp. 118–22.

Media: See pp. 126–32.

GOVERNMENT

Norway is a constitutional monarchy. The 165-member Parliament (Storting) is elected under a system of proportional representation by universal adult suffrage for a four-year term. In order to legislate, the Storting divides itself into two houses – the Lagting (containing one quarter of the members) and the Odelsting (containing the remaining three quarters of the members). The King appoints a Prime Minister who commands a majority in the Storting. The PM, in turn, appoints a Council of Ministers who are responsible to the Storting. The main political parties include the Labour Party (DnA), the Conservative Party (H), the Progress Party (FP), the Socialist Left Party (SVP), the Christian Democratic Party (KrF), the Centre Party (SP), the Red Electoral Alliance and the Liberal Party (Venstre). At the general election held September 1993 these parties obtained the following number of seats in the Storting. A Labour Party government was formed in October 1993.

Party	Seats
Labour	67
Centre (SP)	32
Conservatives	28
Christian Democrats	13
Socialist Left	13
Party of Progress	10
Liberals	1
Red Electoral Alliance	1
Total	*165*

King: HM King Harald V (succeeded upon the death of his father, 17 January 1991).

THE CABINET
Prime Minister: Gro Harlem Brundtland.
Minister of Agriculture: Gunhild Oyangen.
Minister for Children and Family Affairs: Grete Berget.
Minister of Church Affairs: See below.
Minister of Cultural Affairs: Ase Kleveland.
Minister of Defence: Jorgen Kosmo.
Minister of Development Cooperation: Kari Nordheim-Larsen.
Minister of Education and Research, and Minister of Church Affairs: Gudmund Hernes.
Minister for the Environment: Thorbjorn Berntsen.
Minister of Finance: Sigbjorn Johnsen.
Minister of Fisheries: Jan Henry T. Olsen.
Minister of Foreign Affairs: Johan Jorgen Holst.
Minister of Government Administration: Nils Olav Totland.
Minister of Health: Werner Christie.
Minister of Industry and Energy: Jens Stoltenberg.
Minister of Justice: Grete Faremo.
Minister of Local Government and Labour: Gunnar Berge.
Minister of Social Affairs: Grete Knudsen.
Minister of Trade and Shipping: Bjorn Tore Godal.
Minister of Transport and Communications: Kjell Opseth.

DEPENDENCIES
The following European dependencies are part of the kingdom of Norway.

Svalbard (includes Bear Island (Bjornoya)) *Area:* 62 924 km² (24 295 sq mi). *Population:* 3700 (1990 est) – about two-thirds of the population are Russian miners. *Capital:* Longyearbyen.

Jan Mayen *Area:* 380 km² (147 sq mi). *Population:* no permanent population.

GEOGRAPHY
Norway's coastline is characterized by fjords, a series of long, deep, narrow inlets formed by glacial action. (Norway's coastline measures 2650 km excluding the fjords but 21 347 km including the fjords.) The greater part of Norway comprises highlands of hard rock. Permanent glaciers occur in the southwest. The principal lowlands are along the Skagerrak coast and

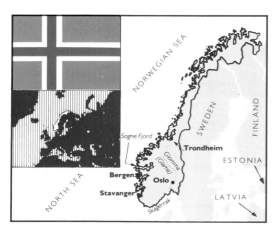

around Oslofjord and Trondheimsfjord. *Principal rivers*: Glomma (Glama), Lågen, Tanaelv. *Highest point*: Galdhøpiggen 2469 m (8098 ft).

Norway's temperate climate is the result of the warming Gulf Stream. Summers are remarkably mild for the latitude, while winters are long and very cold. Precipitation is heavy – over 2000 mm (80 in) in the west, with marked rain shadows inland. Norway has the nickname 'The Land of the Midnight Sun and at the North Cape the Sun does not set between the middle of May and end of July; conversely the Sun does not rise between the middle of November and the end of January.

Svalbard (formerly known as Spitsbergen) is a bleak archipelago in the Arctic. The island of Spitsbergen is exploited for its coal. Jan Mayen is an active volcanic island situated between Norway and Greenland.

ECONOMY
Norway enjoys a high standard of living. Only a small proportion of the land can be cultivated, and agriculture – which is heavily subsidized – is chiefly concerned with dairying and fodder crops. Timber is a major export of Norway, over one half of which is forested. The fishing industry is an important foreign-currency earner, and fish farming – which has been encouraged by government development schemes – is taking the place of whaling and deep-sea fishing. Manufacturing – which has traditionally been concerned with processing fish, timber and iron ore – is now dominated by petrochemicals and allied industries, based upon large reserves of petroleum and natural gas in Norway's sector of the North Sea. Petroleum and natural gas supply over one third of the country's export earnings. The development of industries such as electrical engineering has been helped by cheap hydroelectric power.

Labour force (1991)

Sector	Number employed
Industry	335 000
Agriculture	128 000
Construction	140 000
Public utilities	23 000
Trade, restaurants and hotels	357 000
Transport and communications	160 000
Finance, etc.	150 000
Services and administration	735 000
Other (including unemployed)	120 000
Total	*2 148 000*

For information on the Norwegian currency see pp. 104–5, on GNP see p. 125, on imports and exports see pp. 112–13 and on the national budget see pp. 134–36.

RECENT HISTORY
Norway came under the rule of the kings of Sweden after the Napoleonic Wars, although a separate Norwegian Parliament was allowed a considerable degree of independence. Growing nationalism in Norway placed great strains upon the union with Sweden, and in 1905 – following a vote by the Norwegians to repeal the union – King Oscar II of Sweden gave up his claims to the Norwegian crown to allow a peaceful separation of the two countries. After a Swedish prince declined the Norwegian throne, Prince Carl of Denmark was confirmed as King of Norway – as Haakon VII – by a plebiscite. Norway was neutral in World War I, and declared neutrality in World War II, but was occupied by German forces (1940) who set up a puppet government under Vidkun Quisling. After the war, Norway joined NATO and agreed in 1972 to enter the EC, but a national referendum rejected membership. In 1992, a Norwegian reapplication for EC membership became a serious option. In the 1990s Norwegian diplomacy has been notably active, for example, in bringing about the Israeli-Palestinian peace accord.

Norwegian Counties (Fylker)

Fylker capitals

A: Arendal
B: Bergen
Bd: Bodo
D: Drammen
H: Hamar
K: Kristiansand
L: Leikanger
Ll: Lillehammer
M: Molde
Ms: Moss
O: Oslo
S: Stavanger
Sk: Skien
St: Steinkjer
Tn: Trondheim
Tr: Tromso
V: Vadso

SWEDEN

Official name: Konungariket Sverige (Kingdom of Sweden).

Member of: UN, EFTA, CSCE, Council of Europe, OECD.

Area: 449 964 km² (173 732 sq mi).

Population: 8 644 000 (1992 est).

Capital: Stockholm 1 471 000 (city 679 000; Huddinge 74 000; Täby 57 000, Solna 52 000; 1992 est).

Other major cities: Göteborg (Gothenburg) 720 000 (city 432 000), Malmö 466 000 (city 235 000), Uppsala 171 000, Linköping 124 000, Orebro 122 000, Norrköping 121 000, Västeras 120 000, Jönköping 112 000, Helsingborg 110 000, Boras 102 000, Sundsvall 94 000, Umea 93 000, Lund (part of the Malmö agglomeration) 90 000, Eskilstuna 90 000, Gavle 89 000, Södertälje 82 000, Halmstad 81 000, Karlstad 77 000, Skelleftea 76 000, Kristianstad 72 000, Växjö 70 000, Lulea 69 000 (all including suburbs; 1992 est).

Languages: Swedish (official); see pp. 77–9.

Religion: Lutheran (85%); see pp. 80–81.

Education: See pp. 86–90.

Defence: See pp. 122–24.

Transport: See pp. 118–22.

Media: See pp. 126–32.

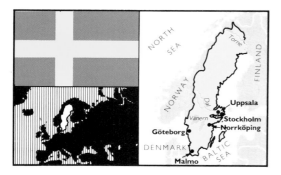

GOVERNMENT

Sweden is a constitutional monarchy in which the King is ceremonial and representative head of state without any executive role. The 349-member Riksdag (Parliament) is elected for three years by universal adult suffrage by proportional representation. The Speaker of the Riksdag nominates a Prime Minister who commands a parliamentary majority. The PM, in turn, appoints a Cabinet of Ministers who are responsible to the Riksdag. The main political parties are the Social Democratic Labour Party (SDAP), the (conservative) Moderate Party (MS), the Liberal Party (FP), the Centre Party (CP), the Christian Democratic Party (KdS), the (right-wing) New Democracy Party (ND) and the (former Communist) Left Party. At the general election held on 15 September 1991 these parties obtained the following number of seats in the Riksdag and a coalition of MS, FP, CP and KdS members was formed.

Party	Seats
Social Democratic Labour Party (SDAP)	138
Moderate Party (MS)	80
Liberal Party (FP)	33
Centre Party (CP)	31
Christian Democratic Party (KdS)	26
New Democracy (ND)	25
Left Party	16
Total	349

King: HM King Carl XVI Gustaf (succeeded upon the death of his grandfather, 15 September 1973).

THE CABINET

Prime Minister: Carl Bildt (MS).

Deputy Prime Minister and Minister of Social Welfare: Bengt Westerberg (FP).

Minister of Adult Education: Beatrix Ask (MS).

Minister of Agriculture: Karl Erik Olsson (CP).

Minister of Aid and Human Rights: Alf Svensson (KdS).

Minister for the Civil Service: Inger Davidsson (KdS).

Minister of Constitutional and Civil Law: Reidunn Laurén (ind).

Minister of Defence: Anders Björck (MS).

Minister of Education: Per Uckel (MS).

Minister for the Environment: Olof Johansson (CP).

Minister for Europe: Ulf Dinkenspiel (ind).

Minister of Finance: Anne Wibble (FP).

Minister of Fiscal Affairs and Financial Markets: Bo Lundgren (FP).

Minister of Foreign Affairs: Baroness Margaretha af Ugglas (MS).

Minister of Health and Social Security: Bo Könberg (FP).

Minister of Housing: Birgit Friggebo (FP).

Minister of Industry and Trade: Per Westerberg (MS).

Minister of Justice: Gun Hellsvik (MS).

Minister of Labour: Borje Hornlund (CP).

Minister of Physical Planning: Görel Thurdin (KdS).

Minister of Social Welfare: See above.

Minister of Transport and Communications: Mats Odell (KdS).

GEOGRAPHY

The mountains of Norrland – in the north and along the border with Norway – cover two thirds of the country. Norrland is characterized by fast-flowing rivers with many falls and rapids which have been utilized for hydroelectric power. The courses of these rivers from the Scandinavian Highlands to the Baltic Sea include many lakes. There are about 90 000 lakes in Sweden. The largest lakes – Vänern, Vättern and Malaren – are situated in central Sweden, Svealand. In the south are the low Smaland Highlands, which hardly rise above 150 m (500 ft) and the fertile lowland of Skane, which forms Sweden's most important agricultural region. Sweden's Baltic coastline is rocky and indented with many hundreds of small wooded islands. The Baltic also contains two large Swedish islands – Gotland (which lies almost halfway between the Swedish mainland and Latvia) and Oland (which adjoins the Swedish mainland). All of Sweden shows the results of either glacial erosion or glacial deposition. *Principal rivers*: Göta, Ume, Torne, Angerman, Klar, Dal. *Highest point*: Kebnekaise 2123 m (6965 ft). Sweden experiences long cold winters and warm summers, although the north – where snow remains on the mountains for eight months – is more severe than the south, where Skane has a relatively mild winter.

ECONOMY

Sweden's high standard of living has been based upon its neutrality in the two World Wars, its cheap and plentiful hydroelectric power, and its mineral riches. The country has about 15% of the world's uranium deposits, and large reserves of iron ore that provide the basis of domestic heavy industry and important exports to Western Europe. Agriculture – like the bulk of the population – is concentrated in the south. The principal products include dairy produce, meat (including reindeer), barley, sugar beet and potatoes. (There is some concern about the future of Sweden's subsidized agriculture within an enlarged European Community.)

Vast coniferous forests are the basis of the paper, board and furniture industries, and large exports of timber. Heavy industries include motor vehicles (Saab and Volvo), aerospace and machinery, although the ship-building industry – in the 1970s the world's second largest – has ceased to exist. Sweden has been badly hit by the recession in the early 1990s and has suffered rising unemployment and a falling GNP.

Labour force (1991)

Sector	Number employed
Industry	890 000
Mining	11 000
Agriculture	143 000
Construction	312 000
Public utilities	37 000
Commerce, trade	624 000
Finance, etc.	397 000
Transport and communications	318 000
Services and administration	1 698 000
Other	115 000
Total	*4 545 000*

For information on the Swedish currency see pp. 104–5, on GNP see p.125, on imports and exports see pp. 112–13 and on the national budget see pp. 134–36.

RECENT HISTORY

The union of Norway and Sweden was dissolved in 1905 when King Oscar II (reigned 1872–1907) gave up the Norwegian throne upon Norway's vote for separation. During and after World War I (1914–18) there was a sudden worldwide demand for many of the industrial products of neutral Sweden – steel, paper pulp, ball bearings, matches, etc. The result was a dramatic increase in Sweden's industrial output and capacity, and a corresponding change from a rural agricultural to an urban industrial society. Sweden experienced an unprecedented boom but – like the rest of Europe – the country suffered during the Great Depression in the early 1930s. As a result Sweden began to develop what was to become a comprehensive welfare state under successive social democratic governments. In the period 1945–50 in particular Sweden underwent a programme of intense social reform.

Although Sweden declared itself to be neutral in World War II (1939–45), the country was forced to allow the transit of German troops across Swedish soil after the fall of Norway (1940). Sweden has been a prime mover in promoting unity and harmonization among the Nordic countries, for example through the Nordic Council. The country has also assumed a moral leadership on world, social and environmental issues but was jolted by the (unclaimed) assassination of PM Olof Palme (1986). Sweden has been an enthusiastic supporter of the United Nations and has participated in many UN humanitarian operations. The country's influence in the Third World has been helped by the fact that Sweden was not a colonial power – its last overseas possession, a small West Indian island, was relinquished in the 19th century.

Although the country was strictly neutral throughout the Cold War, Sweden maintained impressive armed forces, in particular a modern air force. In the 1990s economic necessity has obliged Sweden to dismantle aspects of the welfare system. The country has also become a candidate for EC membership.

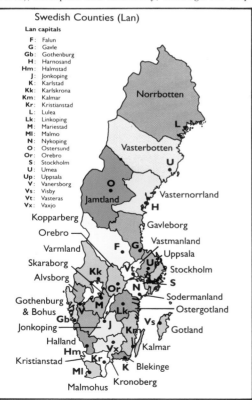

Swedish Counties (Lan)

Lan capitals

F :	Falun
G :	Gavle
Gb :	Gothenburg
H :	Harnosand
Hm :	Halmstad
J :	Jonkoping
K :	Karlstad
Kk :	Karlskrona
Km :	Kalmar
Kr :	Kristianstad
L :	Lulea
Lk :	Linkoping
M :	Mariestad
Ml :	Malmo
N :	Nykoping
O :	Ostersund
Or :	Orebro
S :	Stockholm
U :	Umea
Up :	Uppsala
V :	Vanersborg
Vs :	Visby
Vt :	Vasteras
Vx :	Vaxjo

Norrbotten

Vasterbotten

Jamtland

Vasternorrland

Kopparberg

Orebro

Varmland

Skaraborg

Alvsborg

Gothenburg & Bohus

Jonkoping

Halland

Kristianstad

Malmohus

Gavleborg

Vastmanland

Uppsala

Stockholm

Sodermanland

Ostergotland

Gotland

Kalmar

Blekinge

Kronoberg

SWITZERLAND

Official name: Schweizerische Eidgenossenschaft (German) or Confédération suisse (French) or Confederazione Svizzera (Italian) or Confederaziun Helvetica (Romansch); (Swiss Confederation).
Member of: EFTA, CSCE, OECD, Council of Europe.
Area: 41 293 km² (15 943 sq mi).
Population: 6 834 000 (1992 est).
Capital: Berne (Bern) 299 000 (city 134 000; 1990 est).
Other major cities: Zürich 839 000 (city 343 000), Geneva (Genève) 389 000 (city 165 000), Basel 359 000 (city 170 000), Lausanne 263 000 (city 123 000), Lucerne (Luzern) 161 000 (city 59 000), St Gallen 126 000 (city 73 000), Winterthur 108 000 (city 86 000), Biel/Bienne 83 000 (city 53 000), Thun 78 000 (city 38 000), Lugano 69 000 (city 25 000), Neuchâtel 66 000 (city 33 000), Fribourg (Freiburg) 57 000 (city 34 000) (1990 est).
Languages: German, French, Italian, Romansch – all official; see pp. 77–9.
Religions: Roman Catholic (47%), Reformed Churches (43%); see pp. 80–81.
Education: See pp. 86–90; **Defence:** See pp. 122–24; **Transport:** See pp. 118–22; **Media:** See pp. 126–32.

GOVERNMENT

Switzerland is a federal republic in which the governments of the 20 cantons and 6 half cantons have considerable powers. The Federal Assembly comprises the 46-member Council of States and the 200-member National Council. The former is directly elected for three or four years with two members from each canton and one from each half canton; the latter is elected for four years by universal adult suffrage by proportional representation. The Federal Assembly elects a seven-member Federal Council (Cabinet) for four years. The Council appoints one of its members to be President for one year. Political parties include the (liberal) Radical Democratic Party (FDPS), the Social Democratic Party (SD), the (conservative) Christian Democratic Party (CDVS), the (centre) Swiss People's Party (SVP), the

Ecologists, the Liberal Party, the Independent Alliance, the Automobile Party, the (right-wing) Swiss Democrats and the (former Communist) Labour Party. At the general election held on 20 October 1991 these parties obtained the following number of seats. An SD, FDPS, CDVS and SVP coalition was formed.

Party	Seats
Radical Democratic Party	44
Social Democratic Party	43
Christian Democratic People's Party	37
Swiss People's Party	25
Greens	14
Liberal Party	10
Independent Alliance	9
Automobile Party	8
Swiss Democrats	5
Others	5
Total	200

President: (for 1993) Adolf Ogi (see below).

THE FEDERAL COUNCIL (CABINET)

Minister of Defence: Kaspar Villiger (FDPS). *Minister of Finance:* Otto Stich (SD). *Minister of Foreign Affairs:* René Felber (SD). *Minister for Home Affairs:* Flavio Cotti (CDVS). *Minister of Justice and the Police:* Arnold Koller (CDVS). *Minister for the Public Economy:* Jean-Pascal Delamuraz (FDPS). *Minister of Transport, Communications and Energy:* Adolf Ogi (SVP).

CANTONS

Population figures are 1990 estimates. Canton capitals bear the same name as their canton except where indicated. * = half canton **Aargau** *Area:* 1404 km² (542 sq mi). *Population:* 490 000. **Appenzell Ausser Rhoden*** *Area:* 243 km² (94 sq mi). *Population:* 51 000. *Capital:* Herisau. **Appenzell Inner Rhoden*** *Area:* 172 km² (66 sq mi). *Population:* 14 000. *Capital:* Appenzell. **Basel-Land*** *Area:* 428 km² (165 sq mi). *Population:* 229 000. *Capital:* Liestal. **Basel-Stadt*** *Area:* 37 km² (14 sq mi). *Population:* 190 000. *Capital:* Basel. **Berne (Bern)** *Area:* 6049 km² (2336 sq mi). *Population:* 937 000. **Fribourg (Freiburg)** *Area:* 1670 km² (645 sq mi). *Population:* 204 000. **Geneva (Genève)** *Area:* 282 km² (109 sq mi). *Population:* 373 000. **Glarus** *Area:* 684 km² (264 sq mi). *Population:* 37 000. **Graubünden (Grisons)** *Area:* 7109 km² (2745 sq mi). *Population:* 169 000. *Capital:* Chur. **Jura** *Area:* 838 km² (324 sq mi). *Population:* 65 000 (1990 est). *Capital:* Delémont. **Lucerne (Luzern)** *Area:* 1494 km² (577 sq mi). *Population:* 315 000. **Neuchâtel** *Area:* 797 km² (308 sq mi). *Population:* 159 000. **St Gallen** *Area:* 2016 km² (778 sq mi). *Population:* 415 000. **Schaffhausen** *Area:* 298 km² (115 sq mi). *Population:* 71 000. **Schwyz** *Area:* 908 km² (351 sq mi). *Population:* 108 000. **Solothurn** *Area:* 791 km² (305 sq mi). *Population:* 224 000. **Thurgau** *Area:* 1006 km² (388 sq mi). *Population:* 202 000. *Capital:* Frauenfeld. **Ticino** *Area:* 2811 km² (1085 sq mi). *Population:* 283 000. *Capital:* Bellinzona. **Unterwalden Nidwalden*** *Area:* 274 km² (106 sq mi). *Population:* 32 000. *Capital:* Stans. **Unterwalden Obwalden*** *Area:* 492 km² (190 sq mi). *Population:* 28 000. *Capital:* Sarnen. **Uri** *Area:* 1075 km² (415 sq mi). *Population:* 34 000 (1990 est). *Capital:* Altdorf. **Valais (Wallis)** *Area:* 5231 km² (2020 sq mi). *Population:* 244 000. *Capital:* Sion. **Vaud** *Area:* 3211 km² (1240 sq mi). *Population:* 572 000. *Capital:* Lausanne. **Zug** *Area:* 239 km² (92 sq mi). *Population:*

84 000 (1990 est). **Zürich** *Area*: 1729 km² (668 sq mi). *Population*: 1 145 000.

GEOGRAPHY

The parallel ridges of the Jura Mountains lie in the northwest on the French border. The south of the country is occupied by the Alps. Between the two mountain ranges is a central plateau that contains the greater part of Switzerland's population, agriculture and industry. *Principal rivers*: Rhine (Rhein), Rhône, Aare, Inn, Ticino. *Highest point*: Dufourspitze (Monte Rosa) 4634 m (15 203 ft). Altitude and aspect modify Switzerland's temperate climate. Considerable differences in temperature and rainfall are experienced over relatively short distances.

ECONOMY

Switzerland's neutrality has allowed it to build a reputation as a secure financial centre. Zürich is one of the world's leading banking and commercial cities. The country enjoys one of the world's highest standards of living. Industry – in part based upon cheap hydroelectric power – includes engineering (from turbines to watches), textiles, food processing (including cheese and chocolate), pharmaceuticals and chemicals.

Dairying is important in the agricultural sector, and there is a significant timber industry. Tourism and the international organizations based in Switzerland are major foreign-currency earners. Foreign workers – in particular Italians – help alleviate the country's labour shortage. For information on currency see pp. 104–5, on the GNP see p. 125, on imports and exports see pp. 112–13 and on the national budget see pp. 134–36.

Labour force (1991)

Sector	Number employed
Industry and construction	1 246 000
Agriculture	197 000
Trade, restaurants, hotels	735 000
Finance, etc.	380 000
Transport and communications	215 000
Services and administration	795 000
Total	*3 568 000*

RECENT HISTORY

Neutrality enabled Switzerland to escape involvement in the two World Wars and made it the ideal base for the Red Cross (1863), the League of Nations (1920), etc. Switzerland avoids membership of any body it considers might compromise its neutrality – a referendum in 1992 confirmed that Switzerland should not join the EEA.

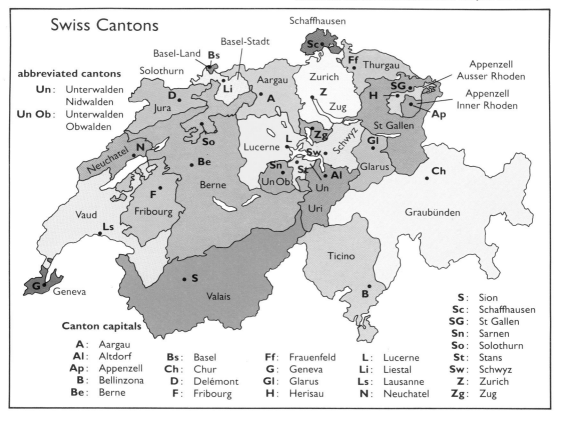

Swiss Cantons

abbreviated cantons

Un: Unterwalden Nidwalden
Un Ob: Unterwalden Obwalden

Canton capitals

A: Aargau						**S**: Sion
Al: Altdorf	**Bs**: Basel	**Ff**: Frauenfeld	**L**: Lucerne	**St**: Stans		**Sc**: Schaffhausen
Ap: Appenzell	**Ch**: Chur	**G**: Geneva	**Li**: Liestal	**Sw**: Schwyz		**SG**: St Gallen
B: Bellinzona	**D**: Delémont	**Gl**: Glarus	**Ls**: Lausanne	**Z**: Zurich		**Sn**: Sarnen
Be: Berne	**F**: Fribourg	**H**: Herisau	**N**: Neuchatel	**Zg**: Zug		**So**: Solothurn

ANDORRA

Official name: Les Valls d'Andorrà (The Valleys of Andorra).

Member of: UN, CSCE.

Area: 467 km² (180 sq mi).

Population: 55 400 (1991 est.)

Capital and major towns: Andorra la Vella 33 400 (town 20 400), Les Escaldes (part of the Andorra la Vella built-up area) 13 000, Encamp 7 000 (1990 est.)

Languages: Catalan (30%; official), Spanish (59%), French (6%).

Religion: Roman Catholic (90%). Andorra lies within the Spanish diocese of Urgel.

Education: Education is compulsory between the ages of six and 14. Instruction is provided in Catalan and French. There are no institutes of higher education but students attend universities in France and Spain.

Defence Andorra has neither armed forces nor a defence budget.

Transport Andorra has neither railways nor an airport. There are 220 km (138 mi) of roads.

Media There is a single daily newspaper and a commercial radio station.

GOVERNMENT

Andorra has joint heads of state (co-princes) – the president of France and the Spanish bishop of Urgel – who delegate their powers to permanent representatives who retain certain rights of veto under the new constitution approved by a referendum in 1993. Until December 1993 there was a traditional 28-member General Council – four councillors from each parish – which was elected for four years by universal adult suffrage. The new 28-member legislative body comprises 14 members elected by parish constituencies and 14 members elected on a national list. After 1981 the General Council chose an Executive Council (government); under the new constitutional arrangements the government will be responsible to the legislature. The 1993 referendum also

approved the establishment of political parties. The last general election held under the old system was on 5 and 12 April 1992; the first elections to be held under the new constitution are scheduled for December 1993.

Heads of state (co-Princes): Dr Juan Martí Alansis, Bishop of Urgel, and François Mitterrand, President of the French Republic.

THE CABINET

Head of government (President of the Executive Council): Oscar Ribas Reig.

Minister of Agriculture and the Natural Patrimony: Marc Moles.

Minister of Education: Josep Dalleres.

Minister of Finance, Commerce and Industry: Josep Casal.

Minister of Health, Labour and Welfare: Bibiana Rossa.

Minister of Public Services: Albert Montaner.

Minister of Tourism and Sport: Xavier Espot.

GEOGRAPHY

Situated in the eastern Pyrenees, Andorra comprises two principal river valleys and is surrounded by mountains. *Principal river:* Valira. *Highest point:* Pla del'Estany 3011 m (9678 ft). Andorra is mild in spring and summer, but cold for six months, with snow in winter.

ECONOMY

The economy used to be based mainly on sheep and timber. Tourism has been encouraged by the development of ski resorts and by the duty-free status of consumer goods, and the country receives over 10 000 000 tourists a year.

Labour force (1991)

Sector	Number employed
Industry/construction	8 700
Agriculture	150
Services (including education, health)	19 300
Total	28 200

Andorra uses both French and Spanish currencies.

The principal imports are various consumer goods imported for sale in duty-free shops.

Imports (1990)

Sector	% of imports
Perfume, alcoholic beverages, tobacco	14%
Electrical consumer goods	12%
Transport equipment	10%
Clothes	7%

Exports (1990)

Sector	% of exports
Clothes	52%
Mineral water	15%
Cattle	8%
Electrical consumer goods	8%

RECENT HISTORY

The country's joint allegiance to French and Spanish co-princes has made difficulties for Andorra in obtaining international recognition. However, reforms in 1993 included a new constitution, the legalization of political parties and trade unions, a separate judiciary, independent diplomatic representation and UN membership.

CYPRUS

Official name: Kypriaki Dimokratia (Greek) or Kibris Cumhuriyeti (Turkish) (The Republic of Cyprus).

Member of: UN, Commonwealth, CSCE, Council of Europe.

Area: 9251 km² (3572 sq mi) – of which 3355 km² (1295 sq mi) are in the Turkish-controlled zone.

Population: 756 000 (1992 est) – 570 000 in the Greek Cypriot zone; 186 000 in the Turkish-controlled zone.

Capital and major cities: Nicosia 338 000 (including 39 000 in Lefkosa, the Turkish-controlled zone), Limassol 135 000, Larnaca 63 000 (1990 est).

Languages: Greek (75%), Turkish (24%; including Turkish settlers).

Religions: Orthodox (75%), Sunni Islam (19%).

Education: Education is compulsory between the ages of five and a half and 12 (seven and 15 in the Turkish zone). There is a single university.

Defence: The National Guard is 10 000; Greek Cypriots are liable to 26 months' conscriptions. In the north there is a Turkish Cypriot regular force of 4000.

Transport: There are no railways. Paphos and Larnaca have international airports.

GOVERNMENT

A 56-member House of Representatives is elected by universal adult suffrage in the Greek Cypriot community for five years – an additional 24 seats for the Turkish Cypriot community remain unfilled. An executive President – who appoints a Council of Ministers – is elected from the Greek Cypriot community by universal adult suffrage for a five-year term. There is provision in the constitution for a Vice President to be similarly elected from the Turkish Cypriot community. In 1975, the administration of the Turkish Cypriot community unilaterally established the 'Turkish Republic of Northern Cyprus', which is unrecognized internationally except by Turkey. The main political parties in the Greek Cypriot zone are the (conservative) Democratic Rally (DISY), the Liberal Party, AKEL (the Communist Party), the Democratic Party and the Socialist Party (EDEK). In elections in the Greek Cypriot zone held on 19 May 1991 the parties gained the following seats:

Party	Seats
Democratic Rally	20
AKEL	18
Democratic Party	11
Socialist Party	7
Total	56

The Democratic Party/Liberal Rally formed a new government in May 1991.

President: Glafcos Clerides.

THE CABINET

Minister of Agriculture and Natural Resources: Kostas Petrides.

Minister of Commerce and Industry: Stelios Kiliaris.

Minister of Communications and Works: Adamos Adamides.

Minister of Defence: Kostas Eliades.

Minister of Education: Kleri Angelidou.

Minister of Finance: Phedros Ekonomides.

Minister of Foreign Affairs: Alekos Michaelides.

Minister of Health: Manolis Christophides.

Minister of the Interior: Dinos Michaelides.

Minister of Justice and Public Order: Alekos Evangelou.

Minister of Labour and Social Insurance: Andreas Moushioutas.

GEOGRAPHY

The south of the island is covered by the Troodos Mountains. Running east to west across the centre of Cyprus is a fertile plain, north of which are the Kyrenian Mountains and the Karpas Peninsula. *Principal rivers*: Seranhis, Pedieas. *Highest point*: Mount Olympus 1951 m (6399 ft).

ECONOMY

Potatoes, fruit, wine, clothing and textiles are exported from the Greek Cypriot area, in which ports, resorts and an international airport have been constructed to replace facilities lost since partition. The Turkish Cypriot area relies heavily on aid from Turkey. Tourism is important in both zones. In September 1993 the exchange rate was 0.49 Cypriot pounds to 1US$.

RECENT HISTORY

British administration in Cyprus was established in 1878. During the 1950s, Greek Cypriots – led by Archbishop (later President) Makarios III (1913–77) – campaigned for Enosis (union with Greece). The Turkish Cypriots advocated partition, but following a terrorist campaign by the Greek Cypriot EOKA movement, a compromise was agreed. In 1960 Cyprus became an independent republic. Power was shared by the two communities, but the agreement broke down in 1963, and UN forces intervened to stop intercommunal fighting. The Turkish Cypriots set up their own administration. When pro-Enosis officers staged a coup in 1974, Turkey invaded the north. Cyprus was effectively partitioned and the Turkish Cypriots established the 'Turkish Republic of Northern Cyprus' (since 1975 with Rauf Denktas as President). Over 200 000 Greek Cypriots were displaced from the north, into which settlers arrived from Turkey. Since then, UN forces have manned the 'Attila Line' between the Greek south and Turkish north, but attempts to reunite Cyprus as a federal state have been unsuccessful.

MALTA

Official name: Repubblika Ta'Malta (Republic of Malta).

Member of: UN, Commonwealth, CSCE, Council of Europe.

Area: 316 km² (122 sq mi).

Population: 360 000 (1991 est.).

Capital: Valletta 204 000 (city 9200; 1991 est.).

Other main towns: Birkirkara 21 000, Qormi 20 000, Hamrun 14 000 and Sliema 14 000 are part of the Valletta agglomeration (1991 est.).

Languages: Maltese and English (official).

Religions: Roman Catholic (official; 98%). There are two dioceses – the archdiocese of Malta based on Valletta and a bishopric on Gozo.

Education: Education is compulsory between the ages of five and 16. There is a single university.

Defence: The total armed strength in 1993 was 1650. Military service is voluntary.

Transport: There are 1553 km (965 mi) of roads. Malta has no railways. There is an international airport at Luqa near Valletta.

Media: There are three daily newspapers – two published in Maltese, one in English. The Malta Broadcasting Authority is an independent statutory authority; there are several private radio stations.

GOVERNMENT

The 65-member House of Representatives is elected by universal adult suffrage under a system of proportional representation for five years. The President – whose role is ceremonial – is elected for five years by the House. The President appoints a Prime Minister and a Cabinet who command a majority in the House. The main political parties are the (conservative) National Party, the Malta Labour Party and the Democratic Alternative. As a result of elections held on 22 February 1992 the parties gained the following number of seats:

Party	Seats
Nationalist Party	34
Malta Labour Party	31
Total	65

A Nationalist Party government was formed.

President: Dr Censu Vincent Tabone.

THE CABINET

Prime Minister: Eddie Fenech Adami.
Deputy Prime Minister and Minister for Foreign Affairs: Prof. Guido de Marco.
Minister of Economic Services: Dr George Bonello du Puis.
Minister of Education and the Development of Human Resources: Dr Ugo Mifsud Bonnici.
Minister of the Environment: Michael Falzon.
Minister of Finance: John Dalli.
Minister of Food, Agriculture and Fisheries: Lawrence Gatt.

Minister of Foreign Affairs: (see above).
Minister for Gozo: Anton Tabone.
Minister of Home Affairs and Social Development: Dr Louis Galea.
Minister of Justice: Dr Joe Fenech.
Minister of Social Security: Dr George Hyzler.
Minister of Transport and Communications: Dr Francis Zammit Dimech.
Minister of Youth and Sport: Dr Michael Frendo.

GEOGRAPHY

The three inhabited islands of Malta, Gozo and Comino consist of low limestone plateaux with little surface water. There are no significant rivers. *Highest point:* an unnamed point, 249 m (816 ft).

ECONOMY

The main industries are footwear and clothing, food processing and beverages, and ship repairing. Tourism is the main foreign-currency earner. Malta is virtually self-sufficient in agricultural products. Machinery and transport equipment represent 47% of Maltese imports and 29.3% of exports. Footwear and clothing represent about 27% of exports.

The Maltese currency is the lira which is divided into 1000 mils and 100 cents. In September 1993 the exchange rate was 0.38 Maltese Lira to 1US\$.

RECENT HISTORY

As a British colony (from 1814), Malta became a vital naval base, and the island received the George Cross for its valour in World War II. Malta gained independence in 1964. Maltese political life has been polarized between the National Party and the Maltese Labour Party. Dom Mintoff – Labour PM (1971–84) – developed close links with Communist and Arab states, notably Libya. Malta has an association agreement with the European Community and applied for full membership of the Community in 1990.

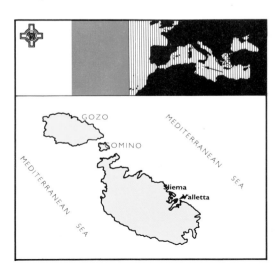

MONACO

Official name: Principauté de Monaco (Principality of Monaco).

Member of: UN, CSCE.

Area: 2.21 km² (0.85 sq mi).

Population: 29 900 (1990 census).

Capital: Monaco 1200 (1990 census).

Other major towns: Monte-Carlo 13 200, La Condamine 12 700, Fontvieille 2800 (1990 census).

Languages: French (official), Monegasque.

Religion: Roman Catholic (90%). The principality forms a single archdiocese.

Education: Education is compulsory between the ages of six and 16. There are no higher education institutions.

Defence: There is a small palace guard.

Transport: There are 50 km (31 mi) of roads and 1.7 km (1 mi) of railway track. There is a heliport at Fontvieille.

Media: There is a Monegasque edition of the French daily *Nice-Matin*. There are commercial radio and television stations.

GOVERNMENT

Monaco is a constitutional monarchy. Legislative power is jointly held by the Prince and the 18-member National Council, which is elected by universal adult suffrage for five years. Executive power is held by the Prince, who appoints a four-member Council of Government headed by the Minister of State, a French civil servant chosen by the sovereign. There are no political parties, but political groups include the (majority) Liste Campora and the Liste Médicin. At elections in January 1993 the groups obtained the following seats:

Group	Seats
Liste Campora	15
Liste Médecin	2
Independent	1
Total	18

Prince: HSH Prince Rainier III (succeeded upon the death of his grandfather, 9 May 1949).

THE CABINET

Minister of State: Jacques Dupont. *Chief of the*

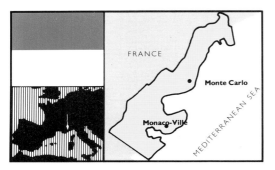

Cabinet: Denis Ravera. *Councillor of Finance and Economic Affairs:* Jean Pastorelli. *Councillor of the Interior:* Michel Eon. *Councillor of Public Works and Social Affairs:* Bernard Fautrier.

GEOGRAPHY

Monaco consists of a rocky peninsula and a narrow stretch of coast. Since 1958 the area of the principality has increased by one fifth through reclamation of land from the sea. *Principal river:* Vésubie. *Highest point:* on Chemin de Révoirés 162 m (533 ft).

ECONOMY

Monaco depends upon real estate, banking, insurance, light industry and tourism.

RECENT HISTORY

The greater part of the principality was lost – and eventually annexed by France – in 1848. Since 1861 Monaco has been under French protection. Prince Rainier III granted a liberal constitution in 1962.

SAN MARINO

Official name: Serenissima Repubblica di San Marino (Most Serene Republic of San Marino).

Member of: UN, CSCE, Council of Europe.

Area: 61 km² (23 sq mi).

Population: 23 700 (1992 est.).

Capital: San Marino 9000 (city 4200; Borgo Maggiore 4200; 1991 est.).

Other main town: Seravalle 7300 (1991 est.).

Language: Italian.

Religion: Roman Catholic (official; 95%). San Marino forms part of the diocese of San Marino-Montefeltre (most of whose territory is in Italy).

Education: Education is compulsory from six to 14. There are no institutions of higher education.

Defence: There is a small Voluntary Military Force. Male citizens can be conscripted in an emergency.

Transport: There are 237 km (147 mi) of roads. A funicular links San Marino and Borgo Maggiore.

Media: There are no daily newspapers in San Marino where the Italian daily press circulates. There are commercial radio and television stations.

GOVERNMENT

The 60-member Great and General Council is elected by universal adult suffrage for five years. The Council elects two of its members to be Captains-Regent, who jointly hold office as heads of state and of government for six months. The Captains-Regent preside over a 10-member Congress of State – the equivalent of a Cabinet – which is elected by the Council for five years. The main political parties are the (conservative) Christian Democratic Party (PDCS), the Socialist Party (PSS), the Democratic Progressive Party (PDP), the Popular Alliance (AP), the Democratic Movement (MD) and the Reformed Communist Party (RC). At elections on 30 May 1993 the following seats were gained:

Party	Seats
Christian Democrats (PDCS)	26
Socialist Party (PSS)	14
Democratic Progressive Party (PDP)	11
Popular Alliance (AP)	4
Democratic Movement	3
Reformed Communist Party	2
Total	*60*

A PDCS-PSS coalition was formed in June 1993.

THE CABINET (CONGRESS OF STATE)

Secretary of State for Finance and the Budget: Clelio Galassi (PDCS).

Secretary of State for Foreign and Political Affairs: Gabriele Gatti (PDCS).

Secretary of State for Internal Affairs, Civil Protection and Justice: Antonio Volpinari (PSS).

Minister of State for Labour and Cooperation: Sante Canducci (PDCS).

Minister of State for Commerce: Ottaviano Rossi (PDCS).

Minister of State for Education and Culture: Emma Rossi (PSS).

Minister of State for the Environment: Piernatalino Mularoni (PDCS).

Minister of State for Health and Social Security: Renzo Ghiotti (PDCS).

Minister of State for Industry and Handicrafts: Fiorenzo Stolfi (PSS).

Minister of State for Transport, Communications, Tourism and Sport: Augusto Casali (PSS).

GEOGRAPHY

The country is dominated by the triple limestone peaks of Monte Titano, the highest point at 739 m (2424 ft). There are no significant rivers. San Marino has a Mediterranean climate with warm summers, mild winters and moderate rainfall.

ECONOMY

Tourism, in particular visitors on excursions, is the mainstay of the economy. In an effort to diversify, manufacturing – particularly leather, footwear, textiles and ceramics – has been encouraged. There are no figures available for Sammarinesi imports or exports. San Marino uses Italian currency (qv).

RECENT HISTORY

San Marino's independence was recognized by the new Kingdom of Italy (1862). In 1957 a bloodless 'revolution'

replaced the Communist-Socialist administration that had been in power since 1945.

VATICAN CITY

Official name: Stato della Città del Vaticano (State of the Vatican City). Also known as the Holy See.

Member of: CSCE, UN (observer).

Area: 0.44 km² (0.17 sq mi).

Population: 750 (1989 est).

Languages: Italian and Latin (both official).

Religion: The Vatican is the headquarters of the Roman Catholic Church.

GOVERNMENT

The Pope is elected Bishop of Rome and head of the Roman Catholic Church for life by the Sacred College of Cardinals. The Vatican City is administered by a Pontifical Commission appointed by the Pope.

Pope: HH (His Holiness) Pope John Paul II (elected 16 October 1978).

GEOGRAPHY

The state comprises the Vatican City, a walled enclave in Rome, plus a number of Roman churches (including St John Lateran) and the papal villa at Castelgandolfo.

RECENT HISTORY

The Vatican City is all that remains of the once extensive Papal States. When the French troops protecting the Pope were withdrawn in 1870, Italian forces entered Rome, which became the capital of Italy. Pope Pius IX (reigned 1846–78) retreated into the Vatican, from which no Pope emerged until 1929, when the Lateran Treaties provided for Italian recognition of the Vatican City as an independent state. Since the 1960s the Papacy has again played an important role in international diplomacy, particularly under Popes Paul VI (reigned 1963–78) and John Paul II (1978–).

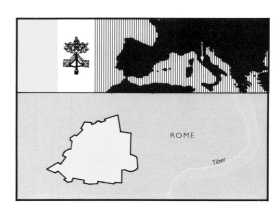

POPULATION

Most of the figures in the following tables relate to the period 1990–92.

THE COUNTRIES OF WESTERN EUROPE

Country	Area	Population	Year	Density per km²
Belgium	30 519 km²	10 022 000	1992	328.4
Denmark	43 092 km²	5 162 000	1992	119.8
France	543 965 km²	57 456 000	1992	105.6
Germany	357 050 km²	79 754 000	1991	223.4
Greece	131 957 km²	10 269 000	1991	77.8
Ireland	70 282 km²	3 523 000	1991	50.1
Italy	301 277 km²	57 104 000	1991	189.5
Luxembourg	2 586 km²	390 000	1992	150.8
Netherlands	41 785 km²	15 129 000	1992	362.1
Portugal	92 072 km²	10 421 000	1991	113.2
Spain	504 782 km²	39 952 000	1991	79.1
UK	244 103 km²	57 561 000	1992	235.8
Austria	83 855 km²	7 812 000	1991	93.2
Finland	338 145 km²	5 029 000	1992	14.9
Iceland	103 001 km²	260 000	1992	2.5
Liechtenstein	160 km²	29 400	1991	183.8
Norway	386 958 km²	4 274 000	1992	11.0
Sweden	449 964 km²	8 644 000	1992	19.2
Switzerland	41 293 km²	6 834 000	1992	165.5
Andorra	467 km²	55 400	1991	118.6
Cyprus	9 251 km²	756 000	1992	81.7
Malta	316 km²	360 000	1991	1 139.2
Monaco	2.21 km²	29 900	1990	13 529.4
San Marino	61 km²	23 700	1992	388.5
Vatican City	0.44 km²	750	1989	1 704.5

BIRTH AND DEATH RATES

Country	Population projection 2000	Population projection 2010	Population change 1980–90
Belgium	10 236 000	10 512 000	-0.1%
Denmark	5 184 000	5 171 000	0.4%
France	59 245 000	61 784 000	4.2%
Germany	83 231 000	87 056 000	1.5%
Greece	10 406 000	10 463 000	4.2%
Ireland	3 492 000	3 458 000	9.4%
Italy	57 274 000	56 270 000	1.1%
Luxembourg	395 000	403 000	2.5%
Netherlands	15 855 000	16 403 000	5.7%
Portugal	9 756 000	9 642 000	5.3%
Spain	39 879 000	40 317 000	4.4%
UK	59 021 000	59 962 000	1.6%
Austria	8 091 000	8 201 000	0.5%
Finland	5 064 000	5 036 000	4.1%
Iceland	276 000	293 000	1.1%
Liechtenstein	33 300	38 500	7.7%
Norway	4 426 000	4 550 000	3.1%
Sweden	8 938 000	9 157 000	1.6%
Switzerland	7 028 000	7 049 000	4.6%

MALE-FEMALE RATIO

Country	% of males	% of females	Year of figures
Belgium	48.9%	51.1%	1991
Denmark	49.3%	50.7%	1992
France	48.7%	51.3%	1990
Germany	48.3%	51.7%	1991
Greece	49.0%	51.0%	1991
Ireland	49.7%	50.3%	1991
Italy	48.6%	51.4%	1991
Luxembourg	48.8%	51.2%	1991
Netherlands	49.4%	50.6%	1990
Portugal	48.3%	51.7%	1990
Spain	49.1%	50.9%	1992
UK	48.8%	51.2%	1991
Austria	47.9%	52.1%	1990
Finland	48.5%	51.5%	1991
Iceland	50.1%	49.9%	1991
Liechtenstein	48.9%	51.1%	1992
Norway	49.4%	50.6%	1991
Sweden	49.4%	50.6%	1991
Switzerland	48.9%	51.1%	1991

MARRIAGE AND DIVORCE

Country	Marriage rate per 1000	Divorce rate per 1000	Year of figures
Belgium	6.5	2.0	1990
Denmark	6.1	2.7	1990
France	5.1	1.9	1990
Germany	6.5	1.6	1990
Greece	5.9	0.6	1990
Ireland	5.2	*	1989
Italy	5.4	0.4	1990
Luxembourg	6.0	2.0	1990
Netherlands	6.4	1.9	1990
Portugal	7.3	0.9	1990
Spain	5.5	1.4	1991
UK	6.8	2.9	1990
Austria	5.6	2.1	1990
Finland	5.0	2.9	1989
Iceland	4.5	1.9	1990
Liechtenstein	6.3	1.2	1991
Norway	5.2	2.4	1990
Sweden	4.2	2.3	1991
Switzerland	6.8	2.0	1990

* divorce is not available in Ireland.

POPULATION BY AGE

Country	aged under 15	15–29	30–44	45–59	60–74	over 75
Belgium	18.1%	21.8%	22.5%	16.9%	14.1%	6.6%
Denmark	17.0%	22.4%	21.9%	18.4%	13.3%	7.0%
France	19.1%	22.6%	22.8%	15.6%	12.8%	7.1%
Germany	16.2%	22.2%	21.3%	19.9%	13.3%	7.1%
Greece	19.8%	22.1%	19.8%	19.2%	13.1%	6.0%
Ireland	28.9%	24.7%	18.8%	12.8%	10.7%	4.1%
Italy	17.8%	24.1%	20.1%	18.6%	13.5%	5.9%
Luxembourg	17.1%	22.3%	23.3%	18.5%	12.8%	6.0%
Netherlands	18.2%	24.6%	23.7%	16.2%	11.9%	5.4%
Portugal	22.7%	24.6%	18.8%	16.5%	12.6%	4.8%
Spain	18.4%	25.1%	20.6%	16.5%	12.1%	7.3%
UK	19.2%	22.5%	21.0%	16.6%	13.7%	7.0%
Austria	17.4%	23.9%	20.8%	17.5%	13.3%	7.1%
Finland	19.3%	20.5%	24.6%	17.1%	12.9%	5.6%
Iceland	24.7%	24.7%	22.4%	13.4%	10.2%	4.6%
Liechtenstein	19.4%	24.8%	25.4%	16.8%	9.5%	4.1%
Norway	19.0%	22.9%	22.1%	15.1%	13.8%	7.1%
Sweden	18.0%	20.7%	21.2%	17.4%	14.7%	8.0%
Switzerland	17.2%	22.1%	23.0%	18.3%	12.7%	6.7%

Figures are 1988–91 estimates

URBAN-RURAL RATIO

Country	urban dwellers	rural dwellers	Year of figures
Belgium	96.6%	3.4%	1991
Denmark	84.8%	15.2%	1990
France	74.3%	25.7%	1990
Germany	85.3%	14.7%	1990
Greece	62.5%	37.5%	1990
Ireland	57.1%	42.9%	1990
Italy	67.1%	32.9%	1991
Luxembourg	85.9%	14.1%	1991
Netherlands	88.5%	11.5%	1990
Portugal	33.6%	66.4%	1990
Spain	78.4%	21.6%	1990
UK	91.5%	8.5%	1991
Austria	53.9%	46.1%	1991
Finland	61.7%	38.3%	1992
Iceland	91.0%	9.0%	1990
Liechtenstein	46.5%	53.5%	1992
Norway	75.0%	25.0%	1990
Sweden	83.4%	16.6%	1990
Switzerland	59.7%	40.3%	1991

MIGRATION

Following the collapse of the former Soviet Union and its East European satellites the number of migrants to Western Europe greatly increased. In 1992 some 2 000 000 immigrants entered EEA countries both driven by war and oppressive regimes and attracted by economic opportunity.

Recent migrants to Europe come from four main regions:

The former Soviet bloc Since the mid-1980s nearly 3 000 000 people have moved from the former Soviet bloc to Western Europe. Germany has been the principal goal of this migration. Over one half of the migrants from the former Soviet bloc have been ethnic Germans – mainly from Romania, Russia and Ukraine – who have a legal right of abode in Germany. Germany has also been the major destination for gypsies from Romania. Albanians – fleeing from the lowest standard of living in Europe – have chosen Italy and Greece as well as Germany as suitable destinations.

The former Yugoslavia The civil wars in the former Yugoslavia have displaced over 2 500 000 people, mainly Bosnian Muslims and (to a lesser extent) Bosnian Croats. Since 1991 nearly three quarters of a million people from the former Yugoslavia have sought refuge in the countries of Western Europe.

Turkey Up to 3 000 000 Turks live in EEA countries as economic migrants. For some years, nearly 2 000 000 Turks have made an important contribution to the German economy as *Gastarbeiter* (guest workers).

North Africa About 2 000 000 people from Morocco, Algeria and Tunisia live in Western Europe, mainly in France, which is the former colonial power in North Africa, and also in Spain.

In the 1990s there has been increased racial intolerance in some EEA countries. In Germany, for example, attacks on Turkish and other immigrants by a growing number of right-wing extremists has become a major concern. In response to an increasing number of immigrants – arriving at a time when unemployment rates are high – Germany has instituted restrictions upon entry, in particular along the Polish and Czech borders. (This, in turn, has led to the Czech Republic establishing stricter border controls along its frontier with Slovakia.) France, too, has introduced strict immigration laws. It is ironic that these new controls should be imposed at a time when the Single European Market has brought free movement within the EC and so soon after the fall of the Iron Curtain.

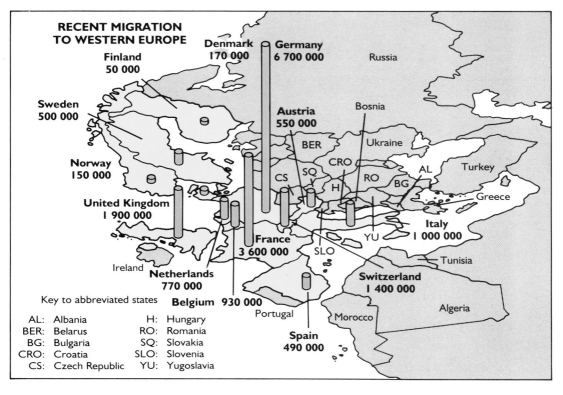

RECENT MIGRATION TO WESTERN EUROPE

Denmark 170 000
Germany 6 700 000
Russia
Finland 50 000
Sweden 500 000
Austria 550 000
Bosnia
BER
Ukraine
Norway 150 000
CRO
AL
Turkey
CS
SQ
RO
BG
H
Greece
United Kingdom 1 900 000
Italy 1 000 000
YU
France 3 600 000
SLO
Ireland
Tunisia
Netherlands 770 000
Switzerland 1 400 000
Belgium 930 000
Algeria
Portugal
Morocco
Spain 490 000

Key to abbreviated states

AL:	Albania	H:	Hungary
BER:	Belarus	RO:	Romania
BG:	Bulgaria	SQ:	Slovakia
CRO:	Croatia	SLO:	Slovenia
CS:	Czech Republic	YU:	Yugoslavia

BIRTH AND DEATH RATES

Compared with many Third World countries the birth rate in Western Europe is low. Uganda, for example, has a birth rate of 52.2 per thousand. By comparison, Italy has the lowest crude birth rate of any sovereign country and a list of the ten countries in the world with the lowest birth rates would also include Greece, San Marino, Spain, Germany, Portugal, Austria, Belgium and Denmark. The figures for the death rates per thousand for West European countries are not as low as might be expected. This is because a number of EEA countries have a relatively high proportion of elderly people (see p. 74). With the exception of Japan, Australia and Canada, the ten countries in which people have the highest life expectancy are all in Western Europe. Japan has the world's highest life expectancy, followed by Iceland, Sweden, Switzerland and Spain.

BIRTH RATE

Country	Birth rate per 1000 of population	Year of figure	% of legitimate births	% of illegitimate births
Belgium	12.4	1990	90.8%	9.2%
Denmark	12.4	1990	54.9%	45.1%
France	13.3	1991	69.9%	30.1%
Germany	11.4	1990	89.5%	10.5%
Greece	10.1	1990	97.8%	2.2%
Ireland	15.7	1991	85.5%	14.5%
Italy	9.8	1990	93.7%	6.3%
Luxembourg	12.9	1990	87.1%	12.9%
Netherlands	13.2	1990	88.6%	11.4%
Portugal	11.8	1990	85.5%	14.5%
Spain	10.2	1990	92.0%	8.0%
UK	13.8	1991	71.3%	28.7%
Austria	12.0	1991	76.4%	23.6%
Finland	13.1	1991	80.8%	19.2%
Iceland	17.6	1991	44.8%	55.2%
Liechtenstein	14.2	1991	92.3%	7.7%
Norway	14.3	1991	61.4%	38.6%
Sweden	14.4	1991	53.0%	47.0%
Switzerland	12.6	1991	93.9%	6.1%

DEATH RATE

Country	Death rate per 1000 of population	Year of figure
Belgium	10.5	1990
Denmark	11.9	1990
France	9.2	1991
Germany	11.6	1990
Greece	9.2	1990
Ireland	9.0	1990
Italy	9.3	1990
Luxembourg	9.9	1990
Netherlands	8.6	1990
Portugal	10.4	1990
Spain	8.5	1990
UK	11.2	1991
Austria	10.6	1991
Finland	9.8	1991
Iceland	6.9	1991
Liechtenstein	6.4	1991
Norway	10.5	1991
Sweden	11.0	1991
Switzerland	9.0	1991

LIFE EXPECTANCY

Country	Life expectancy - males	Life expectancy - females
Belgium	72.4 yrs	79.1 yrs
Denmark	72.0 yrs	77.7 yrs
France	73.0 yrs	81.1 yrs
Germany	71.6 yrs	78.1 yrs
Greece	72.6 yrs	77.6 yrs
Ireland	71.0 yrs	76.7 yrs
Italy	73.2 yrs	79.7 yrs
Luxembourg	70.6 yrs	77.9 yrs
Netherlands	73.7 yrs	79.7 yrs
Portugal	70.6 yrs	77.6 yrs
Spain	74.4 yrs	80.3 yrs
UK	72.4 yrs	78.0 yrs
Austria	72.5 yrs	79.0 yrs
Finland	70.8 yrs	78.9 yrs
Iceland	75.7 yrs	80.3 yrs
Liechtenstein	69.5 yrs	73.6 yrs
Norway	73.4 yrs	79.8 yrs
Sweden	74.4 yrs	80.2 yrs
Switzerland	74.0 yrs	80.8 yrs

Figures are for 1990.

LANGUAGE

Although most West European countries are dominated by a single language, many have significant linguistic minorities. Only Belgium and Switzerland, and to a lesser extent Spain, are truly multilingual.

BELGIUM

Acute rivalry between Belgium's two principal linguistic communities has been a major feature of recent Belgian history (see p. 25). In 1993, the country adopted what is effectively a federal system with three regions based upon linguistic divisions – Flemish-speaking Flanders in the north, French-speaking Wallonia in the south and bilingual Brussels.

Flemish may be regarded as a dialect of Dutch rather than a separate language. There are several spoken dialects of Flemish, but the written language is virtually the same as Dutch. The version of French spoken by the Walloons has its own distinct accent and vocabulary. A small minority of German speakers in the areas of Eupen and Malmédy in the Ardennes enjoys autonomy in cultural matters.

Brussels is officially a bilingual 'island' within Flanders. The city was originally Flemish-speaking but after Belgium became independent in 1830, and French assumed a major role in the Belgian administration, the capital gradually attracted more French speakers. Today, central Brussels is mainly French-speaking and the suburbs are Flemish-speaking.

Languages spoken in Belgium	% speaking each language as a first language
Flemish	nearly 58%
French	42%
German	under 1%

About 10% of the population is officially bilingual (Flemish-French).

DENMARK

The first language of almost all of the population of 'metropolitan' Denmark is Danish, a North German language that only became distinct from Swedish in the 11th and 12th centuries. There is a very small German-speaking minority (c. 8 000) in South Jutland.

In the autonomous territory of the Faeroes most people speak Faeroese, a North German language related to Icelandic rather than Danish, as a first language.

Languages spoken in Denmark	% speaking each language as a first language
Danish	99%
Faeroese	under 1%
German	very small minority

FRANCE

The French language is taught and spoken throughout France although there are significant minority tongues that have gained official recognition. Occitan, Breton, Corsican, Catalan, Basque and Alsatian (German) are taught at secondary school level in their appropriate regions.

Occitan (also known as Provençal and Langue d'Oc) is a Romance language that is closely allied to Catalan. It is spoken in parts of Languedoc and Provence. All 1 500 000 Occitan speakers speak French as a first language. Alsatian is a German dialect spoken in Alsace and parts of northern Lorraine. Breton, a Celtic language related to Welsh and Cornish, is a first language in parts of western Brittany and, owing to a recent revival in interest in the language, is understood by a growing number of Bretons. Catalan and Basque are spoken in areas adjoining Spain – Catalan in rural districts of Roussillon and Basque in southwest Aquitaine. Corsican is a dialect of Italian and is closely related to the dialect spoken in rural Tuscany. Flemish is spoken in areas adjoining the Belgian province of West Flanders.

The largest linguistic minority in France is Arabic which is the first language of immigrants from Algeria, Tunisia and Morocco and their descendants. There is also a significant Portuguese community in Paris.

Languages spoken in France	% speaking each language as a first language
French	93.2%
Arabic	2.5%
German (Alsatian)	2%
Portuguese	1%
Breton	under 1.0%
Others (Catalan, Basque, Flemish, Corsican)	under 0.5%

GERMANY

The German language is the first tongue of the overwhelming majority of the population of Germany. The German linguistic group includes not only the standard German language but also a number of dialects that linger mainly in rural areas. These include Swabian, Bavarian, Franconian, Middle Franconian and Upper Saxon. Modern Low German, a distinct dialect, is spoken in rural areas in northern Germany.

The largest linguistic minority is Turkish, the first language of a considerable number of guest workers (see p. 75) who have migrated to Germany from Turkey. Traditional linguistic minorities include Frisian and Sorb. Frisian, a West Germanic language more closely related to English than to German, is spoken in the Frisian Islands and in western coastal districts of Schleswig-Holstein. Sorb (or Lusatian), a Slavic tongue related to Polish and Czech, is spoken in rural areas of eastern Germany adjoining Poland and the Czech Republic.

Languages spoken in Germany	% speaking each language as a first language
German	over 96%
Turkish	2.1%
Frisian	small minority
Sorb	small minority

GREECE
Modern Greek, the only Hellenic language, is a direct descendant of Ancient Greek. There are several small linguistic minorities in Greece. Macedonian (a Slavic language that is very closely related to Bulgarian) is spoken in some rural areas adjoining the Former Yugoslav Republic of Macedonia. There are Turkish minorities in Thrace and Albanian minorities in Epirus and parts of Western Macedonia. Minorities speaking Vlach – a dialect of Romanian – are found in several locations in northern Greece. There are at least two Vlach dialects including one which incorporates elements of Albanian.

Languages spoken in Greece	% speaking each language as a first language
Greek	over 96%
Macedonian	1.5%
Turkish	0.9%
Albanian	0.6%
Vlach	under 0.5%

IRELAND
The Irish language (the official language of the Republic of Ireland) is taught in all schools in the Republic. About 31% of adults claim to be able to understand the language, but it is only spoken as a first language by about 80 000 people in the Gaeltacht of Kerry, Galway, Mayo and Donegal and by 100 000 elsewhere in the Republic. English is universally understood in the Republic of Ireland.

Languages spoken in Ireland	% speaking each language as a first language
Irish	about 5%
English	over 94%

ITALY
Italian, a Romance language, is the official language of the Italian Republic. Minorities include Sardinian (a dialect of Italian), German (which is the majority language in Bolzano province in the north of Trentino-Alto Adige), French (the majority language in Valle d'Aosta) and a very small Slovene minority near Trieste. The Rhaetic languages Ladin and Friulian are related to Italian but do not seem to be closely related to Romansch (see Switzerland, below). Ladin is spoken in isolated areas near the border with the Swiss canton Graubünden; Friulian is spoken near the Slovene border.

Catalan, Albanian and Greek remain in a few very small pockets where Spanish, Albanian and Greek influences were important in past periods of history. These languages are all declining and tend to be spoken largely by older people. Albanian occurs in Puglia and Sicily, Greek in Sicily and Catalan in Sardinia.

Languages spoken in Italy	% speaking each language as a first language
Italian	over 94%
Sardinian	2.7%
Rhaetic languages	1.2%
German	under 0.5%

French — under 0.5%
Others – Catalan, Slovene, Greek and Albanian

LUXEMBOURG
Letzeburgish, a Germanic language, is the national language and is understood by about three-quarters of the population. French and German are universally understood in the Grand Duchy and both are used as languages of instruction in schools. French is the language of government and administration; German is the language of commerce. Immigrants from Portugal form an important linguistic minority.

Languages spoken in Luxembourg	% speaking each language as a first language
Letzeburgish	72.5%
German	universal/10% (first)
Portuguese	9%
French	universal/6% (first)

NETHERLANDS
Dutch, a Low German tongue, is the official language. It is the first language of the overwhelming majority of the population and is universally understood in the Netherlands and is the first language of those who also speak Frisian. Turks, who have migrated to the Netherlands to work, now form the largest linguistic minority. Ambonese, an Indonesian language, has been introduced by immigrants from the former Dutch East Indies.

Languages spoken in the Netherlands	% speaking each language as a first language
Dutch†	over 96%
Turkish	1.2%
Ambonese	small minority

† including Frisian (2.8%)

PORTUGAL
Almost alone among West European countries, Portugal has no linguistic minorities. The country has various ethnic minorities from former colonies but all speak Portuguese, a Romance language.

Languages spoken in Portugal	% speaking each language as a first language
Portuguese	virtually 100%

SPAIN
The language that is internationally known as Spanish is, in fact, Castilian, a Romance language that is universally understood in Spain. It is, however, the first language of under 75% of the population.

Catalan – a Romance language closely linked to Occitan (see France, above) – is the majority language in Catalonia and the Balearic Islands. The Valencian dialect of Catalan is much influenced by Castilian. Basque – a language that appears to be unrelated to any other Indo-European tongue – is the majority language in rural areas and small towns in the Basque Country and Navarre. The Basque language has been a powerful vehicle of local nationalist feeling in the past few decades. Galician is a Romance language that is closely related to Portuguese. It is spoken in country districts of Galicia and has experienced a great revival in Galician cities since the 1970s.

Languages spoken in Spain	% speaking each language as a first language
Castilian (Spanish)	72.3%
Catalan	16.3%
Galician	8.1%
Basque	2.3%

UNITED KINGDOM
The English language is the most widely understood language in the world. Speakers of various languages of the Indian sub-continent, in particular Bengali, Gujarati, Hindi, Punjabi and Urdu, make up just under 2% of the population of the UK. Welsh, a Celtic language, is understood by about one-fifth of the population of the Principality but those who speak Welsh as a first language are largely confined to parts of north and west Wales. Gaelic, another Celtic language, is spoken by under 1% of the population of Scotland and is confined to the far west of the Scottish Highlands and the Western Isles.

Languages spoken in the UK	% speaking each language as a first language
English	over 98%
Indian languages (see above)	under 2%
Welsh	0.05%
Gaelic	0.014%

AUSTRIA
The overwhelming majority of Austrians speak German, the official language. Minority languages include Magyar (Hungarian) in Burgenland, Croat in Burgenland, Slovene in Carinthia and pockets of Czech.

Languages spoken in Austria	% speaking each language as a first language
German	over 96%
Slovene	under 2%
Croat	1.8%
Magyar (Hungarian)	0.2%
Czech	small minority

FINLAND
There are two official languages in Finland – Finnish (the majority language, which is related to Magyar and Estonian) and Swedish. Swedish-speaking Finns are concentrated in southern and western coastal areas and in the Aland Islands. In the far north there are about 2000 Lapps.

Languages spoken in Finland	% speaking each language as a first language
Finnish	nearly 94%
Swedish	nearly 6%
Lapp	small minority

ICELAND
The entire population of Iceland speaks Icelandic (the official language), a Nordic tongue that is related to Norwegian.

LIECHTENSTEIN
The population of Liechtenstein is German-speaking.

NORWAY
Apart from a tiny minority in the far north that speaks Lapp, the Norwegians speak a single North German language. However, Norwegian has two distinct dialects – Bokmaal (which predominates in urban areas) and Landsmaal or Nynorsk (which is spoken in rural districts).

Languages spoken in Norway	% speaking each language as a first language
Norwegian Bokmaal	nearly 80%
Norwegian Landsmaal	nearly 20%
Lapp	small minority

SWEDEN
Swedish (the official language) is a North German language that is closely related to Danish. The use of local dialects has decreased. There is a small Lapp minority in Norrbotten. Small linguistic minorities among immigrants in Stockholm and Gothenburg include Turkish and Croat.

Languages spoken in Sweden	% speaking each language as a first language
Swedish	nearly 100%
Lapp	small minority

SWITZERLAND
Three of the major cultural traditions of Western Europe – French, German and Italian – come together in Switzerland and these three tongues are all official languages. German is spoken in the north, centre and east of Switzerland. There are six traditional German-Swiss dialects but in 1945 a standardized *Schywzerdütsch* was recognized. Schywzerdütsch differs from standard German in pronunciation, vocabulary and, to a small extent, in spelling. The Italian spoken in Ticino is the same in pronunciation as that spoken in neighbouring parts of north Italy. Twelve Franco-Swiss patois have been recognized but none of these appears in a written form. French is spoken in western Switzerland.

Romansch, a Rhaetic language (see Italy, above), was added as the fourth official language in 1945. More nearly related to French than to Italian, Romansch is spoken in north and west Graubünden. Ladin, another Rhaetic language (see Italy), is spoken in the Engadine. Immigrants from south and east European states – including Serbs and Croats – make up 6% of the population.

Languages spoken in Switzerland	% speaking each language as a first language
German (Schwyzerdütsch)	65%
French	18%
Italian	10%
Romansch (with Ladin)	under 1%
Others (see above)	6%

RELIGION

Belgium The Roman Catholic Church has a leading role in Belgian life. Belgium comprises one archdiocese – Mechelen-Brussels – and seven dioceses. Church attendance in Flanders is higher than in Wallonia.

Denmark The Evangelical Lutheran Church – the established national Church – has ten coequal dioceses. Church attendance has declined in recent decades.

France The Roman Catholic Church – disestablished since 1905 – has a leading role although only about 15% of French Catholics attend Mass regularly. France comprises 95 dioceses, 18 of which are archbishoprics – Aix and Arles, Albi, Auch, Avignon, Besançon, Bordeaux, Bourges, Cambrai, Chambéry, Lyon, Marseille, Paris, Rennes, Reims, Rouen, Sens, Toulouse and Tours. Metz and Strasbourg dioceses owe direct allegiance to Rome. Under 40% of the parishes have a resident priest.

Germany Church attendance in the north and in the former GDR is lower than in the rest of Germany. The EKD (Evangelische Kirche in Deutschland) – a federation of (mainly) regional Lutheran Churches – has the greatest attendance and is strongest in the north and east. The Roman Catholic Church is organized into 24 dioceses including five archdioceses – Bamberg, Cologne, Freiburg, Munich and Paderborn. Meissen and Berlin dioceses owe direct allegiance to Rome. Roman Catholicism is strongest in the south and west.

Greece The Orthodox Church is legally the national Church. Proselytizing from it is forbidden by law. Greece is divided into 66 dioceses, each headed by a metropolitan (bishop); the head of the Athens diocese is an archbishop and Primate of Greece. By West European standards, Church attendance is high.

Ireland Ireland has one of the highest proportions of practising Christians in Europe. The Roman Catholic Church plays a leading role in Irish life. The whole island of Ireland comprises a single ecclesiastical jurisdiction under the Archbishop of Armagh. Within the Republic of Ireland there are three archdioceses – Cashel and Emly (with six suffragan bishoprics), Dublin (three) and Tuam (five) – and five dioceses under the archdiocese of Armagh.

Italy Under the 1929 Lateran Treaty, the Roman Catholic Church is recognized as the official Church of Italy. The Church is organized into the Holy See (see p.72), the Patriachate of Venice and 57 other archdioceses – Acerenza, Amalfi, Ancona, Bari, Benevento, Bologna, Brindisi, Cagliari, Camerino, Campobasso, Capua, Catania, Catanzaro, Chieti, Cosenza, Crotone, Fermo, Ferrara, Florence, Foggia, Gaeta, Genoa, Gorizia, Laciano, L'Aquila, Lecce, Lucca, Manfredonia, Matera, Messina, Milan, Modena, Monreale, Naples, Oristano, Otranto, Palermo, Perugia, Pescara, Pisa, Potenza, Ravenna, Reggio Calabria, Rossano, Salerno, Sant'Angelo, Siena, Sorrento, Spoleto, Siracusa, Taranto, Trani, Trento, Turin, Udine, Urbino and Vercelli. There are 158 other dioceses headed by bishops. Six archbishops and 24 of the bishops owe direct allegiance to the Pope. About one quarter of the population is practising.

Luxembourg Luxembourg comprises a single archdiocese that owes allegiance directly to Rome.

Netherlands The Roman Catholic Church – the largest religious denomination – is organized into one archdiocese (Utrecht) and six other dioceses. Only about 20% of Dutch Catholics regularly attend Mass. The Dutch Reformed Church is organized into 74 districts; the Reformed Churches (Calvinist) have 12 synods.

Portugal Although not an established Church, Roman Catholicism has a leading role in Portuguese life. Portugal is divided into three archdioceses – Braga (with seven suffragan dioceses), Evora (two) and Lisbon (five). Over one half of the population attends Mass in the north, but practising Catholics represent less than 10% of the population in the south.

Spain The Concordat of 1979 regulates the relationship between the state and the Roman Catholic Church. Spain is divided into 13 archdioceses and 53 other dioceses – Barcelona (with no suffragan dioceses), Burgos (four suffragan dioceses), Granada (five), Madrid (no suffragans), Oviedo (three), Pamplona (four), Santiago de Compostela (four), Seville (six), Tarragona (six), Toledo (four), Valencia (six), Valladolid (five) and Zaragoza (five). Ciudad Real diocese owes direct allegiance to Rome. About two-fifths of the population are regularly practising Catholics.

United Kingdom The Church of England is the established English Church although its practising membership represents only 4% of the population. It is organized into two archdioceses – Canterbury (with 29 other dioceses within the province) and York (13 other dioceses). The (Presbyterian) Church of Scotland – the national Church of Scotland – is organized into 12 synods.

Austria The Roman Catholic Church, which has a leading role in Austria, has two archdioceses – Salzburg (with four suffragan dioceses) and Vienna (three).

Finland There are two national Churches: the Evangelical Lutheran Church of Finland – with one archdiocese (Turku) and seven other dioceses – and the Orthodox Church of Finland (under the archbishop of Kuopio). Church attendance is higher than in any other Scandinavian country.

Iceland The Evangelical Lutheran Church of Iceland – the national Church – has one archdiocese (Rekyjavik) and two other dioceses.

Liechtenstein The country is part of the Swiss Roman Catholic diocese of Chur.

Norway The Evangelical Lutheran Church of Norway – the national Church – is organized into 11 coequal dioceses. Church attendance figures are in decline.

Sweden The Evangelical Lutheran Church of Sweden – the national Church – is organized into one archdiocese (Uppsala) and 12 other dioceses. About one half of the population never attends Church.

Switzerland The Roman Catholic Church in Switzerland is organized into six coequal dioceses that owe direct allegiance to Rome. Eighteen Reformed Churches – mainly organized on a cantonal basis – form the Federation of Swiss Protestant Churches. The south and east are mainly Catholic; the north and west have a Protestant majority.

RELIGIOUS COMPOSITION OF THE POPULATION

Principal religions and the percentage of the population professing them

Belgium
Roman Catholic 86%
Islam 1% Protestant 1% non-religious 11% others 1%

Denmark
Lutheran 89%
other Protestant Churches 1% Roman Catholic 1% non-religious 9%

France
Roman Catholic 74%
Islam 4% Protestant Churches 4% non-religious 18%

Germany
Lutheran and Lutheran tradition 43%
Roman Catholic 36% Islam 2% non-religious 18% others 1%

Greece
Greek Orthodox 98%
Islam 1% other Christians (Roman Catholic 0.5% Protestant and others 0.5%)

Ireland
Roman Catholic 93%
Anglican 3% other Protestants 1% non-religious 3%

Italy
Roman Catholic 83%
non-religious 16% others 1%

Luxembourg
Roman Catholic 95%
Protestant Churches 1% non-religious 4%

Netherlands
Roman Catholic 36%
Dutch Reformed 19% Reformed (Calvinist) 8% non-religious 33% Islam 2% others (includes other Protestants) 2%

Portugal
Roman Catholic 94%
non-religious 4% others (including Protestants) 2%

Spain
Roman Catholic 95%
non-religious 3% Islam 1% others (including Protestants) 1%

UK
Anglican 55% (practising 4% non-practising 51%)
Roman Catholic 9% Presbyterian 3% Methodist 2% Islam 2% Hindu 1% other Christian Churches 4% non-religious 24%

Austria
Roman Catholic 84%
Lutheran 6% other Protestant Churches 1% Islam 1% non-religious 8%

Finland
Lutheran 88%
Finnish Orthodox 1% non-religious 11%

Iceland
Lutheran 93%
Roman Catholic 1% non-religious 7%

Liechtenstein
Roman Catholic 87%
Lutheran 8% non-religious 5%

Norway
Lutheran 88%
Roman Catholic 1% other Protestant Churches 2% non-religious 9%

Sweden
Lutheran 85%
Roman Catholic 2% non-religious 12%

Switzerland
Roman Catholic 47% **Reformed Churches 43%**
Islam 2% non-religious 8%

URBANIZATION

On the map, opposite, major urban concentrations within Western Europe can be discerned. These include groups of large cities in northwest Germany (the Essen-Ruhr agglomeration, greater Düsseldorf and greater Cologne), in the Low Countries, in southeast and northern England and in northern France. Northern Italy also boasts several major urban areas. A series of 'satellite cities' around London can be identified in southeast England but Paris, which is the largest city in Europe, does not have a similar series of smaller satellites.

The lack of urban development in large areas of Scandinavia, Iberia and Greece is also apparent. Greece, for example, has only two cities with over half a million inhabitants, while Portugal has two cities with over a million inhabitants and no other place with over 100 000. In Norway not even Oslo has over half a million people. By contrast the Essen-Ruhr agglomeration in Germany actually contains several cities with over half a million inhabitants.

In the following table the population figures in the final column relate to the agglomeration or urban area: that is the city, its suburbs and the surrounding built-up area and not to local government districts. By using this definition for the urban area of every city listed below – and in the text (pp. 24–72 and pp. 143–83) – a more accurate comparison of size has been possible.

A table listing the largest cities in Eastern and Central Europe will be found on p. 185.

LARGEST CITIES OF WESTERN EUROPE

City	Country	Date of census estimate	Details	Population
Paris	France	1990	(city 2 175 000)	9 063 000
London	UK	1991	(Grtr. London 6 803 000)	7 825 000
Madrid	Spain	1991	(city 3 121 000)	4 846 000
Essen	Germany	1991	(city 627 000)	4 700 000
Milan	Italy	1990	(city 1 432 000)	3 670 000
Berlin	Germany	1991	(city 3 446 000)	3 590 000
Barcelona	Spain	1991	(city 1 707 000)	3 400 000
Athens	Greece	1991	with suburbs	3 097 000
Rome	Italy	1990	(city 2 791 000)	2 985 000
Naples	Italy	1990	(city 1 206 000)	2 905 000
Birmingham	UK	1991	(city 995 000)	2 326 000
Manchester	UK	1991	(city 433 000)	2 281 000
Lisbon	Portugal	1990	(city 950 000)	2 131 000
Vienna	Austria	1991	(city 1 533 000)	2 045 000
Hamburg	Germany	1991	(city 1 669 000)	1 924 000
Oporto	Portugal	1990	(city 450 000)	1 695 000
Glasgow	UK	1991	(city 688 000)	1 648 000
Leeds	UK	1991	(city 706 000)	1 543 000
Stockholm	Sweden	1992	(city 679 000)	1 471 000
Munich	Germany	1991	(city 1 229 000)	1 465 000
Cologne	Germany	1991	(city 960 000)	1 419 000
Copenhagen	Denmark	1992	(city 465 000)	1 337 000
Frankfurt	Germany	1991	(city 654 000)	1 268 000
Lyon	France	1990	(city 422 000)	1 262 000
Turin	Italy	1990	(city 992 000)	1 114 000
Stuttgart	Germany	1991	(city 592 000)	1 091 000
Marseille	France	1990	(city 808 000)	1 087 000
Amsterdam	Netherlands	1992	(city 713 000)	1 080 000
Rotterdam	Netherlands	1992	(city 590 000)	1 060 000
Valencia	Spain	1991	(city 777 000)	1 060 000
Helsinki	Finland	1992	(city 498 000)	1 005 000
Brussels	Belgium	1992	with suburbs	951 000
Dublin	Ireland	1991	(city 478 000)	921 000
Antwerp	Belgium	1992	(city 465 000)	917 000
Düsseldorf	Germany	1991	(city 578 000)	913 000

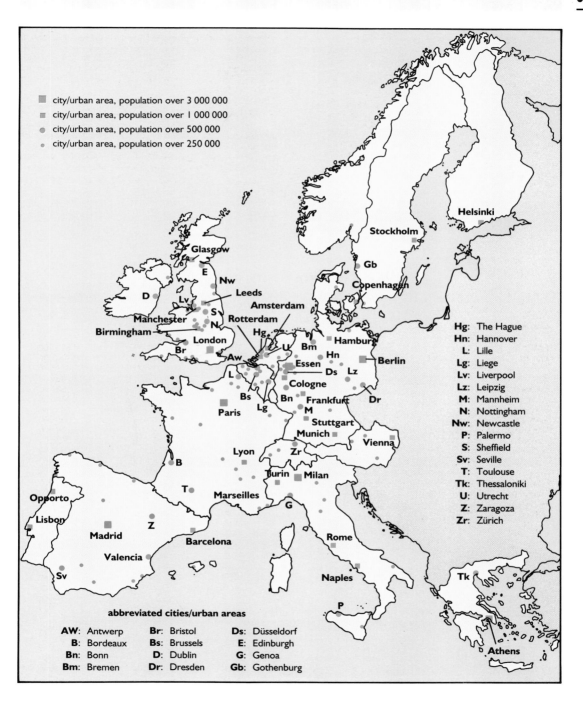

city/urban area, population over 3 000 000
city/urban area, population over 1 000 000
city/urban area, population over 500 000
city/urban area, population over 250 000

Helsinki

Stockholm

Glasgow
E
Nw
Leeds
D
Lv
S
Amsterdam
Manchester
N
Rotterdam
Birmingham
Br
London
Aw
L
Bs
Lg
Paris

Gb
Copenhagen

Hg.
U
Bm
Hn
Hamburg
Essen
Ds
Lz
Berlin
Cologne
Bn
Frankfurt
M
Dr
Stuttgart
Munich

Hg: The Hague
Hn: Hannover
L: Lille
Lg: Liege
Lv: Liverpool
Lz: Leipzig
M: Mannheim
N: Nottingham
Nw: Newcastle
P: Palermo
S: Sheffield
Sv: Seville
T: Toulouse
Tk: Thessaloniki
U: Utrecht
Z: Zaragoza
Zr: Zürich

Vienna

Lyon
Zr
B
Turin
Milan
T
Marseilles
G

Opporto
Lisbon
Z
Madrid
Barcelona
Valencia
Sv

Rome

Naples

Tk

P

Athens

abbreviated cities/urban areas

AW: Antwerp	Br: Bristol	Ds: Düsseldorf
B: Bordeaux	Bs: Brussels	E: Edinburgh
Bn: Bonn	D: Dublin	G: Genoa
Bm: Bremen	Dr: Dresden	Gb: Gothenburg

WELFARE

The countries of the EEA all have some form of welfare state, although the extent of the provision of health care, pensions and benefits, etc., varies from one country to another. In some countries – for example, Sweden and the UK – economic necessity, resulting from recession, has led to cuts in the health service.

BELGIUM Social welfare – administered by the National Office for Social Security – is paid for by contributions from employers and employees. Family allowances, health insurance, unemployment benefit, old-age pensions, etc., are provided. Only in the cases of widows, orphans, pensioners and the disabled is medical care completely free.

DENMARK Denmark was one of the first countries to introduce a comprehensive welfare system. Taxation and employers' contributions pay for a range of benefits including old-age pensions, unemployment benefit, sickness and disability payments, and the health service. Since the mid-1980s some benefits have been paid according to individual means.

FRANCE Contributions from employers, employees and the self-employed pay for a comprehensive system of welfare benefits including old-age pensions, unemployment benefit, maternity benefit, sickness and disability payments and very substantial family allowances. The overwhelming majority of GPs are involved in the state health scheme. Patients pay for treatment and prescriptions and are then reimbursed in part or in full depending upon individual circumstances. France already spends over 6% of its GDP (gross domestic product) on health care – almost the highest percentage in Europe – and the amount is increasing sharply. Although facilities are of the very highest standard – there have been, for example, no hospital wards since 1977 when rooms for one, two or three patients were introduced – there has been little rationalization, with expensive specialist equipment provided at too many smaller hospitals which are unable to use these facilities often. A minimum national hourly wage is in force.

GERMANY Germany has comprehensive welfare insurance which is administered by autonomous local and state organizations and non-profit-making companies. Old-age pensions (the highest in Europe), unemployment benefit, sickness and disability payments, and maternity benefit are paid. Sickness benefit covers all medical expenses. The German health care system has been widely held to be a model for the rest of Europe but by the middle of 1993 it was reeling under the strain of huge increases in the cost of treatment and drugs. The problem is increased by an ageing population – by the year 2030 over 35% of Germany's population will be over 60, compared with 20% today.

GREECE Wage earners are covered by a state insurance scheme; voluntary schemes operate for salaried staff and the self-employed. All workers are entitled to receive sickness benefit and old-age pensions.

IRELAND Compulsory social insurance – paid for by employers and employees – covers old-age pensions, widows' pensions, invalidity and disability payments, sickness payments, and dental and optical benefits. People of inadequate means receive benefits under a non-contributory scheme. Not all benefits are available to the self-employed. Health care is free to people on low incomes and is paid for by others at one of two rates, according to their means.

ITALY The social security system – the Instituto Nazionale della Previdenza Sociale – provides old-age pensions, unemployment benefit, disability payments, and family and other allowances. Compensation for industrial injuries is operated under a separate scheme. A national health insurance scheme operates and a comprehensive health care scheme provides free treatment, etc., for certain categories of people, although those in employment make minimum payments for treatment, medical examinations, etc.

LUXEMBOURG Compulsory social insurance is operated by several semi-public bodies and not by the government. Various benefits – including old-age pensions, invalidity payments and health payments – are available and are paid for by either employers' or employeees' contributions (or a combination of both) according to the individual benefit. Health insurance is compulsory for the employed and self-employed but is voluntary for the rest of the population.

NETHERLANDS Insurance schemes cover old-age pensions, maternity payments, widows' and orphans' pensions, sickness and disability and other payments, and medical expenses. Participation in the health scheme is compulsory for workers who earn below a certain salary and also for old-age pensioners. Insurance payments are made by employers and employees; in the case of pensioners, health-care payments are taken from pensions.

PORTUGAL A contributory state social welfare scheme provides old-age pensions, disability payments, family allowances and health care. Unemployment benefit is covered by a separate scheme and is not universally available.

SPAIN Taxation and employers' and employees' contributions pay for a national social welfare system which includes old-age pensions, disability payments, unemployment benefit, accident and maternity benefit. Participation in the National Insurance Scheme is compulsory for all employed and self-employed persons.

UK Earnings-related contributions by employees and employers pay for a compulsory National Insurance Scheme which includes old-age pensions, and sickness, maternity, unemployment and other benefits. The National Health Service – which is not funded by insurance – provides free medical and hospital treatment, although charges are made for dental work, eye tests, spectacles and prescriptions for all except pensioners, children, those receiving benefit and other exempted persons.

AUSTRIA Compulsory insurance provides a range of earnings-related benefits including old-age pensions, maternity, sickness and invalidity and other payments. Separate insurance schemes cover unemployment benefit and family allowances.

FINLAND A comprehensive social welfare system – paid for by taxation and contributions by employers and employees – provides old-age pensions, sickness and disability payments, maternity allowances, child and housing allowances, and various care provisions. Sickness payments cover most but not all of the costs of medical treatment and most individuals are required to pay some hospital fees.

ICELAND Health care is provided for by compulsory health insurance. The social security system – which is paid for by taxation, and employers' and employees' contributions – provides old-age pensions, maternity payments, and widows' pensions. Unemployment benefit is available only through schemes operated through membership of certain trade unions.

LIECHTENSTEIN Insurance schemes for old-age pensions, sickness, accidents and bereavement are compulsory. The state pays family allowances and unemployment benefit.

NORWAY Taxation and employers' and employees' contributions finance the compulsory National Pension Scheme which provides for old-age pensions, disability, widows' and other pensions. Medical care is also provided by the state.

SWEDEN The extensive Swedish welfare state has been trimmed by economic necessity in the 1990s. Payment is made by the National Pension Fund – contribution to which is compulsory – for old-age pensions, disability benefit, and sickness, unemployment and other benefits. Contributions are made by employers and employees, and from taxation.

SWITZERLAND Insurance schemes to provide old-age, widows' and invalids' pensions are compulsory. All salaried employees are obliged to contribute to an insurance scheme for unemployment benefit. There is no national health service but most Swiss are insured under the terms of the Federal Insurance Law.

PUBLIC HEALTH FUNDING

Almost all of the states of Western Europe face a number of similar problems that have made public health care a major political issue. These problems include: an ageing population (making the provision of health care more costly); rising unemployment (which makes increasing demands upon the public purse); falling birthrates (which adds to the 'greying' of the population); and ever-higher costs for the provision of medicines, treatment and hospitalization. These problems have forced governments to look at the costs of health care and the public provision of health services. At the same time, most governments have given increased emphasis to the prevention of illness. This is echoed in the Maastricht Treaty which states that the EC has a clear legal duty to help prevent diseases by promoting education, public information and research. Various health initiatives are envisaged and research is currently concentrated on AIDS, cancer and drug abuse. A

European Public Health Alliance – an umbrella organization for over four dozen national and international bodies – has been formed to help explore and exchange ideas in the health debate.

The amount that each country spends on health care varies widely. Those with the highest expenditure – as a percentage of GDP – are as follows:

PUBLIC EXPENDITURE ON HEALTH CARE

Country	% of GDP spent on public care (1990)
Sweden	7.8%
France	6.6%
Belgium	6.0%
Netherlands	5.9%
Italy	5.9%
Germany	5.9%
Ireland	5.8%
Austria	5.7%
Denmark	5.1%
UK	5.0%

An alternative measure of public health expenditure is the cost per head of the population in each country. Those with the highest expenditure are as follows:

HEALTH CARE (COST PER HEAD)

Country	Health care expenditure per person in ECUS (1993)
Sweden	1690
Germany	1380
France	1370
Austria	1220
Denmark	1140
Netherlands	1050
Belgium	1020
Italy	1020

The measure of 'efficiency' in public health is both difficult and controversial. One of the many possible measures of efficiency that have been suggested is the average amount of time that patients referred to hospital have to wait before seeing a surgical specialist. The EEA countries in which the longest such delays occur are as follows:

DELAY BEFORE SEEING A HOSPITAL SPECIALIST

Country	Average number of days patients referred to hospital have to wait before seeing a surgical specialist
UK	38 days
Norway	32 days
Portugal	27 days
Denmark	25 days
Ireland	24 days
Switzerland	14 days
Netherlands	11 days
Spain	10 days
Italy	10 days

EDUCATION

Free compulsory education begins at five years of age in the UK and the Netherlands, but at six or seven in most other EEA states. Nursery or pre-primary education is not universal in any EEA country although it is, probably, most widely available in Belgium where 90% of those eligible attend nursery school. In Western Europe primary and secondary education is generally provided by the state or by local authorities. In the Netherlands, Belgium and Ireland denominational schools are common but, although these may be described as non-state schools, they receive public funding. In Denmark, Germany, Greece, Italy, Luxembourg, Portugal, the UK and all seven EFTA countries, between 90% and 100% of pupils attend state schools. The highest percentages of private schools are to be found in Belgium (60%), Ireland (28%), the Netherlands (72%) and Spain (31%).

Tertiary education is provided at universities and university-level institutions (see pp. 88–90) and other colleges offering advanced courses. The percentage of students in each country going on to tertiary education varies (see below).

Country	No. of students in tertiary education per 100 000	Year of the figure
Belgium	2 604	1989
Denmark	2 486	1991
France	2 842	1991
Germany	2 844	1992
Greece	2 104	1988
Ireland	2 219	1990
Italy	2 379	1991
Luxembourg†	1 421	1992
Netherlands	2 819	1990
Portugal	1 524	1992
Spain	2 655	1989
UK	1 954	1990
Austria	2 638	1991
Finland	3 315	1991
Iceland	2 154	1991
Liechtenstein	n/a	n/a
Norway	2 858	1991
Sweden	2 196	1991
Switzerland	2 018	1991

† includes Luxembourgeois students abroad.

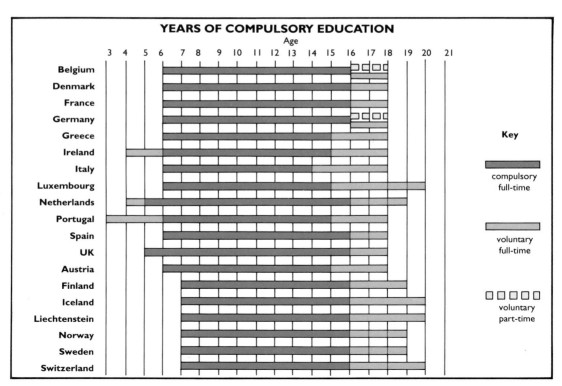

YEARS OF COMPULSORY EDUCATION

Key

compulsory full-time

voluntary full-time

voluntary part-time

PRIMARY SCHOOLS

Country	number of schools	number of primary school teachers	number of primary school pupils	teacher:student ratio
Belgium	4 608	71 065	755 610	1:10.6
Denmark†	3 000	62 700	632 175	1:10.1
France	44 131	309 875	4 062 245	1:13.1
Germany	30 165	359 255	5 167 680	1:14.4
Greece	8 178	39 125	868 335	1:22.2
Ireland	3 428	20 320	560 835	1:27.6
Italy	24 387	195 020	3 060 560	1:15.7
Luxembourg	238	1 765	26 610	1:15.1
Netherlands	9 443	82 560	1 540 000	1:18.7
Portugal	11 439	63 660	1 013 475	1:15.9
Spain	20 251	118 695	3 156 185	1:26.6
UK	24 268	216 160	4 617 740	1:21.4
Austria	3 386	29 405	371 970	1:12.7
Finland†	4 845	42 165	583 675	1:13.9
Iceland*	265	3 200	58 640	1:18.3
Liechtenstein	14	115	1 890	1:16.4
Norway	3 406	33 960	475 345	1:14.0
Sweden	4 649	100 030	881 525	1:8.8
Switzerlandß	n/a	n/a	404 155	n/a

* includes both primary and secondary level.

ß In Switzerland education below tertiary level is the responsibility of the cantons. National figures are not available.

† Includes lower secondary (for pupils up to the age of 13); see also secondary schools.

SECONDARY SCHOOLS

Country	number of schools	number of secondary school teachers	number of secondary school pupils	teacher:student ratio
Belgium	2 123	114 630	825 920	1:7.2
Denmark†	157	7 500	71 880	1:9.6
France	11 325	413 300	5 402 300	1:13.1
Germany‡	11 040	293 880	3 731 000	1:12.7
Greece	2 765	44 890	708 550	1:15.8
Ireland	493	11 630	213 790	1:18.4
Italy	9 992	113 560	2 275 580	1:20.0
Luxembourg	24	1 920	7 590	1:3.9
Netherlands	1 284	94 440	697 000	1:7.4
Portugal	1 116	73 200	856 920	1:11.7
Spain	22 633	200 630	3 611 860	1:18.0
UK	4 876	234 290	3 395 700	1:14.5
Austria	2 013	57 550	436 930	1:7.6
Finland†	464	6 180	101 625	1:16.4
Iceland*	265	3 200	58 640	1:18.3
Liechtenstein	8	80	1 090	1:13.6
Norway	843	20 650	237 050	1:11.5
Sweden	489	30 115	292 050	1:9.7
Switzerlandß	n/a	n/a	384 780	n/a

* includes both primary and secondary level.

† Upper secondary; see also primary schools. ‡ Excludes vocational schools.

ß In Switzerland education below tertiary level is the responsibility of the cantons. National figures are not available.

Figures are for 1989–90.

Comparison between countries is difficult as the definitions of 'primary', or first level, and 'secondary', or second level, education – and the age at which transfers are made between them – vary from state to state.

UNIVERSITIES

BELGIUM Students at private (Roman Catholic) universities outnumber those at state universities by more than 2:1. Louvain (founded 1425) – the oldest Belgian university – was divided on linguistic lines in 1970 when a new campus was built at Wavre.

Antwerp* (university centre; 2000 students), Antwerp St Ignatius*† (4000), Brussels Free University† (23 000), Brussels St Aloysius*† (1000), Brussels St Louis*† (1000), Gembloux* (agriculture; 1000), Ghent (13 000), Liège 10 000, Limburg*† (at Hasselt; 1000), Louvain† (Flemish; Catholic; 23 000), Louvain† (French; Catholic; at Woluwe; 18 000), Mons Catholic*† (1000), Mons-Hainaut (at Mons; 2000), Mons Polytechnic (university status; 1000), Notre Dame de la Paix*† (at Namur; 1000).

DENMARK After Copenhagen (1479) no Danish university was founded until 1829. The first provincial university (Aarhus) was founded in 1928. Three more provincial universities were added after 1964.

Aalborg* (university centre; 5000 students), Aarhus (13 000), Copenhagen (26 000), Copenhagen Technical (6000), Odense (7000), Roskilde* (university centre; 4000), Royal Veterinary and Agricultural University (at Frederiksberg; 3000).

FRANCE Medieval French universities included Paris (founded after 1100), Montpellier (1220), Toulouse (1229), Grenoble (1339), Aix (1413), Bordeaux (1441) and Rennes (1461). By the 1970s, some universities had grown so large that they had become unwieldy – Paris had over 200 000 students. Therefore, the university sector was restructured – larger universities were divided and several new universities were founded.

Aix-Marseille I Provence (at Marseille; 19 000 students), Aix-Marseille II (at Marseille; 19 000), Aix-Marseille III (at Aix; 18 000), Angers (12 000), Avignon (3000), Bordeaux I (19 000), Bordeaux II (15 000), Bordeaux III (15 000), Burgundy (at Dijon; 21 000), Caen (23 000), Catholic University of the West† (at Angers; 5000), Clermont-Ferrand I (10 000), Clermont-Ferrand II Blaise Pascal (14 000), Compiègne (3000), Corsica (at Corti; 2000), Franche-Comté (at Besançon; 16 000), Grenoble I Joseph Fourier (14 000), Grenoble II Pierre Mendès-France (19 000), Grenoble III Stendhal (6000), Grenoble National Polytechnic (university status; 3000), Lille I Lille Flandres Artois (19 000), Lille II (18 000), Lille III Charles de Gaulle (22 000), Lille University and Polytechnic† (13 000), Limoges (12 000), Lorraine National Polytechnic (university status; at Nancy; 3000), Lyon I Claude-Bernard (23 000), Lyon II Lumière (20 000), Lyon III Jean Moulin (15 000), Lyon Catholic† (7000), Metz (11 000), Montpellier I (18 000), Montpellier II Languedoc (11 000), Montpellier III Paul Valéry (16 000), Nancy I (15 000), Nancy II (17 000), Nantes (26 000), Nice (22 000), Orléans (12 000), Paris I Panthéon-Sorbonne (37 000), Paris II Panthéon-Assas (19 000), Paris III Sorbonne Nouvelle (19 000), Paris IV Paris-Sorbonne (24 000), Paris V René Descartes (32 000), Paris VI Pierre et Marie Curie (22 000), Paris VII (30 000), Paris VIII Vincennes à St Denis (22 000), Paris IX Paris-Dauphine (6000), Paris X Paris-Nanterre (32 000), Paris XI Paris-Sud (25 000), Paris XII Paris-Val de Marne (18 000), Paris

XIII Paris-Nord (14 000), Paris Catholic Institute†* (15 000), Pau (11 000), Perpignan (5000), Picardy (at Amiens; 10 000), Poitiers (22 000), Reims (21 000), Rennes I (24 000), Rennes II Upper Brittany (13 000), Saint-Etienne Jean Monnet (12 000), Savoy (at Chambéry; 7000), Strasbourg I Louis Pasteur (14 000), Strasbourg II (11 000), Strasbourg III Robert Schuman (8000), Toulon (5000), Toulouse I (15 000), Toulouse II Le Mirail (20 000), Toulouse III Paul Sabatier (22 000), Toulouse Catholic Institute†* (2000), Toulouse National Polytechnic (university status; 3000), Tours François Rabelais (22 000), Upper Alsace (at Mulhouse; 5000), Valenciennes (8000), West Brittany (at Brest; 16 000).

GERMANY Germany's medieval universities include Heidelberg (1366), Cologne (1388), Leipzig (1409), Rostock (1419), Greifswald (1456), Freiburg (1457), Munich (1471), Mainz (1477) and Tübingen (1477). Since 1960, 35 new universities have been created. The universities in the former GDR have been reformed since reunification.

Aachen Rhenish-Westphalian Technical (37 000 students), Augsburg (13 000), Bamberg Otto-Friedrich (8000), Bayreuth (9000), Berlin Humboldt (21 000), Berlin Technical (35 000), Bielefeld (14 000), Bochum Ruhr (36 000), Bonn Rhenish Friedrich-Wilhelm (38 000), Bremen (13 000), Brunswick Technical Carolo Wilhelmina (17 000), Chemnitz Technical (10 000), Clausthal Technical (4000), Cologne (54 000), Cologne Sport (6000), Darmstadt Technical (18 000), Dortmund (22 000), Dresden Friedrich List Technical (5000), Dresden Technical (10 000), Duisburg (16 000), Düsseldorf Heinrich-Heine (16 000), Eichstätt Catholic (3000), Erlangen-Nürnberg Friedrich-Alexander (28 000), Essen (18 000), Frankfurt Johann Wolfgang Goethe (34 000), Freiberg Bergakemie (3000), Freiberg Albert-Ludwig (24 000), Giessen Justus-Liebig (21 000), Göttingen Georg-August (30 000), Greifswald Ernst-Moritz-Arndt (4000), Halle-Wittenberg Martin Luther (9000), Hamburg (43 000), Hamburg-Harburg Technical (2000), Hannover (28 000), Hannover Medical (4000), Hannover Veterinary (2000), Heidelberg Ruprecht-Karl (28 000), Hildesheim (3000), Hohenheim (6000), Ilmenau Technical (3000), Jena Friedrich Schiller (5000), Kaiserslautern (9000), Karlsruhe Fredericiana (21 000), Kassel (15 000), Kiel Christian-Albrecht (19 000), Koblenz Management (under 1000), Konstanz (9000), Leipzig (15 000), Leipzig Technical (10 000), Leuna-Merseburg Carl Schorlemmer Technical (3000), Lübeck Medical (1000), Magdeburg Technical Otto von Guericke (4000), Mainz Johannes Gutenberg (26 000), Mannheim (10 000), Marburg Philipp (17 000), Munich Ludwig-Maximilian (60 000), Munich Military (3000), Munich Technical (24 000), Munich Ukrainian (n/a), Münster Westphalian Wilhelm (46 000), Oldenburg (11 000), Open University (at Hagen; 30 000), Osnabrück (9000), Paderborn (16 000), Passau (8000), Regensburg (13 000), Rostock (6000), Saarland (at Saarbrücken; 20 000), Siegen (12 000), Speyer (postgraduate; 1000), Stuttgart (21 000), Trier (10 000), Tübingen Eberhard-Karl (25 000), Ulm (6000), Weimar Architecture (3000), Wismar Technical (2000), Wuppertal Bergish (17 000), Würzburg Bavarian Julius-Maximilian (18 000).

GREECE The first Greek universities – the Capodistrian and National Technical in Athens – were founded in the 1830s. The first provincial university was the Aristotelian in Thessalonika (1925). Five provincial universities were founded in the 1960s and 1970s.

Aegean (at Athens; 2000 students), Athens Agriculture* (1000), Athens American College†* (5000), Athens National Capodistrian (45 000), Athens National Technical (8000), Athens Panteios* (8000), Athens School of Economics* (5000), Athens School of Fine Art (under 1000), Crete (at Rethymnon; 1000), Crete Technical (at Khania; 1000), Ioannina (9000), Macedonia (at Thessalonika; 7000), Patras (9000), Piraeus* (11 000), Thessalonika Aristotelian (56 000), Thrace Demokritos (at Komotini; 7000).

IRELAND Trinity College, the University of Dublin, was founded in 1592. The 19th-century colleges of the National University – reorganized as a federal university in 1908 – cater for the majority of Ireland's undergraduates. Two new universities were created in 1989.

Cork University College‡ (7000 students), Dublin City (4000), Dublin Trinity College (9000), Dublin University College‡ (13 000), Galway University College‡ (6000), Limerick (6000), Maynooth St Patrick's College‡/the Pontifical University (3000).

ITALY Many of Italy's largest universities were founded in the Middle Ages, including Bologna (c.1000), Parma (1064), Modena (1175), Perugia (1200), Padua (1222), Naples (1224), Siena (1240), Macerata (1290), Rome La Sapienza (1303), Florence (1321), Pisa (1343), Pavia (1361), Ferrara (1391), Turin (1404), Catania (1434) and Genoa (1471). Between 1960 and 1990, 14 new universities were founded. A number of universities are run by the Roman Catholic Church.

Ancona (7000 students), Gabriele d'Annunzio (at Chieti; 4000), Bari (68 000), Basilicata (at Potenza; 2000), Bergamo† (4000), Bologna (74 000), Brescia (9000), Cagliari (27 000), Calabria (at Cosenza; 7000), Camerino (5000), Cassino (Frosinone; 7000), Catania (35 000), Catania† (3000), Ferrara (5000), Florence (51 000), Genoa (36 000), L'Aquila (7000), Lecce (12 000), Macerata (6000), Messina (31 000), Milan (157 000), Milan Luigi Bocconi† (commercial; 10 000), Milan Modern Languages Institute† (3000), Milan Polytechnic (university status; 30 000), Milan Sacro Cuore† (Catholic; 22 000), Modena (9000), Molise (at Campobasso; 2000), Naples (117 000), Naples Naval (2000), Naples Orientale (8000), Naples Suor Orsola Benincasa† (4000), Padua (50 000), Palermo (43 000), Parma (18 000), Pavia (23 000), Perugia (20 000), Pisa (30 000), Reggio Calabria (4000), Rome La Sapienza (186 000), Rome LUISS† (Social Studies; 3000), Rome Maria SS Assunta† (1000), Rome Tor Vergata (4000), Salerno (26 000), Sassari (9000), Siena (13 000), Turin (73 000), Turin Polytechnic (university status; 10 000), Trento (8000), Trieste (16 000), Tuscia (at Viterbo; 2000), Udine (7000), Urbino† (12 000), Venice (27 000), Venice Architecture* (at Venice; 9000), Verona (11 000).

LUXEMBOURG Luxembourg University Centre (1000 students).

NETHERLANDS The universities of Leiden (founded 1575), Groningen (1614), Amsterdam (1632) and Utrecht (1636) are ancient foundations. The university sector has several specialized institutions of university status. Agricultural University (at Wageningen; 6000 students), Amsterdam (27 000), Amsterdam Catholic Theology† (under 1000), Amsterdam Free University (12 000), Delft Technology (15 000), Eindhoven Technology (7000), Erasmus (at Rotterdam; 18 000), Groningen (18 000), Leiden (18 000), Limburg (at Maastricht; 6000), Netherlands School of Business* (at Breukelen; under 1000), Nijmegen Catholic† (13 000), Open University (at Heerlen; 50 000), Theological University of the Christian Reformed Churches† (at Apeldoorn; under 1000), Theological University of the Reformed Churches† (at Kampen; under 1000), Theological University of the Reformed Churches in the Netherlands† (at Kampen; under 1000), Theological and Pastoral University† (at Heerlen; under 1000), Tilburg Brabant Catholic (9000), Twente (at Enschede; 7000), Utrecht (23 000), Utrecht Catholic Theology† (under 1000), Utrecht Humanist Studies (under 1000).

PORTUGAL The university of Coimbra was founded in 1290 and remained the only university in Portugal until 1911 when Lisbon and Oporto were founded. Ten new universities were created in the 1970s and 1980s.

Algarve (at Faro; 1000 students), Aveiro (4000), Azores (at Ponta Delgada; 1000), Beira Interior (at Covilhã; 2000), Coimbra (13 000), Evora (2000), Infante Dom Henrique† (at Oporto; 4000), Lisbon (17 000), Lisbon Catholic† (8000), Lisbon Luis de Camões† (5000), Lisbon Lusiada (3000), Lisbon New University (7000), Lisbon Technical (14 000), Minho (at Braga; 6000), Oporto (18 000), Tras-os-Montes/Alto Duoro (at Vila Real; 4000).

SPAIN Spain's oldest universities include Salamanca (1218), Valladolid (1293), Barcelona (1450), Zaragoza (1474), Valencia (1500), Santiago (1501), Seville (1502), Madrid (1508) and Granada (1532). Some universities are run by Roman Catholic religious orders. Eighteen new universities were created between 1960 and 1989.

Alcalá de Henares (15 000 students), Alicante (11 000), Balearic Islands (at Palma de Mallorca; 9000), Barcelona (81 000), Barcelona Autonomous (36 000), Basque Country (at Bilbao; 47 000), Cádiz (15 000), Cantabria (at Santander; 12 000), Castile-La Mancha (at Ciudad Real; 12 000), Catalonia Polytechnic (university status; at Barcelona; 17 000), Comillas Pontifical† (at Madrid; 16 000), Córdoba (14 000), Deusto† (at Bilbao; 14 000), Extremadura (at Badajoz and Cáceres; 12 000), Granada (56 000), Iberoamerican University (postgraduate; at Salamanca; under 1000), La Laguna (16 000), León (10 000), Madrid Autonomous (28 000), Madrid Complutense (127 000), Madrid Carlos III (under 1000), Madrid Polytechnic (university status; 43 000), Málaga (23 000), Murcia (26 000), Navarre† (at Pamplona; 15 000), Navarre Public (at Pamplona; 5000), Open University (at Madrid; 104 000), Oviedo (29 000), Salamanca (24 000), Salamanca Pontifical† (9000), Santiago de Compostela (35 000), Seville (47 000), Valencia (55 000), Valencia Polytechnic (university status; 19 000), Valladolid (36 000), Zaragoza (40 000).

UNITED KINGDOM After Oxford (1249), Cambridge (1284), St Andrews (1411), Glasgow (1451), Aberdeen (1495), and Edinburgh (1583) no British universities were founded until Durham and London in the 1830s. The 14 large 'civic' universities were founded between 1851 (Manchester) and 1957 (Leicester). Between 1961 and 1967, 21 universities were created. In 1992–93, 40 polytechnics and colleges became universities.

Aberdeen (7000 students), Aberystwyth University College** (4000), Anglia Polytechnic University (at Chelmsford and Cambridge; 4000), Aston (at Birmingham; 4000), Bangor University College of North Wales** (3000), Bath (4000), Belfast Queen's University (10 000), Birmingham (10 000), Bournemouth (at Poole; 7000), Bradford (5000), Brighton (7000), Bristol (9000), Brunel (at Uxbridge, London; 4000), Buckingham† (1000), Cambridge (14 000), Cardiff Medical College** (1000), Cardiff University College** (9000), Central England (at Birmingham; 9000), Central Lancashire (at Preston; 8000), City (in London; 4000), Coventry (5000), Cranfield (3000), De Montfort (at Leicester and Milton Keynes; 10 000), Derby (4000), Dundee (6000), Durham (6000), East Anglia (at Norwich; 5000), East London (7000), Edinburgh (13 000), Essex (at Colchester; 4000), Exeter (6000), Glamorgan (at Pontypridd; 6000), Glasgow (13 000), Glasgow Caledonian (11 000), Greenwich (in London; 8000), Heriot-Watt (at Edinburgh; 8000), Hertfordshire (at Hatfield and Hertford; 9000), Huddersfield (7000), Hull (7000), Humberside (at Hull; 7000), Keele (4000), Kent (at Canterbury; 5000), Kingston (in London; 5000), Lampeter St David's University College** (1000), Lancaster (6000), Leeds (14 000), Leeds Metropolitan (9000), Leicester (7000), Liverpool (10 000), Liverpool John Moores (11 000), London (51 000), London Guildhall (6000), Loughborough (7000), Luton (8000), Manchester (13 000), Manchester UMIST* (Institute of Science and Technology) (5000), Manchester Metropolitan (18 000), Middlesex (in London; 9000), Napier (at Edinburgh; 6000), Newcastle-upon-Tyne (10 000), North London (6000), Northumbria (at Newcastle; 10 000), Nottingham (10 000), Nottingham Trent (11 000), Open University (at Milton Keynes; 73 000), Oxford (14 000), Oxford Brookes (8000), Paisley (4000), Plymouth (9000), Portsmouth (9000), Reading (8000), Robert Gordon (at Aberdeen; 5000), St Andrews (4000), Salford (5000), Sheffield (11 000), Sheffield Hallam (12 000), South Bank (in London; 9000), Southampton (8000), Staffordshire (at Stoke and Stafford; 7000), Stirling (4000), Strathclyde (at Glasgow; 9000), Sunderland (7000), Surrey (at Guildford; 4000), Sussex (at Brighton; 6000), Swansea University College** (6000), Teeside (at Middlesbrough; 5000), Thames Valley (in London and Slough; 15 000), Ulster (at Coleraine and Belfast; 10 000), Warwick (at Coventry; 7000), Westminster (in London; 8000), West of England (at Bristol; 9000), Wolverhampton (9000), York (5000).

AUSTRIA The ancient foundations of Vienna (1365) and Graz (1586) are the largest universities.

Graz Karl-Franzens (27 000 students), Graz Music and Dramatic Art (2000), Graz Technical (12 000), Innsbruck Leopold-Franzens (25 000), Klagenfurt (5000), Leoben Mining and Metallurgy (2000), Linz Academy of Art* (under 1000), Linz Johannes Kepler (12 000), Salzburg (12 000), Salzburg Mozarteum (music and performing art; 2000), Vienna (71 000), Vienna Academy of Fine Arts* (under 1000), Vienna Agricultural (7000), Vienna

Applied Arts (1000), Vienna Economics and Business (19 000), Vienna Music and Dramatic Art (3000), Vienna Technical (19 000), Vienna Veterinary (2000).

FINLAND Only Helsinki (1640) and the Industrial Arts (1871) universities predate the 20th century. Seven universities were founded in the 1960s and 1970s.

Abo (Swedish language; at Turku/Abo; 5000 students), Helsinki (28 000), Helsinki School of Economics* (4000), Helsinki Technology (12 000), Helsinki Veterinary College* (under 1000), Industrial Arts University (at Helsinki; 1000), Joensuu (6000), Jyväskylä (8000), Kuopio (3000), Lappeenranta (2000), Lapland (at Rovaniemi; 2000), Oulu (10 000), Swedish School of Economics* (at Helsinki; 2000), Swedish School of Social Work* (at Helsinki; under 1000), Tampere (14 000), Tampere Technology (5000), Turku (11 000), Turku School of Economics* (1000), Vaasa (2000).

ICELAND The University of Iceland (at Rekyjavik; 4000 students) was founded in 1911.

LIECHTENSTEIN There are no university-level institutes.

NORWAY Apart from Oslo (1811) and the Agricultural University (1859), Norway's universities are 20th-century foundations.

Bergen (13 000 students), Free Faculty of Theology* (at Oslo; under 1000), Nordland* (university centre; at Morkved; 1000), Norwegian Academy of Music* (at Oslo; under 1000), Norwegian Veterinary College* (at Oslo; under 1000), Norwegian School of Economics* (at Bergen; 2000), Norwegian School of Management* (at Oslo; 4000), Norwegian University of Agriculture (near Oslo; 2000), Norwegian University of Sport (at Oslo; under 1000), Oslo (22 000), Oslo Architecture School* (3000), Rogaland* (university centre; at Stavanger; 3000), Tromso (4000), Trondheim (13 000).

SWEDEN Uppsala (founded 1477) and Lund (1668) were the only Swedish universities until the 1820s. Since 1960, 14 universities have been founded.

Boras (3000 students), Chalmers Technology (at Gothenburg; 5000), Gothenburg (22 000), Halmstad (2000), Jököping (3000), Kalmar (3000), Karlstad (4000), Linköping (10 000), Lulea (5000), Lund (23 000), Orebro (5000), Ostersund (2000), Royal Institute of Technology* (at Stockholm; 9000), Skövde (2000), Stockholm (26 000), Sundsvall-Härnösand (3000), Swedish University of Agriculture (at Uppsala; 3000), Umea (10 000), Uppsala (18 000), Växjo (4000).

SWITZERLAND The universities of Basel, Zürich, Berne, Lausanne and Geneva were founded between 1460 and 1559. Since Neuchâtel was founded in 1909 there have been no new foundations.

Basel (7000 students), Berne (8000), Fribourg (6000), Geneva (13 000), Lausanne (7000), Lausanne Federal Polytechnic* (4000), Neuchâtel (3000), St Gallen School of Economics* (4000), Swiss Federal Institute of Technology* (at Zürich; 11 000), Zürich (19 000).

† private universities. * institutes of university status. ‡ part of the National University of Ireland. ** constituents of the federal University of Wales.

HOUSING

By world standards, the housing stock of Western Europe is modern and relatively uncrowded. By contrast, the average number of persons per room in Romania is 1.5, in Algeria 2.5, in Nigeria 3, in Jamaica 4.3 and in Djibouti over 6.

HOUSING OWNERSHIP

Country	% of housing owner occupied	% of housing rented	% of other units[1]
Belgium	59%	36%	5%
Denmark	54%	45%	1%
France	54%	40%	6%
Germany	39%	60%	1%
Greece	39%	58%	3%
Ireland	68%	21%	11%
Italy	59%	36%	5%
Luxembourg	59%	41%	
Netherlands	43%	57%	
Portugal	57%	39%	4%
Spain	57%	25%	18%
UK	67%	33%	
Austria	48%	36%	16%
Finland	68%	24%	8%
Iceland	70%	30%	
Liechtenstein	54%	42%	4%
Norway	40%	57%	3%
Sweden	56%	40%	4%
Switzerland	30%	67%	3%

[1] vacant, communal and holiday homes.

NUMBER OF DWELLING UNITS[1]

Country	Number of dwelling units
Belgium	3 600 000
Denmark	2 375 000
France	21 535 000
Germany	34 435 000
Greece	4 000 000
Ireland	1 050 000
Italy	17 550 000
Luxembourg	130 000
Netherlands	5 800 000
Portugal	3 240 000
Spain	12 350 000
UK	22 620 000
Austria	3 280 000
Finland	2 120 000
Iceland	71 000
Liechtenstein	9 500
Norway	1 770 000
Sweden	3 830 000
Switzerland	3 150 000

[1] houses, flats and other sub-units of larger structures; figures exclude second and holiday homes. The figures are for the period 1987–90.

SIZE OF DWELLING UNITS[1]

Country	Average number of rooms per dwelling	Average number of persons per room
Belgium	5.0	0.5
Denmark	3.8	0.6
France	3.9	0.7
Germany	4.1	0.6
Greece	3.3	0.9
Ireland	3.7	1.0
Italy	4.0	0.8
Luxembourg	5.4	0.5
Netherlands	4.1	0.7
Portugal	5.0	0.8
Spain	4.4	1.4
UK	3.8	0.6
Austria	4.3	0.6
Finland	3.5	0.6
Iceland	4.8	0.9
Liechtenstein	3.0	1.4
Norway	4.1	0.6
Sweden	3.4	0.6
Switzerland	3.8	0.6

[1] houses, flats and other sub-units of larger structures; figures exclude bathrooms, wcs and hallways. The figures are for the period 1986–90.

AGE OF HOUSING

Country	Built prior to 1950	Built 1950–70	Built since 1970
Belgium	49%	32%	19%
Denmark	44%	26%	30%
France	38%	17%	45%
Germany	37%	35%	28%
Greece	30%	48%	22%
Ireland	55%	17%	28%
Italy	31%	47%	22%
Luxembourg	62%	20%	18%
Netherlands	28%	30%	42%
Portugal	47%	23%	30%
Spain	39%	42%	19%
UK	54%	29%	17%
Austria	45%	33%	22%
Finland	25%	22%	53%
Iceland	41%	10%	49%
Liechtenstein	27%	42%	31%
Norway	44%	38%	18%
Sweden	33%	37%	30%
Switzerland	53%	28%	19%

The figures are for the period 1986–92.

UNEMPLOYMENT

In the majority of the countries of Western Europe the days of full employment have gone. The 1980s witnessed considerable economic growth, but worries about the Gulf War influenced a mild slowdown in growth. Most economic theorists expected that this would be only a temporary phenomenon and that Western economies would bounce back. Instead the states of Western Europe have experienced either very slow growth (as is the case of the UK) or recession (for example, Sweden and Finland) ever since.

Short-term prospects remain gloomy and few economists predict any real improvement before 1995. EC countries, in particular, have been hit by high interest rates that have resulted from the monetary policies of the German Bundesbank following German reunification (1990; see p. 23). The result of merging East and West Germany into a single economy which could be prone to inflation was high German interest rates in an attempt to cool down the economy. In several Western European countries the economic pressures proved too great and their currencies were devalued. Germany, France, Belgium and the Netherlands still have high interest rates and remain in recesssion. Other EEA states, such as the UK, whose currencies have been devalued and whose interest rates have been slashed, are edging slowly out of recession.

In such an economic climate consumer confidence is low and spending – and therefore demand and industrial production – have fallen. The result is unemployment. This has been added to by cuts in public-sector jobs as Western governments have reduced their spending as a means of combatting a growing deficit.

There are now nearly 19 000 000 people unemployed in the EEA states and fear of unemployment has become the greatest obstacle to economic recovery.

Information on employment and the relative strengths of each of the principal sectors of the labour force of each EEA country will be found in entries for individual states, pp. 24–67. The statistics below relate to 1993.

Belgium has 550 000 people unemployed, that is 12.1% of the labour force. Belgium's economy is export led and the country has suffered through a fall in demand from its principal trading partner, Germany. The government has taken austerity measures but the economy remains in recession.

Denmark has 336 000 people unemployed, that is 12% of the labour force. It is hoped that a combination of reductions in income tax, cuts in interest rates and government schemes to promote employment in areas of long-term unemployment will create employment opportunities in 1994–95.

France has 3 140 000 people unemployed, that is 11.5% of the labour force. France's GDP is shrinking as consumer demand continues to fall. Unemployment is rising and is expected to peak at nearly 3 500 000 by 1994. Measures are being taken to stimulate demand but high interest rates remain a problem.

Germany has 3 090 000 people unemployed, that is 10.5% of the labour force. Largely as a result of the costs of reunification Germany is suffering its deepest recession for 40 years. Unemployment is rising – with nearly 15% of the labour force in the former East Germany out of work – and is expected to reach 3 500 000 by 1994.

Greece has 150 000 people unemployed, that is 9% of the labour force. High inflation, high interest rates and low productivity hamper economic recovery. Unemployment continues to rise.

Ireland has 293 000 people unemployed, that is 21.7% of the labour force. The highest rate of unemployment in the EC owes much to low investment rates. On the plus side Ireland enjoys low interest rates and a low level of inflation.

Italy has 2 960 000 people unemployed, that is 10.5% of the labour force. Recession began in 1992 and has been deepened by government cuts that were made to tackle a very large public deficit. Despite low wage increases and rises in productivity unemployment is expected to rise.

Luxembourg has 3000 people unemployed, that is 2.3% of the labour force.

The Netherlands have 359 000 people unemployed, that is 5% of the labour force. The Dutch economy depends heavily upon trade, in particular with Germany. As a result the Netherlands have shared in the recession that has gripped Western Europe.

Portugal has 365 000 people unemployed, that is 5.3% of the labour force. Portugal has been immune from some of the effects of the recession, in part owing to the country's low labour costs.

Spain has 3 300 000 people unemployed, that is 16.4% of the labour force. Cuts in public spending and schemes to create employment have been instituted in an attempt to drag the Spanish economy out of recession. Although the effective devaluation of the peseta has improved competitiveness, unemployment is rising sharply.

The UK has 2 910 000 people unemployed, that is 10.4% of the labour force. Low interest rates and a competitive pound appear to have produced a very tentative recovery and unemployment is no longer rising.

Austria has 204 000 people unemployed, that is 5.3% of the labour force.

Finland has 283 000 people unemployed, that is 11% of the labour force. The collapse of the economy of Russia, formerly a major trading partner, has deepened the recession in Finland where unemployment is at its highest since the 1930s.

Iceland has 5000 people unemployed, that is 4.6% of the labour force.

Liechtenstein has 30 people unemployed, that is 0.2% of the labour force.

Norway has 117 000 people unemployed, that is 5.5% of the labour force. Despite high interest rates, the recession in Norway is not as deep as in her neighbours.

Sweden has 561 000 people unemployed, that is 14% of the labour force. Sweden – in the grip of its deepest recession for 60 years – has moved from full employment to 14% unemployment in a few years.

Switzerland has 71 000 people unemployed, that is 2% of the labour force. The Swiss economy has, in part, remained cushioned from the effects of recession. Unemployment has tended to hit temporary foreign workers rather than Swiss nationals.

STANDARDS OF LIVING

The countries of Western Europe enjoy high a standard of living. This may be measured by comparing the GNP (gross national product) per head in each state.

The following data relates to 1992 estimates.

GNP per head

Country	GNP per head (US$)
Belgium	22 600
Denmark	28 200
France	23 900
Germany	24 120
Greece	7 600
Ireland	14 700
Italy	20 200
Luxembourg	31 080
Netherlands	21 400
Portugal	7 600
Spain	13 600
UK	17 300
Austria	23 800
Finland	24 400
Iceland	22 580
Liechtenstein	21 020
Norway	28 200
Sweden	29 600
Switzerland	35 500

Possession of a car, a telephone and a television set are indicators of a high standard of living.

Car ownership

Country	Persons per car
Liechtenstein	1.5
France	2.0
Luxembourg	2.0
Germany	2.1
Sweden	2.2
Finland	2.3
Norway	2.3
Belgium	2.4
Italy	2.4
UK	2.5
Denmark	2.7
Spain	2.7

Telephone ownership

Country	Persons per receiver
Liechtenstein	0.7
Sweden	1.1
Switzerland	1.1
Denmark	1.2
France	1.2

Television ownership

Country	Persons per receiver
Denmark	2.0
Finland	2.0
France	2.0
Spain	2.0
Germany	2.1

EC SOCIAL POLICY

The Maastricht Treaty (see p. 19), which was signed in 1993 by the 12 members of the European Community (EC), included an agreement on social policy (see below). This reflects the original Treaty of Rome which stressed the need for 'social cohesion' in the Community.

EC social policy does not represent a major problem for any of the four candidates whose applications for membership are currently being negotiated. Austria, for example, has already adopted many EC directives in this field ahead of membership. High levels of social welfare and excellent working conditions are traditional in Norway, Sweden and Finland, all of which already fulfil almost all of the conditions of the Social Charter (see below).

THE SOCIAL CHARTER

A principal objective of the Maastricht Treaty is to raise living standards generally and improve working conditions. The Treaty expands the powers of the EC authorities to make new Community-wide rules on social affairs, building upon established policies contained in the 'Community Charter of Fundamental Human Rights'.

Areas covered by these provisions include:
- equal treatment for men and women in employment (including equal pay);
- terms and conditions of employment contracts;
- the treatment of temporary workers;
- conditions relating to collective redundancies;
- minimum health and safety at work standards; and
- the participation of the workforce in company decision-making.

At Maastricht, the Social Chapter was endorsed by the governments of 11 EC member-states but not by the UK. The view of the British government is that the European Community should respect the diversity of employment practices in member states and allow members to continue with their own policies. Thus, for the present, the UK is not subject to Social Chapter provisions nor does it have to pay for them.

Implementing the Social Chapter provisions will be costly and other EC members have already complained that the refusal of the British government to recognize the Social Chapter has put it at an 'unfair' competitive advantage.

CHARTER OR CHAPTER?

Some public confusion has arisen over the use of the terms 'Social Charter' and 'Social Chapter'. Both terms appear in the press and seem to be used concerning the same thing.

The Social Charter is the popular name for the Community Charter of Fundamental Human Rights (see above).

The Social Chapter is that part of the Maastricht Treaty that refers to the Social Charter.

REGIONAL POLICY IN THE EC

Community policy is aimed at reducing economic disparities between regions. This is to be achieved by means of various funds including the European Regional Fund and the European Social Fund (see below). Community policy in this area has five principal objectives:

Objective 1: To promote the development and structural adjustment of regions whose development is lagging behind (that is, those regions in which the per capita GDP is less than 75% of the Community average), see map and below.

Objective 2: To convert the regions, frontier regions and parts of regions (including employment areas and urban communities) that are seriously affected by industrial decline.

Objective 3: To combat long-term unemployment and facilitate the integration into working life of young people and of persons exposed to exclusion from the labour market.

Objective 4: To facilitate the adaptation of workers to industrial changes and to changes in production systems.

Objective 5: To promote rural development by speeding up the adjustment of agricultural structures in the framework of the reform of the Common Agricultural Policy (CAP; see p. 96) and to facilitate the development and structural adjustment of rural areas.

The less-developed regions – concerned by Objective 1, above – are as follows.

Belgium The entire province of Hainaut.

Denmark No less-developed regions.

France The island and region of Corsica – comprising the départements of Haute-Corse and Corse-du-Sud – plus the arrondissements of Avesnes, Douai and Valenciennes in the Nord département, Nord-Pas-de-Calais region (which form a contiguous industrial unit with the Belgian province of Hainaut).

The French overseas départements of Guadeloupe, Guyane (French Guiana), Martinique and Réunion have also been granted less-developed region status under the terms of Objective 1.

Germany The Länder of Brandenburg, Mecklenburg-West Pomerania, Saxony, Saxony-Anhalt and Thuringia, plus that part of the city of Berlin that was formerly included in East Germany – in other words, the whole of the former German Democratic Republic.

Greece The entire country.

Ireland The entire Republic of Ireland.

Italy The regions of Basilicata, Calabria, Campania, Molise, Puglia, Sardinia and Sicily. The region of Abruzzi was retained on the list of less-developed

regions for a non-renewal period of three years (1994–96).

Luxembourg No less-developed regions.

Netherlands The province of Flevoland was added to the list of less-developed regions under the terms of Objective 1 in 1993.

Portugal The entire country including the autonomous regions of the Azores and Madeira.

Spain The regions of Andalusia, Asturias, the Canary Islands, Cantabria, Castile-Leon, Castile-La Mancha, Extremadura, Galicia, Murcia and Valencia, plus the Spanish enclaves in North Africa – Ceuta and Melilla

UK The whole of Northern Ireland is a less-developed region under the terms of Objective 1. In 1993 the Scottish regions of Highland and the Western Isles and the English former administrative county of Merseyside were added to the list.

REGIONAL FUNDS

European Community regional aid is paid through the Structural Fund, which is an 'umbrella' covering several funds including the Regional Development Fund, the Social Fund and the Agricultural Guidance Fund. These funds represent an ambitious shift of resources from the most prosperous regions of the EC to its poorer regions. For the period 1993–99, a total of Ecu 141 billion (£107 billion) of regional aid has been allocated. This sum is three times the size of the Marshall Aid Plan which restored the shattered economies of the countries of Western Europe after the Second World War.

However, not all EC states have used their full allocation of aid. Ireland has utilized 97% of the aid it received between 1989 and 1993. Portugal and the UK have used 90% and Spain and Greece have used 80% of their allocation on a wide variety of projects. In Spain, for example, EC funds have made an major contribution towards seven airport expansion schemes, the Madrid-Seville high-speed rail link, water management schemes and new telephone systems. Italy, on the other hand, has taken up only 68% of its allocation of EC funds.

The EC funds allocated to individual countries over the period 1989–93 were:

Country	Ecus allocated (1989–93)	£ sterling allocated (1989–93)	Ecus per head
Spain	15 800 000 000	11 976 000 000	411
Italy	12 100 000 000	9 172 000 000	212
Portugal	8 515 000 000	6 454 000 000	864
Greece	8 220 000 000	6 231 000 000	801
France	7 400 000 000	5 609 000 000	130
UK	7 125 000 000	5 401 000 000	128
Germany	7 000 000 000	5 306 000 000	88
Ireland	4 510 000 000	3 419 000 000	1280
Belgium	1 090 000 000	826 000 000	109
Netherlands	900 000 000	682 000 000	60
Denmark	420 000 000	318 000 000	81
Luxembourg	79 000 000	60 000 000	206

Less-Developed Regions of the EC

Western Isles

Highland

Northern Ireland

DENMARK

IRELAND

UNITED KINGDOM

Merseyside

NETHERLANDS

Flevoland

Mecklenburg-West Pomerania

Valenciennes

Saxony-Anhalt

East Berlin

Brandenburg

Douai

Hainaut

Saxony

Nord-Pays-de-Calais

Thuringia

GERMANY

Avesnes

LUXEMBOURG

BELGIUM

Galicia

FRANCE

Asturias

Cantabria

Castile-Leon

PORTUGAL

SPAIN

ITALY

less-developed regions

Valencia

Corsica

Abruzzi

Basilicata

GREECE

Andalusia

Sardinia

Puglia

Campania

Extre-madura

Murcia

Castile-La Mancha

Calabria

Sicily

AGRICULTURE

THE EC COMMON AGRICULTURAL POLICY

The Common Agricultural Policy (CAP) is the name given to the body of policies adopted by the EC towards agriculture and the import and export of agricultural products. It was one of the first and perhaps most important common policies introduced by the EC. Its significance lies not only in its agricultural objectives, but as a symbol of the Community's desire for economic and political union. It has accounted for the lion's share of the Community's budget (see p. 13), and its effects have been wide ranging and often controversial.

The CAP's objectives were set out in the Treaty of Rome (1957) which established the European Economic Community. The principal means by which these were to be achieved were decided at a conference at Stresa in Italy in 1958. After further negotiations, the basic regulations for the operation of a Community policy for agriculture were agreed by 1962 and the delicate matters of the level of agricultural prices and Community finance by 1968. The policy applied to the six original member states and covered all their major agricultural products. Subsequently, it has been extended to new members.

THE OBJECTIVES OF THE CAP

The principal objectives of the CAP – set out in Article 39 of the Rome Treaty – are to increase agricultural productivity; to ensure a fair standard of living for the agricultural community; to stabilize markets; and to ensure supplies to consumers at reasonable prices. Three guiding principles have governed the operation of the policy. Firstly, Market Unity, which means a single EC market for agricultural products, devoid of national barriers and with common policies. Secondly, Community Preference, which means that within the EC the agricultural products of member states should be more favourably treated than those from countries outside the EC. Thirdly, Financial Solidarity, which means that the expenditure attributable to the policy should be met from the Community's budget and that any revenue generated by the policy (for example, import taxes) should go to the EC's budget.

The policies employed by the EC to achieve its agricultural objectives fall into two broad categories – price support policies and structural policies, a classification reflected in the division of the EC's agricultural budget between its Guaranteed Section (price support) and its Guidance Section (structure policies). The purpose of price support policy is to ensure common market prices for EC farming products at levels that provide reasonable farming incomes and security of food supplies. The level of prices necessary to achieve these objectives are decided annually by the EC's Council of Ministers.

However, there are two potential threats to the realization of these prices. The first is foreign competition. World agricultural product prices have generally been substantially lower than those desired by the EC for its farmers. Consequently, unrestricted agricultural imports would result in EC target prices not being achieved. To prevent this the EC controls the price and quantity of agricultural imports. The systems used are frequently complex but the basic mechanism has consisted of import taxes (called variable levies) which increase the price of imports to the required levels, thus preventing them from undercutting EC target prices. Conversely, a tax can be applied to EC exports in the unlikely event of EC prices being below those outside the EC in order to reduce their flow and ensure an adequate supply of food within the EC. The second threat to the achievement of the EC's target prices for agricultural products is that the EC's farmers can push prices down by over-supplying the market. To avoid this, the EC can purchase agricultural products from its own farmers when prices fall below predetermined minimum levels (hence the notorious butter mountains and wine lakes that have been widely reported in the press).

Structural policies which have generally accounted for a small percentage of the EC's expenditure on agriculture – as little as 5% in many years – have been concerned with direct payments to farmers for a multiplicity of reasons such as capital investment, special aid for particularly poor farming regions and so forth.

HOW SUCCESSFUL IS THE CAP?

There is no clear and unequivocal answer to the question of how successful the CAP has been in achieving its objectives. On the one hand, there has been an enormous growth in agricultural output, productivity and trade. However, many products have become over supplied and have required large expenditures on their storage, or disposal on world markets at much lower prices than were paid for them. The budgetary costs of the CAP have therefore escalated to an extent which threatens political harmony and the further development of the EC.

There are serious question marks over the efficiency of a policy aimed at supporting poor farmers which provides financial support for all farmers, regardless of their income. Thus, some 80% of agricultural support is alleged to go to just 20% of EC farmers because, under a CAP-type price support policy, the amount of financial support a farmer receives largely depends upon the level of output of his farm.

Consumers have also paid higher prices for their food than they might otherwise have done, although this has not been a political issue. There are various reasons for this – in particular, there has been a long history of this type of support for agriculture in most of the EC member states, with the notable exception of the UK. Furthermore, as people have become better off, the cost of food has become of less significance to them.

An important and developing issue in recent years has been concern over the environmental damage from the intensification of agricultural production which in many cases the CAP has encouraged. There has also been international criticism of the CAP by food exporting countries because they are denied access to the EC market and because there is evidence that EC agricultural production and exports have depressed world market prices, although this may have benefited some of the world's food importers. A reduction in the level of EC support for its agriculture has been a major issue in international negotiations to promote world trade.

CAP REFORM

Consequently, the pressures for CAP reform have intensified in recent years and most people, including farmers, have recognized the need for fairly radical changes. Thus, in May 1992, the EC's Council of Ministers reached an agreement on CAP reform which has been described as historic, and is the culmination of a long process of reform begun in the mid 1980s. It brings to an end a period of great uncertainty about the future direction of policy for at least the next three years and probably for the rest of the decade. The agricultural objectives of the Treaty of Rome and the CAP's three underlying principles remain intact. However, there is a significant change in the method of support for EC farming. There will be less emphasis on price support and more on direct payments to farmers – thus breaking the link between income support and production and allowing farm prices to be cut. However, direct payments will not be open-ended, but controlled by quotas and ceilings and, in some cases, linked to a farmer's willingness to take land out of production (set-aside) and undertake environmental conservation work.

In the future, unless there is some unpredictable crisis in world food supplies, the EC market will become more open and there will be less opportunity to dispose of EC agricultural products on world markets at subsidized prices. With only limited growth expected in the consumption of agricultural products this will mean a more competitive environment for EC farmers. It may also mean that further efforts will be needed to control production and the EC now has in place the policies to do this for all the major agricultural commodities. A tightening of quotas is quite likely in the future. In the short term (the next three years), it is the EC's intention that farmers be fully compensated for price cuts. In the longer term, it is uncertain whether full compensation will continue to be available since there are likely to be further internal and external pressures for a reduction in domestic support. An enlargement of the EC could add to these pressures since agriculture, for example, in some of the Eastern European countries, has considerable potential for expansion.

Finally, it is important to emphasize that the EC is not unique in providing support for its agriculture. All the industrial countries have large and sometimes complex agricultural policies. There have been various attempts to measure the levels of government involvement in agriculture so that objective international comparisons can be made. Thus, for example, one estimate made by the Organization for Economic Cooperation and Development (OECD) of the level of subsidy to the EC's agriculture in 1990 was $82 billions or 48% of the value of the EC's agricultural production. Comparable figures for other countries were: Japan $31 billions or 68%; the USA $36 billions or 30%; Canada $6 billions or 41%; Sweden $3 billions or 59%; Switzerland $5 billions or 78%; Finland $5 billions or 72%.

WEST EUROPEAN FARMING PRODUCTS

Beef (1990)
Germany	2 005 000 tonnes
France	1 716 000 tonnes
Italy	1 166 000 tonnes
UK	958 000 tonnes
Netherlands	478 000 tonnes
Spain	446 000 tonnes
Ireland	441 000 tonnes
Belgium	320 000 tonnes
Austria	213 000 tonnes

Butter (1990)
Germany	695 000 tonnes
France	539 000 tonnes
Netherlands	177 000 tonnes
UK	134 000 tonnes
Ireland	132 000 tonnes
Denmark	93 000 tonnes
Belgium	90 000 tonnes
Italy	80 000 tonnes
Sweden	69 000 tonnes

Cow's milk (1990)
Germany	33 500 000 tonnes
France	27 250 000 tonnes
UK	14 750 000 tonnes
Netherlands	11 250 000 tonnes
Italy	10 650 000 tonnes
Spain	6 168 000 tonnes
Ireland	5 600 000 tonnes
Denmark	4 730 000 tonnes
Switzerland	3 840 000 tonnes

Eggs (hen's) (1990)
Germany	998 000 tonnes
France	906 000 tonnes
Italy	682 000 tonnes
UK	647 000 tonnes
Spain	621 000 tonnes
Netherlands	615 000 tonnes
Belgium	158 000 tonnes
Greece	127 000 tonnes
Sweden	117 000 tonnes

Pig meat (1990)
Germany	4 668 000 tonnes
France	1 840 000 tonnes
Spain	1 720 000 tonnes
Netherlands	1 632 000 tonnes
Italy	1 278 000 tonnes
Denmark	1 168 000 tonnes
UK	947 000 tonnes
Belgium	815 000 tonnes
Austria	465 000 tonnes

Sheep meat (1900)
UK	347 000 tonnes
Spain	200 000 tonnes
France	150 000 tonnes
Greece	85 000 tonnes
Italy	69 000 tonnes
Ireland	58 000 tonnes
Germany	52 000 tonnes
Norway	26 000 tonnes
Portugal	25 000 tonnes

LAND TENURE

Country	Owner operated	Rented	State	Other*
Belgium	28%	71%	1%	negligible
Denmark	64%	36%	negligible	negligible
France	65%	34%	negligible	1%
Germany	60%	5%	negligible	35%
Greece	c. 85%	n/a	n/a	n/a
Ireland	c. 70%	n/a	n/a	n/a
Italy	81%	7%	negligible	12%
Luxembourg	50%	50%	negligible	negligible
Netherlands	97%	2%	negligible	1%
Portugal	68%	9%	negligible	23%
Spain	76%	4%	negligible	20%
UK	73%	27%	negligible	negligible
Austria	59%	2%	negligible	39%
Finland	79%	21%	negligible	negligible
Iceland	n/a	n/a	n/a	n/a
Liechtenstein	85%	12%	3%	negligible
Norway	65%	35%	negligible	negligible
Sweden	48%	15%	negligible	37%
Switzerland	36%	59%	1%	4%

* Mainly land owned by companies, educational and religious establishments, etc, and farmed for them by managers.

SIZE OF AGRICULTURAL HOLDINGS

Country	1–5 ha	5–10 ha	10–20 ha	20–50 ha	over 50 ha
Belgium	28%	18%	24%	24%	6%
Denmark	2%	16%	26%	39%	17%
France	18%	12%	19%	33%	18%
Germany	30%	18%	22%	24%	6%
Greece	69%	20%	7%	3%	1%
Ireland	16%	15%	29%	31%	9%
Italy	68%	17%	9%	4%	2%
Luxembourg	19%	10%	12%	33%	26%
Netherlands	25%	18%	25%	27%	5%
Portugal	73%	15%	7%	3%	2%
Spain	53%	19%	12%	9%	7%
UK	14%	13%	15%	25%	33%
Austria	34%	17%	21%	21%	7%
Finland	35%	21%	24%	18%	2%
Iceland	25%	12%	24%	36%	3%
Liechtenstein	59%	13%	13%	14%	1%
Norway	18%	13%	16%	24%	29%
Sweden	15%	20%	22%	27%	16%
Switzerland	42%	15%	27%	15%	1%

1 ha equals 2.471 acres

NUMBER OF HOLDINGS OVER 1 ha

Country	Total number of farming holdings	Country	Total number of farming holdings
Belgium	79 800	**Austria**	292 000
Denmark	86 000	**Finland**	199 000
France	912 000	**Iceland**	6 000
Germany	671 000	**Liechtenstein**	310
Greece	704 000	**Norway**	171 000
Ireland	217 000	**Sweden**	97 000
Italy	1 974 000	**Switzerland**	92 000
Luxembourg	3 800		
Netherlands	117 000	1 ha equals 2.471 acres	
Portugal	384 000		
Spain	1 540 000		
UK	243 000		

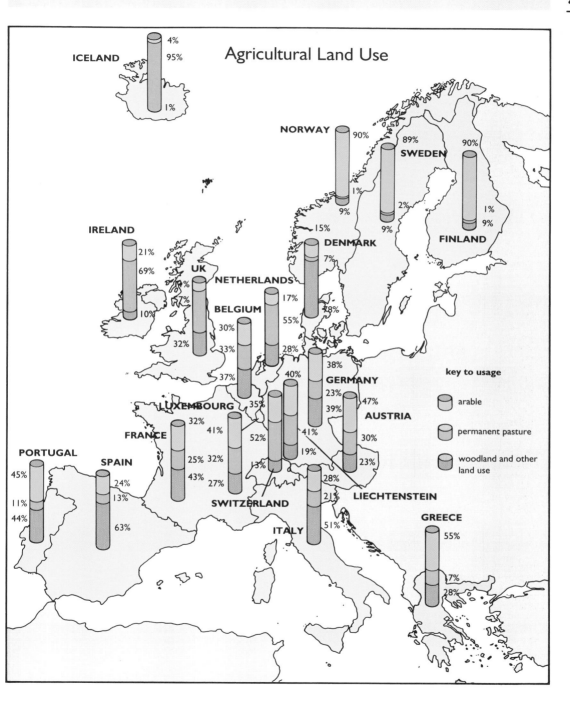

Agricultural Land Use

ICELAND 4% 95% 1%

NORWAY 90% 1% 9%

SWEDEN 89% 2% 9%

FINLAND 90% 1% 9%

IRELAND 21% 69% 10%

UK 7% 32%

NETHERLANDS 17% 55% 28%

BELGIUM 30% 33% 37%

DENMARK 15% 7% 78%

GERMANY 38% 23% 39%

LUXEMBOURG 35% 41% 19% 28%

SWITZERLAND 40% 13% 21%

FRANCE 32% 25% 43%

AUSTRIA 47% 30% 23%

LIECHTENSTEIN

PORTUGAL 45% 11% 44%

SPAIN 24% 13% 63%

ITALY 32% 27% 51%

52% 41%

GREECE 55% 17% 28%

key to usage

arable

permanent pasture

woodland and other land use

AVERAGE ANNUAL PRODUCTION OF CROPS (in tonnes)

Country	Wheat	Barley	Grain maize	Potatoes	Sugar beet
Belgium	1 345 000	640 000	55 000	1 785 000	6 195 000
Denmark	3 085 000	5 120 000	nil	1 320 000	3 410 000
France	31 390 000	9 915 000	12 440 000	5 100 000	29 545 000
Germany	15 795 000	13 310 000	1 440 000	17 520 000	28 900 000
Greece	2 350 000	515 000	2 190 000	1 045 000	2 540 000
Ireland	525 000	1 490 000	nil	635 000	1 420 000
Italy	7 805 000	1 640 000	6 170 000	2 380 000	14 115 000
Luxembourg	35 000	60 000	nil	25 000	nil
Netherlands	985 000	255 000	1 000	6 880 000	7 680 000
Portugal	435 000	70 000	675 000	1 090 000	8 000
Spain	5 585 000	10 280 000	3 315 000	5 080 000	7 875 000
UK	13 270 000	8 250 000	nil	6 170 000	8 090 000
Austria	1 430 000	1 410 000	1 530 000	900 000	2 445 000
Finland	475 000	1 655 000	nil	905 000	135 000
Iceland	nil	nil	nil	15 000	nil
Liechtenstein	500	400	*	1 000	negligible
Norway	165 000	580 000	nil	460 000	nil
Sweden	1 740 000	1 935 000	nil	1 230 000	2 545 000
Switzerland	595 000	335 000	240 000	790 000	925 000

Figures are an average for the period 1989–90. * No grain maize but 28 000 tonnes of maize are grown p.a. making it the principal crop.

LIVESTOCK

Country	Total number of beef and other cattle	Total number of dairy cattle	Total number of sheep	Total number of pigs	Total number of goats
Belgium	2 330 000	835 000	145 000	6 270 000	n/a
Denmark	1 470 000	770 000	111 000	280 000	n/a
France	16 220 000	5 275 000	11 500 000	12 220 000	700 000
Germany	13 620 000	6 770 000	4 000 000	34 870 000	470 000
Greece	445 000	240 000	9 760 000	1 145 000	6 000 000
Ireland	4 640 000	1 390 000	6 000 000	1 070	n/a
Italy	5 355 000	2 880 000	11 575 000	8 840 000	570 000
Luxembourg	155 000	60 000	8 000	70 000	n/a
Netherlands	21 915 000	1 920 000	1 950 000	13 790 000	n/a
Portugal	945 000	400 000	4 220 000	2 665 000	n/a
Spain	3 410 000	1 595 000	24 500 000	15 950 000	4 530 000
UK	8 955 000	2 890 000	30 065 000	7 340 000	n/a
Austria	1 610 000	950 000	310 000	3 770 000	15 000
Finland	860 000	505 000	65 000	1 350 000	n/a
Iceland	45 000	30 000	700 000	12 000	n/a
Liechtenstein	4 000	2 000	3 000	3 000	n/a
Norway	620 000	335 000	2 300 000	710 000	n/a
Sweden	1 125 000	555 000	395 000	2 175 000	n/a
Switzerland	1 065 000	785 000	420 000	1 860 000	20 000

Figures are for 1990.

VITICULTURE

Country	Wine – annual production (hectolitres)	Country	Wine – annual production (hectolitres)
France	61 070 000	**Austria**	3 070 000
Germany	10 900 000	**Liechtenstein**	800
Greece	4 140 000	**Switzerland**	1 320 000
Italy	59 700 000		
Luxembourg	143 000		
Portugal	7 730 000		
Spain	30 730 000		
UK	20 000		

FORESTRY

The wood industry plays an important role in the economies of several West European countries. In Finland, for example, wood and wood products account for about 40% of export earnings. Over 75% of Finland is wooded and forests are the country's most important natural resource. There are government programmes to replace depleted areas of forest but the cost of transporting timber from some of the more remote areas that are now being exploited is high. Wood and pulp are among Finland's principal exports.

Productive forests cover much of Sweden and over 75% of central Sweden is wooded. The state owns about 25% of Sweden's forests and comprehensive legislation governs harvesting and reafforestation. Wood, wood pulp and paper are among Sweden's principal exports.

Norway, too, is heavily wooded – the area of commercial forest exceeds that of farmland by a ration of 8:1 (see p. 99). Forestry, although not conducted on such a scale in Norway as it is in Finland and Sweden, is economically very important. Over 60% of Norway's forests are owned by farmers and, as many Norwegian farms are too small to be able to rely upon income from crops and animals alone, forestry makes a significant addition to farmers' earnings.

Austria is a major exporter of untreated timber, producing wood from small privately-owned farms as well as from traditional large estates and state-owned plantations which, together, form the most considerable forests of central Europe.

Switzerland has long recognized the importance of forests to both the national economy and ecology. Forests protect settlements and communications from the danger of avalanches and help prevent erosion. Stringent forestry laws forbid any diminution of the area covered by forests – about one quarter of the country.

Alpine and Scandinavian forests have been seriously damaged by acid rain, but Britain has the highest percentage of damaged trees in Europe – 67%.

WOOD PRODUCTION

Country	Production of sawn softwood (m³)	Production of sawn hardwood (m³)
Belgium	625 000	225 000
Denmark	450 000	400 000
France	5 960 000	2 930 000
Germany	8 110 000	1 570 000
Greece	200 000	225 000
Ireland	290 000	6 000
Italy	730 000	1 100 000
Luxembourg	30 000	40 000
Netherlands	160 000	220 000
Portugal	1 700 000	290 000
Spain	1 990 000	610 000
UK	1 600 000	260 000
Austria	5 690 000	220 000
Finland	7 460 000	70 000
Iceland	nil	nil
Liechtenstein	20 000	negligible
Norway	2 350 000	10 000
Sweden	11 280 000	220 000
Switzerland	1 440 000	180 000

Paper Production

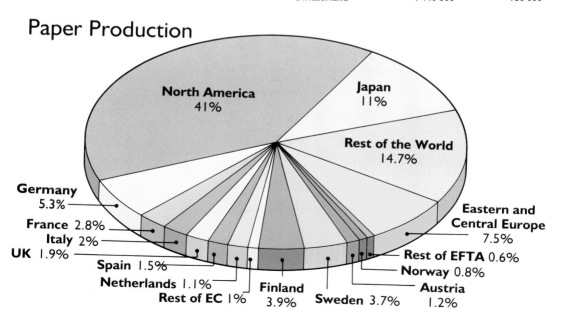

North America 41%

Japan 11%

Rest of the World 14.7%

Germany 5.3%

France 2.8%

Italy 2%

UK 1.9%

Spain 1.5%

Netherlands 1.1%

Rest of EC 1%

Finland 3.9%

Sweden 3.7%

Eastern and Central Europe 7.5%

Rest of EFTA 0.6%

Norway 0.8%

Austria 1.2%

FISHING

The fishing industry plays a major role in the economies of three West European countries – Iceland, Norway and Denmark. In Iceland, fishing and fish-processing employ over 11% of the labour force and fisheries products account for nearly three quarters of the country's export earnings. In Denmark the fishing industry accounts for nearly 6% of export earnings. In Norway fish products are responsible for 6% of export earnings.

The northeast Atlantic – including the English Channel, the Irish Sea, the North Sea and the Baltic Sea – is the major fishing ground for most of the countries of Western Europe. However, catches are declining owing to overfishing, and EC and other measures have been adopted to conserve stocks. The European Community has imposed stringent quotas, or licences, to reduce the pressure on fish stocks. In 1990 the EC imposed a compulsory eight-day period in every month during which EC vessels may not leave port. Other EC conservation measures include limits upon the size and horsepower of fishing vessels. There has been no agreement concerning the size of the mesh of nets but various EC measures on quality and packing have been adopted.

The EC Common Fisheries Policy (CFP), which came into effect in 1983 after long and acrimonious negotiations, is concerned with access to fishing grounds. It defines a 200-nautical mile (370-km) zone around EC coasts (excluding the Mediterranean). Within the 200-mile zone, vessels from all EC member states have access. The CFP also defines a six-nautical mile (11.1–km) exclusive zone adjoining each member state, within which only vessels from that country have access, and a further zone between six and 12 nautical miles from the shore within which 'the historic rights' of other member states are recognized.

Early in the 1990s the EC Commission proposed a reduction of 40% in the Community's fishing fleet. However, such a reduction would be difficult to implement, particularly as the principal fishing ports tend to be in isolated regions which have few other resources or employment opportunities. The political consequences of implementing such cuts discourage some governments from taking action. The EC has, however, made financial provisions to help areas that would be hit by decommissioning schemes and a reduction in the fishing fleets of most EC nations has begun.

France has reduced its fishing fleet by 10%. This has resulted in a loss of some 2000 fishing jobs. The UK has let market forces dictate the size of its declining fishing fleet. Spain faces problems on several fronts. Fishing is an important factor in the economy of one region, Galicia, thus any substantial reduction in the size of the fleet would have a disproportionate effect upon a single region. At the same time, Spain is having difficulty in obtaining access to fishing grounds for its considerable long-distance fishing fleet. Until 1990, when Namibia extended its territorial waters and imposed licence restrictions, Spanish vessels took a large catch from the southeast Atlantic.

Fish consumption in the EEA countries is rising. Portugal and Iceland have the highest consumption per capita with annual totals of 60.1 kg and 92.4 kg respectively. Austria is at the other end of the scale with an annual consumption of 7.2 kg per capita. The growth in demand for fish is particularly marked in Spain, France and Germany, which are now all major importers of fish. Reduced EC catches (see above) mean that the Community is no longer self-sufficient.

Overfishing is a worldwide problem and fishing is a significant problem in the Community's relations with a number of countries. Canada claims that EC vessels have overfished an area of the Grand Banks in the northwest Atlantic that straddles the border between Canadian and international waters. Canada believes this fishing to be illegal and claims that, as a result of EC overfishing, over 30% of Canada's fleet has had to be laid off and considerable economic hardship has been experienced in Nova Scotia and Newfoundland. The EC refutes these claims but has temporarily imposed its own ban on taking cod from the area because the EC's quotas have been filled.

The importance of fishing to the Icelandic economy caused that country to extend its territorial waters in 1964 and again in 1972. On both occasions British opposition to the extensions resulted in clashes between British vessels and Icelandic coastal patrols – the so-called 'cod wars'. More recently Iceland's determination to protect an exclusive right to these waters threatened to derail talks between the EC and the EFTA upon setting up the EEA. Iceland's stance concerning fishing rights could prevent her from eventually joining the EC.

FISHING TRADE

Country	Imports (tonnes)	Exports (tonnes)
Belgium	231 000	48 000
Denmark	433 000	1 583 000
France	775 000	305 000
Germany	1 177 000	430 000
Greece	92 000	20 000
Ireland	42 000	162 000
Italy	678 000	83 000
Luxembourg[1]		
Netherlands	619 000	602 000
Portugal	184 000	91 000
Spain	669 000	272 000
UK	922 000	381 000
Austria	66 000	600
Finland	112 000	3 600
Iceland	8 000	592 000
Liechtenstein[2]		
Norway	218 000	708 000
Sweden	148 000	120 000
Switzerland	103 000	800

[1] figures included with Belgium. [2] figures included with Switzerland.

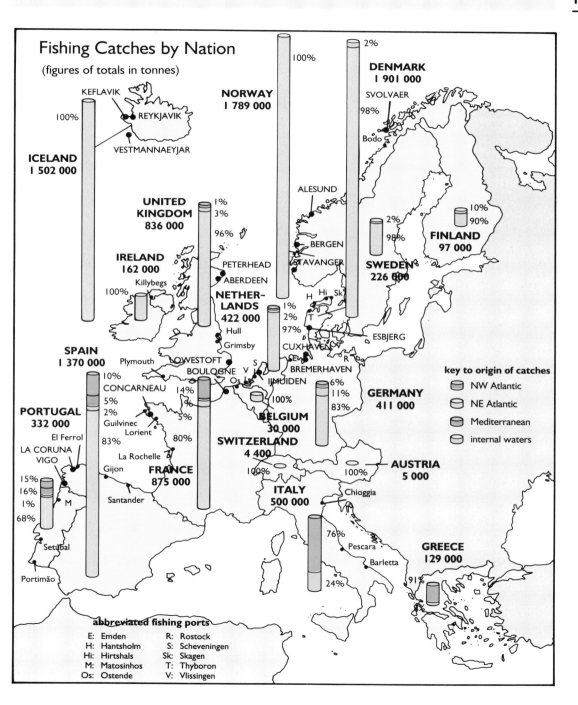

MONEY

Part of the Maastricht Treaty envisages an ever closer monetary union and an eventual single currency (see below and p. 19), but, in the meantime, the countries of Western Europe have their own national currencies.

CURRENCIES

BELGIUM
Unit: Belgian franc of 100 centimes.
Exchange rate: (November 1993) 1US$ = 36.77 Belgian francs.
Coins: 50 centimes, and 1, 5, 20 and 50 francs.
Notes: 100, 500, 1000, 5000 and 10 000 Belgian francs.
Bank of issue: Banque Nationale de Belgique (National Bank of Belgium), Brussels; founded 1850.

DENMARK
Unit: Danish krone (plur. kroner) of 100 ore.
Exchange rate: (November 1993) 1US$ = 6.81 Danish kroner.
Coins: 25 and 50 ore, and 1, 5, 10 and 20 kroner.
Notes: 50, 100, 500 and 1000 kroner.
Bank of issue: Danmarks Nationalbank (National Bank of Denmark), Copenhagen; founded 1818.

FRANCE
Unit: Franc of 100 centimes.
Exchange rate: (November 1993) 1US$ = 5.93 francs.
Coins: 2, 5, 10, and 20 centimes, and 1, 2, 5 and 10 francs.
Notes: 10, 20, 50, 100, 200 and 500 francs.
Bank of issue: Banque de France (Bank of France), Paris; founded 1800.

GERMANY
Unit: Deutschemark (DM) of 100 pfennig (plur. pfennige).
Exchange rate: (November 1993) 1US$ = 1.69 DM.
Coins: 1, 2, 5, 10 and 50 pfennige, and DM 1, 2 and 5.
Notes: DM 5, 10, 20, 50, 100, 200, 500 and 1000.
Bank of issue: Deutsche Bundesbank (German Federal Bank), Frankfurt; founded 1957.

GREECE
Unit: Drachma (which, in theory, is divided into 100 lepta although the smaller unit is no longer in use; plur. drachmai).
Exchange rate: (November 1993) 1US$ = 241.87 drachmai.
Coins: 1, 2, 5, 10, 20, 50 and 100 drachmai.
Notes: 500, 1000 and 5000 drachmai.
Bank of issue: Bank of Greece, Athens; founded 1928.

IRELAND
Unit: Irish pound or punt (IR£) of 100 pence.
Exchange rate: (November 1993) 1US$ = £IR 0.72.
Coins: 1, 2, 5, 10, 20 and 50 pence, and IR£1.
Notes: IR£5, 10, 20 and 50 notes.
Bank of issue: Bank Ceannais na hEireann (Central Bank of Ireland), Dublin; founded 1942.

ITALY
Unit: Lira (plur. lire).

Exchange rate: (November 1993) 1US$ = 1651.42 lire.
Coins: 5, 10, 20, 50, 100, 200 and 500 lire.
Notes: 1000, 2000, 5000, 10 000, 20 000, 50 000 and 100 000 lire.
Bank of issue: Banca d'Italia (Bank of Italy), Rome; founded 1893.

LUXEMBOURG
Unit: Luxembourg franc of 100 centimes. Belgian currency is also in circulation.
Exchange rate: (November 1993) 1US$ = 36.77 Luxembourg francs.
Coins: 1, 5, 20 and 50 Luxembourg francs; 50 Belgian centimes.
Notes: 100 and 1000 Luxembourg francs.
Bank of issue: Institut Monétaire Luxembourgeois (Luxembourg Monetary Institute), Luxembourg – the equivalent of a central bank; founded 1983.

THE NETHERLANDS
Unit: Gulden (fl.) of 100 cents.
Exchange rate: (November 1993) 1US$ = 1.90 fl.
Coins: 5, 10 and 25 cents, and 1, 2½ and 5 fl.
Notes: 10, 25, 50, 100, 250 and 1000 fl.
Bank of issue: De Nederlandsche Bank NV (The Netherlands Bank), Amsterdam; founded 1814.

PORTUGAL
Unit: Escudo (which, in theory, is divided into 100 centavos, although the smaller unit is no longer in use).
Exchange rate: (November 1993) 1US$ = 174.41 escudos.
Coins: ½, 1, 2½, 5, 10, 20, 25 and 50 escudos.
Notes: 100, 500, 1000 and 5000 escudos.
Bank of issue: Banco de Portugal (Bank of Portugal), Lisbon; founded 1846.

SPAIN
Unit: Peseta (which, in theory, is divided into 100 céntimos, although the smaller unit is no longer used).
Exchange rate: (November 1993) 1US$ = 135.28 pesetas.
Coins: 1, 2, 5, 10, 25, 50, 100, 200 and 500 pesetas.
Notes: 1000, 2000, 5000 and 10 000 pesetas.
Bank of issue: Banco de España (Bank of Spain), Madrid; founded 1829.

UNITED KINGDOM
Unit: pound (sterling) divided into 100 pence.
Exchange rate: (November 1993) 1US$ = £0.675.
Coins: 1p, 2p, 5p, 10p, 20p, 50p and £1.
Notes: (Bank of England) £5, £10, £25, and £50; (Scottish banks) £5, £10, £25, £50 and £100.
Bank of issue: Bank of England, London; founded 1694. In Scotland, notes are also issued by the Bank of Scotland, the Royal Bank of Scotland and the Clydesdale Bank.

AUSTRIA
Unit: Schilling of 100 Groschen.
Exchange rate: (November 1993) 1US$ = 11.91 Schilling.
Coins: 2, 5, 10, and 50 Groschen, and 1, 5, 10, 20, 25, 50, 500 and 1000 Schilling.
Notes: 20, 50, 100, 500, 1000 and 5000 Schilling.
Bank of issue: Osterreichische Nationalbank (national Bank of Austria), Vienna; founded 1922.

FINLAND
Unit: Markka (plur. markkaa) of 100 pennis (sing.

penni).
Exchange rate: (November 1993) 1US$ = 5.80 markkaa.
Coins: 10 and 50 pennis, and 1 and 5 markkaa.
Notes: 10, 50, 100, 500 and 1000 markkaa.
Bank of issue: Suomen Pankki (Bank of Finland), Helsinki; founded 1811.

ICELAND
Unit: Króna (plur. kronur) of 100 aurar (sing. eyrir).
Exchange rate: (November 1993) 1US$ = 71.57 kronur.
Coins: 10 and 15 aurar, and 1, 5, 10 and 50 kronur.
Notes: 100, 500, 1000 and 5000 kronur.
Bank of issue: Sedlabanki Islands (Central Bank of Iceland), Reykjavik; founded 1961.

LIECHTENSTEIN Uses Swiss currency (see below).

NORWAY
Unit: Norwegian krone (plur. kroner) of 100 ore.
Exchange rate: (November 1993) 1US$ = 7.38 kroner.
Coins: 10 and 50 ore, and 1, 5 and 10 kroner.
Notes: 50, 100, 500 and 1000 kroner.
Bank of issue: Norges Bank (Bank of Norway), Oslo; founded 1816.

SWEDEN
Unit: Krona (plur. kronor) of 100 öre.
Exchange rate: (November 1993) 1US$ = 8.20 kronor.
Coins: 10 and 50 öre, and 1 and 5 kronor.
Notes: 10, 20, 50, 100, 500 and 1000 kronor.
Bank of issue: Sveriges Riksbank (Swedish Central Bank), Stockholm; founded 1668.

SWITZERLAND
Unit: Swiss franc of 100 centimes or Rappen.
Exchange rate: (November 1993) 1US$ = 1.50 Swiss francs.
Coins: 5, 10, 20 and 50 centimes, and 1, 2 and 5 francs.
Notes: 10, 20, 50, 100, 500 and 1000 francs.
Bank of issue: Schweizerische Nationalbank/Banque nationale de Suisse (National Bank of Switzerland), Zürich and Berne; founded 1907.

STOCK EXCHANGES

Belgium Brussels (Société de la Bourse de Valeurs Mobilières de Bruxelles). There are also stock exchanges in Antwerp, Ghent, and Liège.

Denmark Copenhagen (Kobenhavns Fondsbors).

France Paris (La Bourse de Paris). There also stock exchanges in Bordeaux, Lille, Lyon, Marseille, Nancy, and Nantes.

Germany Frankfurt (Wertpapierbörse). There are also stock exchanges in Berlin, Bremen, Düsseldorf, Hamburg, Hannover, Munich, and Stuttgart.

Greece Athens Stock Exchange.

Ireland Dublin Stock Exchange. There is also a stock exchange in Cork.

Italy Milan (Borsa Valori). There are stock exchanges at Genoa, Naples, Rome, and Turin.

Luxembourg Luxembourg (Société de la Bourse de Luxembourg).

The Netherlands Amsterdam (Vereniging voor der Effectenhandel). There is also a stock exchange in Rotterdam.

Portugal Lisbon (Borsa de Valores de Lisboa). There is also a stock exchange in Oporto.

Spain Madrid (Bolsa de Madrid). There are also stock exchanges in Barcelona, Bilbao and Valencia.

UK London (The Stock Exchange). There are also stock exchanges at Aberdeen, Belfast, Birmingham, Bradford, Bristol, Cardiff, Glasgow, Manchester, and Newcastle.

Austria Vienna (Wiener Börsekammer).

Finland Helsinki Stock Exchange.

Iceland There is no stock exchange in Iceland.

Liechtenstein There is no stock exchange in Liechtenstein.

Norway Olso (Olso Bors). There are also stock exchanges in Alesund, Bergen, Drammen, Fredrikstad, Haugesund, Kristiansand, Kristiansund, Stavanger, and Trondheim.

Sweden Stockholm Stock Exchange.

Switzerland Zürich (Effektenbörsenverein and Bourse Suisse de Commerce). There are also stock exchanges in Basel, Berne and Geneva.

THE ERM AND THE ECU

The ERM (the Exchange Rate Mechanism) is an agreement between certain members of the EC to limit the movement of their currencies. It is not a totally fixed system: members agree a set of exchange rates against each other's currencies and a margin on either side of these *central rates* to allow for daily movements. Pressure on their currencies forced the exit of the UK and Italy from the ERM in September 1992. This was followed by a series of devaluations of the Spanish and Portuguese currencies. Economic uncertainty led to pressure on the Irish punt and the French franc in July 1993 that finally obliged the EC central banks' governors to widen ERM fluctuation margins to 15%. The result is now a vacuum at the heart of European monetary policy.

The ECU is a unit of account, based upon a basket of European currencies, used as a reserve asset in the ERM. ECU is an abbreviation for European Currency Unit; the écu was also a late medieval French coin. The ECU is widely envisaged as the eventual single European currency, and a limited number of ECU coins has already been made in Belgium, where they are legal tender. Commemmorative ECU coins have been issued in France, Ireland and Spain.

Maastricht outlined three stages towards monetary union. The first stage envisaged the 'convergence' of member states in monetary affairs. Currencies of member states were to be regulated through the ERM but the virtual collapse of that system in July 1993 has postponed monetary union. The second stage was the establishment of a central European bank. The first steps have been taken towards such a bank, which is to be situated in Frankfurt, Germany.

INDUSTRY AND PRODUCTION

The countries of Western Europe form one of the world's three major industrial blocs – the other two being North America (the USA and Canada) and East Asia (Japan, South Korea, China and Taiwan).

INDUSTRIAL REGIONS

Within the EEA a number of regions may be identified where industry is concentrated. The principal industrial regions include:
- the Ruhr (Germany), based originally upon a major coalfield. This region concentrates upon heavy industry but also has a share of modern high technology industries. The Ruhr includes the Essen conurbation which contains some 4 700 000 people.
- northern England, comprising six distinct industrial regions, most of which were originally coalfields (Merseyside based upon Liverpool, Greater Manchester, South Yorkshire based upon Sheffield, West Yorkshire based upon Leeds-Bradford, Teesside based upon Middlesbrough and Tyneside based upon Newcastle).
- northern France-southern Belgium, forming an almost continuous belt of industrial towns stretching from the old coalfields around Lens and Béthune in France, through Lille and Charleroi to Liège in Belgium.
- Lombardy and Piedmont (Italy), where cities such as Turin and Milan and their neighbours house a considerable part of Italian industry. The industrial heartland of Italy owes more to position – in easy contact with the rest of Europe – rather than to local raw materials.
- Catalonia (Spain), where Barcelona forms the heart of Spain's principal industrial region.
- Saxony (Germany), an historic industrial region which has suffered high levels of unemployment and decline since German reunification.
- West Midlands (England), where Birmingham, Coventry and Wolverhampton are the major centres within an industrial region that specializes in engineering.

Other major industrial regions include the following cities and their surroundings: London, Paris, Rotterdam, Glasgow, Hamburg, Munich, Frankfurt, Stuttgart, Madrid, Marseille, Antwerp, Amsterdam, Berlin, Copenhagen, Lisbon and Stockholm.

EC INDUSTRIAL POLICY

The earliest purpose of the Community was industrial cooperation. The European Coal and Steel Community (founded 1952) – and now part of the EC – removed trade barriers in coal, coke, iron and steel. Initially through the use of quotas, the steel industry was restructured and EC aid and loans have been awarded to regions in which workers in the steel and coal industries have lost their jobs. The coal industry, in particular, has declined: in the UK, for example, coal production has slumped owing to falling demand and overseas competition.

The European textile and shipbuilding industries have also been badly hit by competition. Some traditional European textile regions have almost stopped production, while in many ports the shipbuilding industry has ceased to exist. For example, the Swedish shipbuilding industry – once one of the largest in the world – has disappeared.

The growth industries, on the other hand, include electrical consumer goods and information technology. The EC has promoted a joint strategy concerning the latter.

Other important EC initiatives concern the harmonization of company law within the Community, the standardization of safety devices, labelling and technical matters, the liberalization of government procurement and regulations regarding the merger of large multi-national companies.

PRODUCTION

The figures below relate to production of major manufactures and mineral ores in EEA countries. Unless otherwise indicated, the figures are for 1990.

MANUFACTURING

ALUMINIUM

Country	Tonnes	% of world total
World	23 600 000	100.0%
Germany	1 335 000	5.6%
Norway	870 000	3.7%
Italy	610 000	2.6%
France	570 000	2.4%
UK	555 000	2.4%
Spain	430 000	1.8%
Greece	155 000	0.7%
Sweden	130 000	0.6%
Austria	130 000	0.6%
Switzerland	100 000	0.4%
Iceland	90 000	0.4%

CARS

Country	Number	% of world total
World	34 000 000	100.0%
Germany	4 620 000	13.6%
France	3 210 000	9.4%
Italy	1 970 000	5.8%
Spain	1 700 000	5.0%
UK	1 300 000	3.8%
Belgium	1 120 000	3.3%
Sweden	400 000	1.2%
Netherlands	135 000	0.4%
Portugal	90 000	0.3%

CEMENT

Country	Tonnes	% of world total
World	1 140 000 000	100.0%
Germany	40 000 000	3.5%

Italy	40 000 000	3.5%
Spain	28 100 000	2.5%
France	26 500 000	2.3%
UK	15 600 000	1.4%
Greece	14 000 000	1.2%
Belgium	6 900 000	0.6%
Portugal	6 000 000	0.6%
Switzerland	5 500 000	0.5%
Austria	4 900 000	0.4%
Netherlands	3 700 000	0.3%
Sweden	2 500 000	0.2%
Finland	1 670 000	0.1%
Denmark	1 660 000	0.1%
Ireland	1 320 000	0.1%
Norway	1 250 000	0.1%

COMMERCIAL VEHICLES

Country	Number	% of world total
World	14 000 000	100.0%
France	555 000	4.0%
Germany	350 000	2.5%
Spain	310 000	2.2%
UK	275 000	2.0%
Italy	245 000	1.8%
Sweden	70 000	0.5%
Portugal	60 000	0.4%
Netherlands	30 000	0.2%

COPPER

Country	Tonnes	% of world total
World	15 330 000	100.0%
Germany	750 000	4.9%
Belgium	335 000	2.2%
Italy	290 000	1.9%
UK	250 000	1.6%
Spain	205 000	1.3%
France	195 000	1.3%
Sweden	115 000	0.8%
Finland	55 000	0.4%
Norway	45 000	0.3%
Austria	45 000	0.3%

FERTILIZER (NITROGENOUS)

Country	Tonnes	% of world total
World	85 150 000	100.0%
Germany	2 300 000	2.7%
Netherlands	1 700 000	1.7%
France	1 450 000	1.5%
Italy	1 300 000	1.3%
UK	1 100 000	1.1%
Spain	960 000	1.1%
Belgium	700 000	0.8%
Greece	420 000	0.5%
Finland	295 000	0.3%
Ireland	270 000	0.3%
Austria	230 000	0.3%
Portugal	170 000	0.2%
Sweden	170 000	0.2%

FERTILIZER (PHOSPHATES)

Country	Tonnes	% of world total
World	41 550 000	100.0%
France	940 000	2.3%
Germany	640 000	1.5%
Spain	440 000	1.0%
Italy	410 000	1.0%
Netherlands	370 000	0.9%
Belgium	330 000	0.8%
Greece	260 000	0.6%
UK	250 000	0.6%
Finland	220 000	0.5%
Norway	200 000	0.5%
Denmark	130 000	0.3%
Austria	110 000	0.3%
Sweden	110 000	0.3%

IRON AND FERRO-ALLOYS

Country	Tonnes	% of world total
World	506 000 000	100.0%
Germany	32 725 000	6.5%
France	14 410 000	2.9%
UK	12 490 000	2.8%
Italy	12 000 000	2.4%
Belgium	9 420 000	1.9%
Spain	6 000 000	1.2%
Netherlands	4 960 000	1.0%
Austria	3 440 000	0.7%
Sweden	2 740 000	0.5%
Luxembourg	2 730 000	0.5%
Finland	2 280 000	0.5%
Norway	900 000	0.2%
Portugal	360 000	0.1%

LEAD

Country	Tonnes	% of world total
World	5 830 000	100.0%
Germany	800 000	8.6%
UK	350 000	6.0%
France	270 000	4.6%
Italy	180 000	3.0%
Spain	115 000	2.0%
Belgium	95 000	1.6%
Sweden	72 000	1.2%
Netherlands	42 000	0.7%
Austria	22 000	0.4%
Ireland	12 000	0.2%

NICKEL

Country	Tonnes	% of world total
World	865 000	100.0%
Norway	55 000	6.4%
UK	26 000	3.0%
Greece	16 000	1.8%
Finland	13 000	1.5%
France	10 000	1.2%
Austria	3 000	0.3%
Germany	3 000	0.3%

PETROLEUM PRODUCTS

Country	Tonnes	% of world total
World	2 860 000 000	185 000
Germany	96 000 000	3.4%
UK	81 000 000	2.8%
Italy	77 200 000	2.7%
France	68 000 000	2.4%
Netherlands	55 000 000	1.9%
Spain	46 000 000	1.6%
Belgium	24 000 000	0.8%
Sweden	15 500 000	0.5%
Greece	15 000 000	0.5%
Norway	9 800 000	0.3%
Portugal	9 400 000	0.3%
Denmark	8 000000	0.3%
Finland	8 000 000	0.3%

RADIO SETS

Country	Number	% of world total
World	105 700 000	100.0%
Germany	6 400 000	6.0%
France	2 080 000	2.0%
Portugal	1 190 000	1.1%
Belgium	1 160 000	1.1%
UK	400 000	0.3%

RUBBER (SYNTHETIC)

Country	Tonnes (1989–90)	% of world total
World	7 000 000	100.0%
Germany	680 000	9.7%
France	520 000	7.4%
Italy	295 000	4.2%
UK	295 000	4.2%
Netherlands	235 000	3.4%
Belgium	120 000	1.7%
Spain	80 000	0.8%
Finland	30 000	0.4%

SHIPBUILDING

Country	Tonnes	% of world total
World	14 700 000	100.0%
Germany	865 000	5.9%
Denmark	405 000	2.8%
Spain	380 000	2.6%
Italy	350 000	2.4%
Netherlands	160 000	1.1%
Finland	160 000	1.1%
France	110 000	0.8%
Norway	80 000	0.5%
UK	75 000	0.5%
Belgium	55 000	0.4%
Portugal	25 000	0.2%

STEEL

Country	Tonnes	% of world total
World	685 000 000	100.0%
Germany	45 600 000	6.7%
Italy	25 000 000	3.7%
UK	18 000 000	2.6%
France	16 800 000	2.5%
Spain	12 000 000	1.8%
Belgium	11 425 000	1.7%
Netherlands	5 410 000	0.8%
Austria	4 560 000	0.7%
Sweden	4 450 000	0.6%
Luxembourg	3 480 000	0.5%
Finland	2 855 000	0.4%
Switzerland	1 000 000	0.1%
Greece	960 000	0.1%

TELEVISION SETS

Country	Number	% of world total
World	100 600 000	100.0%
Germany	4 205 000	4.2%
UK	3 020 000	3.0%
Italy	2 330 000	2.3%
France	2 185 000	2.2%
Spain	1 300 000	1.3%
Belgium	920 000	0.9%
Finland	625 000	0.6%
Austria	570 000	0.6%
Portugal	485 000	0.5%
Sweden	350 000	0.3%
Denmark	110 000	0.1%

TYRES

Country	Number (1988–90)	% of world total
World	950 000 000	100.0%
France	61 400 000	6.5%
Germany	57 100 000	6.0%
Italy	45 000 000	4.7%
UK	30 000 000	3.2%
Spain	20 000 000	2.1%
Finland	20 000 000	2.1%
Portugal	3 400 000	0.4%
Sweden	2 600 000	0.3%

ZINC

Country	Tonnes	% of world total
World	8 570 000	100.0%
Germany	480 000	5.6%
Belgium	310 000	3.6%
France	295 000	3.4%
Spain	260 000	3.0%
Italy	250 000	2.9%
Netherlands	200 000	2.3%
Finland	165 000	1.9%
UK	125 000	1.5%
Norway	120 000	1.4%
Austria	27 000	0.3%
Sweden	8 000	0.1%
Portugal	5 000	0.1%

MINERALS

Although, with relatively few exceptions, the countries of Western Europe are not major producers of minerals, many of the following products are important in the economies of individual states.

BAUXITE

Country	Tonnes	% of world total
World	106 600 000	100.0%
Greece	2 575 000	2.4%
France	720 000	0.7%

CHROMIUM ORE

Country	Tonnes	% of world total
World	12 000 000	100.0%
Finland	450 000	3.8%
Greece	65 000	0.5%

COAL

See Energy, p. 111.

COAL (lignite/brown coal)

See Energy, p. 111.

COPPER ORE

Country	Tonnes	% of world total
World	9 130 000	100.0%
Portugal	103 000	1.1%
Sweden	70 000	0.8%
Spain	28 000	0.3%
Norway	20 000	0.2%
Finland	15 000	0.2%

IRON ORE

Country	Tonnes	% of world total
World	965 000 000	100.0%
Sweden	13 000 000	1.4%
France	2 600 000	0.3%
Spain	2 300 000	0.2%
Norway	1 300 000	0.1%
Austria	700 000	0.1%

LEAD ORE

Country	Tonnes	% of world total
World	3 340 000	100.0%
Sweden	82 000	2.5%
Spain	65 000	2.0%
Ireland	32 000	1.0%
Greece	25 000	0.7%
Italy	15 000	0.4%
Germany	9 000	0.3%
Norway	3 000	0.1%

MAGNESITE

Country	Tonnes	% of world total
World	20 000 000	100.0%
Austria	1 100 000	5.5%
Greece	800 000	4.0%
Spain	450 000	2.3%

MERCURY

Country	Tonnes	% of world total
World	5 540	100.0%
Spain	715	12.9%
Finland	100	1.8%

NATURAL GAS

See Energy, p. 111.

NICKEL ORE

Country	Tonnes	% of world total
World	865 000	100.0%
Greece	16 000	1.9%
Finland	11 000	1.3%
Germany	1 500	0.2%
Norway	1 300	0.2%

OIL

See Energy, p. 111.

SILVER

Country	Tonnes	% of world total
World	14 650	100.0%
Spain	250	1.7%
Sweden	200	1.7%
Germany	70	0.5%
Greece	60	0.4%
Finland	30	0.2%

TIN ORE

Country	Tonnes	% of world total
World	223 000	100.0%
UK	4 000	1.8%
Spain	2 000	0.9%
Germany	2 000	0.9%

URANIUM

Country	Tonnes	% of world total
World	65 000	100.0%
Germany	3 000	8.1%
France	2 800	7.6%
Spain	150	0.2%
Portugal	100	0.2%

ZINC ORE

Country	Tonnes	% of world total
World	7 140 000	100.0%
Spain	265 000	3.7%
Ireland	170 000	2.4%
Sweden	170 000	2.4%
Germany	65 000	0.9%
Finland	60 000	0.8%
Italy	45 000	0.6%
Greece	25 000	0.4%

ENERGY

EC activities in the realm of energy began with the establishment of the European Coal and Steel Community (ECSC) in 1952 and continued with the beginning of the European Atomic Energy Community (Euratom) in 1958.

EURATOM

Euratom encouraged the development of nuclear energy in the Community. It encouraged research and the exchange of information and established common procedures throughout the Community's nuclear industry. Euratom also introduced a common market for nuclear fuels in 1959. The Joint Research Centre conducts research on nuclear safety and the management of radioactive waste.

EC ENERGY POLICY

The Community has striven to develop an overall energy policy. The EC introduced its *internal energy market* in 1990. This encourages the sale of both gas and electricity across the Community's internal borders and coordinates investment in energy within EC member-states. The Community has also worked to reduce levels of the emission of the so-called 'greenhouse gases', in particular carbon dioxide, which are responsible for global warming. The Community is also studying plans to introduce an energy tax.

The principal aims of the present European Community energy initiatives covering the decade 1985–95 are:
- to reduce the dependence upon oil to 40% of overall Community energy requirements;
- to reduce the importation of oil into the Community to 30% of overall Community energy requirements;
- to reduce the proportion of electricity generated by oil-burning power stations to 15% of the electricity consumed within the Community;
- to improve energy efficiency by 20%;
- to increase the use of new sources of energy; and
- to encourage the use of renewable sources of energy throughout the Community.

JET

The JET (Joint European Torus) is an experimental thermonuclear machine which has been developed to pioneer new processes of nuclear fusion. JET members include all European Community member-states plus Sweden and Switzerland.

COAL

The coalfields of Western Europe were one of the resources upon which the Industrial Revolution was based. Typically, the older coalfields are the site of major industrial towns and heavy industry. However, these coalfields are no longer able to compete with imported coal from Poland, the USA, Vietnam and other producers. Coal produced from the Ruhr in Germany, for example, sells for three times the price of coal offered on the world market. British coal, too, is expensive when compared with imports. The result is a dramatic contraction of the industry throughout Western Europe.

The principal remaining coalfields are:

In Belgium The Sambre-Meuse coalfield in Wallonia, which was the basis of much of Belgium's industry, has now ceased production. The remaining coalfield is in Kempenland on the borders of Limburg and Antwerp provinces.

France The principal remaining coalfield in France is the Nord field which is based upon Lens, Béthune, Douai and Valenciennes. A handful of smaller coalfields produce a significant amount of coal.

Germany Based upon Essen and its neighbours, the large Ruhr coalfield is the base of Germany's largest industrial region. Coal production has gradually moved north to the concealed field in the Lippe valley but production has fallen dramatically as, without the use of subsidies, German coal has been unable to compete with imports. Lignite is important in central and eastern Germany, in particular in the states of Saxony and Saxony-Anhalt. These lignite fields were greatly developed by the government of the former East Germany.

Italy Northern Italy produces a small amount of lignite.

Spain Spanish coal mining is now confined to the north, largely in the Leon-Oviedo coalfield. Production fell by one half between 1989 and 1991. Lignite production exceeds that of bituminous coal.

UK The British coal mining industry is sharply declining. The labour force of the industry was reduced by one half between October 1992 and October 1993. Only 19 pits remain open – one each in South Wales, Scotland and Northumberland, two in the West Midlands and 14 in the Yorkshire-Nottinghamshire field.

Norway Norway's small coal mining industry is confined to the Arctic archipelago of Svalbard.

COAL (BITUMINOUS)

Country	Tonnes	% of world total
World	3 560 000 000	100.0%
UK	70 000 000	1.8%
Germany	66 400 000	1.7%
France	11 000 000	0.3%
Spain	8 600 000	0.2%
Belgium	635 000	
Norway	300 000	
Portugal	220 000	

COAL (LIGNITE/BROWN COAL)

Country	Tonnes	% of world total
World	1 175 000 000	100.0%
Germany	360 000 000	30.6%
Greece	52 000 000	4.4%
Spain	21 300 000	1.8%
Austria	2 500 000	0.2%
France	2 100 000	0.2%
Italy	1 500 000	0.1%

NATURAL GAS

Several of the countries of Western Europe have important reserves of natural gas, both inland and beneath the continental shelf, in particular in the North Sea.

Denmark The production of natural gas from the Danish sector of the North Sea and from the Jutland peninsula is economically important.

France The most important centres for the production of natural gas in France are Parentis-Lacq in Aquitaine and Fuveau in southern France.

Germany The greater part of Germany's natural gas is produced in the Weser and Ems valleys and the Hannover region of Lower Saxony and from the Halle and Cottbus areas in eastern Germany.

Ireland The Kinsale Head gasfield, off the southern coast of Ireland, meets all of Ireland's natural gas requirements.

Italy The production of natural gas in Italy is concentrated in Umbria and Tuscany.

Netherlands Natural gas has been produced in the northeastern provinces of the Netherlands in economically important quantities for the past four decades. The Groningen field is the most significant Dutch field and the largest field in Western Europe.

Spain The Utrillas field in eastern Spain is the most important source of natural gas in the country.

UK Apart from small, but significant, gasfields on the mainland, most of the British production of natural gas comes from the North Sea.

Norway The Norwegian sector of the North Sea is a major producer of natural gas. The Frigg and Ekofisk fields are the most important. Exploration for natural gas is being undertaken in Svalbard.

Country	cubic metres	% of world total
World	1 960 000 000 000	100.0%
Netherlands	81 660 000 000	3.3%
UK	49 000 000 000	2.6%
Norway	27 280 000 000	1.6%
Italy	16 910 000 000	0.9%
Germany	13 500 000 000	0.8%
Denmark	3 750 000 000	0.2%
France	3 690 000 000	0.2%
Ireland	1 600 000 000	0.1%
Austria	1 330 000 000	0.1%
Spain	1 310 000 000	0.1%

OIL

Denmark Oil production from the Danish sector of the North Sea makes a significant contribution to the economy of a country with few natural resources.

France The Parentis-Lacq field in Aquitaine is the most important French oilfield.

Germany Oil production in Germany, in significant quantities, is limited to the Weser-Ems region of Lower Saxony.

Greece Offshore oilfields in the northern Aegean are responsible for Greece's small but growing domestic production.

Italy Commercial oil production in Italy is virtually restricted to the Gela-Ragusa field in Sicily.

Netherlands Dutch oil production comes from the Groningen area.

Spain Spanish oil production is growing and maritime exploration for reserves continues.

UK At the start of the 1990s the UK was virtually self-sufficient in oil from the North Sea, although production is expected to begin to decline. The largest fields are Brent, Forties, Ninian and Piper.

Austria There has been small-scale commercial oil production in northern Austria – which also produces natural gas – for the past six decades.

Norway Since Norway's first oil well in the North Sea was drilled in 1966 the country has become a major oil producer. North Sea oil accounts for about 12% of Norway's GDP. The most important field is the Frigg field.

Country	Tonnes	% of world total
World	3 150 000 000	100.0%
Norway	102 600 000	3.6%
UK	94 200 000	3.1%
Denmark	7 600 000	0.2%
Italy	4 600 000	0.1%
Germany	3 700 000	0.1%
Netherlands	3 500 000	0.1%
France	3 100 000	0.1%
Austria	1 200 000	
Spain	1 100 000	
Greece	600 000	

ELECTRICITY PRODUCTION

Some West European countries, such as France, rely heavily upon nuclear power to produce electricity. Coal-burning power stations used to be the basis of electricity generation in countries such as Britain, but gas-fired power stations have become increasingly popular. Other countries such as Sweden and Switzerland – which have many fast-flowing rivers – rely largely upon HEP and are able to export electricity.

Country	kwh p.a.
Germany	562 800 000 000
France	398 600 000 000
UK	318 990 000 000
Italy	216 890 000 000
Spain	157 200 000 000
Sweden	142 580 000 000
Norway	121 850 000 000
Netherlands	74 550 000 000
Belgium	68 130 000 000
Switzerland	54 100 000 000
Finland	53 390 000 000
Austria	50 480 000 000
Ireland	39 200 000 000
Denmark	32 960 000 000
Greece	31 870 000 000
Portugal	25 800 000 000
Iceland	4 430 000 000
Luxembourg	1 390 000 000
Liechtenstein	53 800 000

FOREIGN TRADE

The leading import and export commodities and the major trading partners for EEA countries are given.

BELGIUM

Imports: 3 842 477 000 000 Belgian francs (1991) – chemicals (11.5%), road vehicles/parts (9.9%), petroleum (6.0%), diamonds (5.4%), electrical machinery (4.7%). Trading partners for imports: Germany (23.5%), Netherlands (17.2%), France (15.8%), UK (8.4%), USA (4.8%), Italy (4.5%). *Exports:* 3 746 929 000 000 Belgian francs (1991) – road vehicles/parts (15.1%), chemicals (13.8%), diamonds (12.5%), iron and steel (7.0%), textiles/yarn (5.2%). Trading partners for exports: Germany (23.2%), France (18.6%), Netherlands (13.3%), UK (7.6%), Italy (5.9%), USA (3.7%).

DENMARK

Imports: 205 871 000 000 kroners (1991) – industrial machinery (9.9%), road vehicles/parts (5.8%), petroleum/ petroleum products (5.1%), office machinery (4.6%), transport equipment (4.6%). Trading partners for imports: Germany (22.1%), Sweden (10.9%), UK (8.0%), USA (6.3%), France (6.2%), Netherlands (5.7%), Norway (5.6%). *Exports:* 228 549 000 000 kroners (1991) – meat/meat products (9.7%), fish (5.9%), furniture (4.2%), industrial machinery (4.2%), dairy products (3.7%), medica/ pharmaceutical products (3.6%). Trading partners for exports: Germany (22.5%), Sweden (11.5%), the USA (10.3%), France (5.9%), Norway (5.5%).

FRANCE

Imports: 1 266 788 700 000 francs (1991) – chemicals (10.7%), road vehicles/parts (9.4%), industrial machines (7.6%), petroleum (7.3%), general electrical apparatus (5.1%), office machinery (4.3%). Trading partners for imports: Germany (18.8%), Italy (11.6%), Belgium and Luxembourg (8.8%), USA (8.2%), UK (7.2%), Netherlands (5.1%), Spain (4.7%). *Exports:* 1 142 183 000 000 francs (1991) – chemicals (13.5%), road vehicles/parts (11.9%), industrial machinery (7.3%), electrical machinery (5.3%), iron and steel (4.3%), power generating machinery (3.7%), cereals (3.7%), wine (3.7%). Trading partners for exports: Germany (17.2%), Italy (11.4%), UK (9.5%), Belgium and Luxembourg (9.5%), Spain (6.3%), USA (6.1%), Netherlands (5.6%).

GERMANY

Imports: 643 914 000 000 DM (1991) – road vehicles/parts (10.2%), chemicals (8.4%), food/live animals (8.3%), petroleum (6.2%), clothing (6.2%), industrial machinery (5.6%), electrical apparatus (5.3%). Trading partners for imports: France (12.2%), Netherlands (9.7%), Italy (9.3%), Belgium and Luxembourg (7.1%), UK (6.6%), USA (6.6%), Japan (6.1%). *Exports:* 665 813 500 000 DM (1991) – road vehicles/parts (15.4%), industrial machinery (13.1%), chemicals (12.7%), general electrical apparatus (7.1%), iron and steel (3.6%), textiles, fabric and yarn (3.3%). Trading partners for exports: France (13.1%), Italy (9.2%), Netherlands (8.4%), UK (7.6%), Belgium and Luxembourg (7.3%), USA (6.2%), Austria (5.9%).

GREECE

Imports: 3 921 522 000 000 drachmae (1991) – road vehicles/ parts (11.1%), chemicals (10.4%), petroleum (9.1%), industrial machinery (7.0%), general transport equipment (5.9%), textiles, fabric and yarn (5.5%). Trading partners for imports: Germany (19.4%), Italy (14.2%), France (7.8%), Japan (6.6%), Netherlands (6.0%), UK (5.4%). *Exports:* 1 579 967 000 000 drachmae (1991) – clothing (20.2%), vegetables/fruit (13.7%), petroleum/petroleum products (8.6%), textiles, fabric and yarn (6.2%), iron and steel (4.7%), tobacco (4.5%). Trading partners for exports: Germany (23.9%), Italy (16.7%), France (7.5%), UK (6.8%), USA (5.7%), Netherlands (3.4%), Cyprus (2.9%).

IRELAND

Imports: IR£12 853 384 000 (1991) – chemicals/related products (13.3%), office machinery (9.1%), general electrical apparatus (7.8%), industrial machinery (6.2%), road vehicles/ parts (5.2%). Trading partners for imports: UK (41.4%), USA (15.0%), Germany (8.2%), Japan (5.0%), Netherlands (4.4%), France (4.4%). *Exports:* –IR£15 024 639 000 (1991) – chemicals/related products (17.7%), office machinery (16.5%), general electrical apparatus (7.0%), meat/meat preparations (5.9%), dairy products (4.1%). Trading partners for exports: UK (31.9%), Germany (12.7%), France (9.5%), USA (8.7%), Netherlands (6.6%), Belgium and Luxembourg (4.9%).

ITALY

Imports: 225 769 800 000 000 lire (1991) – industrial machinery (18.5%), chemicals (11.0%), road vehicles/parts (10.4%), petroleum (8.4%), iron and steel (3.3%), textiles (3.2%). Trading partners for imports: Germany (20.9%), France (14.2%), Netherlands (5.7%), UK (5.7%), USA (5.6%), Belgium and Luxembourg (4.9%), Switzerland (4.4%). *Exports:* 209 746 500 000 000 lire (1991) – industrial machinery (27.5%), road vehicles/parts (8.1%), clothing (6.9%), chemicals (6.7%), food/live animals (5.6%), textiles (5.5%). Trading partners for exports: Germany (21.0%), France (15.2%), USA (6.9%), UK (6.7%), Spain (5.1%), Switzerland (4.2%), Belgium and Luxembourg (3.4%).

LUXEMBOURG

Imports: 277 110 000 000 Luxembourg francs – machinery/ electrical apparatus (18.7%), transport equipment/road vehicles (14.2%), base metals/manufactures (14.1%), mineral products/petroleum (11.9%). Trading partners for imports: Belgium (39.2%), Germany (30.0%), France (11.9%), Netherlands (4.1%). *Exports:* 214 353 000 000 Luxembourg francs (1991) – base metals/manufactures including iron and steel (35.5%), machinery/electrical apparatus (12.7%), plastics (12.6%). Trading partners for exports: Germany (29.6%), France (17.3%), Belgium (17.1%), Netherlands (5.1%), UK (5.1%).

THE NETHERLANDS

Imports: 236 565 000 000 guilders (1991) – electrical and non-electrical machinery (22.6%), chemicals (10.5%), petroleum (8.0%), road vehicles/parts (7.6%), clothing (4.1%). Trading partners for imports: Germany (25.6%), Belgium and Luxembourg (14.2%), UK (8.7%), USA (8.1%), France (7.6%), Italy (3.7%), Japan (3.7%). *Exports:* 249 051 000 000 guilders (1991) – electrical and non-electrical machinery

(17.9%), chemicals (16.1%), petroleum/petroleum products (6.5%), transport equipment/road vehicles (5.7%), fruit/vegetables (4.3%). Trading partners for exports: Germany (29.4%), Belgium and Luxembourg (14.3%), France (10.7%), UK (9.3%), Italy (6.4%), USA (3.9%).

PORTUGAL

Imports: 4 048 797 000 000 escudos (1991) – road vehicles/parts (15.3%), chemicals (8.9%), industrial machinery (8.4%), petroleum (7.0%), textiles, fabric and yarn (6.4%), general electric apparatus (4.3%). Trading partners for imports: Spain (16.6%), Germany (15.0%), France (12.8%), Italy (10.2%), UK (7.1%), Netherlands (6.9%). *Exports:* 2 453 041 000 000 escudos (1991) – clothing (21.2%), footwear (8.8%), road vehicles/parts (6.5%), electrical machinery (5.6%), cork/wood manufactures (4.4%), chemicals (4.2%). Trading partners for exports: Germany (19.2%), Spain (14.7%), France (14.2%), UK (10.1%), Netherlands (5.4%), Angola (4.5%).

SPAIN

Imports: 8 898 365 600 000 pesetas (1991) – electrical and non-electrical machinery (24.8%), petroleum (11.9%), road vehicles/parts (10.8%), chemicals (7.9%), textiles (4.5%). Trading partners for imports: Germany (17.6%), France (16.5%), Italy (10.9%), USA (8.7%), UK (8.2%), Japan (5.1%), Netherlands (3.8%). *Exports:* 5 630 558 600 000 pesetas (1991) – road vehicles/parts (19.6%), electrical and non-electrical machinery (15.5%), fruit/vegetables (7.6%), chemicals (6.0%), general electrical apparatus (5.0%). Trading partners for exports: France (22.1%), Germany (17.6%), Italy (12.6%), UK (8.5%), Portugal (7.3%), USA (5.4%).

UNITED KINGDOM

Imports: £118 786 000 000 (1991) – chemicals (9.2%), food/live animals (8.7%), road vehicles/parts (8.6%), office machinery (6.4%), industrial machinery (6.0%), general electrical apparatus (6.0%). Trading partners for imports: Germany (16.8%), USA (11.5%), France (9.3%), Netherlands (8.4%), Japan (5.7%), Italy (5.4%), Belgium and Luxembourg (4.6%). *Exports:* £104 877 000 000 (1991) – chemicals/chemical products (13.1%), industrial machinery (8.8%), road vehicles/parts (8.2%), petroleum/petroleum products (6.5%), office machinery (6.3%), general electrical apparatus (5.4%). Trading partners for exports: Germany (12.6%), France (11.1%), USA (10.8%), Netherlands (7.9%), Italy (5.9%), Belgium and Luxembourg (5.6%), Ireland (5.1%).

AUSTRIA

Imports: 591 898 400 000 Schillings (1991) – road vehicles/parts (12.0%), industrial machinery (9.7%), clothing (4.8%), office machinery (3.9%), petroleum (3.7%), textiles, yarn, fabric (3.7%). Trading partners for imports: Germany (43.0%), Italy (8.8%), Japan (4.8%), France (4.4%), Switzerland (4.2%), USA (3.9%). *Exports:* 479 029 100 000 Schillings (1991) – industrial machinery (12.2%), chemicals (8.9%), paper (6.2%), road vehicles/parts (5.6%), iron and steel (5.6%). Trading partners for exports: Germany (39.0%), Italy (9.4%), Switzerland (6.4%), France (4.3%), UK (3.6%), Hungary (3.0%), Netherlands (3.0%).

FINLAND

Imports: 87 744 000 000 markkaa (1991) – electrical and non-electrical machinery (24.7%), chemicals (11.6%), petrol-eum (9.5%), road vehicles/parts (7.7%). Trading partners for imports: Germany (16.9%), Sweden (12.3%), Russia (8.4%), UK (7.7%), USA (6.9%), Japan (6.0%). *Exports:* 92 841 600 000 markkaa (1991) – paper, paperboard and manufactures (28.1%), electrical and non-electrical machinery (20.7%), chemicals (6.9%), transport equipment (6.8%), iron and steel (6.3%). Trading partners for exports: Germany (15.4%), Sweden (13.9%), UK (10.4%), USA (6.1%), France (5.9%), Netherlands (5.0%), Russia (4.9%).

ICELAND

Imports: 104 129 000 000 kronur (1991) – machinery/transport equipment (35.7%), manufactured goods (17.1%), petroleum (8.1%), chemicals (8.1%), food/live animals (7.1%). Trading partners for imports: Germany (12.7%), USA (12.6%), Netherlands (9.8%), Denmark (8.4%), UK (8.0%), Sweden (7.4%). *Exports:* 91 560 000 000 kronur – fish/fish products (79.4%), aluminium (8.8%). Trading partners for exports: UK (23.4%), USA (12.6%), Germany (12.1%), France (10.1%), Japan (7.9%), Spain (4.9%).

LIECHTENSTEIN

Imports: included with those of Switzerland, see below.
Exports: 2 246 100 000 Swiss francs (1991).

NORWAY

Imports: 165 181 200 000 kroner (1991) – transport equipment/road vehicles (15.2%), industrial machinery (9.3%), chemicals (8.9%), food/live animals (5.2%), general electrical apparatus (5.2%). Trading partners for imports: Sweden (15.3%), Germany (14.1%), UK (8.7%), Denmark (7.3), USA (7.3%), Netherlands (5.3%). *Exports:* 220 316 300 000 kroner (1991) – petroleum/petroleum products (40.3%), natural gas (8.3%), transport equipment (mainly maritime) (7.7%), non-ferrous metals (7.6%), fish (6.5%), chemicals (6.3%). Trading partners for exports: UK (26.5%), Germany (11.1%), Sweden (10.3%), Netherlands (7.9%), France (7.5%), Denmark (5.6%), USA (4.7%).

SWEDEN

Imports: 289 923 000 000 kroner (1991) – chemicals (10.6%), road vehicles/parts (7.8%), petroleum (7.6%), food/live animals (6.1%), clothing (5.3%). Trading partners for imports: Germany (18.5%), USA (8.7%), UK (8.6%), Denmark (7.8%), Norway (6.9%), Finland (6.2%), France (5.1%). *Exports:* 326 008 000 000 kroner (1991) – road vehicles/parts (13.1%), paper/paperboard (11.2%), chemicals (9.2%), wood pulp/waste paper (8.1%), iron and steel (5.7%), telecommunications equipment (4.8%). Trading partners for exports: Germany (15.0%), UK (9.7%), Norway (8.4%), USA (8.3%), Denmark (7.2%), France (5.8%), Netherlands (5.6%).

SWITZERLAND

Imports: 95 031 800 000 Swiss francs (1991) – electrical/non-electrical machinery (19.9%), road vehicles/parts (6.4%), clothing (5.4%), chemicals (5.0%), petroleum (3.6%). Trading partners for imports: Germany (32.8%), France (10.9%), Italy (10.0%), USA (7.3%), UK (5.5%), Japan (4.3%), Netherlands (4.1%). *Exports:* 87 946 500 000 Swiss francs (1991) – electric and non-electric machinery (13.8%), chemicals (10.4%), precision instruments/clocks and watches (6.4%), textiles/clothing (2.5%). Trading partners for exports: Germany (11.4%), France (4.6%), Italy (4.2%), USA (3.9%), UK (3.2%), Japan (2.1%), Austria (2.0%).

TRADE FAIRS

Trade fairs play an important part in the economic life of the countries of Western Europe. Some trade fairs are open to the general public; others are specialized events with access only to the trade.

Trade and other exhibitions are increasing in importance and every major West European city has centres either used or adapted for exhibitions or purpose-built halls.

The most important trade fairs held in the countries of the EEA include the following:

Belgium
Brussels holds 25 or more major trade fairs each year at the Foire Internationale de Bruxelles. Ghent holds several annual trade fairs at the International Fair of Flanders.

Denmark
Copenhagen stages several large trade fairs each year.

France
With the exception of the exhibitions held in Paris (which attract very large attendances), French trade fairs tend to be smaller than their counterparts in Germany, Italy and Britain. Other important French trade fairs and exhibitions are held in Lyon, Bordeaux, Grenoble, Lille, Marseille, Metz, Strasbourg and Toulouse.

Germany
There are over 80 major annual German trade fairs held in centres in all parts of the country. The most notable German international trade fair is held each spring at Leipzig, which stages a total of about 20 international and national fairs. The principal exhibition centres of the former West Germany are Hamburg (the Ernst-Merck-Halle centre) and Hannover, which has staged the annual German Industries Fair (now known as the Hannover Fair) since 1947. Berlin, Munich and Stuttgart all have several venues staging important trade fairs and exhibitions. Specialized trade fairs include those held at Nürnberg (an international toy fair) and Offenbach (leather goods), while Frankfurt (which is famous for its book fair) has held international trade fairs since 1240. Other large trade exhibitions are staged at Cologne, Düsseldorf, Essen, Friedrichshafen, Saarbrücken and Wiesbaden.

Greece
The major trade exhibition in Greece is the Helexpo general trade fair which is held annually in Thessalonika.

Italy
The Fiera Campionaria de Milano – staged in Milan – is one of the major trade exhibitions in Europe. Bari holds the annual Fiera del Levante (a large Occidental-Oriental trade fair) and the International Agriculture and Horse Fair in Bologna is one of the largest of its type in the continent. Other major trade fairs in Italy are held

at Turin, Verona and Genoa. Trade fairs are also staged at Bolzano, Florence, Padua, Palermo, Parma, Rimini, Rome and Vicenza.

Netherlands
Utrecht stages a number of major trade fairs including the Royal Dutch Industries Fair. Amsterdam also stages important trade exhibitions.

Portugal
Lisbon and Braga are the venues of the most important trade fairs in Portugal.

Spain
The Feria de Barcelona is one of the principal trade fairs of Europe. Building on the success of the World Trade Fair, which was held in 1992, Seville has joined Barcelona and Madrid as one of the major Spanish exhibition centres. Bilbao and Valencia also stage important trade fairs.

United Kingdom
The National Exhibition Centre in Birmingham has attracted some of the major trade exhibitions that were formerly held in London. However, London retains a considerable number of important exhibition venues. Other major centres for trade fairs and exhibitions include Liverpool, Glasgow, Manchester and Bristol. Stoneleigh, near Coventry, stages the largest agricultural trade fair.

Austria
Vienna stages three general major fairs that are open to the public and two dozen other exhibitions, while Wels holds biennial agricultural fairs. Ried holds agricultural and leisure fairs in alternate years.

Finland
A variety of important international trade fairs are held at the Helsinki Fair Centre.

Norway
Oslo is the principal centre for trade fairs in Norway.

Sweden
The Malmö trade fair is the most important trade exhibition in Sweden. Both Stockholm and Gothenburg also stage a number of trade fairs during the year.

Switzerland
Switzerland takes advantage of its central position within Western Europe to stage a number of successful trade fairs including the Swiss Industries Fair (in Basel), the National Fair (in Lausanne) and the Swiss Agricultural and Dairy Farming Fair (in St Gallen). Zürich is also the venue of a number of important trade fairs.

key to map on opposite page

● Trade fairs that attract over 2 000 000 visitors per year

● Trade fairs that attract over 1 000 000 visitors per year

● Trade fairs that attract over 500 000 visitors per year

• Other important trade fairs

Trade Fairs

MAJOR COMPANIES

In the 1980s and 1990s the trend has been towards a more integrated world economy and the growth of multinational companies. The top 100 multinational companies are thought to account for almost one fifth of the world's productive assets and a greater proportion of world trade. Many of the largest multinational firms are based in the USA or Japan but a growing number are based in Western Europe. The diagram (opposite) compares the total assets of the largest non-financial (i.e. non-banking and insurance) multinational companies. In 1990, the most recent year for which comparable figures are available, the leading companies in Western Europe were:

Alcatel Alsthom
Ownership: French multinational. *Principal interests:* the telecommunications industry. *Total assets:* US$ 38 200 000 000.

Asea Brown Boveri
Ownership: Swiss-Swedish multinational. *Principal interests:* the electrical industry. *Total assets:* US$ 30 200 000 000.

Bayer
Ownership: German multinational. *Principal interests:* the chemical industry. *Total assets:* US$ 25 400 000 000.

British Petroleum
Ownership: British multinational. *Principal interests:* the oil industry. *Total assets:* US$ 59 300 000 000.

Daimler-Benz
Ownership: German multinational. *Principal interests:* the car and commercial vehicle construction industry. *Total assets:* US$ 48 800 000 000.

Electrolux
Ownership: Swedish multinational. *Principal interests:* the electrical industry. *Total assets:* US$ 11 700 000 000.

Elf Aquitaine
Ownership: French multinational*. *Principal interests:* the oil industry. *Total assets:* US$ 42 600 000 000.

ENI
Ownership: Italian state-owned multinational. *Principal interests:* the petrochemical industry. *Total assets:* US$ 60 500 000 000.

Ferruzzi/Montedison
Ownership: Italian multinational. *Principal interests:* diversified interests in many industries. *Total assets:* US$ 30 800 000 000.

Fiat
Ownership: Italian multinational. *Principal interests:* the car and commercial vehicle construction industry. *Total assets:* US$ 66 300 000 000.

Générale des Eaux
Ownership: French multinational. *Principal interests:* the water industry and a widely diversified range of industries. *Total assets:* US$ 27 900 000 000.

Hanson
Ownership: British multinational. *Principal interests:* widely diversified interests in many industries. *Total assets:* US$ 27 700 000 000.

Hoechst
Ownership: German multinational. *Principal interests:* the chemical industry. *Total assets:* US$ 23 800 000 000.

Michelin
Ownership: French multinational. *Principal interests:* the tyre industry. *Total assets:* US$ 14 900 000 000.

Nestlé
Ownership: Swiss multinational. *Principal interests:* the food industry. *Total assets:* US$ 27 900 000 000.

Péchiney
Ownership: French state-owned multinational. *Principal interests:* the metallurgical industry. *Total assets:* US$ 14 300 000 000.

Petrofina
Ownership: Belgian multinational. *Principal interests:* the oil industry. *Total assets:* 12 300 000 000.

Philips Electronics
Ownership: Dutch multinational. *Principal interests:* the electronics and electrical industries. *Total assets:* US$ 30 600 000 000.

Rhône-Poulenc
Ownership: French multinational*. *Principal interests:* the chemical industry. *Total assets:* US$ 21 400 000 000.

Roche Holding
Ownership: Swiss multinational. *Principal interests:* the pharmaceutical industry. *Total assets:* US$ 17 900 000 000.

Royal Dutch/Shell
Ownership: British-Dutch multinational. *Principal interests:* the oil industry. *Total assets:* US$ 106 000 000 000.

Saint-Gobain
Ownership: French multinational. *Principal interests:* the construction and allied industries. *Total assets:* US$ 17 600 000 000.

Sandoz
Ownership: Swiss multinational. *Principal interests:* the chemical industry. *Total assets:* US$ 10 100 000 000.

Siemens
Ownership: German multinational. *Principal interests:* the electrical industry. *Total assets:* US$ 50 100 000 000.

Stora
Ownership: Swedish multinational. *Principal interests:* the paper industry. *Total assets:* US$ 15 000 000 000.

Thomson
Ownership: French state-owned multinational. *Principal interests:* the electronics industry. *Total assets:* US$ 20 700 000 000.

Total
Ownership: French multinational. *Principal interests:* the oil industry. *Total assets:* US$ 20 800 000 000.

Unilever
Ownership: British-Dutch multinational. *Principal interests:* the food industry. *Total assets:* US$ 24 800 000 000.

Volkswagen
Ownership: German multinational. *Principal interests:* the car and commercial vehicle construction industry. *Total assets:* US$ 41 900 000 000.

* nationalized but scheduled for privatization.

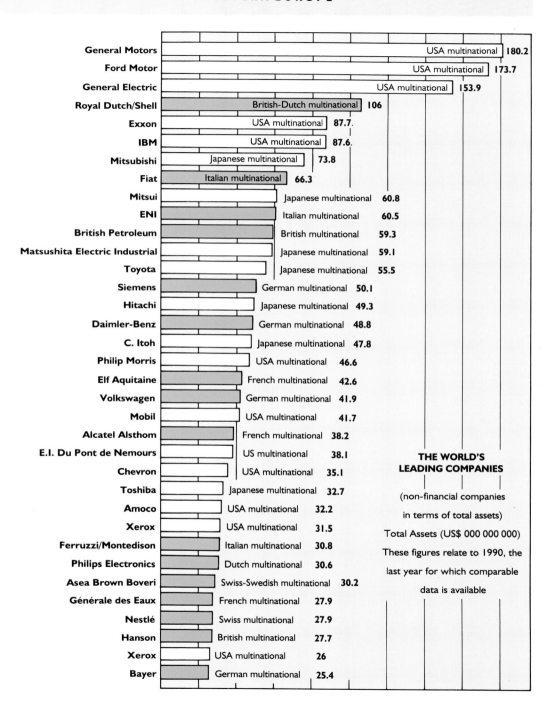

Company	Nationality	Total Assets
General Motors	USA multinational	180.2
Ford Motor	USA multinational	173.7
General Electric	USA multinational	153.9
Royal Dutch/Shell	British-Dutch multinational	106
Exxon	USA multinational	87.7
IBM	USA multinational	87.6
Mitsubishi	Japanese multinational	73.8
Fiat	Italian multinational	66.3
Mitsui	Japanese multinational	60.8
ENI	Italian multinational	60.5
British Petroleum	British multinational	59.3
Matsushita Electric Industrial	Japanese multinational	59.1
Toyota	Japanese multinational	55.5
Siemens	German multinational	50.1
Hitachi	Japanese multinational	49.3
Daimler-Benz	German multinational	48.8
C. Itoh	Japanese multinational	47.8
Philip Morris	USA multinational	46.6
Elf Aquitaine	French multinational	42.6
Volkswagen	German multinational	41.9
Mobil	USA multinational	41.7
Alcatel Alsthom	French multinational	38.2
E.I. Du Pont de Nemours	US multinational	38.1
Chevron	USA multinational	35.1
Toshiba	Japanese multinational	32.7
Amoco	USA multinational	32.2
Xerox	USA multinational	31.5
Ferruzzi/Montedison	Italian multinational	30.8
Philips Electronics	Dutch multinational	30.6
Asea Brown Boveri	Swiss-Swedish multinational	30.2
Générale des Eaux	French multinational	27.9
Nestlé	Swiss multinational	27.9
Hanson	British multinational	27.7
Xerox	USA multinational	26
Bayer	German multinational	25.4

**THE WORLD'S
LEADING COMPANIES**

(non-financial companies
in terms of total assets)

Total Assets (US$ 000 000 000)

These figures relate to 1990, the
last year for which comparable
data is available

TRANSPORT

The establishment of a Community transport policy – to allow the free movement of traffic throughout the EC – is one of the objectives of the Treaty of Rome. The aims of the EC transport policy may be summarized as an intention to:

– harmonize safety regulations;
– harmonize legislation concerning the size of lorries;
– negotiate with non-members concerning transit;
– establish a Community system for paying the costs of infrastructure;
– establish a pricing policy for international road haulage;
– harmonize national taxation systems for commercial vehicles;
– remove any obstacles for an integrated railway system;
– develop an EC air transport policy;
– establish a common commercial maritime policy;
– grant financial assistance to improve road and rail networks by means of projects that are deemed to be of European importance.

Many of these policies and aims would apply within the EEA and already grants have been made to improve road and rail links with Scandinavia.

ROAD TRANSPORT

In terms of the number of persons using means of transport *per annum* and the tonnage of freight handled, road transport is the most important form of transport in Western Europe.

INTERNATIONAL VEHICLE REGISTRATION LETTERS IN EUROPE

A	Austria	H	Hungary
AL	Albania	I	Italy
AND	Andorra	IRL	Ireland
B	Belgium	IS	Iceland
BER*	Belarus	L	Luxembourg
BG	Bulgaria	LR*	Latvia
CH	Switzerland	LT	Lithuania
CRO*	Croatia	M	Malta
CS	Czech Republic	MC	Monaco
CY	Cyprus	MOL*	Moldova
D	Germany	N	Norway
DK	Denmark	NL	Netherlands
E	Spain	P	Portugal
EW*	Estonia	PL	Poland
F	France	RO	Romania
FL	Liechtenstein	RO*	Russia
FR	Faeroe Islands	RSM	San Marino
GB	UK	S	Sweden
GBA	Alderney	SF	Finland
GBG	Guernsey	SLO*	Slovenia
GBJ	Jersey	SQ*	Slovakia
GBM	Isle of Man	TR	Turkey
GBZ	Gibraltar	UKR*	Ukraine
GR	Greece	V	Vatican City
	YU	Yugoslavia	

* indicates a registration that is in use but has not been officially recognized.

TOTAL NUMBER OF VEHICLES

Country	Total number of cars	Total number of lorries and buses	Persons per vehicle
Belgium	3 833 300	401 900	2.4
Denmark	1 590 400	301 400	2.7
France	23 550 000	4 740 000	2.0
Germany	35 512 100	2 764 200	2.1
Greece	1 729 700	792 900	4.1
Ireland	796 400	147 200	3.7
Italy	27 300 000	2 427 000	1.9
Luxembourg	183 400	12 000	2.0
Netherlands	5 509 000	555 000	2.5
Portugal	1 605 000	593 000	4.7
Spain	12 010 700	2 385 200	2.7
UK	19 742 000	2 861 000	2.5
Austria	2 991 300	261 900	2.4
Finland	1 926 300	271 100	2.3
Iceland	119 700	14 500	1.9
Liechtenstein	16 900	1 700	1.5
Norway	1 614 600	383 100	2.1
Sweden	3 605 200	325 100	2.2
Switzerland	3 011 700	285 600	2.1

The figures are for 1991, the last year for which comparable data is available.

TOTAL LENGTH OF ROADS

Country	Length in km	Length in mi
Belgium	137 876	85 672
Denmark	71 063	44 156
France	805 600	500 576
Germany	621 267	386 037
Greece	130 000	80 800
Ireland	92 303	57 354
Italy	302 403	187 904
Luxembourg	5 091	3 163
Netherlands	116 309	72 271
Portugal	70 176	43 605
Spain	324 166	201 427
UK	356 517	221 529
Austria	107 180	66 598
Finland	76 407	47 477
Iceland	11 378	7 070
Liechtenstein	323	201
Norway	88 922	55 253
Sweden	133 673	83 060
Switzerland	71 099	44 179

The figures are for the period 1990–91.

TOTAL LENGTH OF MOTORWAYS

Country	Length in km	Length in mi
Belgium	1 631	1 014
Denmark	650	404
France	7 100	4 412
Germany	11 714	7 279
Greece	116	72
Ireland	24	15
Italy	6 695	4 160
Luxembourg	118	73
Netherlands	2 094	1 301
Portugal	318	198
Spain	2 700	1 678
UK	3 129	1 944
Austria	1 532	952
Finland	225	140
Iceland	nil	nil
Liechtenstein	nil	nil
Norway	437	272
Sweden	936	582
Switzerland	1 515	941

The figures are for 1991–2, the last year for which comparable data is available.

RAIL TRANSPORT

Belgium Belgian railways are operated by the state-run *Société Nationale des Chemins de Fer Belges (SNCB)* /*Nationale Maatschappij der Belgische Spoorwegen (NMBS)*. The country has one of the densest railway networks in the world.
Track length: 3466 km (2154 mi) – of which 2291 km (1424 mi) are electrified. In addition there are 165 km (103 mi) of narrow-gauge railways.

Denmark State-run Danish railways are operated by *DSB*. Construction of a 17.7 km (11 mi) rail link under the Great Belt linking Denmark and Sweden began in 1988. It will consist of two 8 km (5 mi) tunnels and a short stretch of bridge. Originally scheduled to open in 1996, the link is not now expected to open until 1998 or 1999.
Track length: There are 2476 km (1539 mi) of track in Denmark of which 225 km (140 mi) are electrified. In addition there are 523 km (325 mi) of privately-owned branch lines operating passenger and/or freight services.

France Nearly all of the railways in France are operated by the *Société Nationale des Chemins de Fers (SNCF)*. A very small number of branch lines in the country are run independently.
Track length: There are 34 322 km (21 327 mi) of track of which 12 439 km (7729 mi) are electrified. *TGV (train grande vitesse)* services are operated on special tracks between Paris and the major provincial cities. One TGV line runs to the Channel Tunnel (see UK, below).

Germany Two state-run companies – *Deutsche Bundesbahn (DB)* in the former West Germany and *Deutsche Reichsbahn* in the former East Germany – operated passenger and freight services in Germany until *Deutsche Bahn* was founded in 1993. The rationalization of the network in the former East Germany and eventual privatization of all or part of the network are envisaged.
Track length: The combined track length operated by the two state-run companies was 42 000 km (26 098 mi) early in 1993.

Greece State-run Greek railways are operated by *OSE*, except in the Athens area where the local railway is run by *ISAP*.
Track length: There are 2479 km (1540 mi) of track.

Ireland The railways of the Republic are operated by the state-run company *Iarnród Éireann* which is part of *Corás Iompair Éireann (CIE)*.
Track length: Early in 1993 the network comprised 1947 km (1210 mi), but this was extended during the year by the reopening of the Ennis line.

Italy State-run Italian railways are operated by *Ente Ferrovie dello Stato*. A network of high-speed lines (*direttissima*) is being constructed for example between Rome and Naples and Rome and Florence. A number of branch lines and local services – some operating narrow-gauge track – are run by 27 private and other companies.
Track length: The state system has a total track length of 15 983 km (9931 mi). The other lines have a length of just over 3000 km (1860 mi).

Luxembourg The state-run *Société Nationale des Chemins de Fer Luxembourgeois* operates services on 271 km (168 mi) of track.

Netherlands State-run *NV Nederlandse Spoorwegen* operates railway services in the Netherlands. The network was extended in the 1980s with a new line onto Flevoland polder.
Track length: There are 2798 km (1739 mi) of track.

Portugal The state-run Portuguese railway system is run by *CP*. Private companies run a number of mineral lines.
Track length: The state system is 3588 km (2229 mi) long of which 434 km (270 mi) are electrified.

Spain The Spanish railway network is being modernized and extended. A high-speed network will eventually link Madrid with Córdoba and Seville in the west, with Barcelona and the French border in the east and Cádiz and Málaga in the south. The state-run company *RENFE* operates most of the network but other lines are run by four regional and a number of private companies. *Track length:* The state system has a total length of 12 560 km (7804 mi). The four regional companies operate services on 1637 km (1017 mi) of track; private companies operate 217 km (135 mi) of track.

UK *British Rail (BR)* is scheduled to be privatized into 27 cost centres. The private-sector Franco-British consortium Eurotunnel has been awarded the concession to operate (until 2042) a cross-Channel rail tunnel. The main terminals will be (London) St Pancras and, initially, (London) Waterloo and Gare du Nord (Paris) and Gare Centrale (Brussels). The railways in Northern Ireland are run by the *Northern Ireland Railways Company Ltd.* There are over two dozen private preservation lines, many using steam. *Track length:* BR operates 16 583 km (10 304 mi) of track. There are 332 km (206 mi) of track in Northern Ireland.

Austria State-run *OBB* operates 90% of the services in the country. There are 19 private lines. *Track length:* OBB runs 5623 km (3494 mi) of track. Private companies – some operating steam – run 562 km (349 mi) of track.

Finland State-run *VR* operates almost of Finland's railways. There is a small private goods system. *Track length:* VR operates 5863 km (3643 mi) of track; there are 10 km (6 mi) of private line.

Iceland has no railways.

Liechtenstein has 18.5 km (11.5 mi) of railway track which is operated by Austrian railways (OBB; see above).

Norway State-run *Norges Statsbaner (NSB)* operates all the railway track in Norway except for lines run by five private companies. *Track length:* NSB has 4027 km (2502 mi) of track. The private companies run a total of 65 km (40 mi) of track.

Sweden There are plans for the eventual privatization of state-run Swedish railways, *Statens Järnvägar*. About 7252 km (4506 mi) of track are electrified. There are also four private companies. *Track length:* The state-run system comprises 9846 km (6118 mi) of track; the private companies operate 571 km (354 mi) of track.

Switzerland The Swiss railway is characterized by a dense network with many privately-owned country and Alpine lines. The state-run *Schweizerische Bundesbahnen (SBB)* is entirely electrified. There are 120 private companies. *Track length:* SBB has 2998 km (1863 mi) of track. The private companies run 2210 km (1373 mi) of track.

METROS AND RAPID TRANSIT SYSTEMS

Belgium *Metros:* Brussels (length 165 km/103 mi). *Rapid transit (trams):* Antwerp (180 km/112 mi), Brussels (included above), Ghent (29 km/18 mi).

Denmark: *Metros:* Copenhagen (135 km/84 mi).

France: *Metros:* Paris (302 km/188 mi), Lille (25 km/16 mi), Lyon (28 km/17 mi), Marseille (18 km/11 mi). *Rapid transit:* Lille (23 km/14 mi), Grenoble (13 km/8 mi), Nantes (13 km/8 mi), St Etienne (7 km/4 mi), Toulouse (13 km/8 mi).

Germany: *Metros:* Berlin (140 km/87 mi), Munich (63 km/39 mi), Frankfurt (51 km/32 mi), Nuremberg (23 km/14 mi). *Rapid transit:* Rapid transit systems (mainly trams) are in operation in over 50 German cities, including Berlin (72 km/45 mi), Munich (79 km/49 mi) and Wuppertal (overhead railway; 13 km/8 mi).

Greece *Metros:* Athens (29 km/18 mi; plus 18 km/11 mi under construction).

Dublin *Rapid transit:* Dublin (40 km/25 mi).

Italy *Metros:* Milan (66 km/41 mi), Naples (11 km/7 mi), Rome (29 km/18 mi). A system is planned for Turin.

Netherlands *Metros:* Amsterdam (18 km/11 mi), Rotterdam (69 km/43 mi). *Rapid transit:* Amsterdam (124 km/77 mi), Rotterdam (106 km/66 mi), Utrecht (29 km/18 mi), The Hague (117 km/73 mi).

Portugal *Metros:* Lisbon (19 km/12 mi). *Rapid transit:* Lisbon (94 km/58 mi), Oporto.

Spain *Metros:* Madrid (113 km/70 mi), Barcelona (71 km/44 mi). *Rapid transit:* Valencia (113 km/70 mi). There are plans for rapid transit systems in Seville and Bilbao.

UK *Metros:* London (408 km/254 mi), Glasgow (11 km/7 mi), and Liverpool. *Rapid transit:* London (20 km/12 mi), Newcastle (60 km/37 mi), Manchester (24 km/15 mi), Sheffield (29 km/18 mi). Systems are under construction in Birmingham and Nottingham.

Austria *Metro systems:* Vienna (30 km/18 mi).

Finland *Metros:* Helsinki (16 km/10 mi). *Rapid transit:* Helsinki (69 km/43 mi).

Norway *Metros:* Oslo (98 km/61 mi). *Rapid transit:* Oslo (54 km/34 mi).

Sweden *Metros:* Stockholm (108 km/67 mi). *Rapid transit:* Gothenburg (81 km/50 mi), Norrkoping.

AIR TRANSPORT

Belgium Brussels has a major international airport; Antwerp, Charleroi, Liège and Ostende airports also have international airports. The state airline is *SABENA.*

Denmark There is an international airport at Copenhagen; there are 12 regional airports. The state airline is *SAS – Scandinavian Airline Systems*, which is jointly owned by Denmark, Norway and Sweden.

France Paris has two major international airports (see table), Orly and Charles de Gaulle (or Roissy); the third Parisian airport is Le Bourget. Other international airports include Bordeaux, Lille, Lyon, Marseille, Nice, Strasbourg and Toulouse. The state airline is *Air France* (see table); *Air-Inter* operates internal flights.

Germany The leading German airport is Frankfurt International (see table). There are two international airports at Berlin (Tempelhof and Tegfel); other international airports include Cologne-Bonn, Dresden, Düsseldorf, Hamburg, Hannover, Leipzig, Munich and Stuttgart. The state airline is *Lufthansa* (see table).

Greece The principal international airport is at Athens; Alexandroupolis, Andravida, Corfu, Heraklion, Kos, Lesbos, Rhodes and Thessaloniki also have international airports. The state airline is *Olympic Airways*.

Ireland The main international airport in Ireland is Dublin. Cork, Knock, and Shannon also have international airports. The state airline is *Aer Lingus*.

Italy Fiumicino (Rome) is one of Europe's principal airports (see table). Milan has two international airports (Malpensa and Linate). Other international airports include Catania, Florence, Genoa, Naples and Turin. The state airline is *Alitalia* (see table).

Luxembourg Luxembourg has an international airport. *Luxair* is the national airline.

Netherlands Schiphol (near Amsterdam) is one of Europe's main airports (see table). Groningen, Maastricht and Rotterdam also have international airports. The state airline is *KLM* (see table).

Portugal The principal international airport is at Lisbon. Faro, Funchal (Madeira), Oporto, Santa Maria (Azores) and San Miguel (Azores) also have international airports. The state airline is *TAP*.

Spain Barajas (Madrid) is one of Europe's principal airports (see table). Other international airports include Barcelona, Bilbao, Malaga, Palma (Majorca), Seville, Valencia and two principal airports in the Canary Islands. The state airline is *Iberia* (see table).

UK London Heathrow and Gatwick are among the world's principal airports (see table). Other international airports include Belfast, Birmingham, Cardiff, Edinburgh, Glasgow, Leeds/Bradford, Liverpool, London Stansted, Luton and Manchester. The main airline is *British Airways* (see table).

Austria Schwechat, Vienna, is the principal Austrian airport. Graz, Innsbruck, Klagenfurt, Linz and Salzburg also have international airports. The state airline is *Austrian Airlines*.

Finland Helsinki-Vantaa is an international airport. There are over 20 regional airports. The state airline is *Finnair*.

Iceland Keflavik has an international airport. The state airline is *Icelandair*.

Liechtenstein has no airport.

Norway Fornebu, Oslo, is the principal Norwegian airport. Bergen and Stavanger also have international airports. The state airline is *SAS* (see Denmark, above).

Sweden Arlanda, Stockholm, is the principal Swedish airport (see table). Gothenburg and Malmö also have international airports. The state airline is *SAS* (see Denmark, above).

Switzerland Zürich has a major international airport (see table). Basel and Geneva also have international airports. The state airline is *Swissair*.

EUROPE'S MAJOR AIRPORTS

Airport name	City	Country	Terminal passengers	International passengers	Air transport movements
Heathrow Airport	**London**	UK	42 647 000	35 250 000	367 400
Frankfurt International	**Frankfurt**	Germany	28 713 000	21 860 000	308 500
Orly	**Paris**	France	24 330 000	9 210 000	201 700
Charles de Gaulle	**Paris**	France	22 506 000	20 875 000	233 000
Gatwick	**London**	UK	21 047 000	19 650 000	188 200
Barajas	**Madrid**	Spain	15 869 000	7 330 000	158 400
Fiumicino	**Rome**	Italy	15 550 000	8 052 000	165 500
Schiphol	**Amsterdam**	Netherlands	14 895 000	14 800 000	191 500
Arlanda	**Stockholm**	Sweden	14 822 000	6 555 000	252 700
Zürich	**Zürich**	Switzerland	12 277 000	11 585 000	172 200

The figures are for 1990–1, the latest year for which comparable figures are available.

MAJOR EUROPEAN AIRLINES

Airline	Country	Passenger km	Aircraft km	Passengers carried	Total no. of aircraft
Aeroflot	**Russia**	242 174 000	n/a	137 198 000	103
British Airways	**UK**	66 795 000	385 483	25 172 000	228
Lufthansa	**Germany**	41 903 000	375 801	21 613 000	177
Air France	**France**	36 653 000	274 868	15 693 000	121
KLM	**Netherlands**	26 390 000	151 502	6 903 000	57
Alitalia	**Italy**	22 754 000	181 543	18 203 000	119
Iberia	**Spain**	22 112 000	173 594	16 228 000	93

The figures are for 1990–1, the latest year for which comparable figures are available.

MARINE AND INLAND WATERWAY TRANSPORT

In the following text the largest ports in each country are listed in order of the amount of freight that each handles a year.

Belgium *Largest ports:* Antwerp (handles over 102 000 000 tonnes of freight a year; the world's seventh largest port), Zeebrugge, Ostende. *Inland waterways:* 1500 km (932 mi); 99 000 000 tonnes of freight carried a year.

Denmark *Largest ports:* Copenhagen, Aarhus, Aalborg, Esbjerg.

France *Largest ports:* Marseille (handles over 90 300 000 tonnes of freight a year; the world's tenth largest port), Le Havre (handles over 50 000 000 tonnes of freight a year), Dunkerque (handles over 30 000 000 tonnes of freight a year), Rouen, Nantes-St Nazaire, Bordeaux. *Inland waterways:* 14 932 km (9278 mi); 7 600 000 tonnes of freight handled a year.

Germany *Largest ports:* Hamburg (handles over 57 000 000 tonnes of freight a year), Duisburg (an inland port on the Rhine; handles over 40 000 000 tonnes of freight a year), Bremen-Bremerhaven (handles nearly 30 000 000 tonnes of freight a year), Rostock, Wilhelmshaven. *Inland waterways:* 7541 km (4686 mi); over 56 000 000 tonnes handled a year. The Main-Danube Canal (171 km/106 mi), which opened in 1992 has greatly extended the opportunities for inland navigation in Central Europe.

Greece *Largest ports:* Piraeus (Athens), Patras, Thessaloniki.

Ireland *Largest ports:* Dublin, Dun Laoghaire, Cork.

Italy *Largest ports:* Genoa (handles over 40 000 000 tonnes of freight a year), Venice, Trieste, Naples, Palermo.

Luxembourg Barge traffic uses the canalized River Moselle.

Netherlands *Largest ports:* Rotterdam (handles over 288 000 000 tonnes of freight a year; the world's largest port), Amsterdam, IJmuiden. *Inland waterways:* 6340 km (3940 mi); nearly 7 000 000 tonnes of international freight handled a year. Dutch inland waterways carry over 30% of all goods moved within the Netherlands.

Portugal *Largest ports:* Lisbon, Leixoes (Oporto), Setubal, Funchal.

Spain *Largest ports:* Barcelona, Bilbao, Santa Cruz de Tenerife, Gijón, Las Palmas, Seville.

UK *Largest ports:* Immingham-Grimsby (handles about 34 000 000 tonnes of freight a year), London, Milford Haven, Tees-Hartlepool, Southampton, Grangemouth-Leith.

Austria The Danube – 351 km/218 mi in Austria – is used by barge traffic in Austria.

Finland *Largest ports:* Kotka, Helsinki, Turku.

Iceland *Largest port:* Rekyjavik.

Norway *Largest ports:* Narvik, Oslo.

Sweden *Largest ports:* Gothenburg, Helsingborg, Stockholm, Malmö.

Switzerland *Inland waterways:* 2052 km (1275 mi); Basel is an important river port.

DEFENCE

The Maastricht Treaty (see p. 19) envisages closer military cooperation between members of the EC. It is envisaged that this will take place through meetings of EC defence ministers and through the auspices of the WEU (see below).

NATO

The North Atlantic Treaty Organization came into existence in August 1949. NATO is a collective defence organization whose member countries agree to treat an armed attack on any one of them as an attack against all. The North Atlantic Council is the highest authority of the alliance. It comprises 16 permanent representatives – one from each member state – and is chaired by the Secretary General of NATO. The foreign ministers of the member states meet at least twice a year. The defence of the NATO area is the responsibility of the Defence Planning Committee. France is not a member of the DPC, which meets regularly at ambassadorial level and twice a year at ministerial level.

Throughout the Cold War, NATO confronted the (Communist bloc) Warsaw Pact. Upon the collapse of Communism in Eastern Europe (after 1989) and the disbandment of the Warsaw Pact (1991), NATO has at times appeared to struggle to redefine its role; for example, the alliance was unable to influence the civil wars in the former Yugoslavia. By 1993 the Czech Republic, Hungary and Poland were being openly canvassed as future NATO members. Several other East European states were seeking membership, for example Albania.

Headquarters: Brussels, Belgium.

Secretary-General: Manfred Wörner (Germany).

Members: Belgium (founder member), Canada (founder member), Denmark (founder member), France (founder member), Germany (West Germany admitted 5 May 1955; the former East Germany was included as part of reunified Germany 3 October 1990), Greece (admitted 18 February 1952), Iceland (founder member), Italy (founder member), Luxembourg (founder member), Netherlands (founder member), Norway (founder member), Portugal (founder member), Spain (admitted 30 May 1982), Turkey (admitted 18 February 1952), UK (founder member), USA (founder member).

WEU

The West European Union (refounded 1955) seeks to harmonize the security and defence of Western European countries. The WEU was reactivated in 1984 to strengthen NATO.

Headquarters: Brussels, Belgium.

Membership: Belgium, Denmark (observer member), France, Germany, Greece, Iceland (associate member), Ireland (observer member), Italy, Luxembourg, Netherlands, Norway (associate member), Portugal, Spain, Turkey (associate member), UK.

ARMED STRENGTH OF WEST EUROPEAN COUNTRIES

Country	Army personnel	Navy personnel	Air forces personnel	Total (1992; inc. others*)
Belgium	54 100	4 400	17 300	75 800
Denmark	17 100	6 900	8 800	32 800
France	285 000	64 900	91 700	537 300
Germany	203 400	35 000	95 800	398 200
Greece	113 000	19 500	26 800	185 800
Ireland	10 900	1 000	1 000	12 900
Italy	230 000	48 000	76 200	465 600
Luxembourg	800	no navy	no air force	1 600
Netherlands	64 100	15 500	16 000	95 600
Portugal	32 700	15 300	10 300	99 200
Spain	146 000	36 000	35 000	281 600
UK	147 600	58 900	83 200	289 700
Austria	46 000	no navy	6 000	52 000
Finland	27 800	1 800	3 000	32 600
Iceland	no army	no navy	no air force	130
Liechtenstein	nil	nil	nil	nil
Norway	15 900	7 300	9 500	33 400
Sweden	43 500	9 500	7 500	61 100
Switzerland†	1 600	no navy	n/a	676 600

* includes paramilitary police, local defence forces, etc., but excluding reserves. † About 615 000 conscripts serve for a period of training in the army each year and up to 60 000 conscripts serve in the air force for a period of training per annum.

NAVAL STRENGTH OF WEST EUROPEAN COUNTRIES

Country	Aircraft carriers	Destroyers	Frigates	Submarines	Others†
Belgium			4		28
Denmark				5	49
France	1	4	34	18	89
Germany		6	8	22	107
Greece		4	6	10	118
Ireland					7
Italy	2	3	28	8	48
Luxembourg	nil	nil	nil	nil	nil
Netherlands		4	11	5	34
Portugal			11	3	59
Spain	1		15	8	137
UK	2	12	30	19	98
Austria	nil	nil	nil	nil	nil
Finland					58
Iceland					3
Liechtenstein	nil	nil	nil	nil	nil
Norway			5	11	49
Sweden				12	79
Switzerland	nil	nil	nil	nil	nil

† includes corvettes, missile craft, minesweepers, minehunters, auxiliaries, tugs, supply ships, coastal patrol vessels, etc.

PRINCIPAL NAVAL BASES

Belgium: Ostende.

Denmark: Frederikshavn.

France: Cherbourg, Toulon and Brest.

Germany: Wilhelmshaven, Bremerhaven, Kiel, Olpenitz and Rostock.

Greece: Salamis (west of Athens), Patras and Soudha Bay (Crete).

Ireland: Haulbowline Island (Cork).

Italy: La Spezia, Naples, Taranto and Ancona, plus Brindisi and Venice.

The Netherlands: Den Helder, plus Vlissingen, Wil-lemstad (in Curaçao) and Oranjestad (in Aruba).

Portugal: Lisbon and Portimao, plus bases in the Azores and Madeira.

Spain: Ferrol, Rota, Cádiz, Cartagena, Palma de Mallorca, Mahon and Las Palmas.

UK: Devonport (Plymouth), Rosyth (near Dunfermline), Portmouth and Faslane (in Argyll), plus Gibraltar and Hong Kong.

Finland: Upinniemi (near Helsinki) and Turku.

Iceland: Reykjavik.

Norway: Bergen, plus Horten, Ramsund and Tromso.

Sweden: Stockholm, Gothenburg, and Karlskrona.

Belgium Belgium is part of NATO and houses the organization's headquarters. Conscription is compulsory for all male Belgians. The period of training is eight months. In 1993 Belgium formed a European corps with France and Germany.

Denmark Denmark is part of NATO. The Danish armed forces are raised in part from voluntary enlistment and in part from conscription. Male conscripts are selected at the age of 18–19 and are called up at about the age of 20. They are liable to service of between four and 12 months.

France France is a NATO member although it does not formally come under the NATO command structure. In 1993 France formed a European corps with Belgium and Germany. France is. a nuclear power with an estimated 426 nuclear warheads in 1992. Over 15 000 French troops serve overseas in *départements d'outre-mer* (such as Guyane and Martinique), colonial possessions (such as Polynesia) and former colonies (including Djibouti and Gabon). In addition some 45 000 French troops are based in Germany, mainly in Baden-Württemberg. France is a regular participant in UN operations and has undertaken independent action in former French African colonies. Frenchman are subject to conscription normally from the age of 18–19. There are various exemptions, for example, for those who are the sole wage-earner in the family or for those who have had a brother killed in active service. The period of military service is now 10 months.

Germany Troops from the USA, UK, France and Russia are based in Germany, although Russian forces in the former East Germany are scheduled to be withdrawn by the end of 1994. Germany is a NATO member, but has only recently begun to take part in UN operations, for example in Somalia. In 1993 Germany formed a European corps with Belgium and France. German males are subject to compulsory military conscription for 12 months.

Greece Greece is NATO member and has provided bases for the Alliance. In 1993 Greece concluded a mutual defence agreement with Cyprus. Conscription is compulsory for Greek males, normally without any exemptions. The period of training is 19 months for the army, 21 months for the air force and 24 months for the navy.

Ireland Ireland is neutral but has participated in UN operations. Service in the Irish forces is on a voluntary basis.

Italy Italy is a NATO member and has participated in a number of UN operations. The USA maintains a number of bases in Italy. Italian males are subject to compulsory military service of 12 months.

Luxembourg Service in the Luxembourgeois infantry is voluntary. The Grand Duchy belongs to NATO.

Netherlands Until 1993–94 Dutch males were subject to compulsory military service – 12 months in the army and the air force and 12–15 months in the navy. In 1993 universal conscription was abandoned and service, in future, is to voluntary. The country belongs to NATO and regularly participates in NATO exercises and UN operations. Dutch forces are also based abroad in the West Indies.

Portugal Portugal – a NATO member – no longer maintains any forces overseas. The USA maintains a presence in the Azores. Portuguese males are subject to compulsory military service of between 12 and 18 months. It is planned to reduce this period of conscription to four months in 1994.

Spain Spain is NATO's most recent member. The country also participates in UN operations. The USA maintains air force bases in southern Spain. Spanish males are subject to compulsory military training of nine months. Policemen are exempt from conscription.

UK Britain is a nuclear power with an estimated 144 nuclear warheads in 1992. Britain belongs to NATO and regularly contributes to NATO exercises and UN military operations. Over 53 000 British troops are based in Germany, mainly in Lower Saxony and other forces are maintained in Belize, Brunei, Cyprus, the Falkland Islands, Gibraltar, Hong Kong and Nepal. Service in the British forces is on a voluntary basis.

Austria Austria is neutral. All Austrian males serve six months of military service and are liable for 60 days of refresher courses.

Finland Finland is neutral. All Finnish males are subject to military conscription of 240, 285 or 330 days and, following this initial training, are liable to recall to refresher courses of 40–100 days.

Iceland Athough Iceland has no conventional armed forces the country is a NATO member. There is an American presence at Keflavik.

Liechtenstein Liechtenstein has no forces.

Norway Norway is an active NATO member and is the host to regular NATO exercises. The country participates in various UN peace-keeping activities. Conscription is compulsory for all Norwegian males. The initial period of training is 12 months for the army and the air force, and 15 months for the navy. Recruits are liable to recall to regular refresher courses, which in the case of the navy are limited.

Sweden Sweden is neutral but has modern and impressive armed forces. Swedish troops have participated in UN operations. At 18 all Swedish males are subject to conscription although the country's armed forces consist in part of long-term volunteers. Military service lasts for between 7½ and 15 months in the army and navy, and between eight and 12 months in the air force.

Switzerland Switzerland is neutral. All Swiss males are subject to compulsory military service comprising 17 weeks at the age of 20, refresher courses between the ages of 21 and 32, then 39 days training between the ages of 33 and 42 for the *Landwehr* (militia) and a further 13 days training between the ages of 43 and 50 for the *Landsturm* (home guard).

GROSS NATIONAL PRODUCT

The Gross National Product (GNP) of a country is the Gross Domestic Product (GDP; see below) plus net property income – profits, interest and dividends – from abroad.

The Gross Domestic Product of a country is the total amount of goods and services produced by an economy over a one-year period.

GNP OF EEA COUNTRIES (by order)

The figures below relate to 1992 except where indicated.

Germany US$ 1 950 000 000 000
The German economy is the largest in Europe and the second largest in the world. Because of the effects of international recession and the costs of integrating the former East Germany, the German economy declined by about 2% during 1993 (see p. 23 and pp. 32–35). The German GNP is, therefore, now lower than the figure given above.

France US$ 1 360 000 000 000
After annual growth figures of over 1.5% for several years, the French GNP decreased by over 1% in 1993. See also pp. 28–31.

Italy US$ 1 170 000 000 000
Italy's economic problems – a weak lira, high interest rates, major budgetary difficulties and a general lack of business confidence – continue and the Italian economy declined during the year. The 1993 statistics are likely to reveal that the United Kingdom has overtaken Italy to regain third place on the GNP table.

United Kingdom US$ 1 000 000 000 000
Almost alone in Western Europe, the United Kingdom has seen a tentative revival in economic fortunes in 1993. Britain's GNP is probably now larger than that of Italy (see above).

Spain US$ 540 000 000 000
During the 1980s Spain experienced an encouraging growth in GNP. However, Spain's GNP growth rates have declined in the 1990s as the economy dipped into recession.

The Netherlands US$ 330 000 000 000
The Dutch economy has not suffered the effects of recession to quite the same extent as that of many other West European economies.

Sweden US$ 260 000 000 000
Sweden has suffered greatly from the effects of recession and a fall of least 0.3% in GNP is forecast for 1993 and 1994. The Swedish GNP is, therefore, smaller than the 1992 figure given above.

Switzerland US$ 240 000 000 000
The Swiss economy has remained – at least in part – immune from the effects of recession. The country has one of the highest economic growth rates in Western Europe. It is probable that Switzerland will overtake Sweden on the GNP table in the near future.

Belgium US$ 224 000 000 000
The Belgian economy continues to be troubled by a substantial budget deficit and large national debt. High interest rates are an additional problem. The Belgian GNP has not grown during 1993.

Austria US$ 190 000 000 000
Despite the West European recession the Austrian economy has not declined.

Denmark US$ 145 000 000 000
The Danish GNP has risen slowly despite the recession.

Norway US$ 120 000 000 000
Oil and natural gas from the North Sea have enabled Norway to withstand the worst effects of the international recession. Norway experienced growth rates in excess of 2% per annum before the recession.

Finland US$ 105 000 000 000
The Finnish economy has been hit by the sudden decline in trade with what was the Soviet Union, formerly Finland's largest trading partner. Coupled with the effects of recession and high interest rates, this resulted in a decline of 1.5% in the Finnish GNP in 1992 and a further setback in 1993.

Greece US$ 80 000 000 000
Despite government austerity programmes and the effects of international recession, the Greek economy has experienced only a modest decline, largely as a result of the investment of EC funds in Greece's infrastructure.

Portugal US$ 80 000 000 000
Low unemployment is a reflection of the relative health of the Portuguese economy. Inflation remains a problem but Portugal's GNP has remained relatively static and is now probably larger than that of Greece.

Ireland US$ 50 000 000 000
Despite public finance difficulties and high rates of unemployment, Ireland's economy is in a more healthy state than that of many West European countries. Encouraged by low interest rates and EC investment, there are some signs of recovery.

Luxembourg US$ 11 225 000 000
A 1992 estimate.

Iceland US$ 5 456 000 000
The figure given is for 1990.

Liechtenstein US$ 610 000 000
A 1991–92 estimate.

OTHER MAJOR ECONOMIES

The following 1992 estimates are given for comparison.
USA US$ 5 670 000 000 000.
Japan US$ 4 000 000 000 000.
Canada US$ 588 000 000 000.
China US$ 476 000 000 000.

MEDIA

BELGIUM

The Belgian press is divided on linguistic grounds with 18 French-language dailies, 15 Flemish-language and one in German. Some papers are published in several regional editions under different names. The main newspaper titles (with place of publication and average circulation) include:
De Standaard (Flemish) with *Het Nieuwsblad* (Flemish), Brussels, with *De Gentenaar* (Flemish), Ghent, 290 000;
Het Laatste Nieuws (Flemish), Brussels, with *De Nieuwe Gazet* (Flemish), Antwerp, 290 000;
Le Soir (evening; French), Brussels, 200 000;
De Nieuw Gids (Flemish), Brussels, with *Het Volk* (Flemish), Ghent, 190 000;
Gazet van Antwerpen (Flemish), Antwerp, with *Gazet van Mechelen* (Flemish), Malines, 190 000;
Vers l'Avenir (French), Namur, 150 000;
La Lanterne (French), Brussels, with *La Meuse* (French), Liège, 130 000;
Le Journal & Indépendance/Le Peuple (French), with *La Nouvelle Gazette* (French), both published in Charleroi, with *La Province* (French), Mons, 110 000;
Het Belang van Limburg (Flemish), Hasselt, 105 000.

Periodicals are also printed in either Flemish or French although a few appear in both languages. French and Dutch magazines also circulate. The magazines with the highest circulations include:
Kerk en Leven (weekly; Flemish), religious magazine, 800 000;
De Bond (weekly; Flemish), general interest, 340 000;
Vrouw & Wereld (monthly; Flemish), women's magazine, 315 000;
Dag Allemaal (weekly; Flemish), general interest, 300 000;
Humo (weekly; Flemish), general interest and TV listings, 265 000;
Libelle (weekly; Flemish and French editions), women's magazine, 260 000;
TeVe-Blad (weekly; Flemish), TV listings, 250 000;
Jet Limburg (fortnightly; Flemish), regional interest, 240 000;
Flair (weekly; Flemish and French editions), women's magazine, 240 000;
Télémoustique (weekly; French), TV listings, 225 000.

There are three state broadcasting organizations which offer radio and TV channels: RTBF, which broadcasts in French; BRT, in Flemish; and BRF, in German. A subscription channel broadcasts in French and there are French and Flemish commercial channels. British, Dutch, German and French TV channels are also received. There are many local radio stations.

DENMARK

Danish papers have high circulations per head of the population. Denmark's small size and linguistic unity have encouraged a national press. There are nearly 30 regional dailies. The main titles (with place of publication and average circulation) include:
Ekstra Bladet (evening), Copenhagen, 230 000;
B.T., Copenhagen, 210 000 (225 000 Sunday);
Politiken, Copenhagen, 155 000 (200 000 Sunday);
Jyllands-Posten Morgenavisen, Viby, 140 000 (230 000 Sunday);
Berlingske Tidende, Copenhagen, 130 000 (180 000 Sunday);
Jydske Vestkysten, Esbjerg, 130 000 (150 000 Sunday);
Erhvervs-Bladet, Copenhagen, 110 000 copies.

Given the relatively small population of Denmark, Danish magazines enjoy extraordinarily high circulations. Those with the largest circulations include:
Idé-nyt (quarterly), free homes and gardens magazine, 2 400 000;
Samvirke (monthly), consumers' magazine, 700 000;
Beboerbladet (quarterly), home rental magazine, 435 000;
Helse-Familiens Laegemagasin (10 a year), family health magazine, 340 000;
Se og Hor (weekly), TV listings, 315 000;
Familien Journalen (weekly), general interest, 315 000;
Hjemmet (weekly), homes magazine, 280 000;
Vi pa Landet (quarterly), farming magazine, 280 000;
Jyllands Ringens program (5 a year), car and motor cycle magazine, 280 00.

Danmarks Radio-TV is a public corporation. There is also a national commercial channel (TV2). Danmarks Radio operates three national and 10 local stations. There are over 350 local and community radio stations.

FRANCE

Although 16 daily newspapers are published in Paris, France still has a regional rather than a national press. The 55 provincial daily papers dominate sales outside Paris. There are only two Sunday papers in Paris. There are seven large newspaper groups. The main titles (with place of publication and average circulation) include:
Ouest-France, Rennes, 790 000;
Le Figaro, Paris, 785 000;
France-Dimanche (Sunday), Paris, 710 000;
Le Progrès, Lyon, 415 000 (Sunday 540 000);
Le Parisien, Paris, 400 000;
La Voix du Nord, Lille, 395 000;
Sud-Ouest, Bordeaux, 365 000;
Le Monde, Paris, 365 000;
L'Humanité-Dimanche (Sunday), Paris, 360 000;
France-Soir (evening), Paris, 305 000;
L'Equipe (sports), Paris, 300 000;
Le Dauphiné Libéré, Grenoble, 295 000;
La Nouvelle République du Centre-Ouest, Tours, 270 000;
L'Est-Républicain, Nancy, 265 000;
Nice-Matin, Nice, 265 000;
La Montagne, Clermont-Ferrand, 255 000.

The periodicals with the largest sales are television listings magazines. The main periodicals include:
Télé 7 Jours (weekly), TV listings, 3 340 000;
Télé-Poche (weekly), TV listings, 1 800 000;
Modes et travaux (monthly), fashion, 1 500 000;
Sélection du Reader's Digest (monthly), general interest, 1 130 000;

Femme d'Aujourdhui (weekly), women's magazine, 850 000;
Nous Deux (monthly), women's illustrated stories, 825 000;
Paris-Match (weekly), news, 690 000;
Jours de France (weekly), news/fashion, 675 000;
L'Express (weekly), news, 670 000;
Marie-Claire (monthly), women's magazine, 600 000;
Télérama (weekly), TV listings, 525 000;
Le Canard Enchaîné (weekly), satirical magazine, 520 000;
Intimité (weekly), women's illustrated stories, 510 000;
La Vie Catholique, religious magazine, 400 000.

Radio France broadcasts seven main channels through 47 local radio stations. There are over 1700 local commercial radio stations and three commercial stations that are almost national in their coverage. The two state-run TV channels (A2 and FR3) compete with the three private TV channels.

GERMANY

Nearly 400 daily newspapers are published in Germany, most of them confined to small regional sales. For historic reasons there is no national press although *Frankfurter Allgemeine Zeitung, Berliner Zeitung* and *Süddeutsche Zeitung* enjoy national circulations and prestige. 'Tabloid' papers such as *Bild-Zeitung* and *Super!* are increasing in popularity. There are six main newspaper groups. Principal papers (with place of publication and average circulation) include:
Bild-Zeitung, Hamburg and 15 provincial centres, 4 900 000;
Bild am Sonntag (Sunday), Hamburg, 2 400 000;
Westdeutsche Allgemeine Zeitung, Essen, 1 210 000;
Wochenpost (weekly), Berlin, 550 000;
Freie Presse, Chemnitz, 540 000;
Die Zeit (weekly), Hamburg, 490 000;
Sächsische Zeitung, Dresden, 450 000;
Mitteldeutsche Zeitung, Halle, 450 000;
Welt am Sonntag (Sunday), Hamburg, 430 000;
Frankfurter Allgemeine Zeitung, Frankfurt, 390 000;
Süddeutsche Zeitung, Munich, 390 000;
Rheinische Post, Düsseldorf, 390 000;
Super!, Berlin, 370 000;
Berliner Zeitung, Berlin, 370 000;
Nürnberger Nachrichten (evening), Nürnberg, 350 000;
Leipziger Zeitung, Leipzig, 320 000;
Magdeburgische Zeitung, Magdeburg, 320 000;
Express, Cologne, 315 000;
Hamburger Abendblatt (evening), Hamburg, 310 000;
Thüringer Allgemeine, Erfurt, 300 000.

The periodicals – by contrast – are mainly national rather than regional. Those with the largest circulations include:
Hörzu (weekly), TV listings, 3 900 000;
TV Hören + Sehen (weekly), TV listings; 2 690 000;
burda moden (monthly), fashion/cookery, 2 300 000;
Funk Uhr (weekly), TV listings, 2 000 000;
Das Beste aus Readers Digest (monthly), general interest, 1 900 000;
Neue Post (weekly), general interest, 1 750 000;
Stern (weekly), current affairs/general interest,

1 490 000;
FF-dabei (weekly), general interest, 1 490 000;
Der Spiegel (weekly), current affairs, 1 400 000;
Brigitte (fortnightly), women's magazine, 1 300 000;
Bravo (weekly), young people's magazine, 1 190 000;
Neue Revue (weekly), general interest, 1 150 000;
Bild + Funk (weekly), TV listings, 1 040 000;
Bunte Illustrierte (weekly), family magazine, 1 040 000;
Gong (weekly), TV listings, 1 000 000 circulation.

ARD is the coordinating body for radio and TV networks in Germany. Five radio networks – each broadcasting up to five channels – operate throughout the country. There are 15 regional broadcasting organizations. There are three television channels – one produced by ARD, one controlled by a public corporation and a third educational channel.

GREECE

Greece has over 130 daily newspapers most of which have only small regional circulations. A particular feature of the Greek press is afternoon papers which enjoy higher circulations than morning papers. Principal titles (with place of publication and average circulation) include:
Eleftheros Typos (afternoon), Athens, 165 000;
Ta Nea (afternoon), Athens, 135 000;
Eleftherotypia (afternoon), Athens, 110 000;
Apogevmatini (afternoon), Athens, 75 000;
Vradyni (afternoon), Athens, 70 000;
Avriani (afternoon), Athens, 50 000;
Akropolis, Athens, 50 000;
Makedhonia, Thessaloniki, 50 000.

Greek periodicals have a much lower circulation than their counterparts in most other West European countries. The titles with the highest readerships include:
Tilerama (weekly), TV listings, 190 000;
To Vima (weekly), current affairs, 165 000;
Radiotilerash (weekly), TV listings, 135 000;
Tachydromos (weekly), general interest illustrated magazine, 50 000;
Gynaika (fortnightly), women's magazine, 45 000.

The state-owned ERT station provides a national network of radio and TV programmes (three channels). Two commercial stations offer competition but are not available throughout Greece.

IRELAND

Seven daily papers are published in the Republic of Ireland. The seven Irish dailies (with place of publication and average circulation) are:
Irish Independent, Dublin, 155 000;
Evening Herald (evening), Dublin, 130 000;
Evening Press (evening), Dublin, 100 000;
The Irish Times, Dublin, 95 000;
Irish Press, Dublin, 90 000;
Cork Examiner, Cork, 65 000;
Cork Evening Echo (evening), Cork, 30 000.

British newspapers are also available in Ireland. The Sunday papers – which have greater circulations than the dailies – include:

Sunday World, Dublin, 325 000;
Sunday Independent, Dublin, 240 000;
Sunday Press, Dublin, 200 000.

The wide distribution of British magazines means that the Republic of Ireland has relatively few mass-market magazines. Those with the highest sales include:
RTE Guide (weekly), TV listings, 125 000;
Irish Farmers' Journal (weekly), 70 000;
Woman's Way (weekly), women's magazine, 70 000;
Ireland's Own (weekly), family and general interest, 55 000;
IT (monthly), society magazine, 30 000;
U Magazine (monthly), women's magazine, 25 000;
Hot Press (fortnightly), music and leisure, 25 000.

RTE – an autonomous statutory corporation – operates two national TV channels and two national radio channels. British television can be received in most of Ireland. There are over 20 local and one national commercial radio stations.

ITALY

The Italian press is characterized by low circulations compared with other West European countries. The press is concentrated in Milan and Rome and several other provincial centres produce important daily titles. There is no national press but *Corriere della Sera*, *La Repubblica* and *La Stampa* enjoy national circulations and prestige. Of 80 daily papers, the main titles (with place of publication and average circulations) include:
Corriere della Sera (evening), Milan, 850 000;
La Gazetta dello Sport (sports), Milan, 830 000;
La Repubblica, Rome, 800 000;
Corriere dello Sport (sports), Rome, 620 000;
La Stampa, Turin, 570 000;
Stampa Sera (evening), Turin, 570 000;
Il Messaggero, Rome, 390 000;
Il Sole/24 Ore (financial), Milan, 350 000;
Il Resto del Carlino, Bologna, 310 000;
L'Unità, Rome; 250 000 (Sunday 800 000);
La Nazione, Florence, 270 000;
Il Giornale, Milan, 250 000;
Il Mattino, Naples, 225 000.

There are over 9000 periodicals – most with small circulations. However, a few women's, motoring and general interest magazines (some sensationalist in tone and content) attract large readerships. The periodicals with the largest readerships are:
L'Automobile (monthly), motoring, 1 500 000;
Familia Cristiana (weekly), Catholic, 1 050 000;
Gente (weekly), political and current affairs, 900 000;
Oggi (weekly), topical and literary, 700 000;
Quattroruote (monthly), motoring magazine, 700 000;
Panorama (weekly), current affairs, 500 000;
Intimità (weekly), women's magazine, 470 000;
Mille Idee per la Donna (weekly), women's magazine, 360 000;
Confidenze (weekly), women's magazine, 360 000;
Grazia (weekly), women's magazine, 360 000;
Gioia (weekly), women's magazine, 350 000;
Visto (weekly), general interest, 350 000;
Annabella (weekly), women's magazine, 270 000.

Italy has over 450 local commercial TV stations, seven of

which are virtually national, as well as RAI (Radiotelevisione Italiana) – the national network which runs three channels – and a Catholic network. RAI broadcasts national radio channels and there are over 1000 local commercial radio stations.

LUXEMBOURG

Despite its small size and population, the Grand Duchy has five daily newspapers – four national papers (published in French and German) and one local edition of a French paper. These papers (with place of publication and average circulation) are:
Luxemburger Wort/La Voix du Luxembourg, Luxembourg city, 85 000;
Tageblatt/Zeitung fir Letzebuerg, Esch-sur-Alzette, 25 000;
Lëtzebuerger Journal, Luxembourg city, 10 000;
Le Républicain Lorrain, Luxembourg edition, Luxembourg city, 10 000;
Zeitung vum Letzeburger Vollek, Luxembourg city; 8000.

Nearly 20 periodicals are published, but French and German magazines also circulate. The principal Luxembourgeois periodicals are:
Télécran (weekly), TV listings, 37 000;
OGB-L Aktuell (monthly), trade union magazine, 28 000;
Soziale Fortschrett (fortnightly), trade union magazine, 23 000;
Revue (weekly), general interest illustrated, 25 000;
AutoRevue (monthly), motoring, 10 000.

RTL is a private company operating TV and radio programmes inside and outside the state. The TV station broadcasts in French; the radio station broadcasts in French, German and Dutch. Two other organizations operate seven TV stations and a satellite network.

THE NETHERLANDS

The national Dutch press comprises eight newspapers printed in Amsterdam, Rotterdam and the Hague. In addition, there are over 70 daily provincial papers. The majority of newspaper sales are by subscription rather than over-the-counter sales. The main titles (with place of publication and average circulation) include:
De Telegraaf, Amsterdam, 780 000;
Algemeen Dagblad, Rotterdam, 415 000;
De Volkskrant, Amsterdam, 340 000;
Brabants Dagblad, s'Hertogenbosch, with *Eindhovens Dagblad*, Eindhoven, with *Het Nieuwsblad*, Tilburg, 295 000;
NRC Handelsblad (evening), Rotterdam, 240 000;
De Gelderlander, Nijmegen, 170 000;
Haagsche Courant (evening), The Hague, 170 000;
Dagblad Tubantia (evening), Enschede, with *Twentsche Courant/Overijssels Dagblad* (evening), Hengelo, 155 000;
Nieuwblad van het Noorden (evening), Groningen, 140 000;
De Limburger, Maastricht, 140 000;
Trouw, Amsterdam, 120 000;
Rotterdam Dagblad (evening), Rotterdam, 115 000.

The Dutch periodicals with the largest circulations are:
Kampioen (monthly), motoring and travel, 2 600 000;

Veronica (weekly), TV listings, 1 060 000;
AVRO bode (weekly), TV listings, 920 000;
Libelle (weekly), women's magazine, 750 000;
TrosKompas (weekly), TV listings, 720 000;
Margriet (weekly), women's magazine, 590 000; *Privé*
(weekly), women's magazine, 480 000;
NCRV-Gids (weekly), TV listings, 475 000;
Story (weekly), general interest, 420 000;
Micro-Gids (weekly), TV listings, 405 000;
Het Beste uit Reader's Digest (monthly), general interest,
400 000.

NOS/NOB – an autonomous state corporation –
operates three TV channels which broadcast programmes provided by eight broadcasting organizations, each
one of which has a particular social, political or religious character. The associations are allotted time on the
three channels in proportion to their membership. A
commercial network broadcasts from Luxembourg.
There are five national, 10 regional and over 140 local
radio stations.

PORTUGAL

The greater part of the Portuguese daily press was
nationalized after the 1974 revolution. However, major
titles were privatized between 1979 amd 1991. There are
30 daily papers – including six published in Lisbon and
three in Oporto – but circulation figures are very low by
European standards. The main titles (with place of
publication and average circulation) are:
Correio da Manhã, Lisbon, 85 000;
Jornal de Noticias, Oporto, 70 000;
Público, Lisbon, 65 000;
Diário Popular (evening), Lisbon, 65 000;
Diário de Noticias, Lisbon, 60 000;
O Primeiro de Janeiro, Oporto, 50 000;
A Capital (evening), Lisbon, 40 000.

By contrast, sales of magazines – particularly sports, TV
listings and women's magazines – are larger:
TV Guia (weekly), TV listings, 560 000;
Maria (weekly), women's magazine, 390 000;
A Bola (4 a week), sports (mainly soccer), 180 000;
Nova Gente (weekly), general interest, 180 000;
Selecções do Reader's Digest (monthly), general interest,
180 000;
Expresso (weekly), current affairs, 160 000;
Record (4 a week), sports (mainly soccer), 120 000;
Guia-Revista Prática (weekly), women's magazine,
80 000;
O Independente (weekly), current affairs, 80 000;
JL (weekly), arts, 80 000.

Televisão Portuguesa – a state corporation – operates
two TV channels and three regional stations. Two
commercial stations now offer competition. There are
four national and five regional RDP (state corporation)
radio stations as well as one national commercial and
over 300 local radio stations.

SPAIN

Strong historic regional identities and the lack of a
single national language have conspired to prevent the
emergence of a national press in Spain. Only *ABC*, *Ya*
and *El País* circulate Spain. Circulation figures for
Spain's 120 daily papers are low. Local weekly papers
published on a Monday and carrying national and
international news – *Hoja del Lunes* – were a feature of
the Spanish regional press until recently. The principal
papers (with place of publication and average circulation) include:
El País, Madrid, Barcelona, Valencia and Seville,
460 000 (1 050 000 Sunday);
ABC, Madrid and Seville, 360 000 (600 000 Sunday);
La Vanguardia, Barcelona, 195 000 (320 000 Sunday);
La Opinión de Murcia, Murcia, 180 000;
Diario 16 (evening), Madrid, 180 000 (210 000 Sunday);
El Periódico, Barcelona, 160 000 (380 000 Sunday);
El Mundo, Madrid, 145 000 (215 000 Sunday);
As (sports), Madrid, 145 000;
El Correo Español-El Pueblo Vasco, Bilbao, 135 000;
El Observador de la Actualidad, Barcelona, 120 000;
Marca (sports), Madrid, 115 000.

Current affairs, women's and general interest magazines and TV listings guides outsell newspapers in
Spain. The periodicals with the largest sales are:
TP Teleprogramma (weekly), TV listings, 1 400 000;
Estar Viva (monthly), women's magazine, 1 220 000;
Tele Indiscreta (weekly), TV listings, 950 000;
Pronto (weekly), general interest, 925 000;
Hola! (weekly), general interest, 585 000;
Hogar y Moda (weekly), women's magazine, 550 000;
Interviú (weekly), general interest, 495 000;
Panorama Internacional (weekly), general interest,
420 000;
Diez Minutos (weekly), general interest, 380 000;
Lecturas (weekly), women's magazine, 345 000;
Semana (weekly), general interest, 340 000;
Super Pop (fortnightly), teenage, 300 000.

RTVE is a public corporation that controls and coordinates TV and radio. There are seven regional television
companies including those broadcasting in Basque,
Catalan and Galician. RNE runs five national channels
and there are three regional stations broadcasting in
Basque, Catalan and Galician. There are over 300 local
radio stations.

UNITED KINGDOM

The UK has a national rather than a regional press. The
British press is characterized by the popularity of
sensational 'tabloids' which do not exist elsewhere in
Europe. As well as the 12 national newspaper titles there
are 88 regional dailies including Scottish and Northern
Irish papers which may be regarded as 'national' in their
own countries. The main papers (with the place of
publication and average circulation) include:
News of the World (Sunday), London, 4 690 000;
The Sun, London, 3 600 000;
Daily Mirror, London, 2 700 000 copies;
Sunday Mirror (Sunday), London, 2 670 000;
The Mail on Sunday (Sunday), London, 2 070 000;
The People (Sunday), London, 2 055 000;
Daily Mail, London, 1 750 000;
Sunday Express (Sunday), London, 1 725 000;
Daily Express, London, 1 500 000;
The Sunday Times (Sunday), London, 1 200 000;
Sunday Post (Sunday), Dundee, 1 140 000;

Daily Telegraph, London, 1 035 000;
Sunday Mail (Sunday), Glasgow, 880 000;
Daily Star, London, 785 000;
Daily Record, Glasgow, 755 000;
Sunday Telegraph (Sunday), London, 585 000;
The Observer (Sunday), London, 540 000;
Today, London, 535 000;
Evening Standard, London, 500 000;
The Times, published in London, 460 000;
The Guardian, London, 405 000;
The Independent on Sunday (Sunday), London, 405 000;
The Independent, London, 330 000;
Manchester Evening News (evening), Manchester, 330 000;
Daily Sport, London, 300 000;
Financial Times (financial), London, 290 000.

Leisure and women's interest magazines attract large readerships. In recent years British magazines have faced considerable competition from overseas publishers, for example *Prima*, *Best*, and *Bella*. The following magazines have the highest circulations:
Satellite Times, satellite TV listings, 2 900 000;
TV Weekly, TV listings, 2 720 000;
TV First, TV listings, 2 100 000;
TV Quick, TV listings, 2 000 000;
Radio Times, TV listings, 1 590 000;
Reader's Digest, general interest, 1 540 000;
What's On TV, TV listings, 1 400 000;
Take A Break, general interest, 1 300 000;
Bella, women's magazine, 1 200 000;
TV Times, TV listings, 1 115 000;
Viz, humorous magazine, 870 000;
Woman's Weekly, women's magazine, 865 000;
Which?, consumers' magazine, 800 000;
Prima, women's magazine, 740 000;
Woman's Own, women's magazine, 730 000;
Woman, women's magazine, 715 000.

The BBC (British Broadcasting Corporation) – which is financed by licence fees – has five national BBC radio services, plus national regional services in Wales, Scotland and Northern Ireland. There are over 50 BBC regional and local stations. There are two national independent radio stations and 80 independent local and community radio stations. There are four national television stations: BBC 1, BBC 2, ITV (Channel 3; an independent commercial station made up of regional programme contractors) and Channel 4 (an independent commercial station). In addition S4C Welsh Fourth Channel is available only in Wales (instead of Channel Four). British Sky Broadcasting PLC – a satellite channel – offers sport, film, music and news channels.

AUSTRIA

The six daily newspapers published in Vienna – including *Wiener Zeitung* (founded 1730), the oldest daily newspaper in the world – and *Salzburger Nachrichten* comprise Austria's national daily press. There are 12 other daily papers. Major titles (with place of publication and average circulation) include:
Neue Kronen-Zeitung, Vienna, 1 075 000;
Kurier, Vienna, 445 000;
Kleine Zeitung, Graz, 270 000;

Oberösterreichische Nachrichten, Linz, 115 000;
Salzburger Nachrichten, Salzburg, 110 000;
Neue A-Z, Vienna, 105 000;
Tiroler Tageszeitung, Innsbruck, 105 000;
Kleine Zeitung, Klagenfurt, 100 000.

Despite the fact that German periodicals circulate throughout Austria, there is a healthy number of Austrian magazines including a number of news magazines that resemble newspapers. Principal titles include:
auto touring (monthly), motoring and travel, 890 000;
Die ganze Woche (weekly), general interest/current affairs, 820 000;
Oberösterreichische Rundschau (weekly), regional news and general interest, 255 000;
Niederösterreichische Nachrichten (weekly), regional news and general interest, 135 000;
Neue Wochenschau (weekly), new/current affairs, 130 000;
Profil (weekly), political magazine, 105 000;
Samstag (weekly), news/current affairs, 100 000;
Bunte Österreich (weekly), general interest illustrated magazine, 100 000.

ORF – an autonomous state corporation – is the sole provider of radio and TV programmes. It has two TV channels, and three national and 10 regional stations.

FINLAND

The Finnish press is characterized by the independent ownership of its principal titles. The newspaper chains that are common elsewhere in Western Europe do not exist in Finland. There are 65 daily papers – 53 published in Finnish and 12 in Swedish. The titles published in Helsinki have national distributions. Daily papers (with place of publication and average circulation) include:
Helsingin Sanomat, Helsinki, 480 000;
Ilta-Sanomat (afternoon), Helsinki, 225 000;
Iltalehti (afternoon), Helsinki, 115 000 (Saturday 160 000);
Aamulehti, Tampere, 145 000;
Turun Sanomat, Turku, 135 000;
Kaleva, Oulu, 100 000;
Savon Sanomat, Kuopio, 90 000;
Kauppalehti, Helsinki, 85 000;
Keskisuomalainen, Jyväskylä, 80 000.

A number of magazines enjoy very high circulations, given the relatively small population of Finland. Journals published by cooperative societies and retail stores are a particular feature. Principal titles include:
Pirkka (monthly), consumers' and general interest magazine, free in retail stores, 1 705 000;
Yhteishyvä (monthly), consumers' and general interest magazine, free in cooperative stores, 425 000;
Kauppa ja Koti (monthly), consumers' and general interest magazine, free in retail stores, 420 000;
Valitut Palat (monthly), Finnish Reader's Digest, 345 000;
Me (10 a year), family magazine, free to cooperative society members, 305 000;
Aku Ankka (weekly), children's magazine, 305 000;
Seura (weekly), family journal, 275 000;
Apu (weekly), family journal, 255 000;
Akava (monthly), economics and administration,

205 000;
Kotivinkki (11 a year), family magazine, 205 000.

Television and radio are provided by the state-controlled YLE network. Its three TV channels also broadcast programmes made by two commercial companies which lease broadcasting time. YLE has two national radio stations and a number of regional stations. There are over 30 local radio stations. Broadcasting is in both Finnish and Swedish.

ICELAND

A very small domestic market limits the size of the Icelandic press to six daily papers, four of which support particular political parties although the two largest are independent. The daily papers (with place of publication and average circulation) are:
Morgunbladid, Rekyjavik, 50 000;
Timinn, Reykjavik, 30 000;
Thjódviljinn, Rekjavik, 15 000;
Althýdubladid, Rekjavik, 9000;
Dagur, Akureyri, 6000 copies.
Iceland has a surprisingly large number of magazines and other periodicals. The following have the largest circulations:
Sjónvarpsvísir Stödvar (monthly), general interest, 50 000;
Pressan (weekly), current affairs, 17 000;
Mannlif (monthly), general interest, 15 000;
Hús og hibýli (6 a year), homes and domestic, 15 000;
Vikan (fortnightly), news/general interest, 14 000;
Samúel (monthly), leisure, motoring, sport, 13 000.

There are two TV channels – one state-owned (Rikisút-varpid), one commercial (Stöd 2). There are two state-owned and one privately-owned radio station.

LIECHTENSTEIN

There are two daily newspapers, each of which is the organ of one of the two major political parties. These papers (with place of publication and average circulation) are:
Liechtensteiner Vaterland, Vaduz, 9000;
Liechtensteiner Volksblatt, Schaan, 8000.

There are no magazines published in Liechtenstein. Swiss radio and TV are received in the principality.

NORWAY

Norway has over 60 daily papers most of which are confined to relatively small regions. However, a few Oslo titles have achieved a national readership. The principal newspapers (with place of publication and average circulation) include:
Verdens Gang, Oslo, 365 000;
Dagbladet, Oslo, 220 000;
Aftenposten, Oslo, 195 000;
Bergens Tidende, Bergen, 100 000;
Adresseavisen, Oslo, 90 000;
Arbeiderbladet, Oslo, 50 000;
Faedrelandsvennen, Kristiansand, 50 000;
Drammens Tidende og Buskeruds Blad, Drammen, 45 000.

Among the wide selection of Norwegian magazines motoring, family, TV listings and farming periodicals are the most popular. The highest sales are achieved by:
Motor (monthly), motoring, 445 000;
Se og Hor (weekly), TV listings, 315 000;
Hjemmet (weekly), family magazine, 290 000;
Norsk Ukeblad (weekly), family magazine, 260 000;
Donald Duck & Co (weekly), children's magazine, 210 000;
Allers (weekly), farming magazine, 160 000;
Det Beste (monthly), Norwegian Reader's Digest, 160 000;
Familien (fortnightly), family magazine, 155 000;
Kontor (querterly), business, 140 000;
Vi Menn (weekly), men's magazine, 120 000;
Bondebladet (weekly), farming magazine, 115 000.

NRK – an autonomous state corporation – has a monopoly on radio and TV broadcasting. It operates two national, 17 regional and several community radio stations.

SWEDEN

Although there are nearly 60 regional daily newspapers, the most influential titles are those published in Stockholm. The four leading Stockholm papers virtually constitute a national press. A significant number of Swedish papers are owned by trade unions or political parties. The main papers (with place of publication and average circulation) are:
Expressen (evening), Stockholm, 560 000 copies (Sunday 680 000);
Dagens Nyheter, Stockholm, 395 000 (Sunday 455 000);
Aftonbladet (evening), Stockholm, 365 000 (Sunday 460 000);
Göteborgs-Posten, Gothenburg, 275 000 (Sunday 315 000);
Svenska Dagbladet, Stockholm, 230 000;
Dag (evening), Gothenburg, 190 000 (Sunday 250 000 copies);
Arbetet, Malmö, 115 000;
Sydsvenska Dagbladet Snällposten, Malmö (Sunday 140 000);
Dagens Industri (business), Stockholm, 80 000;
Nya Wermlands-Tidningen, Karlstad, 75 000;
Nerikes Allehanda, Orebro, 70 000;
Ostgöta Correspondenten, Linköping, 70 000.

Swedish magazines enjoy a wide circulation. Family and domestic titles are the most popular. As well as those titles listed below, the magazines of trade unions also enjoy a wide readership – the magazine of the Union of Municipal Workers, for instance, has a circulation of over 670 000. The principal magazines include:
Var Bostad (11 a year), house and home, 970 000;
ICA Kuriren (weekly), house and home, 540 000;
Land (weekly), farming, 400 000;
Aret Rund (weekly), family journal, 315 000;
Hemmets Veckotidning (weekly), family journal, 305 000;
PRO-Pensionarën (10 a year), pensioners' magazine, 290 000;
Hemmets Journal (weekly), family magazines, 290 000;
Allers (weekly), family magazine, 285 000;
Vi Bilägare (fortnightly), cars, hobbies, home, 250 000;

Kalle Anka & Co (weekly), children's magazine, 225 000;
Motor (monthly), motoring, 200 000.

Sveriges Radio (SR) – an autonomous state corporation
– operates two TV channels. There are also two commercial channels. SR operates four national radio stations.
There are 24 local and over 10 community radio stations.

SWITZERLAND

Four national languages and a strong local identity in
individual cantons have encouraged the existence of
many (107) daily papers. However, only 14 of these titles
have a readership of over 50 000. There is no national
press but *Journal de Genève* and *Neue Zürcher Zeitung*
have international reputations. The principal papers
(with place of publication and average circulation)
include:
Blick (German), Zürich, 385 000;
Tages Anzeiger Zürich (German), Zürich, 270 000;
Le Matin (French), Lausanne, 160 000;
Neue Zürcher Zeitung (German), Zürich, 150 000;
Berner Zeitung (German), Berne, 125 000;
Baseler Zietung (German), Basel, 115 000;
La Suisse (French), Geneva, 110 000;
24 heures (French), Lausanne, 95 000;
Luzerner Zeitung (German), Lucerne, 80 000;
St Gallet Tagblatt (German), St Gall, 70 000;
Der Bund (German), Berne, 60 000;
Tribune de Genève (French), Geneva, 60 000;
Luzerner Neuste Nachrichten (German), Lucerne, 55 000.

French, German and Italian magazines circulate in
Switzerland. Nevertheless, there are many Swiss maga-
zines, some with high circulations. They include:
Touring (fortnightly; French, German and Italian),
travel/tourism, 1 120 000;
Der Schweizerische Beobachter (fortnightly; German),
general interest illustrated, 410 000;
Trente jours (monthly; French), general interest,
400 000;
Das Beste aus Reader's Digest (monthly; French and
German editions), general interest, 335 000;
Tele (weekly; German), TV listings, 285 000;
Schweizer Familie (weekly; German), family, 240 000;
Radio-TV (weekly; French), TV listings, 225 000;
Schweizer Illustrierte (weekly; German), general inter-
est illustrated, 205 000;
Meyers Modeblatt (weekly; German), fashion, 200 000;
Tes-Revue (monthly; German), touring, 200 000;
Glücks-Post (monthly; German), general interest,
190 000;
Ski (7 a year; French, German and Italian), skiing,
110 000;
Weltwoche (weekly; German), current affairs, 105 000;
Femme d'aujourdhui (weekly; French), women's maga-
zine, 105 000;
Annabelle (fortnightly; German), women's magazine,
105 000.

RTSR broadcasts radio and TV programmes in French,
DRS in German and RTSI in Italian. These three
societies constitute SBC, a private company that fulfils
a public broadcasting duty. There are three TV channels
and three SBC radio stations in each main language and
a number of local private commercial stations.

THE ARTS

The number of arts festivals held in the countries of
Western Europe is increasing. The following list
includes most of the principal festivals and gives a
flavour of what is on offer at some of the other events.

Belgium The Festival of Flanders, a music festival, is
held in several Flemish towns between April and October. Its counterpart in the south of Belgium, the Festival
of Wallonia, is held in a number of venues from September to November. The autumn also sees the annual Liège
Nuits de Septembre music festival.

Denmark The Copenhagen dance festival is held in
May.

France Probably the most famous arts festivals held in
France are the Aix-en-Provence music festival, which is
held in July and August, the Cannes international film
festival (May) and a drama and dance festival held in
Avignon in July and August. Other festivals include
Arles (music, dance and drama – held in July), the Bach
festival in Mulhouse (held in June), the Berlioz festival
in Lyon (held in September) and the Strasbourg choral
festival (held in March and April). Lille stages a music,
dance, drama and folklore festival from October to
November, while Paris hosts a dance festival from
September to December and a music festival in January.

Germany The Berlin film festival, which is held in
February and March, and the Wagner festival, which is
held at Bayreuth in July and August, are among the
many important German arts festivals. The most important music festivals are the Handel festival held at Halle
(in June), the Bach festivals at Ansbach (in July and
August) and at Leipzig (in September), and the Beet-
hoven festival at Bonn (from May to September). Berlin
stages a music, dance and drama festival from September
to October, while Wiesbaden hosts a music, ballet and
drama festival in May.

Greece The most famous arts festivals in Greece are the
Epidavros music and drama festival, which is held in the
summer, and the Athens international music and drama
festival, which is held at the same time.

Ireland Ireland has a number of international festivals
but none is as well-known as the Wexford opera festival,
which is held from October to November.

Italy The Venice film festival, held in August and
September, probably attracts more public attention
than any other Italian arts festival. In May and June,
Florence stages a music festival with an emphasis on
opera; in September and October, Perugia holds a sacred
music festival. Bergamo and Brescia stage a music
festival in April and May, while the biennial Venice
contemporary music festival takes place in September.
Music, dance and drama feature in the Spoleto festival
every June and July.

Luxembourg The Echternach music festival is held
annually in May and June.

Netherlands The Festival of Holland, a major festival of music, dance and drama, is staged in June in three cities – Amsterdam, The Hague and Rotterdam.

Portugal The principal Portuguese arts festival is held at Estoril every June when music, dance and drama are featured.

Spain Cuenca stages a festival of religious music at Easter, while the Barcelona festival of music, dance and drama is staged in October. In June and July, Granada holds a festival of music, dance and folklore.

UK The largest music festival in Britain is the Promenade Concerts which are held between June and September. Other major music festivals include the Aldeburgh opera festival (held in June), the Glyndebourne opera season (held from May to August) and the Three Choirs Festival, which is held alternately in Gloucester, Hereford and Worcester from August to September. Cheltenham stages a music and literature festival in July, while the Glasgow Mayfest (held appropriately in May) stages drama, music and dance. The Edinburgh Festival (held in August and September) features dance, music and, in particular, innovative drama. Although of relatively recent origin, the Brighton Festival has become an important showcase for music, dance and drama. The Welsh National Eisteddfod – a festival of folklore, music, dance and drama – is held alternately in north and south Wales at different venues.

Austria The Mozart festival, which is held in Salzburg each July and August, is one of the most prestigious European arts festivals. The Bregenz summer music festival is held in July and August on the famous lakeside stage with seating for 6300 in the auditorium. The Graz festival of music, dance and drama is held in October and November, while the Linz music festival is held in the early autumn. Vienna, one of major cultural centres of Europe, stages music, dance and drama festivals between March and June.

Finland The national Finnish enthusiasm for opera is reflected in the Savonlinna opera festival which is held in July. The Helsinki music and dance festival is staged in August and September.

Iceland The Rekyjavik arts festival is held in June.

Norway The principal Norwegian arts festival is the Bergen festival of music, dance and drama, which is staged in May and June.

Sweden The most famous of the Swedish arts festivals is the unique opera festival that is held in the 18th-century court theatre at the Drottningholm royal palace, near Stockholm, between May and September.

Switzerland The Lucerne international music festival (held in August and September) is one of Europe's major arts festivals. Other Swiss festivals include the Lausanne music, dance and drama festival (held between May and July), the Montreux-Vevey music festival (staged from August to October) and the Zürich and Fribourg music festivals, staged respectively in June and July.

LEADING EUROPEAN ORCHESTRAS

Among the many outstanding symphony and other orchestras in the countries of Western Europe are the following:

Denmark
The Danish National Radio Symphony Orchestra (founded 1925), based in Copenhagen.

France
The French Philharmonic Orchestra (Radio France; founded 1976), based in Paris.
Orchestre de Paris (founded 1967).
Orchestre National de France (founded 1934), based in Paris.

Germany
The Bavarian Radio Symphony Orchestra (founded 1949), based in Munich.
Berlin Philharmonic Orchestra (founded 1882).
Dresden State Orchestra (which can be traced to 1548).
Gewandhaus Orchestra of Leipzig (founded 1781).
Stuttgart Chamber Orchestra (founded 1945).
Südwestfunk Orchestra (founded 1946), based in Baden-Baden.

Italy
Santa Cecilia Orchestra (founded 1907), based in Rome.

Netherlands
Royal Concertgebouw Orchestra (founded 1888), based in Amsterdam.

Spain
National Orchestra of Spain (founded 1940), based in Madrid.

United Kingdom
Hallé Orchestra (founded 1858), based in Manchester.
London Philharmonic Orchestra (founded 1932).
London Symphony Orchestra (founded 1904).
The Royal Liverpool Philharmonic Orchestra (founded 1840s).
The Royal Philharmonic Orchestra (founded 1946), based in London.
The Royal Scottish Orchestra (founded 1891), based in Glasgow.

Austria
Concertus Musicus Wien (founded 1953), based in Vienna.

Finland
Helsinki Philharmonic Orchestra (founded 1882).

Norway
Oslo Philharmonic Orchestra (founded 1871).

Sweden
Stockholm Philharmonic Orchestra (founded 1902).

Switzerland
Orchestre de la Suisse Romande (founded 1918), based in Geneva.

NATIONAL BUDGETS

BELGIUM

Revenue: 1 898 066 million Belgian francs (1991) – direct taxation 726 471 million francs (38% of revenue), regional taxes 708 848 million francs (37%), VAT, etc. 187 230 million francs (10%), customs and excise 149 879 million francs (8%).

Expenditure: 2 322 005 million Belgian francs (1991) – regional budgets 775 612 million francs (33% of total expenditure), government departments 575 484 million francs (25%), pensions 238 802 million francs (10%), defence 101 506 million francs (4%).

DENMARK

Revenue: 279 855 million kroner (1991) – income and property tax 127 614 million kroner (46% of total revenue), customs and excise 121 239 million kroner (43%).

Expenditure: 318 177 million kroner (1991) – social affairs 75 649 million kroner (24% of total expenditure), education 20 476 million kroner (6%), defence 15 814 million kroner (4%), justice 7 0162 million kroner (2%), finance 3 523 million kroner (1%).

FRANCE

Revenue: 1 082 127 million francs (1991) – VAT 586 965 million francs (53% of total income), income tax 243 830 million francs (22%), corporation tax 154 500 million francs (14%), petroleum revenue 113 600 million francs (10%).
Expenditure: 1 177 190 million francs (1991) – education and culture 277 613 million francs (24% of total expenditure), social services and health 223 175 million francs (19%), public authorities and administration 147 944 million francs (13%), defence 15 814 million francs (4%).

GERMANY

Revenue: 1 542 503 million DM (1991) – taxation 1 086 662 million DM (70% of total revenue).
Expenditure: 1 647 577 million DM (1991) – no breakdown of this figure was available at the time of going to press.

GREECE

Revenue: 3 812 400 million drachmae (1989) – indirect taxation 1 501 970 million drachmae (28% of total revenue), credit receipts 1 051 800 million drachmae (20%), direct taxation 616 065 million drachmae (12%).

Expenditure: 3 812 400 million drachmae (1989) – health, welfare, education and social services 2 776 295 million drachmae (52% of total expenditure), defence 101 700 million drachmae (2%).

IRELAND

Revenue: 9 312 million IR£ (1991) – income tax 3 406 million IR£ (37% of total revenue), VAT 2 230 million IR£ (24%), customs and excise 1 846 million IR£ (20%), corporation tax 678 million IR£ (7%).

Expenditure: 9 648 million IR£ (1991) – social welfare 1 941 million IR£ (20% of total expenditure), health 1 402 million IR£ (15%), education 1 343 million IR£ (14%), defence 372 million IR£ (4%), industry and labour 264 million IR£ (3%), agriculture, fisheries, etc. 286 million IR£ (3%).

ITALY

Revenue: 410 127 544 million lire (1991) – property and income tax 184 290 086 million lire (45%), business tax and duties 94 200 749 million lire (23%), customs and sales 35 985 185 million lire (9%), state monopolies 6 385 531 million lire (2%).

Expenditure: 535 253 686 million lire (1991) – Treasury 284 934 538 million lire (53% of expenditure), Interior 55 645 257 million lire (10%), labour and social welfare 51 311 295 million lire (10%), education 40 911 207 million lire (8%), defence 24 332 433 million lire (5%).

LUXEMBOURG

Revenue: 110 237 million Luxembourgeois francs (1990) – income tax 48 575 million francs (44% of total revenue), sales tax 15 846 million francs (14%), customs and duties 10 321 million francs (9%).

Expenditure: 109 814 million Luxembourgeois francs (1990) – social services 28 910 million francs (26% of total expenditure), transport and power 16 437 million francs (15%), education 15 486 million francs (14%), administration 7 752 million francs (7%), health and housing 6 807 million francs (6%).

NETHERLANDS

Revenue: 187 502 million guilders (1991) – income tax 66 843 million guilders (36% of total revenue), sales tax 39 930 million guilders (21%), corporation tax 18 566 million guilders (10%), excise duties 10 349 million guilders (6%), natural gas revenue 7 264 million guilders (4%).

Expenditure: 206 841 million guilders (1991) – social services and health 51 948 million guilders (25%), education and culture 34 870 million guilders (17%), defence 14 144 million guilders (7%), transport and public works 12 066 million guilders (6%), housing and planning 12 298 million guilders (6%), agriculture 8 513 million guilders (4%).

PORTUGAL

Revenue: 2 591 million escudos (1989) – taxes on goods and services 940 million escudos (36% of total revenue), social services contributions 658 million escudos (25%), income and profit tax 605 million escudos (23%).

Expenditure: 2 493 million escudos (1989) – social services and welfare 641 million escudos (26% of total expenditure), education 275 million escudos (11%), health 225 million escudos (9%), public services 171 million escudos (7%), defence 147 million escudos (6%).

SPAIN

Revenue: 12 541 000 million pesetas (1992) – direct taxation 6 026 900 million pesetas (48% of total revenue), indirect taxation 5 277 100 million pesetas (42%), estate taxes 688 600 (5%).

Expenditure: 13 701 765 million pesetas (1992) – health 1 687 096 million pesetas (12%), labour and social services 1 243 710 million pesetas (9%), public works and transport 1 077 534 million pesetas (8%), education and science 1 035 636 million pesetas (8%), defence 785 369 million pesetas (6%).

UK

Revenue: £221 131 million (1991) – taxes on expenditure £83 023 million (38% of total revenue), income tax £75 105 million (34%), National Insurance £36 643 million (17%).

Expenditure: £227 529 million (1991) – social services £73 870 million (32% of total expenditure), health £30 934 (14%), education £29 522 million (13%), defence £27 336 (12%).

AUSTRIA

Revenue: 595 187 million Schillings (1991) – direct taxation 178 817 million Schillings (30% of total revenue), indirect taxation 176 480 million Schillings (30%).

Expenditure: 595 187 million Schillings (1991) – goods and services 119 330 million Schillings (20% of total expenditure), public bodies 74 903 million Schillings (13%), interest on public debt 42 103 million Schillings (7%), regional authorities 42 103 million (7%).

FINLAND

Revenue: 167 959 million markkaa (1991) – indirect taxes 74 127 million markkaa (44% of total revenue), direct taxes 41 054 million markkaa (24%).

Expenditure: 167 959 million markkaa (1991) – health and social services 51 918 million markkaa (31% of total expenditure), education 29 506 million markkaa (18%), agriculture and forestry 13 320 million markkaa (8%), transport and communications 10 533 million markkaa (6%), defence 8 866 million markkaa (5%).

ICELAND

Revenue: 134 709 million kronur (1991) – indirect taxes 79 560 million kronur (59% of total revenue), direct taxes 45 219 million kronur (34%).

Expenditure: 160 467 million kronur (1991) – education, health, and welfare 72 800 million kronur (45.4% of total expenditure), agriculture and fisheries 11 572 million kronur (7.2%), communications 11 440 million kronur (7.1%), general administration 8 157 million kronur (5.1%).

LIECHTENSTEIN

Revenue: 439.4 million Swiss francs (1991).

Expenditure: 361.8 million Swiss francs (1991).

NORWAY

Revenue: 356 750 million kroner (1991) – purchase tax 65 600 million kroner (18% of total revenue), petroleum extraction tax 29 950 million kroner (8%), income and property tax 19 960 million kroner (6%), alcohol tax 6 159 million kroner (2%).

Expenditure: 408 010 million kroner (1991) – social services 92 975 million kroner (23% of total expenditure), education 31 345 million kroner (8%), communications 25 716 million kroner (6%), defence 22 430 million kroner (6%).

SWEDEN

Revenue: 381 984 million kroner (1992) – taxes on goods and services 186 238 million kroner (49% of total revenue), social security fees 81 060 million kroner (21%), property tax 25 999 million kroner (7%), income and profit tax 23 882 million kroner (6%).

Expenditure: 482 162 million kroner (1992) – health and social services 131 013 million kroner (27% of total expenditure), education 50 912 million kroner (11%), labour 38 590 million kroner (8%), defence 37 745 million kroner (8%), transport and communications 18 810 million kroner (4%).

SWITZERLAND

Revenue: 33 490 million Swiss francs (1991) – indirect taxes 16 282 million francs (49% of total revenue), taxes on income and wealth 12 884 million francs (38%).

Expenditure: 35 501 million Swiss francs (1991) – social services 8 091 million francs (23%), defence 6 202 francs (17%), communications and energy 5 585 million francs (16%), financial services 4 586 million francs (13%), agriculture and forestry 3 078 million francs (9%), education 2 655 million francs (7%).

THE ENVIRONMENT

The European Community has instigated several environmental Action Programmes whose aims can be summarized as: a reduction of pollution; a reduction of nuisance; to protect natural resources; to organize environmental research; to prevent further pollution; to improve environmental monitoring techniques; to cooperate with developing countries on enviromental issues; and to make environmental protection an integral part of all social and economic planning. The Community has brought out over 200 directives and other pieces of environmental legislation over the past 20 years. These range from regulations on water pollution and air pollution to the transport of toxic waste, and from water treatment to noise abatement. In December 1992 the EC adopted a broad strategy document which is now being implemented. It highlights five areas where environmental problems are worst: industry, agriculture, energy, transport and tourism.

DIFFERING STANDARDS

Despite the role played by EC directives, in practice, the countries of Western Europe have widely differing environmental standards. Austria, Switzerland and the Scandinavian countries rate highly in matters such as water pollution, energy efficiency, sewage treatment, the designation and running of natural parks and nature reserves, and in the disposal of household waste. Less developed countries such as Portugal and Spain have far lower rates of air pollution and car use than the states of northern Europe; the Iberian countries also have far lower rates of refuse production. However, they – and Greece – generally have lower standards of sewage treatment and water pollution than northern Europe. West Germany had one of the best environmental records in Western Europe. Reunification has changed Germany's ranking in any table of environmental progress. The former GDR was badly polluted. Its heavy industries were major polluters and a united Germany now faces a major task cleaning up the east.

GLOBAL WARMING

The transportation systems of the world, especially aviation and motor vehicles, are responsible for the release of vast quantities of nitrous oxides, carbon dioxide, lead and benzine into the atmosphere. These all contribute to the greenhouse effect, that is the slow warming of Earth. This will have an impact upon climate and many human activities. Western Europe is currently responsible for the emission of almost 12% of global carbodioxide emissions. In the countries of Western Europe all forms of transport consume 44% of all petroleum used a year. In some countries strenuous efforts have been made to increase the energy efficiency of transportation systems and some progress has been made to reduce the usage of the private car – local government and company measures taken in Germany are notable in this respect.

HOUSEHOLD RUBBISH

The disposal of household rubbish is a major environmental problem in Western Europe. The EC produces over 100 000 000 tonnes of household rubbish per annum – only about 20% of which is recycled. Until recently much hope was placed in the value of recycling waste material but in Germany the problems associated with recycling have brought the issue of the disposal of packaging waste to the country's political agenda. A scheme was set up in Germany whereby waste for recycling is placed in special yellow bins supplied by DSD, the company established to run Germany's recycling initiative. The problem is that – with most German households taking part – the scheme has been too popular and too much waste has been collected. Tens of thousands of tonnes of waste material have mounted up and, in an attempt to clear the backlog, Germany has begun to export the material for recycling to its neighbours. This has had a knock-on effect. Cheap – and even free – waste material from Germany imported into Britain has undermined part of the commercial recycling schemes in the UK. France has taken a lead in sponsoring the burning of rubbish with energy recovery and burning household waste to produce energy has as much prominence as recycling in French waste policy.

THE EFFECT OF PUBLIC PROJECTS

Major projects, such as motorways, dams, HEP plants and reservoirs, can have a destructive effect on the environment. It is sometimes difficult to balance the benefits derived from a project and the environmental harm that it might do. One of the most controversial schemes in Europe is the Acheloös scheme in Greece where – with the construction of two vast dams and 18 km (11 mi) of tunnels – Greece's HEP capacity will be drastically improved and irrigation water will be diverted to Thessaly where it is badly needed. The reverse side of the coin is the drowning of 14 villages, the famous monastery of Myrophillo and severe damage to the Missolonghi wetlands, one of the most important wetlands for birds in Europe.

ACID RAIN

Coal-fired power stations and other industrial processes emit sulphur dioxide and nitrogen oxides, which, when combined with atmospheric moisture, create acid rain (dilute sulphuric acid or nitric acid). Acid rain damages forests, plants and agriculture, raises the acid level in lakes and ground water, killing fish, and contaminating drinking water. The Black Forest in Germany has been steadily losing its trees through *Waldsterben* ('tree death'), but Britain has the highest percentage of damaged trees in Europe – 67%. In southern Norway 80% of lakes are devoid of fish life and Sweden has 20 000 acidified lakes: in both cases the source of the pollution is primarily Britain.

POLLUTION OF BEACHES

The EC 'Blue Flag' Campaign is awarded annually to beaches and ports that attain a high standard of environmental quality and also provide beach amenities, environmental education and information. Water samples must comtain fewer than 100 faecal coliforms/100 ml of water.

TOURISM

Tourism has been one of the major growth industries of the second half of the 20th century. It plays a significant role in the economies of most EEA states. Three 'waves' of tourists may be identified. Mainly in the summer, large numbers of tourists journey from northern Europe to southern Europe for holidays with guaranteed sunshine. Winter tourists from lowland Western Europe visit mountainous areas – in particular the Alps and the Pyrenees – for skiing. Thirdly, tourists from outside Europe, especially from North America, come to the continent because of its historic towns and buildings.

BELGIUM
The principal tourist attractions of Belgium are the historic cities of Flanders (Bruges and Ghent) and the Ardennes uplands of Wallonia. While these areas attract international tourism, a third significant tourist region, the Flemish coast, has a largely Belgian clientele. Out of a total of about 10 000 000 foreign visitors a year to Belgium, Brussels receives the largest number but the majority of these come to Belgium for business reasons.

DENMARK
One third of the 7 700 000 tourists visiting Denmark spend their time at camping sites and similar holiday centres, mainly in Jutland. The majority of these visitors are from Germany, Sweden and the UK. Other tourist attractions include Copenhagen, the Baltic island of Bornholm and the Legoland theme park (which is Denmark's largest single tourist site).

FRANCE
A particular feature of tourism in France is the very high proportion of French holidaymakers who choose destinations within France rather than abroad. Nevertheless, the country receives, on average, 38 300 000 foreign tourists a year.

The principal tourist season is remarkably short, with most French people taking their holidays in July and August. There is also an important winter season for skiing, mainly in the Alps. Leading tourist attractions include the seaside resorts of Brittany and the Atlantic coast (which attract more French than foreign tourists), the Loire Valley and its chateaux, Provence and the coastal resorts of the Côte d'Azur and Languedoc, the valleys of the Dordogne, mountain resorts of the Alps and the Pyrenees, and, overwhelmingly, Paris, which has more foreign tourists than any other French tourist region.

GERMANY
Germany receives fewer foreign tourists than any other major West European country. Tourism is an important industry but the majority of visitors at major tourist attractions in Germany – for example North Sea and Baltic coastal resorts – are Germans. Nevertheless, about 14 500 000 foreign visitors a year come to Germany. The principal attractions are the Rhineland, the Bavarian Alps, the Black Forest, spas and historic towns in southern Germany, and, increasingly, Thuringia (in the former East Germany).

GREECE
Tourism is a major industry and one of the most important sources of foreign currency. Some 8 500 000 foreign visitors take holidays in Greece every year, the majority for summer holidays in the Aegean and Ionian islands, the Dodecanese and Crete. Visitors from Germany outnumber those from Scandinavia and the UK. Apart from Athens (which is the country's principal tourist destination), the Greek mainland has fewer resorts, although developments near historic sites such as Delphi and Olympia and in the Chalcidice peninsula are important.

IRELAND
Tourism is vigorously promoted and people of Irish descent from North America and the UK make up a considerable proportion of the 3 000 000 foreign visitors that Ireland receives per annum. Increasing numbers of visitors come from EC countries and tourism is the mainstay of some small communities in Kerry, Clare, Galway and Cork, where self-catering accommodation is an important foreign-currency earner. However, Dublin remains the largest single tourist centre.

ITALY
Tourism is a major earner of foreign currency for Italy and over 55 000 000 foreign visitors are received per annum – 22% of these visitors are German, 22% are Swiss and 20% are French. Rome attracts large numbers of Catholic pilgrims and visitors to Roman antiquities. Other historic cities that are important on the tourist map include Venice, Florence, Siena and Pisa. Major attractions include Naples and the Neapolitan Riviera, Adriatic resorts (such as Rimini), the coastal resorts of Sardinia and Liguria, the lakes of northern Lombardy (Como, Maggiore, etc.) and Alpine skiing resorts.

LUXEMBOURG
Nearly 900 000 foreign visitors come to the Grand Duchy every year. This total includes business people and others going to EC and banking institutions in the capital as well as tourists to the castles and valleys of the Osling uplands in the north.

NETHERLANDS
German, British and American tourists account for over one half of the 3 700 000 foreign visitors received by the Netherlands per annum. The principal attractions include Amsterdam, the tulip fields of Holland, historic cities such as Utrecht and Delft, and the Dutch countryside with its windmills and canals. The seaside resorts of the Dutch coast tend to attract more domestic than foreign tourists.

PORTUGAL
Tourism – in particular to the coastal resorts of the Algarve which have developed in the last three decades – is a major foreign-currency earner. Other important tourist regions include Lisbon and adjoining coastal resorts and the island of Madeira. On average, Portugal receives about 18 500 000 foreign visitors, of whom 70% are Spanish.

SPAIN

Tourism makes a major contribution to the Spanish economy. Over 53 500 000 foreign visitors come to Spain per annum – of whom 20% are Portuguese, 14% German and 12% British. The principal attractions for foreign visitors are the Costa del Sol, Costa del Azahar, Costa Dorada, Costa Brava, the Balearic Islands (mainly Mallorca and Minorca) and the Canary Islands. The majority of these visitors are on package holidays. Independent travel to historic sites in the interior is being promoted.

UNITED KINGDOM

Invisible earnings from tourism have become an important part of Britain's balance of payments. Just over 18 000 000 foreign visitors take holidays in the UK per annum. Of this total, 13% are French, 13% German and 13% American. The overwhelming majority of visitors include London on their itinerary. Other major destinations include Oxford, the Cotswolds, Stratford-upon-Avon and Scotland. There has been a significant decline in the number of people staying in British seaside resorts, which tend to cater for domestic rather than foreign visitors.

AUSTRIA

Winter and summer visitors to the Austrian Alps and tourists to historic cities such as Vienna and Salzburg make a major contribution to Austria's foreign-currency earnings. Just over 19 000 000 foreign holidaymakers visit Austria per annum. Over one half of these visitors are German.

FINLAND

Finland's main tourist attractions include Helsinki, the lakes of central Finland and the Aland Islands (which enjoy duty-free status). Over 2 800 000 foreign visitors go to Finland per annum; the majority are either Scandinavian or German.

ICELAND

About 150 000 foreign visitors a year go to Iceland, many attracted by its unique volcanic landscape.

LIECHTENSTEIN

The principality attracts holidaymakers on day trips to Vaduz as well as skiers visiting the Alpine resort of Malbun. Just under 100 000 people stay in Liechtenstein per annum.

NORWAY

Nearly 4 000 000 foreign visitors go to Norway per annum – the majority of them are Scandinavian, German and British. The spectacular fjord coastline, the mountainous interior and the 'Midnight Sun' are among the principal attractions, but the high cost of living in Norway has discouraged some potential tourists.

SWEDEN

The rural scenery of Sweden is one of the country's major tourist attractions and one quarter of foreign visitors to Sweden stay in camps and hostels rather than hotels. Other tourist goals include Stockholm (which has the nickname 'the Venice of the North'), Malmo, Uppsala, skiing resorts and the island of Gotland where the walled medieval city of Visby is a major attraction. The majority of Sweden's 7 200 000 foreign visitors are from other Scandinavian countries or from Germany.

SWITZERLAND

Switzerland is a popular destination for independent and package holidaymakers, but the country's high cost of living has discouraged the mass tourism experienced by much of Mediterranean Europe. Alpine and lakeside resorts attract skiers in winter and sightseers in summer and some resorts specialize in catering for an upmarket clientele. Some 37 000 000 foreign visitors go to Switzerland per annum.

WORLD HERITAGE SITES

The World Heritage Convention of UNESCO (a UN agency) has established a list of World Heritage sites to protect areas of outstanding natural and cultural importance throughout the world. Most of these sites are major tourist attractions. World Heritage Sites in EEA include:

France The principal World Heritage Sites include: Amiens (cathedral), Arles (Roman remains), Chambord (chateau and park), Chartres (cathedral), Fontainebleau (park and palace), Fontenay (palace), Mont-Saint-Michel, Nancy (place Stanislas), Nîmes (Pont du Gard), Orange (Roman remains), St-Savin-sur-Gartempe (church), Versailles (palace and park), Vézelay (basilica), and Vézère (caves).

Germany Aachen (cathedral), Brühl (castles), Hildesheim (cathedral), Lübeck (old town), Speyer (cathedral), Trier (monuments), Wies (church), and Würzburg (palace).

Greece Athens (Acropolis), Bassae (temple of Apollo Epicurius), and Delphi (site).

Italy Florence (city centre), Pisa (Duomo square), Rome (city centre), Santa Maria delle Grazie (church and convent), Valcamonica (engraved rocks), and Venice (lagoon and canals).

Portugal Angra do Herismo (in the Azores), Batalha (monastery), Evora (town centre), Lisbon (Tower of Belém, etc.), and Tomar (convent).

Spain The principal World Heritage Sites include: Altamira (cave), Avila (old town), Barcelona (Casa Mila, park and Güell palace), Burgos (cathedral), Caceres (old town), Compostella (old town), Cordoba (mosque), Granada (Alhambra), Madrid (Escurial), Segovia (old town and aqueduct)), Teruel (old town), and Toledo (old town).

United Kingdom Avebury (stone circle), Bath (city centre), Beaumaris (castle), Blemheim Palace, Caernarfon (castle), Canterbury (cathedral and St Martin's), Conwy (castle), Durham (cathedral and castle), Giant's Causeway, Harlech (castle), Ironbridge (gorge, bridge and industrial museum), London (Westminster Abbey and Palace of Westminster; Tower of London), St Kilda (island), Stonehenge (stone circle), and Studley Royal Gardens and Fountains Abbey.

Norway Alta (ancient art), Bergen (old town), and Urnes (wooden church).

Switzerland Berne (old town), Saint-Jean-des-Soeurs (convent), and Sankt Gallen (convent).

CENTRAL

AND EASTERN EUROPE

A CHANGING MAP

The map of Eastern and Central Europe changed dramatically in the early 1990s. The dissolution of the Soviet Union, the fragmentation of Yugoslavia in a series of civil wars and the 'velvet divorce' of the Czechs and Slovaks saw the creation of over a dozen new European countries. It would be rash to predict that this upheaval is over. The conflicts in Bosnia-Herzegovina continue and could spread back to Croatia. Kosovo – where the majority Albanian population is denied rights by the Serbians – is a tinderbox and could involve Albania. Macedonia remains a major issue for Greece which denies its right to exist, at least under the name Macedonia, and any dispute over the new republic could

involve Greece, Albania, Bulgaria and Turkey in a general Balkan war. Also, the union between Serbia and Montenegro is, at best, uneasy.

Away from the former Yugoslavia other potential flashpoints include Moldova (where the issue of Russian secessionists remains unsolved), Estonia (where the Russian community around Narva wishes to secede), and Ukraine (where possible Russian territorial claims in the Donets region and Crimea have unsettled relations between Moscow and Kiev). Irredentist feelings among the large Magyar population outside Hungary – particularly in Slovakia and Romania – could also be a source of unrest and change.

THE NEW EASTERN AND CENTRAL EUROPE

Country	1989 area	1987–89 pop.	1993 area	1991–93 pop.
Czechoslovakia	127 905 km²	15 624 000	dissolved	dissolved
Czech Republic	part of Czechoslovakia	part of Czechoslovakia	78 880 km²	10 302 000
Hungary	93 036 km²	10 640 000	93 036 km²	10 337 000
Poland	312 683 km²	37 764 000	312 683 km²	38 273 000
Slovakia	part of Czechoslovakia	part of Czechoslovakia	49 025 km²	5 290 000
USSR (Soviet Union)	22 402 200 km²	286 717 000	dissolved	dissolved
Estonia	part of USSR	part of USSR	45 226 km²	1 562 000
Latvia	part of USSR	part of USSR	64 589 km²	2 606 000
Lithuania	part of USSR	part of USSR	65 200 km²	3 761 000
Belarus	part of USSR	part of USSR	207 546 km²	10 297 000
Moldova	part of USSR	part of USSR	33 702 km²	4 373 000
Russia	part of USSR	part of USSR	17 075 400 km²	148 543 000
Ukraine	part of USSR	part of USSR	603 700 km²	51 944 000
Albania	28 748 km²	3 083 000	28 748 km²	3 303 000
Bulgaria	110 912 km²	8 974 000	110 912 km²	9 005 000
Romania	237 500 km²	23 112 000	237 500 km²	22 749 000
Turkey	779 452 km²	50 665 000	779 452 km²	58 376 000
Bosnia	part of Yugoslavia	part of Yugoslavia	51 129 km²	2 500 000
Croatia	part of Yugoslavia	part of Yugoslavia	56 538 km²	4 784 000
Macedonia	part of Yugoslavia	part of Yugoslavia	25 713 km²	2 034 000
Slovenia	part of Yugoslavia	part of Yugoslavia	20 251 km²	1 966 000
Yugoslavia	255 804 km²	23 411 000	102 173 km²	10 407 000

MARKET ECONOMICS AND NATIONALISM IN EASTERN EUROPE

The year of the Single European Market (see p. 17) was a sombre one for Eastern Europe. As economic conditions worsened in most of Western Europe during 1993, the East showed even fewer signs of sustained improvement, although real progress was made in 1992–93 on privatization, on the rationalization of state industry, on the setting up of new intra-regional trading and payments arrangements, and on the development of stable economic and financial relationships with the West.

Eastern Europe has seen falls in output (by as much as 33% in Lithuania in 1992) and high rates of inflation tending to hyperinflation (over 2 000% in Russia and Ukraine, an incredible 685 000% in the rump of Yugoslavia by June 1993), associated with menacingly large budget deficits (equivalent to as much as 44% of GNP in Ukraine in 1992). Rising unemployment (already 13% in Slovakia in 1992 and 14.1% in Poland at April 1993) and chronic trading deficits and payments difficulties with the West, particularly on the part of the CIS countries, complete the picture. With continuing deep recession in the world economy and uncertainty about basic economic and political trends in Eastern Europe, the flow of Western aid and investment has remained modest.

However, it is not difficult to find significant exceptions to all these negative trends. Industrial production in Poland is broadly rising, while inflation fell from 70% in 1991 to 45% in 1992. More encouraging, Polish inflation has been brought under control even though the budget remains substantially in deficit. It seems, on the basis of the experience in Poland, that if budgetary deficits can be cut to not much more than 5% of GNP, inflation can be contained. Equally encouraging for other East European states is the indication that the IMF will accept this proposition and release substantial new credits on this basis, as they did for Poland in March 1993. In the Czech Republic, unemployment was recorded at just over 4% in 1992, and while industrial output fell, in accordance with the general regional pattern in 1992, total retail sales grew substantially, with around half of that total being attributable to the private sector.

In Hungary, despite continued difficulties with the budget and signs of growing social discontent with unemployment, inflation and falling real wages, the flow of foreign private investment remains relatively buoyant, with some 50% of the economy now privatized. A sharp fall in agricultural exports in the first half of 1993, partly due to drought, partly to trading difficulties, has almost certainly spoiled Hungary's chances of substantial economic growth this year. But medium-term prospects still look comparatively good.

NATIONALISM AND STATEHOOD

Nationalism has emerged as the most critical area of interaction between political and economic dimensions.

Poland, Hungary and Bulgaria excepted, the entire region has been overtaken by an overwhelming tendency to ethnically based fragmentation. In the Czech-Slovak case the transition has been peaceful, while in Yugoslavia it has produced full-scale civil war. Within the old USSR, with its myriad nationalities, there are cases which might qualify for the soubriquet 'velvet divorce' and a few that have followed the Bosnian model, with the majority coming somewhere in between.

The reemergence of nationalism as a dominant political force in the region was no doubt inevitable once the ideology and repression of Communism had passed, and there can be no questioning the 'legitimacy' of the new nationalisms of Eastern Europe as, in the main, genuinely spontaneous, mass movements. It is equally true to say that, in most cases, those mass movements have found their leaders among the cadres of the old Communist Parties. The emergence of the 'nomenklatura capitalist' – the 'insider' from the old Communist Party apparatus who was able to use his inside knowledge to buy up privatized enterprises at bargain prices – was the key socio-political development of the early transformation period. But, it can be argued, 1992 was the year of the nomenklatura nationalist – the insider from the old apparatus who sees nationalism as a political bandwagon to retain power. Countries as diverse as Croatia, Serbia, Slovenia, Romania, Slovakia and Ukraine are currently all ruled, in the name of nationalism, by men who were formerly high-ranking members of the Communist Party apparatuses of their states. With the exception of President Tudjman of Croatia, in each case they remained in those positions right up until the final collapse of Communism.

A most significant political result in 1992 was the electoral defeat of Vytautus Landsbergis, a nationalist untainted by Communist connections, by nomenklatura nationalist Mykolas Brazauskas in Lithuania, significantly one of the East European countries worst hit by declining output and living standards. There can be no doubt that Brazauskas's victory genuinely represented the will of the Lithuanian people, but his credentials are no stronger than those of President Milosevic of Serbia, President Kravchuk of Ukraine and Prime Minister Meciar of Slovakia, all of whom have won overwhelmingly in (more or less) fair elections in recent years. In contrast, in Russia, Boris Yeltsin, a renegade Communist and at most a moderate nationalist, continues in the top position, while the Czech Republic, after its separation from Slovakia at the end of 1992, elected Vaclav Havel, the archetypal humanist-liberal-dissident, as its first president. But even Russia is only a partial exception, as the Russian Supreme Soviet is dominated by a nomenklatura nationalist opposition that sometimes seems to have more control over government policy than the president himself.

Virtually all the new leaders of Eastern Europe, nationalist or not, can lay claim to democratic credentials, at least at the level of electoral procedures. What is equally true is that under the nomenklatura nationalist regimes, traditionally Communist authoritarian patterns continue to prevail in everyday life. And while privatization programmes are proclaimed universally, they are often, under nomenklatura nationalist regimes, used as a smokescreen for effective nationalization, or simple transfer of property rights from the old Communist state to the new 'nationalist' elites, this representing a perfect marriage betwen nomenklatura nationalism and nomenklatura capitalism.

It would be wrong simply to assume that nomenklatura nationalist regimes are, by their very nature, bound to produce worse economic policies than more liberal-democratic regimes. It is nevertheless striking that Ukraine, ruled by a man who perhaps most perfectly epitomizes the nomenklatura nationalist type, has been the slowest of all the ex-Soviet republics to attack the basis issues of economic transformation. It is significant, too, that within Russia – a multinational state in which, over the past year or so, much effective economic power has passed to local leaders – it is the regions under liberal-democratic control, rather than those dominated by old nomenklatura elements, which have made most progress with transformation policies and are having greatest success in attracting foreign business. Again, nomenklatura nationalist regimes have a universally bad record on price stability. Because they tend to see 'the licence to print money' as essentially a political prerogative, and because their populist and sometimes militarist policies tend to generate very high budget expenditures on defence and social security without the economic growth to provide tax receipts to pay for them, nomenklatura nationalist governments tend to run big budget deficits, which they can only finance through the emission of new money. All the 'clean' nationalist regimes of Eastern Europe have a relatively good record on inflation. Virtually all the nomenklatura nationalist regimes are suffering from hyperinflation, or something very near it.

NATIONALIST MYTHS

Behind these policy weaknesses lie problems of attitude that are unlikely to be resolved in the short term. The great political strength of nomenklatura nationalism is that it meets the often crude and poorly articulated yet powerful feelings of territorial and cultural identity amongst the East European masses. Those feelings are often tribal in essence, in that they revolve around historical myths in which particular 'holy grounds', for example Kosovo for the Serbs, play a key role. The reason why this kind of myth-making is so explosive in Eastern Europe is that so often the holy grounds are disputed between two or even three rival myths, as in the case of Bosnia. Typical nomenklatura nationalist attitudes are feudal-bureaucratic rather than tribal in nature, as indeed were nomenklatura attitudes typically in the final, corrupt and degenerate stage of Communism, viewing national ownership of assets as the basis for enjoying the fruits of those assets. But these two sets of attitudes come together through a common obsession with patrimony, with land, natural resources and capital stock (however obsolescent) as treasures to be fought for and cherished. As President Leonid Kravchuk of Ukraine puts it, 'everything on Ukrainian soil is Ukrainian property'. However understandable these attitudes may be, they fit in awkwardly with standard Western notions of delimited and limited property rights, notions which lie at the heart of the capitalist system. It is, then,

perhaps hardly surprising that privatization makes such slow headway under nomenklatura nationalist governments. More insidiously for the long term, the obsession with possession of physical assets dulls the appreciation of the importance of science, technology and human capital as the basis for growth in an industrial economy. Technology was the Achilles' heel of the Communist systems-in-decline. It is likely to be just as big a weakness under nomenklatura nationalism.

CONTRASTING EXAMPLES

Slovakia provides one of the most interesting examples of the dangers, both economic and political, of nomenklatura nationalism in power. Faced with the prospect of rising unemployment, and committed to a rather vague notion of combining market with a more traditional planning approach, Prime Minister Meciar announced in early 1993 plans to increase production and exports of arms, Slovakia's traditional specialization under the Communist division of labour. One respected Central European newspaper presented a nightmare picture of Slovakia, in league with regimes like Iraq and Libya, and also with renegade nomenklatura nationalist elements in Ukraine, turning into a heavily-armed safe haven for international terrorism. Meanwhile, the dispute between Slovakia and Hungary over the Gabcikovo dam on the river Danube, which separates the two states, became increasingly bitter, with Budapest accusing Bratislava of reneging on an EC-sponsored agreement aimed at limiting the ecological damage caused by the project. This drama has unfolded against a background of growing tension between the two states over the treatment of the 600 000-strong Hungarian minority in Slovakia. Yet there were signs towards the middle of 1993 that Meciar was beginning to modify his stance, and to adopt a much more unequivocal position vis-a-vis the role of the market in the economy. The change in approach was marked by a loan agreement signed with the IMF in June 1993. While all of this was a sensible reaction to the $0.5 bn budget deficit that had developed between January and July (about 10% of GNP), it was not a typically nomenklatura nationalist reaction. It is perhaps significant that although Meciar is an old Communist Party activist, he was never a member of the nomenklatura as such. Whether a more reasoned approach to economic policy making will be accompanied by greater statesmanship on the issue of the Hungarian minority remains to be seen.

While the distinction between 'clean' and nomenklatura nationalist regimes is a useful one, it cannot be pushed too far. One utter exception to the pattern is Slovenia, the only one of the Yugoslav successor states to achieve any kind of real political and economic stability. Ruled by a centre-right (Liberal plus Christian Democrat) government and a president – Milan Kucan – who is a classic nomenklatura nationalist, Slovenia reported in May 1993 a monthly rate of inflation of just 1.4% – one of the lowest in the region. A 3% increase in industrial production in the same month probably does not signify a break in the trend, which is still downwards. But the Slovenian government is notably still putting funds into technological and scientific development in a manner totally atypical of nomenklatura national regimes, but calculated to lay a firm base for economic growth for the tiny Alpine republic in the medium-term future. It is true that the Slovenian government has been very slow on privatization, and has sometimes seemed anxious to keep control over assets in its own hands, but Premier Janez Drnovsek promises that 1993 will be a critical year for privatization, following the passage of a law on transformation of ownership in 1992.

PRIVATIZATION

Two main models of privatization are being implemented in the region – the 'top-down' holding company model, based on the German *Treuhandanstalt* system, and widely employed in Poland and in the Yugoslav successor states; and the 'bottom-up' voucher system, pioneered in the former Czechoslovakia and introduced in Russia in late 1992. Starting in May 1992, a substantial proportion of Czech and Slovak industry was privatized in the course of four rounds of selling-off. Citizens were able to purchase booklets of vouchers, each booklet worth 1 000 investment points, for Kcs. 1 000. They could then exchange the vouchers for shares in enterprises, or in the investment funds that have mushroomed at the same time. In the event, some 72% of the vouchers issued over the initial rounds of privatization were exchanged for shares in investment funds.

In Russia the pattern has been different in that the vouchers (privatization cheques) issued have been largely sold for cash (roubles) on the new Russian stock markets. While there is great interest in the idea of investment funds in Russia, there is no proper legislation to cover their activities, and those operating do so very much at their own risk. As a result, Russian citizens are faced with the choice of investing their vouchers directly in enterprises (which is what the new commercial banks advise), or turning them into cash. In practice they have largely done the latter.

There can be no doubt that the Czecho-Slovak voucher initiative has succeeded in creating a viable model of privatization capable of setting up a large number of industrial enterprises on an independently managed basis significantly faster than alternative models. Substantial doubts remain as to the extent to which the voucher system might be used as a way of laundering nomenklatura and mafia money, and there are worries that such elements could start interfering in the management of enterprises. There is, certainly, no evidence from the first year or so of operation of the system that this is going to be a major problem, but it is too early to tell. The history of the Russian voucher experiment has been rather chequered. Initially, the demand for privatization cheques from dealers was fairly buoyant, and this pushed up the value of the rouble against the dollar in December 1992. But demand weakened significantly in January 1993. By the middle of 1993, however, it had made something of a comeback, with the market price of a privatization cheque for the first time matching its nominal value – not altogether surprisingly, perhaps, in the context of monthly inflation at nearly 20%. In the first half of 1993, 2 291 enterprises employing over 3 000 000 people, some 5% of the workforce, were privatised on the basis of voucher auctions. Still, the voucher

scheme remains only a minor element in the Russian privatization programme. By July 1993 about 57% of Russia's small enterprises had been privatized, while more than one third of employees in large enterprises were working in privatized or 'joint-stock' companies. It should be noted, however, that in the Russian context the term joint-stock company is largely a euphemism for management buy-out. In many cases the managers who buy out are members of the old nomenklatura.

INTRA-REGIONAL TRADE

Partly because of the nomenklatura nationalists' inclinations towards self-sufficiency and partly because of the breakdown of the clumsy and inefficient Comecon system which did, nevertheless, provide some kind of a basis for trade, the early years of the post-Communist era saw a dangerous drop in the volume of intra-regional trade. The break-up of the Soviet Union at the end of 1991 produced the same pattern within what had been the dominant Comecon state. Recent developments have offered some hope that the region may begin to move towards economic cooperation. Most significant was the signature, in December 1992, of a Central European Free Trade Agreement (CEFTA), between Poland, the Czech Republic, Slovakia and Hungary (the Visegrad Group). The agreement sets out a path towards free trade between the four by the year 2001, though with all the reservations about 'sensitive' industrial sectors – textiles, steel, cars, and agriculture – with which we are so familiar in the EC. It represents a welcome acceptance on the part of the four that it is better to try to build free trade in your own region than to wait endlessly hoping for admission to the EC. Perhaps most important of all, it is an alliance of the three front-runners in the transformation stakes (Slovakia does not, of course, fit in here), and could, in time, build a new regional market of respectable proportions in East-Central Europe, to which neighbouring states, particularly the Baltic republics and Belarus, would then be drawn.

It is less easy to be sanguine about the January 1993 CIS agreement on the setting up of an Inter-State Bank, which would provide the financial basis for multilateral clearing of trade balances between republics and create a framework for the coordination of monetary and budgetary policy. As long as the rouble remains so weak (as a result of the weakness of Russian economic policy), it will be impossible for an effective rouble zone to be created. At the same time, even weak roubles can be used to finance local budget deficits. Indeed one of the motives behind the clumsy and unpopular attempt in July 1993 by the Russian government (or some sections of it) to take old rouble bills out of circulation was to freeze a substantial proportion of the rouble holdings of other CIS member republics and force them to cooperate more closely with Moscow. In the event, many of the republics reacted by announcing their intention of quitting the rouble zone. The big question now is whether, with the rouble zone effectively defunct, the CIS can survive as a meaningful political and economic forum. In mid-1993 attempts were still continuing, to create a CIS Economic Union. More specifically, separate negotiations were under way on the creation of a 'common agricultural market' within the CIS.

ALBANIA

Official name: Republika e Shqipërise (Republic of Albania).

Member of: UN, CSCE.

Area: 28 748 km² (11 100 sq mi).

Population: 3 303 000 (1991 est).

Capital: Tirana (Tiranë) 224 000 (1990 est).

Other major cities: Durrës 85 000, Elbasan 83 000, Shkodër 82 000, Vlorë 74 000, Korçë 65 000, Fier 45 000, Berat 44 000 (1990 est).

Languages: Albanian (Gheg and Tosk dialects). Tosk is the official language. See also p. 186.

Religions: Sunni Islam (20%), small Greek Orthodox and Roman Catholic minorities. The practice of religion was banned from 1967 to 1990.

Education: Education is compulsory between the ages of seven and 15. (There are plans to raise the school-leaving age to 16.) Higher education students pay fees in accordance with their means. There is one university (Tirana).

Defence: In 1992 the total strength of Albania's armed forces was estimated to be 40 000 (including 22 400 conscripts) – the army had a strength of 27 000, the air force 11 000 and the navy 2 000. Conscription lasts for two years in the army and three years in the other services. Albania has forged informal links with NATO.

Transport: There are 6700 km (4188 mi) of main roads and 10 000 km (6250 mi) of other roads. The ownership of private cars was banned until 1991. There are 509 km (318 mi) of railway track operating both freight and passenger services. The single international airport in Albania is at Rinas, near Tirana. There are no regular internal flights.

Media: Since the collapse of Communism Albania has a free press with 41 daily newspapers, mostly regional and with small readerships. There is a single state-owned radio network (with regional stations) and one state-owned television station.

GOVERNMENT

A 140-member Assembly is elected under a system of proportional representation by universal adult suffrage for four years. The Assembly elects a President who appoints a Chairman (Prime Minister) and a Council of Ministers. The principal political parties are the (centre) Democratic Party (DPA), the (former Communist) Socialist Party (SPA), the Social Democrat Party (SDP), the Union of Human Rights and the Albanian Republican Party (ARP). At the general election held on 22 and 29 March 1992 these parties obtained the following number of seats.

Party	Seats
Democratic Party	92
Socialist Party	38
Social Democratic Party	7
Union of Human Rights	2
Albanian Republican Party	1
Total	*140*

A coalition of DPA, SDP and ARP members and independents was formed.

President: Sali Berisha (*DPA*).

THE CABINET

Prime Minister (Chairman): Aleksandr Meksi (*DPA*).

Deputy Prime Minister (Deputy Chairman) and Minister for Public Order: Bashkim Kopliku (*DPA*).

Minister of Agriculture and Food: Rexhep Uka (*DPA*).

Minister of Construction, Housing and Land Distribution: Ilir Manushi (*DPA*).

Minister of Culture, Youth and Sport: Dhimitër Anagnosti (*DPA*).

Minister of Defence: Safet Xhulali (*DPA*).

Minister of Education: Ylli Vejsiu (*DPA*).

Minister of Finances and the Economy: Genc Ruli (*DPA*).

Minister of Foreign Affairs: Alfred Serreqi (*DPA*).

Minister of Foreign Economic Relations: Artan Hoxha (*DPA*).

Minister of Health and Environmental Protection: Tritan Shehu (*DPA*).

Minister of Industry, Mining and Energy Resources: Abdyl Xhaja (*Independent*).

Minister of Justice: Kudret Cela (*Independent*).

Minister of Labour, Emigration, Social Welfare and the Politically Persecuted: Dashamir Shehi (*DPA*).

Minister of Tourism: Osman Shehu (*DPA*).

Minister of Transport and Communication: Fatos Bitnicka (*ARP*).

Chairman of the State Control Commission: Blerim Cela (*DPA*).

Chairman of the Science and Technology Committee: Maksim Konomi (*DPA*).

General Secretary: Vullnet Ademi (*SDP*).

GEOGRAPHY

Coastal lowlands – including the basins of the rivers Drini (in the north) and Vjosa (in the south) – cover 25% of the country and support most of Albania's agriculture. Mountain ranges cover the rest of the country – the rugged limestone North Albanian Alps, the central uplands (which include Mount Korab, see below) and the lower southern highlands. *Principal rivers*: Semani, Drini, Vjosa. *Highest point*: Mount Korab 2751 m (9025 ft).

The Mediterranean coastal areas experience hot, dry summers and mild, wet winters. The mountainous interior is equally warm in the summer but has cold winters.

ECONOMY

Albania is poor by European standards. The economy is mainly based upon agriculture and the export of chromium (1 010 000 tonnes in 1990). By the end of 1992 almost all of the state-owned cooperative land had been redistributed into private hands. A National Privatization Agency for the privatization of state-owned industry was operating by 1992. In 1990 Albania ended self-imposed economic isolation and sought financial, technical and humanitarian assistance from the West. Nevertheless, the country has experienced short-term famine, continuing emigration and – owing to a shortage of raw materials – a dramatic collapse in industrial output. These economic problems have been added to by a government commitment to pay 80% of their previous salary to workers made redundant because of the raw materials shortage. (For GNP, see p. 187.)

Labour force (1990)

Sector	Number employed
Industry	313 800
Agriculture	203 700
Construction	82 000
Education and culture	63 200
Trade	54 900
Transport and communications	41 900
Health services	40 700
Other	59 200
Total	859 000

Albania runs a large and increasing budget deficit. Declining production means that revenues are falling while severe social and economic problems mean that extra demands are being placed upon the state. The most recent budgetary figures available are those for 1990.

Revenue	Million lekë	% of revenue
National economy	7 326	88%
Non-productive sector	967	12%
Total	8 293	100%

Expenditure	Million lekë	% of expenditure
National economy	5 998	55%
Social security, education, culture, etc.	2 991	28%
Defence	990	9%
Administration	167	2%
Other		6%
Total	10 869	100%

In 1990 Albania imported goods worth 3 795 million new lekë and exported goods worth 2 273 million new lekë. The currency – the new lek (plural lekë) – is divided into 100 qindarka (qintars). In September 1993, the exchange rate was 110.6 lekë to 1 US$.

Imports (1990)

Sector	% of imports
Machinery and equipment	25.2%
Fuels, minerals, metals	24.5%
Plant and animal raw materials	15.7%
Foodstuffs	10.1%
Chemicals and rubber	9.3%
Consumer goods (general)	8.4%
Spare parts	5.7%
Construction materials	1.1%

Exports (1990)

Sector	% of exports
Minerals, metals, electricity	46.8%
Foodstuffs	20.1%
Plant and animal raw materials	17.8%
Consumer goods (general)	12.7%
Chemicals	1.5%
Construction materials	1.1%

RECENT HISTORY

Independence from the Ottoman (Turkish) Empire was declared in 1912. The country was occupied in both the Balkan Wars (1912–13) and World War I, and a stable government within recognized frontiers did not exist until the 1920s. Interwar Albania was dominated by Ahmed Zogu (1895–1961), who made himself king (as Zog I) in 1928 and used Italian loans to develop his impoverished country. He fled when Mussolini invaded in 1939. Communist-led partisans took power when the Germans withdrew (1944). Under Enver Hoxha (1908–85), the regime pursued rapid modernization on Stalinist lines, allied, in turn, to Yugoslavia, the USSR and China, before opting (in 1978) for self-sufficiency and isolation. In 1990, a power struggle within the ruling Communist Party was won by the more liberal wing led by President Alia, who instituted a programme of economic, political and social reforms. The Communist Party retained a majority in multi-party elections held in April 1991, but – as the Socialist Party – was defeated in 1992. The new centrist government faces severe economic problems and the growing threat of major disorders in the Serbian province of Kosovo where ethnic Albanians – who make up 90% of the population – are denied full civil rights by the minority Serbian community.

BELARUS
(BYELORUSSIA)

Official name: Respublika Belarus. Formerly known as Byelorussia.

Member of: UN, CIS, CSCE.

Area: 207 546 km² (80 134 sq mi).

Population: 10 297 000 (1991 est).

Capital: Minsk (Mensk) 1 613 000 (including suburbs; 1990 est).

Other major cities: Gomel (Homyel) 506 000, Mogilev (Mahilyow) 363 000, Vitebsk (Vitsyebsk) 356 000, Grodno (Hrodna) 277 000, Brest 269 000, Bobruysk (Bobrujsk) 223 000 (1990 est).

Languages: Belarussian (also known as Belorussian) (80%), Russian (13%), Polish (4%). See also p. 186.

Religions: Belarussian Orthodox majority, Roman Catholic (5%). The Belarussian Orthodox Church gained independence within the Russian Orthodox Church in 1990 as a separate exarchate.

Education: Education is compulsory between the ages of seven and 17. There are three universities (Gomel, Grodno and Minsk) and four polytechnics.

Defence: In 1992 the total strength of the armed forces was 125 000 (including 95 000 ground forces, 20 000 in the air force and 10 000 air defence). The armed forces are to be reduced to about 95 000. Conscripts serve for 18 months. The last Russian troops are scheduled to be withdrawn from Belarus by 1999.

Transport: There are over 265 600 km (166 000 mi) of roads in Belarus – 85% of the republic's roads are hard-surfaced. There are 5 590 km (3494 mi) of rail track operating both freight and passenger services. Minsk has an international airport.

Media: There are 12 principal (state-owned) daily newspapers and over 190 regional and local papers that appear daily or more than once a week. There is a single (state-owned) radio and television network.

GOVERNMENT

Under new constitutional arrangements a 160-member Assembly (Sejm) and a President – who will appoint a Chairman (Prime Minister) and a Council of Ministers – will be elected by universal adult suffrage for four years. The current legislature is the Supreme Soviet which was elected in March 1990. The principal political groupings are the former Communists, the (former Communist) Belarus for Democracy group and the Belarussian Popular Front. A number of smaller political parties and groups are active. After the breakaway from the former Communists of the Belarus for Democracy group in June 1991, the Assembly elected in March 1990 comprises:

Grouping	Seats
Former Communist group	300
Belarus for Democracy	33
Belarussian Popular Front	27
Total	360

Members of the former Communist group form the government.

President: Stanislav Shushkevich.

THE CABINET

Prime Minister (Chairman): Vyacheslav Kebich.

First Deputy Prime Minister (First Deputy Chairman): Mikhail Myasnikovich.

Deputy Prime Minister and Minister of Education: Mikhail Dziamchuk.

Deputy Prime Minister and Minister of Resources: Siarhey Linh.

Deputy Prime Minister: Stanislav Bryl.

Deputy Prime Minister: Uladzimier Zalamay.

Deputy Prime Minister: Alaksey Shakovich.

Minister of Agriculture and Production: Fiodar Mirachytsky.

Minister of Communications: Ivan Hrytsuk.

Minister of Construction: I. Antonovich.

Minister of the Construction Materials Industry: A. F. Moiseyevich.

Minister of Culture: Yauhen Vaytovich.

Minister of Defence: Col. Gen. Pavel Kozlousky.

Minister of Education: (see above).

Minister of Finance: Stepan Yanchuk.

Minister of Foreign Affairs: Pyatro Krauchanko.

Minister of Forestry: G. Markousky.

Minister of Grain Products: N. Yakusheu.

Minister of Health: Vasil Kazakou.

Minister of Housing and Municipal Affairs: Barys Batura.

Minister of Information: A.L. Butevich.

Minister of Internal Affairs: Uladzmier Yahorau.

Minister of Justice: L. Dashuk.

Minister of Light Industry: Mikalay Huliuyeu.

Minister of Resources: (see above).

Minister of Road Construction and Utilization: Stanislav Yakuta.

Minister of Social Security: T. Krutoutsova.

Minister of Trade: V. V. Baidak.

Minister of Transport: Uladzmier Barodzic.

Minister of Water Economy and Land Reclamation: A. P. Basiukevich.

GEOGRAPHY

Belarus – formerly spelt Byelorussia (meaning White Russia) – comprises lowlands covered with glacial debris in the north, fertile well-drained tablelands and ridges in the centre, and the low-lying Pripet Marshes in the south and east. Much of the country is flat. Forests cover large stretches of Belarus, in particular in the west. *Principal rivers*: Dnepr, Pripyat, Dvina, Neman. *Highest point*: Dzyarzhynskaya Mountain 346 m (1135 ft).

The continental climate is moderated by the proximity of the Baltic Sea. Belarussian winters are considerably milder than those in European Russia to the east.

ECONOMY

Although Belarus has few natural resources, its economy is overwhelmingly industrial. Major heavy engineering, chemical, fertilizer, oil refining and synthetic fibre industries were established as part of the centrally-planned Soviet economy, but output has declined since 1991. Belarus is dependent upon trade with other former Soviet republics from which it imports the raw materials for its industries and upon which it relies as a market for its industrial goods. Problems in maintaining supplies from other former Soviet republics, high rates of inflation and severe cuts in demand for military equipment (which was formerly a major industry) have contributed to the country's severe economic problems. However, the first steps towards establishing a market economy have been made. (For GNP, see p. 187.)

Labour force (1990)

Sector	Number employed
Industry	3 868 000
Agriculture	1 593 000
Education, social services, culture, health services	1 281 000
Construction	985 000
Transport and communications	570 000
Trade and material services	382 000
Other	99 000
Total	*8 778 000*

Imports (1991)

Sector	% of imports
Machinery	35.0%
Consumer goods	13.7%
Chemicals/petrochemicals	12.3%
Petroleum/natural gas	8.6%
Ferrous metals	7.0%
Other industrial products	10.6%
Processed food	7.7%
Agricultural products	5.1%

Exports (1991)

Sector	% of exports
Machinery	46.0%
Consumer goods	17.8%
Chemicals/petrochemicals	12.7%
Processed food	5.4%
Wood and paper	2.6%
Other agricultural products	1.3%
Other	14.2%

Contamination from the Chernobyl accident (see below) affected about 20% of Belarus, causing areas to be sealed off and necessitating the eventual resettlement of up to 2 000 000 people. The disaster has reduced the acreage available to Belarussian agriculture and expenditure to repair the damage caused by Chernobyl represents over 10% of the Belarussian budget.

Agriculture is dominated by raising fodder crops for beef cattle, pigs and poultry. Flax is grown for export and the local linen industry. Extensive forests supply important woodworking and paper industries.

Belarus has been hit by high rates of inflation. Although in September 1993, Belarus – along with five Asiatic former Soviet republics – agreed to maintain the Russian rouble as a common currency (see the entry for Russia, pp. 168–73) a separate Belarussian curency, the rubel, was issued soon afterwards. The most recent budgetary figures available are 1992 estimates.

Revenue	Million roubles	% of revenue
Tax revenue	87 400	97%
Non-tax revenue	2 500	3%
Total	*89 900*	*100%*

Expenditure	Million roubles	% of expenditure
Social security, education, culture, health, etc.	36 300	38%
National economy (includes subsidies	25 800 20 000	27% 21%)
Chernobyl fund	10 800	11%
Defence	8 000	8%
Administration, law and order	4 000	4%
Interest payments	1 200	1%
Reserve fund	1 000	1%
Other		10%
Total	*95 700*	*100%*

RECENT HISTORY

The Belarussians came under Russian rule as a result of the three partitions of Poland (1772, 1793 and 1795). The region suffered some of the fiercest fighting between Russia and Germany during World War I. Following the Russian Revolution, a Byelorussian Soviet republic was proclaimed (1919). The republic was invaded by the Poles in the same year and divided between Poland and the Soviet Union in 1921. Byelorussia was devastated during World War II. In 1945 the Belarussians were reunited in a single Soviet republic. A perceived lack of Soviet concern for the republic at the time of the accident at the Chernobyl nuclear power station (just over the Ukrainian border; see also above) strengthened a reawakening Belarussian national identity. Byelorussia declared independence following the abortive coup by Communist hardliners in Moscow (September 1991) and – as Belarus (pronounced 'By-ella-roose') – received international recognition when the USSR was dissolved (December 1991).

BOSNIA-HERZEGOVINA

Official name: Bosna i Hercegovina (Bosnia-Herzegovina).

Member of: UN, CSCE.

Area: 51 129 km² (19 741 sq mi).

Population: 4 365 000 (1991 census); c. 2 000 000–2 500 000 (late 1992 est; c. 2 000 000 refugees left Bosnia in 1992–3; over 200 000 people have been killed).

Capital: Sarajevo 526 000 (city 416 000; 1991 census); by 1993 the population of Sarajevo was c. 280 000.

Other major cities: Tuzla 130 000 (over 230 000 by 1993), Banja Luka 143 000, Mostar 110 000 (1991 census).

Languages: Serbo-Croat – a single language with two written forms. See also p. 186.

Religions: Sunni Islam (44%), Serbian Orthodox (33%), Roman Catholic (17%).

Education: In theory education is compulsory from seven to 15. Before the Bosnian war there were universities in Banja Luka, Mostar, Tuzla and Sarajevo.

Defence: By late 1993 the forces controlled by the (largely Muslim) Bosnian government numbered 90 000.

Transport: Transport in Bosnia had broken down by 1993. Rail and road links were largely impassable. Sarajevo airport was open intermittently.

Media: The Bosnian government retained control of a single radio and television network in Sarajevo where a daily newspaper continued publication.

GOVERNMENT:

By 1993 government had broken down. Three separate assemblies – largely representing the previous nationally elected Assembly divided upon religio-linguistic lines – had evolved by the autumn of 1993: the (internationally-recognized) government of Bosnia-Herzegovina (largely Muslim), based in Sarajevo; a (Bosnian Serb) government of the self-styled Republika Srpska, based in Pale; and a (Bosnian Croat) government of the self-styled state of Herceg-Bosna, based in Mostar.

President: (of the internationally-recognized government in Sarajevo) Alija Izetbegovic.

GEOGRAPHY

Ridges of the Dinaric Mountains, rising to over 1800 m (6000 ft), occupy the greater part of the country and in places form arid karst limestone plateaux. The north comprises restricted lowlands in the valley of the River Sava. The combined length of two tiny coastlines on the Adriatic – now under Croat control – is less than 20 km (13 mi). *Principal rivers*: Sava, Bosna, Drina. *Highest point*: Maglic 2387 m (9118 ft). The north (Bosnia) has cold winters and warm summers; Herzegovina (the south) enjoys milder winters and warmer summers.

ECONOMY

The economy has been devastated by war since 1992. Central and east Bosnia is forested. Agriculture is a major employer and sheep, maize, olives, grapes and citrus fruit were important. Bosnia has little industry but possesses natural resources including coal, lignite, copper and asphalt.

RECENT HISTORY

A major Bosnian revolt (1875–6) against Turkish rule attracted international concern, but the great powers overrode Bosnia's pan-Slavic aspirations at the Congress of Berlin (1877–8) and assigned Bosnia-Herzegovina to Habsburg Austro-Hungarian rule. In Sarajevo in 1914, Gavrilo Princip, a Bosnian Serb student, assassinated Archduke Franz Ferdinand, the heir to the Austro-Hungarian Empire – an event that helped precipitate World War I. In 1918, Bosnia became part of the new Kingdom of Serbs, Croats and Slovenes, which was renamed Yugoslavia in 1929. Following the German invasion (1941), Bosnia was included in the Axis-controlled puppet state of Croatia. In 1945, when Yugoslavia was reorganized by Marshal Tito on Soviet lines, Bosnia-Herzegovina became a republic within the Communist federation. After the secession of Slovenia and Croatia and the beginning of the Yugoslav civil war (1991), tension grew between Serbs and Croats in Bosnia. The Muslim Bosnians reasserted their separate identity. In 1992, a referendum – which was boycotted by the Serbs – gave a majority in favour of Bosnian independence. International recognition of Bosnia-Herzegovina was gained in April 1992 but Bosnian Serbs, encouraged by Serbia, seized 70% of the country, killing or expelling Muslims and Croats in a campaign of 'ethnic cleansing'. International peace and humanitarian efforts were attempted and, in an attempt to curb the Bosnian Serbs, strict UN sanctions were imposed on Serbia and Montenegro (Yugoslavia). By the autumn of 1993 the Bosnian government controlled only 10% of the country – central Bosnia, and enclaves including Bihac, Goradze and Srbenica. Croat-Muslim fighting flared over control of central Bosnia. In September 1993 a plan for a Union of Republics of Bosnia and Herzegovina was rejected. This envisaged a Serb republic (occupying 51%), a Croat republic (17%) and a Muslim republic (32%; with access to the sea via a land corridor to an inland port on the River Neretva). Any of the three confederal republics would have been allowed to withdraw after two years.

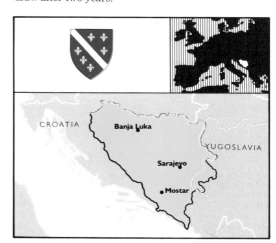

BULGARIA

Official name: Republika Bulgariya (Republic of Bulgaria).

Member of: UN, CSCE, Council of Europe.

Area: 110 912 km² (42 823 sq mi).

Population: 9 005 000 (1991 est).

Capital: Sofia (Sofiya) 1 221 000 (including suburbs; 1990 est).

Other major cities: Plovdiv 379 000, Varna 315 000, Burgas 205 000, Ruse 192 000, Stara Zagora 165 000, Pleven 138 000, Dobrich (formerly Tolbukhin) 116 000, Sliven 112 000, Shumen 111 000 (including suburbs; 1990 est).

Languages: Bulgarian (official; 89%), Turkish (9%). See also p. 186.

Religions: Orthodox (80%) – the Bulgarian Orthodox Church is organized into 11 dioceses under a patriarch based in Sofia; Sunni Islam (8%) – not only the ethnic Turkish minority but also the Pomaks (a minority of ethnic Bulgarian Muslims) follow Islam. There are small Roman Catholic and Protestant minorities.

Education: Education is compulsory between the ages of six and 16. There are four universities (Sofia, Ruse, Gabrovo and Varna). Sixteen other higher education institutions are regarded as having university status.

Defence: In 1992 the total armed strength was 107 000 (including 70 000 conscripts). The army had 75 000 personnel, the air force 20 000 and the navy 10 000. Military service, which is compulsory, lasts 18 months. There is a voluntary militia of over 100 000.

Transport: There are 36 930 km (23 081 mi) of road including 276 km (173 mi) of motorway and 6730 km (4206 mi) of main road. There are 4299 km (2687 mi) of railway track – over one half of which is electrified – operating both passenger and freight services. Inland waterway traffic is important; Ruse and Lom are the principal ports on the River Danube. Varna and Burgas are the most important Bulgarian Black Sea ports. Sofia, Varna and Burgas have international airports.

Media: There are 24 principal daily newspapers (since 1990 including a number of mass circulation independent papers). There is a single state-owned radio and television network.

GOVERNMENT

The 240-member National Assembly is elected every five years by universal adult suffrage using a system of proportional representation. The President – who is directly elected for five years – appoints a Chairman (Prime Minister) and a Council of Ministers that enjoy a majority in the Assembly. The main political parties are the (centre-liberal) Union of Democratic Forces, the (former Communist) Bulgarian Socialist Party, the (mainly Turkish and Pomak) Movement for Rights and Freedom and the United Bulgarian Agrarian People's Union. The UDF is an alliance of 12 parties and political groups. The National Assembly elected on 13 October 1991 comprises:

Party	Seats
Union of Democratic Forces (UDF)	110
Bulgarian Socialist Party (BSP)	106
Movement for Rights and Freedom (MRF)	24
Total	*240*

The coalition government formed in December 1992 comprises non-party experts (academics, business people, etc.) and MRF members.

President: Zhelo Zhelev.

THE CABINET

Prime Minister (Chairman): Lyuben Berov (MRF).

Deputy Prime Minister and Minister of Trade: Valentin Karabashev.

Deputy Prime Minister and Minister of Transport: Neicho Neev.

Deputy Prime Minister and Minister of Labour and Social Affairs: Evgeni Matinchev.

Minister of Agriculture: Georgi Tanev.

Minister of Defence: Valentin Aleksandrov.

Minister of Education, Science and Culture: Martin Todorov.

Minister of the Environment: Valentin Bossevski.

Minister of Finance: Stoyan Aleksandrov.

Minister of Foreign Affairs: Slavi Pashovski.

Minister of Health: Dancho Gogulov.

Minister of Industry: Rumen Bikov.

Minister of Internal Affairs: Col. Viktor Mikhailov.

Minister of Justice: Misho Vulchev.

Minister of Labour and Social Affairs: (see above).

Minister of Territorial Development and Construction: Hristo Totev.

Minister of Trade: (see above).

Minister of Transport: (see above).

GEOGRAPHY

Despite possessing two major mountain chains Bulgaria largely consists of lowlands. The Balkan Mountains run from east to west across central Bulgaria. To the north, low-lying hills and fertile valleys slope down to the River Danube. The Danubian lowland occupies about one third of the country. To the south, another belt of lowland – the Upper Thracian lowland and the Tundzha lowland – separates the Balkan Mountains from the high, rugged Rhodope massif, which includes Bulgaria's highest peak. In the east, a third lowland adjoins the Black Sea. *Principal rivers*: Danube, Iskur, Maritsa. *Highest point*: Musala 2925 m (9596 ft).

The continental north has warm summers and cold winters, while the southeast has a more Mediterranean climate. Except in the mountains, rainfall throughout Bulgaria is only moderate.

ECONOMY

With fertile soils, and few other natural resources, Bulgaria has a strong agricultural base. For nearly half a century, production was centred on large-scale, mechanized cooperatives, but privatization of land began in 1990. The principal crops include: cereals (wheat, maize, barley), fruit (grapes) and, increasingly, tobacco. Agricultural products are the basis of the food-processing, wine and tobacco industries. Eastern bloc grants helped develop industry including engineering, fertilizers and chemicals. Tourism is increasingly important – some 11 000 000 visitors a year are attracted by the Black Sea resorts in the summer and by winter sports facilities in the Balkan Mountains in the winter.

Labour force (1990)

Sector	Number employed
Agriculture	735 200
Forestry	22 400
Manufacturing/utilities	1 384 400
Mining and quarrying	37 800
Construction	336 700
Commerce	372 100
Transport	241 600
Communications	44 700
Finance	24 600
Education/culture	320 000
Health and social security	221 000
Administration	54 500
Other	301 900
Total	4 097 000

Trade patterns have been disrupted in Central and Eastern Europe since 1990–91 when social, economic and political upheavals swept the region. Bulgaria – whose trade links with the USSR had been particularly close – suffered more than most East European countries, with severe shortages of many commodities, particularly industrial raw materials and oil. Industrial production declined, and high rates of inflation (over 100% in 1992) and unemployment have been experienced. However, some progress has been made in the initial stages of the privatization of state-run industries and Bulgaria has moved towards an agreement of association with the European Community. However, Bulgaria's economic problems have not been helped by the lack of a stable government.

Imports (1991)

Sector	% of imports
Machinery	46.2%
Fuels, raw materaisl	33.6%
Chemicals/petrochemicals	4.5%
Agricultural products	4.4%
Other imports	11.3%

Exports (1991)

Sector	% of exports
Machinery	59.1%
Foodstuff	12.1%
Chemicals/fertilizer	3.9%
Metals/minerals/raw materials/fuel	7.7%
Other	17.2%

The value of the Bulgarian currency – the lev (plural leva), which is divided into 100 stotinki – has decreased sharply in the 1990s. In September 1993, the exchange rate was 25.9 leva to 1 US$. The most recent budgetary figures available are estimates for 1992 (see below – in the following table the percentages given for revenue and expenditure apply to 1989–90).

Revenue

	Million leva	% of revenue
National economy, etc.		92%
Non-productive sector		8%
Total	44 500	100%

Expenditure

	Million leva	% of expenditure
National economy		47.2%
Education, culture, health		18.8%
Social security		17.1%
Administration		1.6%
Other		15.3%
Total	53 600	100%

RECENT HISTORY

Bulgaria was on the losing side in the final Balkan War (1913) and in World War I (in which Bulgaria was involved from 1915 to 1918) and forfeited territory to Greece and Romania. In World War II Bulgaria – under King Boris III – joined the Axis powers (1941–44), occupied part of Yugoslavia and annexed Greek Thrace (although these territorial gains were lost after the war). Boris III died under suspicious circumstances in 1943 – it was commonly believed that he was poisoned by order of Hitler. In 1944 a left-wing alliance seized power and the Soviet Red Army invaded. A Communist regime, tied closely to the USSR, was established and the king – Simeon II – was exiled (1946). During the next four and a half decades Bulgaria was the Soviet Union's most loyal ally in the Balkans.

Following popular demonstrations in 1989, the hardline Communist leader Todor Zhivkov (1911–) was replaced by reformers who promised free elections and renounced the leading role of the Communist Party. Free elections were held in June 1990, when the Bulgarian Socialist Party (BSP) – formerly the Bulgarian Communist Party – was returned to power. Faced by severe economic problems, the BSP was unable to govern alone and a coalition government with a non-party prime minister took office in 1991. Short-lived coalitions involving various combinations of the three main parties – the BSP, the (centre-liberal) UDF and the (mainly ethnic Turkish and Pomak) MRF – and non-party independents have followed.

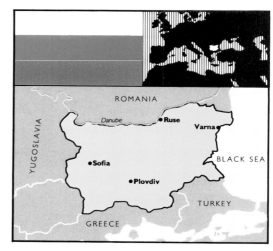

CROATIA

Official name: Republika Hrvatska (The Republic of Croatia).

Member of: UN, CSCE.

Area: 56 538 km² (21 829 sq mi), including the area (25%–30%) that is controlled by Serb forces.

Population: 4 784 000 (1991 census). Since early 1992 Croatia has received over 600 000 refugees from Bosnia.

Capital: Zagreb 934 000 (city 707 000) (1991 census).

Other major cities: Split 207 000 (city 189 000), Rijeka 206 000 (city 168 000), Osijek 165 000 (city 105 000), Zadar 76 000, Pula 62 000, Karlovac 60 000 (1991 census).

Languages: Croat (75%) – the form of Serbo-Croat written in the Latin alphabet, Serb (23%) – the form of Serbo-Croat written in the Cyrillic alphabet. See also p. 186.

Religions: Roman Catholic (77%), Orthodox (11%). The Roman Catholic Church is organized into four archdioceses – Rijeka-Senj, Split-Makarska, Zadar and Zagreb – and eight dioceses.

Education: Education is compulsory between the ages of six and 15. There are four universities – Osijek, Rijeka, Split and Zagreb.

Defence: At the start of 1993 the total armed strength was nearly 110 000 (including over 105 000 in the army, 5000 in the air force and under 1000 in the navy). Compulsory military service lasts 10 months.

Transport: There are 2425 km (1507 mi) of railway track operating both passenger and freight services. There are 27 378 km (17 012 mi) of roads of which 302 km (188 mi) are motorway. Rijeka is an important port on the Adriatic. Zagreb has an international airport; several other regional airports with international services have been closed since 1991.

Media There are nine principal daily newspapers – eight published in Croat; one published in Italian. There is a single (state-owned) radio and television network.

GOVERNMENT

The bicameral Assembly (Sabor) comprises a 138-member Chamber of Representatives (the lower house) elected by universal adult suffrage for four years and a 63-member Chamber of Municipalities (the upper house), comprising three members directly elected from each of the 21 counties into which the republic is divided. An executive President is directly elected for five years. The President appoints a Prime Minister and a Council of Ministers that enjoy a majority in the Chamber of Representatives. The main political parties are the (nationalist) Croatian Democratic Union (CDU), the Croatian Social-Liberal Party (CSLP), the (right-wing nationalist) Croatian Party of Rights (CPR), the Croatian People's Party (CPP), the (former Communist) Social Democratic Party-Party of Democratic Reform (SDP-PDRC), the Croatian Farmers' Party, Dalmatian Action (DA), the Istrian Democratic Assembly (IDA), the Rijeka Democratic Alliance (RDA), and the Serbian

People's Party. At a general election for the Chamber of Representatives held on 2 August 1992 these parties gained the following number of seats:

Party	Seats
Christian Democratic Union	85
Christian Social-Liberal Party	14
Social Democratic Party-Party of Democratic Reform	11
Croatian People's Party	6
DA-IDS-RDA Alliance	6
Croatian Party of Rights	5
Croatian Farmers' Party	3
Serbian People's Party	3
Independents	5
Total	*138*

A CDU government was formed in August 1992.

President: Franjo Tudjman.

THE CABINET

Prime Minister: Hrvoje Sarinic.
Deputy Prime Minister: Dr Mate Granic.
Deputy Prime Minister: Mladen Vedris.
Deputy Prime Minister: Ivan Milas.
Deputy Prime Minister: Vladimir Seks.
Minister of Agriculture and Forestry: Dr Ivan Majdak.
Minister of Defence: Gojko Susak.
Minister of Education and Culture: Vesna Gerardi-Jurkic.
Minister of Energy, Shipbuilding and Industry: Franjo Kajfez.
Minister of Environmental Protection and Construction: Zdenko Karakas.
Minister of Finance: Dr Zoran Jasic.

Minister of Foreign Affairs: Dr Zdenko Skrabalo.
Minister of Health: Juraj Njavro.
Minister of the Interior: Ivan Jarnjak.
Minister of Justice and Administration: Ivica Crnic.
Minister of Labour and Social Welfare: Josip Juras.
Minister of Maritime Affairs, Transport and Communications: Ivica Mudrinic.
Minister of Tourism and Trade: Branko Miksa.
Ministers without portfolio: Dr Zvonimir Baletic, Cedomir Pavlovic, Dr Smiljko Sokol.

GEOGRAPHY

Croatia is shaped like a crescent. The country comprises three principal distinct regions – Slavonia in the east is a fertile region of plains in the Sava and Danube valleys; central Croatia is a region of hills around Zagreb; Dalmatia is a coastal region separated from central Croatia by barren limestone (karst) ranges running parallel to the Adriatic coast. There are over 600 offshore islands. The Dubrovnik area is detached from the rest of Croatia by part of Croatian-held Bosnia. Serb occupation of part of Croatia means that the north and south of the republic are now linked only by the Maslenica bridge, an estuarine crossing north of Zadar. *Principal rivers:* Sava, Danube, Drava. *Highest point:* Troglav 1913 m (6275 ft).

The interior is colder and drier than the Mediterranean coast. Only the mountains receive more than a moderate rainfall.

ECONOMY

Croatia has important mineral resources including bauxite and oil. Slavonia grows cereals, potatoes and sugar beet. Manufacturing – aluminium, textiles and chemicals – dominates the economy. In 1991–3 the economy was damaged by the Yugoslav civil war, and the lucrative Dalmatian tourist industry collapsed. Many businesses have gone bankrupt and the country suffers high rates of inflation, severe unemployment, falling industrial and agricultural GNP, the cost of maintaining over 600 000 refugees and the expense of repairing war damage. By the middle of 1993, nearly 40% of the country's industrial capacity had either been destroyed or damaged owing to war or had been taken by Serbian forces.

Labour force (1991)

Sector	Number employed
Industry	462 000
Agriculture, fishing, forestry	62 000
Construction	98 000
Education and culture	94 000
Trade	142 000
Transport and communications	110 000
Catering, tourism	42 000
Finance, business	56 000
Health and social services	102 000
Other	136 000
Total	*1 304 000*

Because of high rates of inflation, industrial collapse and the effects of the continuing wars in the former Yugoslavia, the most recent available budgetary figures for Croatia – 1990, that is before independence – have been rendered meaningless. The following figures for imports and exports also no longer reflect the current situation but do give an indication of which goods and commodities are the most significant.

Imports (1991)

Sector	% of imports
Machinery, transport equipment	21.9%
Fuels	17.4%
Chemicals	13.5%
Foodstuffs	10.6%
Consumer goods (general)	9.1%

Exports (1991)

Sector	% of exports
Machinery, transport equipment	23.4%
Clothing	17.8%
Chemicals	12.1%
Foodstuffs	7.7%

The Croatian currency – the Croatian dinar (which is divided into 100 para) – has declined in value owing to the collapse of the Croatian economy and high inflation (in 1992 running at over 1000%). In September 1993 the exchange rate was 5081 dinars to 1US$.

RECENT HISTORY

In 1868 Croatia gained autonomy within the kingdom of Hungary, which was part of the Habsburg Austro-Hungarian Empire. A Croat national revival looked increasingly to independent Serbia to create a South ('Yugo') Slav state. After World War I when the Habsburg Empire was dissolved (1918), the Croats joined the Serbs, Slovenes and Montenegrins in the state that was to become Yugoslavia in 1929. However, the Croats soon resented the highly centralized Serb-dominated kingdom and a Croat terrorist organization, the Utase, became active. In 1934 the Utase assassinated (the Serb) King Alexander I of Yugoslavia when he was on a state visit to France.

Following the German invasion of Yugoslavia (1941), the occupying Axis powers set up an 'independent' Croat puppet kingdom – with an Italian prince as nominal king. Ante Pavelic, the head of the Croatian government from 1941 to 1945, had been the leader of the Utase terrorists before World War II. The Croat government adopted harsh anti-Serb policies including expulsions, massacres and forced conversions of Serbs to Roman Catholicism. In 1945 Croatia was reintegrated into a federal Communist Yugoslav state by Marshal Tito, but after Tito's death (1980), the Yugoslav experiment faltered in economic and nationalist crises.

Separatists came to power in Croatia in free elections (1990) and declared independence (June 1991). Serb insurgents, backed by the Yugoslav federal army, occupied 25%–30% of Croatia including those areas with an ethnic Serb majority – Krajina and parts of Slavonia. The fierce Serbo-Croat war came to an uneasy halt in 1992 after Croatian independence had gained widespread diplomatic recognition and a UN peace-keeping force was agreed. By mid-1993 Croats controlled about 20% of Bosnia-Herzegovina where an embryo Croat state – Herceg-Bosna – was effectively established. Intermittent hostilities between Croats and Serbs recommenced in 1993 with attention focussed on the region of the Maslenica bridge (see above).

CZECH REPUBLIC

Official name: Ceská Republika (Czech Republic).

Member of: UN, CSCE, Council of Europe, CEFTA.

Area: 78 880 km² (30 456 sq mi).

Population: 10 302 000 (1991 census).

Capital: Prague (Praha) 1 212 000 (1991 census).

Other major cities: Brno 388 000, Ostrava 328 000, Olomouc 224 000, Zlin 197 000, Plzen 174 000, Ceské Budejovice 173 000, Hradec Kralové 163 000, Pardubice 162 000, Liberec 160 000 (1991 census).

Languages: Czech (94%), Slovak (4%). See also p. 186.

Religions: Roman Catholic (39%), Hussite (8%). The Roman Catholic Church is organized into five dioceses and two archdioceses – Prague and Olomouc. The Hussite Church is organized into five dioceses. The (Presbyterian) Evangelical Church of Czech Brethren is also numerically important.

Education: Education is compulsory between the ages of six to 16. There are 14 universities – Prague (5 including the famous Charles University), Brno (4), Plzen, Liberec, Pardubice, Ostrava, and Olomouc.

Defence: Following the division of the armed forces of the former Czechoslovakia (January 1993), the new Czech armed forces had a total armed strength of about 48 000. Compulsory military service is 18 months; the period served is scheduled to be reduced to 12 months.

Transport: There are 9500 km (5938 mi) of railway track operating both passenger and freight services. Prague has a metro system. There are 55 517 km (34 698 mi) of roads including 362 km (226 mi) of motorway. Inland waterways are used for navigation and Prague on the Vltava and Ustí nad Labem on the Elbe are significant river ports. Ruzyně (Prague), Brno, Ostrava and Karlovy Vary are international airports.

Media: There are 22 principal daily newspapers (one half of which are printed in Prague). There is a single radio and television network with regional studios and broadcasts.

GOVERNMENT

The bicameral Parliament comprises a 200-member Chamber of Deputies (the lower house) which is elected under a system of proportional representation by universal adult suffrage for four years and an 81-member Senate (the upper house) which is directly elected for six years. A President – whose role is largely ceremonial – is elected for a four-year term by an electoral college comprising the two houses of Parliament. The President appoints a Prime Minister who, in turn, appoints a Council of Ministers that commands a majority in the Chamber. The main political parties are the (conservative) Civic Democratic Party (CDP), the Left Bloc (an electoral alliance including the Communist Party), the Social Democratic Party, the Liberal Social Union (an electoral alliance of the Socialist Party, the Agrarian Party and the Green Party), the (conservative) Civic Democratic Union-Czech People's Party (CDU-CPP), the (right-wing nationalist) Association for the Republic-Czech Republic Party, the Social Democratic Party, the (centrist) Civic Democratic Alliance, the (Moravian and Silesian nationalist) Movement for Autonomous Democracy-Society for Moravia and Silesia (MADMS) and the Christian Democratic Party (CD).

At elections held on 5–6 June 1992 the representation of the parties in the lower house was as follows:

Party	Seats
Civic Democratic Party (CDP)	76
Socialist Party	35
Social Democratic Party	16
Liberal Social Union	16
Christian Democratic Union-People's Party (CDU-CPP)	15
Association for the Republic-Czech Republican Party	14
Civic Democratic Alliance (CDA)	14
MADMS	14
Total	200

A coalition CDP, CDU-CPP, CDA and CD government was formed in June 1992.

President: Václav Havel.

THE CABINET

Prime Minister: Václav Klaus (CDP).

Deputy Prime Minister and Minister of Agriculture: Josef Lux (CDU-CPP).

Deputy Prime Minister: Jan Kalvoda (CDA).

Deputy Prime Minister and Minister of Finance: Ivan Kocárnik (CDP).

Minister of Agriculture: (see above).

Minister of Control: Igor Nemec (CDP).

Minister of Culture: Jindrich Kabát (CDU-CPP).

Minister of Defence: Antonín Baudys (CDU-CPP).

Minister of Economic Competition: Stanislav Belehrádek (CDU-CPP).

Minister of the Economy: Karel Dyba (CDP).

Minister of Education: Petr Pitha (CD).

Minister of the Environment: Frantisek Benda (CD).

Minister of Finance: (see above).

Minister of Foreign Affairs: Josef Zieleniec (CDP).

Minister of Health: Petr Lom (CDP).

Minister of Industry and Trade: Vladimír Dlouhý (CDA).

Minister of Justice: Jiri Novák (CDP).

Minister of the Interior: Jan Ruml (CDP).

Minister of Labour and Social Affairs: Jindrich Vodicka (CDP).

Minister of Privatization: Jiri Skalický (CDA).

Minister of Transport: Jan Stráský (CDP).

GEOGRAPHY

The west – Bohemia – is an elevated basin drained by the rivers Elbe and Vltava and their tributaries and surrounded by mountains – the uplands of the Bohemian Forest in the west and south, the Ore Mountains and Giant Mountains in the north and the Bohemian-Moravian Highlands in the east. The east – Moravia – is a lowland that separates the Bohemian uplands from the Carpathian Mountains of neighbouring Slovakia. *Principal rivers:* Elbe (Labe), Vltava. *Highest point:* Snezka 1603 m (5259 ft).

The climate tends towards continental with warm summers and cold winters, but there are many local variations owing to relief. Rainfall total are high in the Giant Mountains but only moderate in the Elbe Basin.

ECONOMY

Apart from coal, there are few mineral resources, but the country is heavily industrialized and some areas have suffered heavy pollution. Manufactures include industrial machinery, motor vehicles and consumer goods. Most of the older plant and uneconomic heavy industries of the former Czechoslovakia were situated in Slovakia, thus, when the federation was dissolved (January 1993), the Czech Republic was left with a healthier industrial base than its neighbour. The timber industry is important. The main crops include wheat, potatoes, barley and sugar beet. The Czech Republic is one of the world's leading producers of hops, which are the basis of the major brewing industry.

Labour force (1990)

Sector	Number employed
Industry, utilities	2 248 000
Agriculture, forestry	635 000
Construction	581 000
Education and culture	425 000
Trade, hotel and catering	533 000
Transport and communications	403 000
Health and social services	278 000
Finance	154 000
Other (including unemployed)	798 000
Total	6 055 000

The country is switching from a centrally planned to a free-market economy. Many businesses have been privatized but the much-abused voucher system (see pp. 140–42) is being replaced by more conventional means of extending the private sector. The Czech Republic has attracted considerable foreign investment (80% German) and its economy is increasingly linked to that of Germany. Although the Czech Republic has had a fall in GNP, its economic decline has not been so pronounced as that suffered by most other former Communist countries. The market reforms of the former Czechoslovakia had considerable success in the Czech Lands but led to a high rate of unemployment in Slovakia. This economic disparity was a major factor in the dissolution of Czechoslovakia.

Imports (1990)

Sector	% of imports
Machinery/transport equipment	37.0%
Fuels, minerals, metals	17.3%
Raw materials	8.8%
Foodstuffs	6.8%

Exports (1990)

Sector	% of exports
Machinery, transport equipment	45.4%
Manufactures (general)	22.4%
Chemicals	7.6%
Food and live animals	4.6%

The Czech currency is the koruna, which is divided into 100 halierov. In September 1993 the exchange rate was 28.72 koruny to 1US$. The most recent budgetary figures are estimates based on 1990 figures.

Revenue	Million koruny	% of revenue
Total	320 090	100%

Expenditure	Million koruny	% of expenditure
Total	319 140	100%

RECENT HISTORY

On the collapse of the Habsburg Empire, the Czechs and Slovaks united in an independent state (1918) – largely due to the efforts of Thomas Masaryk, who became Czechoslovakia's first president. In 1938, Hitler demanded that Germany be granted the Sudetenland, where Germans predominated. Lacking allies, Czechoslovakia was dismembered – Bohemia and Moravia became German 'protectorates'. The Nazi occupation included the massacre of the inhabitants of Lidice (1942). Following liberation (1945), a coalition government was formed, but the Communists staged a takeover in 1948. In 1968, moves by Party Secretary Alexander Dubček to introduce political reforms met with Soviet disapproval, and invasion by Czechoslovakia's Warsaw Pact allies. The conservative wing of the Communist party regained control until 1989, when student demonstrations developed into a peaceful revolution led by the Civic Forum movement. Faced by overwhelming public opposition, the Communist Party renounced its leading role and hardline leaders were replaced by reformers. A new government, in which Communists were in a minority, was appointed and Civic Forum's leader – the playwright Václav Havel – was elected president. In 1990 free multi-party elections were held, Soviet troops were withdrawn and the foundations of a market economy were laid. Increased Slovak separatism led to the division of the country in 1993, when the secession of poorer, more rural Slovakia left the more developed Czech Republic as a likely future EC member.

ESTONIA

Official name: Eesti Vabariik (Republic of Estonia).
Member of: UN, CSCE, Council of Europe.
Area: 45 226 km² (17 462 sq mi).
Population: 1 562 000 (1992 est).
Capital: Tallinn 505 000 (city 498 000) (1991 est).
Other major cities: Tartu 114 000, Narva 87 000, Kohtla-Järve 75 000, Pärnu 57 000 (including suburbs; 1991 est).
Languages: Estonian (63%), Russian (31%). See also p. 186.
Religions: Lutheran (30%), Orthodox (10%). The Evangelical Lutheran Church of Estonia – under an archbishop based in Tallinn – is the main denomination. Most Orthodox Christians in Estonia are ethnic Russians and the country forms a diocese of the Russian Orthodox Church.
Education: Education is compulsory between the ages of six and 17 in schools in which the Estonian language is the first language of instruction and the ages of seven and 17 in schools in which the Russian language is the first language of instruction. There are two universities (Tartu and Tallinn).
Defence: The Estonian armed forces, which were reconstituted in 1992, had a total strength of 2000 early in 1993. Military service of 12 months is envisaged. Late in 1993 some 10 000 Russian troops were still stationed in Estonia. No date for their eventual withdrawal has been agreed.
Transport There are 1026 km (641 mi) of railway track of which 132 km (83 mi) are electrified. Both passenger and freight services are run. There are 1194 km (746 mi) of main roads, 2616 km (1635 mi) of secondary roads and 11 001 km (688 mi) of other roads. Communications are centred upon Tallinn, which is a commercial and ferry port and has Estonia's only international airport.
Media There are 164 daily newspapers – the majority are published in Estonian, a minority in Russian. There is a single (state-owned) radio and television service.

GOVERNMENT

A 101-member Assembly (Riigokogu) is elected for four years by universal adult suffrage. The President is elected by the Assembly for a five-year term. The President appoints a Prime Minister and a Council of Ministers who are responsible to the Assembly. The main political parties are the (nationalist) Pro Patria/National Fatherland Party (known in Estonian as Isamaa), the Secure Home Party, the (nationalist) Estonian Popular Front (Rahvarinne), the Moderate Group, the Estonian National Independence Party (ENIP), the Estonian Citizens Group, the Independent Royalists, the Estonian Green Movement, the Estonian Entrepreneurs' Party and the (former Communist) Estonian Democratic Labour Party.

In the elections held for the Assembly on 20 September 1992 only those Estonians, or their descendents, who were citizens of the country in 1940 were able to vote. This electoral roll deprived most of the ethnic Russians of the right to vote. The Assembly comprises:

Party	Seats
Pro Patria/National Fatherland Party	29
Secure Home	17
Estonian Popular Front	15
Moderate Group	12
Estonian National Independence Party (ENIP)	10
Estonian Citizens Group	8
Independent Royalists	8
Estonian Green Movement	1
Estonian Entrepreneurs' Party	1
Total	101

The coalition government formed in September 1992 comprises members of Pro Patria/National Fatherland Front, the Moderate Group and ENIP.
President: Lennart Meri.

THE CABINET

Prime Minister: Mart Laar.
Minister of Agriculture: Jaan Leetsaar.
Minister of Culture and Education: Paul-Eerik Rummo.
Minister of Defence: Hain Rebas.
Minister of the Economy: Toomas Sildmäe.
Minister of the Environment: Andres Tarand.
Minister of Finance: Madis Üürike.
Minister of Foreign Affairs: Trivimi Velliste.
Minister of the Interior: Lagle Parek.
Minister of Justice: Kaido Kama.
Minister of Social Affairs: Marju Lauristin.
Minister of the State Chancellery: Ulo Kaevats.
Minister of Transport and Communications: Andi Meister.
Ministers without portfolio: Lila Hänni, Arvo Niitenberg, Juri Luik.

GEOGRAPHY

Estonia comprises a low-lying gently undulating main-land which only rises above 300 m (984 ft) in the southeast. The north comprises a limestone plateau which ends on the Baltic coast in low cliffs. There are many rivers and lakes including Lake Peipus, which has an area of 3548 km² (1370 sq mi). Much of the country is forested. Estonia has many small and two larger off-shore islands. *Principal rivers:* Narva, Pärnu. *Highest point:* Munamägi 318 m (1042 ft).

Estonia has a moist temperate climate that is characterized by mild summers and cold winters.

ECONOMY

Major industries include engineering and food process-ing. Progress towards the privatization of industry has been made. Gas for heating and industry is extracted from bituminous shale. The important agricultural sector is dominated by dairying but production declined by 25% in 1992. Over 600 farms have been privatized although over 150 large cooperatives remain in state hands.

Labour force (1991)

Sector	Number employed
Industry, mining	257 000
Agriculture, forestry, fishing	100 900
Construction	78 000
Trade, hotels & catering	69 000
Transport and communications	67 500
Finance	4 000
Social and personal services	198 500
Other	15 100
Total	*790 000*

Since 1991 severe economic difficulties have resulted from Estonia's heavy dependency upon trade with Russia. Acute shortages of energy and raw materials have crippled the economy and Estonia's economy declined in tandem with Russia's until a new convertible Estonian currency, the kroon, was introduced in 1992. In September 1993, the exchange rate was 13.13 kroons to 1 US$. Since its introduction the kroon has been extremely stable, largely owing to the centre-right government's cautious monetary policies.

The most recent budgetary figures available are those for 1991, that is before the introduction of the kroon.

Revenue

	Million roubles	% of revenue
Taxation	2 771	41%
Non-taxation receipts	293	4%
Local government revenue	1 970	29%
Extra budgetary funds	1 671	26%
Total	*6 706*	*100%*

Expenditure

	Million roubles	% of expenditure
Central government	1 701	29%
Local goverment	1 952	34%
Social fund	1 722	30%
Other	990	7%
Total	*5 807*	*100%*

Closer links with Scandinavian countries, in particular Finland, have been forged, but trade is still largely with former Soviet republics. Estonia is disadvantaged through not having many products for which there is a market in the European Community or EFTA. Efforts have been made to exploit medieval Tallinn and the country's picturesque scenery to attract tourists.

Imports (1991)

Sector	% of imports
Textiles and clothing	19.0%
Machinery	14.0%
Mineral products	12.0%
Vegetable products	10.1%
Chemicals	7.3%
Food products	5.7%

Exports (1991)

Sector	% of imports
Textiles	26.4%
Machinery	11.6%
Chemicals	11.0%
Live animals and animal products	10.0%
Mineral products	5.2%

RECENT HISTORY

When the Communists took power in Russia (1917), Estonia (which had been ceded by Sweden to Russia in 1721) seceded. The late 19th century had witnessed a steady growth in Estonian nationalism, spurred by a period of intensive Russification in the 1880s and 1890s. Konstantin Päts, who had summoned an Estonian congress during the 1905 abortive Russian revolution, was declared premier in 1917 but a German occupation and two Russian invasions delayed independence until 1919. Estonia's fragile democracy was replaced by the dictatorship of Päts in 1934. The Non-Aggression Pact (1939) between Hitler and Stalin assigned Estonia to the USSR, which invaded and annexed the republic (1940). Estonia was occupied by Nazi Germany (1941–44). When Soviet rule was reimposed (1945), large-scale Russian settlement replaced over 120 000 Estonians who had been killed or deported to Siberia.

In 1988, reforms in the USSR allowed Estonian nation-alists to operate openly. Nationalists won a majority in the republic's parliament, gradually assumed greater autonomy and seceded following the failed coup by Communist hardliners in Moscow (August 1991). The USSR recognized Estonia's independence in September 1991. The country faces a number of problems associated with the presence of a large Russian-speaking minority. In 1992 the introduction of strict Estonian citizenship laws that denied full rights to most Russian-speakers increased tension with Russia, which halted the with-drawal of troops from Estonia. Ethnic Russians make up 35% of the population of Tallinn and form an over-whelming majority in the eastern towns of Narva and Sillamäe. In the 1992 general election very few inha-bitants of these eastern towns qualified to vote (see above). Narva and Sillamäe, near the Russian border, have unsuccessfully sought considerable autonomy and have held unofficial referenda on their status. In 1993 the citizenship law was eased to allow ethnic Russians with residential qualifications and fluency in Estonian to acquire full citizenship.

HUNGARY

Official name: Magyarország (Hungary) or Magyar Köztársaság (The Hungarian Republic)
Member of: UN, CSCE, Council of Europe, CEFTA.
Area: 93 036 km² (35 921 sq mi).
Population: 10 337 000 (1992 est).
Capital: Budapest 1 992 000 (1992 est).
Other major cities: Debrecen 215 000, Miskolc 192 000, Szeged 178 000, Pécs 170 000, Györ 130 000, Nyíregyháza 114 000, Székésfehérvár 109 000, Kecskemét 105 000, Szombathely 86 000, Szolnok 79 000, Tatabánya 73 000 (1992 est).
Language: Magyar (Hungarian) (97%), German (2%), Slovak (1%). See also p. 186.
Religions: Roman Catholic (56%), Calvinist and Lutheran (22%). The Roman Catholic Church in Hungary is organized into three archdioceses – Eger, Esztergom and Kalocsa – and eight dioceses. The leading Protestant Churches are the (Presbyterian Calvinist) Reformed Church of Hungary and the Lutheran Church in Hungary – both of which are headed by a presiding bishop.
Education: Education is compulsory between the ages of six and 14. There are 19 universities – Budapest (7), Debrecen (3), Pécs (2), Szeged (2), Gödöllö, Keszthely, Miskolc, Sopron, Veszprém.
Defence: In mid-1993 the total armed strength of Hungary's forces was 81 000 (of which 64 000 were in the army and 17 000 were in the air force). There was also a border guard of some 20 000 personnel.
Transport: There are 7600 km (4722 mi) of railway track operating passenger and freight services. Budapest has a metro system. There are 105 424 km (65 507 mi) of roads including 335 km (208 mi) of motorway. The Danube is a major inland waterway and enables Hungary, although land-locked, to have a small ocean-going merchant fleet. Ferihegy (Budapest) is an international airport; there are no regional commercial airports.
Media: There are over 30 principal daily newspapers, more than one half of which are published in provincial cities. Cable television competes with the (state-owned) television service. Commercial radio now operates alongside the state-owned radio service.

GOVERNMENT
The 386-member National Assembly is elected for four years by universal adult suffrage. It comprises 58 members elected from a national list under a system of proportional representation, 152 members elected on a county basis and 176 elected from single-member constituencies. The President – who is elected by the Assembly for a maximum of two four-year terms – appoints a Cabinet and a Prime Minister from the majority in the Assembly. The main political parties include the (centre right) Hungarian Democratic Forum (MDF), the (liberal) Alliance of Free Democrats (SzDSz), the Independent Smallholders' Party (FKgP), the (former

Communist) Hungarian Socialist Party (MSzP), the (centre right) Federation of Young Democrats (FIDESz), and the Christian Democratic People's Party (KDNP). In a general election held on 25 March and 8 April 1990 these parties gained the following number of seats:

Party	Seats
Hungarian Democratic Forum	165
Alliance of Free Democrats	92
Independent Smallholders' Party	43
Hungarian Socialist Party	33
Federation of Young Democrats	21
Christian Democratic People's Party	21
Independents	11
Total	386

A coalition government of members of the Hungarian Democratic Forum, the Independent Smallholders' Party and the Christian Democratic People's Party and independents was formed.
President: Arpad Goncz.

THE CABINET
Prime Minister (Chairman): Peter Boross (ind).
Minister of Agriculture: János Szabó (FKgP).
Minister of Defence: Lajos Für (MDF).
Minister of Education and Culture: Ferenc Mádl (ind).
Minister of Environmental Protection and Urban Development: János Gyurko (MDF).
Minister of Finance: Iván Szabó (MDF).
Minister of Foreign Affairs: Géza Jeszenszky (MDF).
Minister of Industry and Trade: János Miklós Latorcaí (MDF).
Minister of the Interior: Peter Boross (ind; see above).
Minister of International Economic Relations: Béla Kádar (ind).
Minister of Justice: István Balsai (MDF).
Minister of Labour: Gyula Kiss (FKgP).
Minister of Transport, Communications and Water: György Schamschula (MDF).
Minister of Welfare: László Surján (KDNP).
Ministers without portfolio: Tibor Fuezessy (KDNP), Balázs Horváth (FKgP), Ferenc József Nagy (FKgP), Ernö Pungor (ind).

GEOGRAPHY
The largest physical region in Hungary is the Great Alfold (or Great Hungarian Plain) which covers most of central and eastern Hungary. The Great Alfold is divided by the valley of the River Tisza. West of the River Danube, a discontinuous belt of low mountains and hills – including the Bakony Mountains – runs from southwest to northeast across the country. These uplands, which are sometimes known as the Transdanubian Mountains, end in thickly wooded highlands in the northeast on the Slovak border. The Transdanubian uplands separate the Great Alfold from the Little Alfold, a more undulating plain than its larger namesake. The Little Alfold has better soils and is more densely populated than the Great Alfold. *Principal rivers:* Danube (Duna), Tisza, Drava. *Highest point:* Kékes 1015 m (3330 ft).

The Hungarian climate is continental with long, hot dry summers and cold winters. Rainfall is moderate throughout the country.

ECONOMY

Nearly one seventh of the labour force is involved in agriculture. Major crops include cereals (maize, wheat and barley), sugar beet, fruit, and grapes for wine. Most of the land has been privatized.

Labour force (1992)

Sector	Number employed
Manufacturing, mining, utilities	1 286 000
Agriculture, forestry	589 000
Construction	273 000
Commerce	564 000
Transport and communications	373 000
Social and personal services	1 157 000
Total	4 242 000

Despite considerable reserves of coal, Hungary imports more than half of its energy needs. Hungary also mines bauxite and brown coal. The steel, chemical fertilizer, pharmaceutical, machinery and vehicle industries are important.

Imports (1990)

Sector	% of imports
Machinery, transport equipment	30.8%
Fuels, lubricants	15.3%
Chemicals	12.5%
Textiles	5.9%
Foodstuffs	4.8%

Exports (1990)

Sector	% of exports
Machinery, transport equipment	22.5%
Chemicals	12.8%
Meat	8.6%
Clothing	7.1%
Vegetables and fruit	5.7%

Since the early 1980s, private enterprise and foreign investment have been encouraged, and between 1989 and 1993 over one half of state-owned industry was privatized. Although Hungary has experienced economic difficulties including unemployment, falling GDP and inflation, Hungary's economic progress has been among the most impressive in Central and Eastern Europe. Hungary is considered to be a prospective member of the OECD and has been invited to apply for eventual membership of the EC.

The most recent budgetary figures are for 1991.

Revenue

	Million forint	% of revenue
Business taxes	493 000	31%
Consumer taxes	287 000	18%
Personal taxes	333 000	21%
Other receipts	476 000	30%
Total	1 589 000	100%

Expenditure

	Million forint	% of expenditure
Education, defence, law, culture, administration, etc.	707 000	43%
Social security	446 000	27%
Investment	128 000	8%
Industry, agriculture	64 000	4%
Other		18%
Total	1 642 000	100%

The Hungarian currency is the forint which is divided into 100 filler. In September 1993 the exchange rate was 93.7 forints to 1US$.

The Hungarian currency is the forint which is divided into 100 filler. In September 1993 the exchange rate was 93.7 forints to 1US$.

RECENT HISTORY

In 1867 Austria granted Hungary considerable autonomy within the Austro-Hungarian Empire (the Dual Monarchy). Hungary, in turn, granted some autonomy to Croatia. However, there was mounting friction between the governments in Vienna and Budapest and between the Hungarian authorities and various linguistic minorities. Defeat in World War I led to a brief period of Communist rule under Béla Kun (1919), then occupation by Romania. In the postwar settlement Hungary lost two thirds of its territory, mainly to Romania (Transylvania) and the new state of Czechoslovakia (Slovakia). After the deposition of the Habsburgs, Hungary remained a monarchy, without a monarch, until 1945. The Regent, Admiral Miklás Horthy (1868–1957), cooperated with Hitler during World War II in an attempt to regain territory, but defeat in 1945 resulted in occupation by the Red Army, and a Communist People's Republic was established in 1949.

The Hungarian Uprising in 1956 was a heroic attempt to overthrow Communist rule, but was quickly suppressed by Soviet forces, and its leader, Imre Nagy, was executed. János Kadar – Communist Party Secretary 1956–88 – tried to win support with economic progress. However, in the late 1980s reformers in the Communist Party gained the upper hand, and talks with opposition groups led to agreement on a transition to a fully democratic, multi-party state. The (Communist) Hungarian Socialist Workers' Party transformed itself into the Socialist Party but was heavily defeated in the first free elections in May 1990 when conservative and liberal parties won most seats. Soviet troops left Hungary in 1990, and the country has joined Western European organizations and established a free-market economy. The status of over 3 000 000 Hungarians who are citizens of Slovakia, Romania and the former Yugoslavia has become an issue. In 1993 Hungary signed a treaty with Ukraine recognizing their present boundary which includes a Hungarian minority within Ukraine.

LATVIA

Official name: Latvija (Latvia).

Member of: UN, CSCE.

Area: 64 589 km^2 (24 938 sq mi).

Population: 2 606 000 (1993 est).

Capital: Riga 897 000 (including suburbs; 1991 est).

Other major cities: Daugavpils 127 000, Liepaja 114 000, Jelgava 74 000, Jürmala 61 000, Ventspils 50 000 (including suburbs; 1991 est).

Languages: Lettish (over 53%), Russian (34%), Belarussian (5%). See also p. 186.

Religions: Lutheran (22%), Roman Catholic (7%), small Russian Orthodox minority. The largest denomination – the Evangelical Lutheran Church of Latvia – is headed by an archbishop based in Riga. There are two Roman Catholic dioceses including Riga archdiocese.

Education: Education is compulsory between the ages of seven and 17. There are two universities in Riga.

Defence: Latvia's armed forces were established in November 1991. The total armed strength (in 1993) was 4900 including 270 in the navy and 53 in the air force. Compulsory military service lasts for 18 months. In late 1993 there were still between 20 000 and 25 000 Russian troops stationed in Latvia; no date for their eventual withdrawal had been agreed (see Recent History, below).

Transport: There are 3297 km (2061 mi) of railway track of which only 271 km (169 mi) are electrified. Both passenger and freight services are operated. There are 20 600 km (12 875 mi) of roads, not all which are asphalted. Riga and Ventspils are important ports on the Baltic Sea; Riga has an international airport.

Media: There are eight main daily newspapers. The majority of these papers publish in Lettish and use the Latin script; a minority publish in Russian and use the Cyrillic script. Latvia has a single radio and television network.

GOVERNMENT

A President – who appoints a Prime Minister and a Cabinet – and a 100-member Assembly (Saeima) are elected by universal adult suffrage for three years. The main political parties are the (right of centre) Latvia's Way (LC), Harmony for Latvia (SL), the Farmers' Union (LZS), the (former Communist) Equality Party, the (radical nationalist) For Fatherland and Freedom (TUB), the (centre-right) Democratic Centre Party (DCP), the (centre-right) Christian Democratic Union (LKDS), and the (radical nationalist) Latvian National Independence Movement (LNNK).

At a general election held in June 1993 the parties obtained the following number of seats:

Party	Seats
Latvia's Way	36
LNNK	15
Harmony for Latvia	13
Farmers' Union	12
Equality	7
For Fatherland and Freedom	6
Christian Democrats	6
Democratic Centre	5
Total	100

A coalition of members of the Latvia's Way Party and the Farmers' Union was formed, but the government is in a minority in the Assembly and has to rely upon parliamentary support from other centrist parties.

President: Guntis Ulmanis (LC).

THE CABINET

Prime Minister: Valdis Birkavs (LC).
Deputy Prime Minister and Minister of State Reform: Märis Gailis (LC).
Deputy Prime Minister and Minister of Economics: Ojärs Kehris (LC).
Deputy Prime Minister and Minister of Justice: Egils Levit (LC).
Minister of Agriculture: Jänis Kinna (LZS).
Minister of Defence: Valdis Pavlovskis (LC).
Minister of Economics: (see above).
Minister of Education, Culture and Science: Jänis Vaivads (LC).
Minister of Environmental and Regional Development: Girts Lükins (LC).
Minister of Finance: Uldis Osis (LC).
Minister of Foreign Affairs: Georgs Andrejevs (LC).
Minister of the Interior: Girts Kristovskis (LC).
Minister of Justice: (see above).
Minister of State Reform: (see above).
Minister of Transport and Communications: Andris Gütmanis (LC).
Minister of Welfare: Jänis Ritenis (LZS).
Minister without portfolio: Edvins Inkens (LC).

GEOGRAPHY

Latvia comprises an undulating plain, lower in the west (traditionally known as Courland) than in the east (traditionally known as Livonia). Ridges of moraine cross the country, impeding drainage and creating widespread peat bogs. Latvia reaches the Baltic Sea and the large Gulf of Riga in a low sandy coastline. *Principal rivers*: Daugava (Dvina or Western Dvina), Lielupe, Aiviekste. *Highest point*: Osveyskoye 311 m (1020 ft).

Latvia has a relatively mild climate with cool, rainy summers and cold winters. There are, on average, only 135 frost-free days per annum.

ECONOMY

Engineering dominates a heavily industrialized economy. Latvia has relied on Russian trade and faces severe difficulties as it begins to introduce a free market. Severe shortages of raw materials – owing to the collapse of the former Soviet trade bloc – resulted in a dramatic decrease in industrial output and a consequent fall in exports. The government has given great importance to the establishment of the services sector of the economy, particularly banking.

Imports (1990)

Sector	% of imports
Machinery	31.3%
Textiles	16.3%
Chemicals	11.6%
Food products	9.9%
Fuel	7.6%

Exports (1990)

Sector	% of exports
Machinery	27.9%
Foodstuffs	21.6%
Textiles	17.3%
Chemicals	12.4%

GNP decreased by 30% in 1992, and rapid inflation became a serious worry. However, cautious economic policies and the introduction of Latvia's own independent currency – the lat – marked a new chapter in the country's economic history. The lat achieved considerable stability and inflation, although still high by West European standards, had fallen to manageable limits by early 1993. In September 1993 the exchange rate was 0.62 lats to 1 US$.

Agriculture specializes in dairying and meat production; potatoes, sugar beet and forestry are also important. The privatization of land began in 1991.

Labour force (1992)

Sector	Number employed
Manufacturing and utilities	371 800
Agriculture	248 000
Construction	130 000
Social security, education	254 000
Trade/hotels and catering	178 000
Transport and communications	107 000
Business and finance	85 000
Administration	24 000
Total	1 397 000

The most recent budgetary figures available are for 1992, that is before the introduction of the lat.

Revenue

	Million roubles	% of revenue
Total	26 899	100%

Expenditure

	Million roubles	% of expenditure
National economy	6 030	22%
Education	3 236	12%
Health care	2 487	9%
Social security	981	4%
Administration	4 298	16%
Other		37%
Total	26 859	100%

RECENT HISTORY

Courland, the part of Latvia west of the River Daugava (Dvina), was an autonomous duchy until it was annexed by Russia in 1795; Livonia (or Vidzeme), the part of Latvia east of the River Daugava, was taken by Russia from Sweden in the 18th century. Under Russian rule, Latvian national consciousness grew throughout the 19th century. Riga became the third largest city in the Russian Empire.

Following the Communist takeover in Russia (1917) and a brief German invasion of Latvia, Latvian nationalists – led by Karlis Ulmanis – declared independence (1918). However, the infant republic was overrun by war when the Soviet Red Army invaded Livonia (1919) and the Latvian government was forced to take refuge in Courland where German troops remained. A force of Baltic-German forces cleared Latvia of Soviet troops but attempted to assume control of the country as a base from which to fight the Red Army. Latvia, aided by a Franco–British naval force, eventually defeated the German forces and an independent internationally-recognized Latvian government took office in 1920. A democratic system lasted until 1936 when Karlis Ulmanis established a dictatorship.

The Non-Aggression Pact (1939) between Hitler and Stalin assigned Latvia to the USSR, which invaded and annexed the republic (1940). After occupation by Nazi Germany (1941–44), Soviet rule was reimposed. Large-scale Russian settlement replaced over 200 000 Latvians who were killed or deported to Siberia. Collective farming was forcibly introduced and the largely Russian–speaking northeast was annexed by Russia.

In 1988, reforms in the USSR allowed Latvian nationalists to operate openly. Nationalists – led by Anatolijs Gorbunovs – won a majority in Latvia's parliament and declared that Latvia's independence had been restored (1990). Latvia refused to participate in the discussions called by Soviet President Mikhail Gorbachov to reform the Soviet Union and troops of the Soviet Ministry of Internal Affairs were deployed. Latvia finally seceded from the Soviet Union following the failed coup by Communist hardliners in Moscow (1991). The USSR recognized Latvia's independence in September 1991. Tension remains concerning the status of the large Russian minority – which includes many retired Russian military and civilian personnel – and the smaller Ukrainian and Belarussian minorities in Latvia. In the Latvian capital, Riga, ethnic Russians make up about 40% of the population. The Russian government has refused to withdraw its last troops from Latvia until it is satisfied that the rights of all ethnic Russians living in the country are fully protected. The first fully democratic Latvian elections since the 1930s were in June 1993.

LITHUANIA

Official name: Lietuva (Lithuania).
Member of: UN, CSCE, Council of Europe.
Area: 65 200 km² (25 174 sq mi).
Population: 3 761 000 (1992 est).
Capital: Vilnius 597 000 (including suburbs; 1992 est).
Other major cities: Kaunas 434 000, Klaipeda 208 000, Siauliai 149 000, Panevezys 132 000 (including suburbs; 1992 est).
Languages: Lithuanian (81%), Russian (10%), Polish (4%). See also p. 186.
Religions: Roman Catholic (80%), Lutheran minority. The Roman Catholic Church in Lithuania is organized into six dioceses including the archdioceses of Vilnius and Kaunas. The second largest denomination is the Lithuanian Evangelical Lutheran Church. There are two Orthodox denominations – the Russian Orthodox Church (of which Lithuania forms an eparchy) and the Lithuanian Old Believers Church.
Education: Education is compulsory between the ages of six and 15. There are four universities – two in Vilnius, two in Kaunas – and two other institutions of higher education that are regarded as being of university status.
Defence: The withdrawal of the last Russian soldiers from Lithuanian soil in September 1993 left the newly-formed Lithuanian forces as the only troops in the country. Early in 1993, the Lithuanian national defence force had a total armed strength of 7000. There is also a National Guard with about 12 500 personnel.
Transport: There are 2007 km (1254 mi) of railway track operating both passenger and freight services. There are about 44 500 km (27 813 mi) of roads. Klaipeda (once known as Memel) is a major commercial port on the Baltic Sea; river transport is important. Vilnius has an international airport.
Media: There are 16 principal daily newspapers and about 450 other papers. Over 90% of the country's press publishes in Lithuanian. Lithuania has a single (state-owned) radio and television network.

GOVERNMENT
The 141-member Parliament (Seimas) is elected for four years under a system of proportional representation involving two rounds of voting by universal adult suffrage. The President is directly elected for five years. The President appoints a Prime Minister, who, in turn, appoints a Cabinet of Ministers. The principal political parties include the (former Communist) Lithuanian Democratic Labour Party, the (nationalist) Citizens' Charter of Lithuania Movement (popularly known as Sajudis), the Lithuanian Social Democratic Party, the Christian Democratic Party of Lithuania, the Polish Union and the Green Party.

The Parliament elected on 25 October and 15 November 1992 comprised:

Party	Seats
Lithuanian Democratic Labour Party	73
Sajudis	30
Christian Democratic Party of Lithuania	16
Lithuanian Social Democratic Party	8
Polish Union	4
Independents	10
Total	*141*

A Cabinet of Democratic Labour Party members and independents was formed in November 1992.
President: Algirdas Mykolas Brazauskas.

THE CABINET
Prime Minister: Bronislovas Lubys.
Minister of Agriculture: Rimantas Karazija.
Minister of Communications and Information: Gintautas Zinteus.
Minister of Culture and Information: Dainius Trinkunas.
Minister of Defence: Audrius Butkevicius.
Minister of Energy: Algimantas Vladas Stasiukynas.
Minister of Finance: Eduardas Vilkelis.
Minister of Foreign Affairs: Povilas Gylys.
Minister of Health: Jurgis Bredikis.
Minister of Housing and Urban Development: Algirdas Vapsys.
Minister of Industry and Trade: Albertas Ambraziejus Sinevicius.
Minister of the Interior: Romasis Vaitiekunas.
Minister of Justice: Jonas Prapiestis.
Minister of Social Security: Teodoras Medaiskis.
Minister of Transportation: Jonas Birziskis.
Minister without portfolio: Algimantas Matulevicius.

GEOGRAPHY
Central Lithuania comprises a low-lying plain crossed by ridges of glacial moraine that are covered with pine

forests. A 100 km (60 mi) sandspit separates a large lagoon – the Kursiu Maries – from the Baltic Sea. Inland from the lagoon lie the low Samogitian Hills, beyond which is the central plain. Hill country in the extreme east and southeast does not attain 300 m (984 ft). A particular feature of the Lithuanian landscape is the large number of small lakes, over 3000 in all. The country's slow-flowing meandering rivers are widely used to float timber to sawmills as well as being dammed for hydro-electric power. *Principal rivers:* Nemunas (Neman), Vilnya, Merkys, Neris. *Highest point:* Juozapine 294 m (964 ft).

The climate of Lithuania is transitional between the maritime climates of northwest Europe and the harsher continental climate of Russia. Winters are cold, summers are warm and rainfall is moderate.

ECONOMY

About 15% of the labour force is engaged in agriculture, principally cattle rearing and dairying in pastures that have been reclaimed from marshes. As well as meat and milk, the main agricultural products are potatoes, flax and sugar beet.

Labour force (1991)

Sector	Number employed
Industry	566 700
Agriculture	245 000
Construction	182 700
Trade, hotel & catering	188 600
Transport and communications	132 500
Services and other	334 000
Total	1 649 500

Much of the country is heavily forested. The engineering, timber, cement and food-processing industries are important. Ship-building is significant at Klaipeda and there are several fishing ports on the Baltic. Lithuania – whose economy is weaker than that of the other two Baltic republics – faces an uncertain future as it dismantles state control and breaks away from the former Soviet trade system. Since 1991 the country's GDP has fallen by over 50%. This has been due to soaring inflation (over 1000% in 1992) and industrial decline – owing to a shortage of raw materials that used to be imported from other former Soviet republics. The collapse of inter-republican trade in what was the USSR has obliged Lithuania to look west but the country has few products that can find a ready market in the European Community or the EFTA.

Imports (1990)

Sector	% of imports
Industrial products	92.1%
Agricultural products	7.9%

Exports (1990)

Sector	% of exports
Foodstuffs	33.5%
Machinery	22.5%

By the beginning of 1993 approaching one third of Lithuania's state-owned industry had been privatized. However, the change of government in the autumn of 1992 signalled a slower pace of change towards a market economy. The adoption of a new Lithuanian currency,

the litas, in 1993 marked a new chapter in the republic's economic history. No longer tied to the fortunes of the Russian rouble, Lithuania has acquired the opportunity for a more independent economic policy. In September 1993 the exchange rate was 4.03 litas to 1 US$.

The most recent budgetary figures available are for 1991, that is before the adoption of the litas. No recent breakdown of expenditure for individual departments is available.

Revenue	Million roubles	% of revenue
Total	12 694	100%
Expenditure	Million roubles	% of expenditure
Total	11 142	100%

RECENT HISTORY

Lithuanian national consciousness grew in the closing decades of the 19th century. Consigned to Russian rule by the partitions of Poland at the end of the 18th century, Lithuania was subject to extensive Russification in every area of public life. Lithuanians rose against Russian rule in 1830–31 and 1863. When German forces invaded in 1915, they encouraged the establishment of a satellite Lithuanian state with a German prince named as king *in absentia*. Augustinas Voldemaras became Lithuania's first prime minister while the country was still under German occupation.

After World War I, the new Lithuanian state became a republic but faced invasions by the Red Army from the east, attempting to reconquer Lithuania, and the Polish army from the west (1919–20) in a dispute over territory. Lithuania lost Vilnius – its traditional capital – in the war against Poland. Internationally recognized boundaries were not established until 1923, by which time the Lithuanian government had transferred to Kaunas. The dictatorship of Augustinas Voldemaras (1926–29) was followed by that of Antonas Smetona (1929–40). The Non-Aggression Pact (1939) between Hitler and Stalin assigned Lithuania to the USSR, which invaded and annexed the republic (1940). Lithuania was occupied by Nazi Germany (1941–44). When Soviet rule was reimposed (1945), large-scale Russian settlement replaced over 250 000 Lithuanians who had been killed or deported to Siberia.

In 1988, reforms in the USSR allowed Lithuanian nationalists to operate openly. Sajudis – the nationalist movement led by a music professor, Vytautas Landsbergis – won a majority in the republic's parliament, but their declaration of independence (1990) brought a crackdown by Soviet forces in Lithuania. Following the failed coup by Communist hardliners in Moscow (in August 1991), the USSR recognized Lithuania's independence. Following the economic collapse of Lithuania (1992–93), Sajudis lost elections to the (former Communist) Lithuanian Democratic Labour Party. The advent to power of the former Communists has meant that the pace of privatization has slowed. However, the new government has pursued a vigorously nationalist path, adopting a new independent currency, the litas, and securing the total withdrawal of Russian troops from Lithuania in September 1993.

MACEDONIA

Official name: (internal) Republika Makedonija (Republic of Macedonia); (international) The Former Yugoslav Republic of Macedonia.

Member of: UN.

Area: 25 713 km² (9928 sq mi).

Population: 2 034 000 (1991 census).

Capital: Skopje (Skoplje) 563 000 (1991 census).

Other major cities: Tetovo 181 000, Kumanovo 136 000, Bitola 122 000 (1991 census).

Languages: Macedonian (67%), Albanian (20%), Turkish (5%). See also p. 186.

Religions: Macedonian Orthodox (over 60%), Sunni Islam (nearly 25%).

Education: Education is compulsory from the age of seven to 15. There are universities at Skopje and Bitola.

Defence: The forces have a total strength of 20 000. Compulsory military service lasts for nine months.

Transport: No recent figures concerning the length of the road or rail networks are available. Skopje has an international airport.

Media: There are four main daily newspapers. There is a single state-owned radio and television service.

GOVERNMENT

The 120-member Assembly (Sobranje) and a President – who appoints a Cabinet and a Prime Minister – are directly elected for four years by universal adult suffrage. The main political parties include the (nationalist) Internal Macedonian Revolutionary Organization (IMRO), the (former Communist) Social Democratic Alliance of Macedonia, the (largely ethnic Albanian) Party of Democratic Prosperity, the Alliance of Reform Forces, the Socialist Alliance-Socialist Party of Macedonia and the (pro-Serb) Party of Yugoslavs. The coalition government comprises independents and members of several parties. IMRO is in opposition. The Assembly elected on 9 December 1990 comprises:

Party	Seats
IMRO	37
Social Democratic Alliance	31
Party of Democratic Prosperity	25
Alliance of Reform Forces	19
Socialist Alliance-Socialist Party	4
Party of Yugoslavs	1
Independents	3
Total	120

President: Kiro Gligorov.

THE CABINET

Prime Minister: Branko Crvenkovski.
The Cabinet includes: *Minister of Defence:* Dr Vlado Popovski. *Minister of the Economy:* Petrus Stefanov. *Minister of Finance:* Dzevdet Hajredini. *Minister of Foreign Relations:* Stevo Crvenkovski. *Minister of Internal Affairs:* Dr Ljubomir Frčkovski.

GEOGRAPHY

Macedonia is a plateau about 760 m (2500 ft) high, ringed by mountains including the Sar range. The central Vardar valley is the main lowland. *Principal rivers:* Vardar, Strumica. *Highest point:* Korab 2753 m (9032 ft).

ECONOMY

Macedonia was the least developed part of the former Yugoslavia. The republic is largely agricultural, raising sheep and cattle and growing cereals and tobacco. The metallurgical, chemical and textile industries partly rely on local resources including iron ore. The economy has been severely damaged by an intermittent Greek economic blockade and the disruption of trade with Serbia (owing to international sanctions against that state). International recognition (April 1993) brought membership of the IMF and some foreign investment. The republic's new currency, the Macedonian dinar, is not yet quoted in exchange markets.

RECENT HISTORY

After centuries of Turkish rule, Macedonia was partitioned following the First Balkan War (1912). Those areas with a Greek-speaking majority were assigned to Greece and the remainder was partitioned between Bulgaria and Serbia, the latter gaining the area comprising the present republic. Bulgaria continued to claim all Macedonia and occupied the region during World War I. In 1918 Serbian Macedonia was incorporated within the new kingdom of Yugoslavia. When Yugoslavia was reorganized on Soviet lines by Marshal Tito in 1945 a separate Macedonian republic was formed within the Communist federation. After Tito's death (1980), the Yugoslav experiment faltered and local nationalist movements arose. Following the secession of Slovenia and Croatia and the outbreak of the Yugoslav civil war (1991), Macedonia declared its own sovereignty. Despite fierce opposition from Greece, which objected to the use of the name 'Macedonia' and denied the existence of a 'Macedonian' people, the republic eventually gained international recognition in 1993.

MOLDOVA

Official name: Republica Moldoveneasca (Republic of Moldova). Formerly known as Moldavia.

Member of: UN, CIS, CSCE.

Area: 33 702 km² (13 012 sq mi).

Population: 4 373 000 (1991 est).

Capital: Chisinau (formerly Kishinev) 720 000 (city 676 000) (1990 est).

Other major cities: Tiraspol 184 000, Balti (formerly Beltsy) 162 000, Benderi (Bender) 132 000 (1990 est).

Languages: Romanian (67%), Ukrainian (13%), Russian (13%), Gagauz (4%). See also p. 186. Moldova no longer uses the Cyrillic script.

Religions: Orthodox majority – there are both Russian Orthodox and Romanian Orthodox Churches. The Orthodox Gagauz minority uses a Turkish liturgy.

Education: Education is compulsory between the ages of seven and 17. There is a university at Chisinau.

Defence: The Moldovan armed forces, which were created in 1991, have a total armed strength of 14 000. There is also a National Guard of about 4000 personnel. Russian troops are also stationed in the Trans-Dnestr region (see below).

Transport: Under one half of the road system is asphalted. The railway network comprises two lines, both of which are important for international freight traffic. Chisinau has an international airport.

Media: The majority of Moldova's 200 newspapers are now published in the Romanian language and the Latin script. There is a single (state-owned) radio and television network.

GOVERNMENT
The current Parliament has 332 members out of the 380 delegates elected to the former Supreme Soviet of Moldavia within the USSR in 1990. The President – who appoints a Prime Minister and a Council of Ministers – was directly elected. A new constitution is to be drafted. The main political groupings are the former Communists, the (coalition) National Alliance including the Popular Front of Moldova and the Christian Democratic Party (which supports integration with Romania), and the Social Democratic Party.

In mid-1993 the Parliament comprised:

Group	Seats
Former Communist Group	210
Popular Front of Moldova	122
Total	332

The government comprises members of the former Communist group.

President: Mircea Snegur.

THE CABINET
Prime Minister: Andrei Sangheli.
The Cabinet includes: *First Deputy Prime Minister:* Nicolae Andronati; *Minister of Defence:* Pavel Creanga;
Minister of the Economy: Sergiu Certan; *Minister of Finance:* Claudia Melnic; *Minister of Foreign Affairs:* Nicolae Tsyu; *Minister of Internal Affairs:* Constantin Antoci.

GEOGRAPHY
Moldova comprises a hilly plain between the River Prut and the Dnestr valley. Moldova experiences a mild, slightly continental climate. *Principal rivers:* Dnestr, Prut. *Highest point:* Balaneshty 430 m (1409 ft).

ECONOMY
Large collective farms produce fruit (particularly grapes for wine), vegetables, wheat, maize, tobacco and sunflower seed. Food processing and machine building are the main industries. Little progress has been made to privatize agriculture and industry. Since 1991 the collapse of the trade system of the former USSR has resulted in serious shortages of raw materials. Moldovan production has fallen and the country has experienced high rates of inflation. Moldova uses the Russian rouble but plans to introduce its own currency, the leu.

RECENT HISTORY
Known as Bessarabia, the area was part of the Romanian principality of Moldavia – within the (Turkish) Ottoman Empire – before being ceded to the Russians in 1812. Briefly restored to Moldavia (1856–78), Bessarabia remained Russian until World War I. An autonomous Bessarabian republic was proclaimed in 1917, but was suppressed by a Russian Bolshevik invasion (1918). The Russians were removed by Romanian forces and Bessarabia was declared, in turn, an independent Moldavian republic and a part of the kingdom of Romania (1918). When Romania entered World War II as a German ally, the USSR reoccupied Bessarabia, which was reorganized as the Moldavian Soviet Republic in 1944. Following the abortive coup by Communist hardliners in Moscow (September 1991), Moldavia declared independence. As Moldova, the republic received international recognition when the Soviet Union was dissolved (December 1991). Civil war broke out in 1992 when Russian and Ukrainian minorities – fearing an eventual reunion of Moldova with Romania – proclaimed the republic of Trans-Dnestr and attempted to secede. The intervention of CIS forces brought an uneasy peace.

POLAND

Official name: Polska Rzecpospolita (Republic of Poland).

Member of: UN, CSCE, Council of Europe.

Area: 312 683 km² (120 727 sq mi).

Population: 38 273 000 (1991 est).

Capital: Warsaw (Warszawa) 1 656 000 (1990 est).

Other major cities: Katowice 1 604 000 (city 367 000; Sosnowiec 260 000; Bytom 230 000; Gliwice 222 000; Zabrze 203 000; Tychy 190 000; Chorzów 132 000), Lódź 848 000, Kraków 751 000, Wroclaw 643 000, Poznań 590 000, Gdańsk 465 000, Szczecin 413 000, Bydgoszcz 382 000, Lublin 351 000, Bialystok 271 000, Czestochowa 258 000, Gdynia 252 000, Rydom 226 000, Kielce 213 000, Torún 210 000, Bielsko-Biala 180 000, Ruda Slaska 170 000, Olsztyn 161 000 (1990 est).

Languages: Polish; see p. 186.

Religion: Roman Catholic (93%), Polish Orthodox (2%).

Education: Education is compulsory between the ages of seven and 14. There are 25 universities (including 14 polytechnics of university status), plus nine other university institutes.

Defence: The army has a total strength of 194 000, the navy has 19 000 personnel and the air force has 83 000. Compulsory conscription lasts for 18 months.

Transport: There are over 363 000 km (227 000 mi) of roads of which 260 km (163 mi) are motorways. The state-owned railways have 26 228 km (16 393 mi) of track. The rivers Vistula, Bug and Oder are important navigable waterways; the main Baltic ports are Gdańsk, Gdynia and Szczecin. Warsaw has an international airport, and there are nine regional airports for domestic flights.

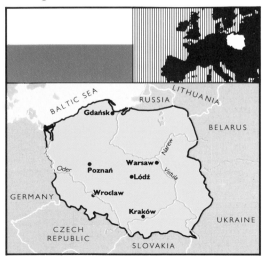

GOVERNMENT

The 100-member Senate – the upper house – and the 460-member Sejm – the lower house – are elected for four years by universal adult suffrage. In the Sejm 391 seats are contested in constituencies and the remaining 69 are elected from party lists. The President – who is directly elected – appoints a Prime Minister who commands a majority in the Sejm. The PM, in turn, appoints a Council of Ministers. The main political parties are the (former Communist) Democratic Left Alliance (SLD), the (centre-left) Polish Peasant Party (PSL), the (centre) Democratic Union (UD), the (former Solidarity) Union of Labour (UP), the (conservative) Confederation for an Independent Poland (KPN), the (independent) Non-Party Block to Support Reform (BBWR), the German Minority of Lower Silesia, and the Social and Cultural Association of Germans from Upper Silesia. At the general election on 19 September 1993 these parties obtained the following number of seats. A coalition of SLD, PSL and UL members and independents was formed in October 1993.

Party	Seats
Democratic Left	171
Polish Peasant Party	132
Democratic Union	74
Union of Labour	41
Confederation for Independent Poland	22
Non-Party Block to Support Reform	16
German minority parties	4
Total	*460*

President: Lech Walesa (elected 1990).

THE CABINET

Prime Minister: Waldemar Pawlak (PSL).
Deputy Prime Minister, Minister of the Economy and Minister of Finance: Marek Borowski (SLD).
Deputy Prime Minister, Minister of Social Policy and Minister of Justice: Wlodzimierz Cimoszewicz (ind).
Deputy Prime Minister, Minister of State Administration and Minister of Education: Aleksander Luczak (SLD).
Minister of Agriculture: Andrzej Smietanko (PSL).
Minister of Culture: Kazimierz Dejmek (PSL).
Minister of Defence: Admiral Piotr Koloziejczyk (ind).
Minister of Education: See above.
Minister of the Economy: See above.
Minister for Environmental Protection, Natural Resources and Forestry: Stanislaw Zelichowski (PSL).
Minister of Finance: See above.
Minister of Foreign Affairs: Andrzej Olechowski (ind).
Minister of Foreign Economic Relations: Leslaw Podkanski (PSL).
Minister of Health: Jacek Zochowski (SLD).
Minister of Industry and Trade: Marek Pol (UP).
Minister of Internal Affairs: Andrzej Milczanowski (ind).
Minister of Justice: See above.
Minister of Labour: Leszek Miller (SLD).
Minister of Social Policy: See above.
Minister of State Administration: See above.

Minister of Transport and Maritime Economy: Boguslaw Liberadzki (ind).
Head of the Council of Ministers' Office: Michal Strak (PSL).
Head of the Central Planning Office: Miroslaw Pietrewicz (PSL).

GEOGRAPHY

Most of Poland consists of lowlands. In the north are the Baltic lowlands and the Pomeranian and Mazurian lake districts. Central Poland is a region of plains. In the south are the hills of Little Poland and the Tatra Mountains, part of the Carpathian chain. *Principal rivers:* Vistula (Wisa), Oder (Odra), Narew. *Highest point:* Rysy 2499 m (8199 ft). Poland's climate tends towards continental with short warm summers and longer cold winters.

ECONOMY

Polish agriculture remains predominantly small-scale and privately owned. Over one quarter of the labour force is still involved in agriculture, growing potatoes, wheat, barley, sugar beet and a range of fodder crops. The industrial sector is large-scale and, until the switch to a free-market economy began in 1990, centrally planned. Poland has major deposits of coal, as well as reserves of natural gas, copper and silver. Engineering, food processing, and the chemical, metallurgical and paper industries are important, but the economic situation has steadily deteriorated since the 1960s. In 1991 Poland imported goods worth 164 259 298 million zlotys and exported goods worth 157 715 913 million zlotys. The currency – zloty – is divided into 100 groszy (sing. grosz). In November 1993, the exchange rate was 20 485.5 zlotys to 1 US$.

Imports (1991)

Sector	% of imports
Electro-engineering products	37.5%
Fuels and power	18.8%
Chemicals	12.6%
Foodstuffs	10.4%
Textiles and clothing	6.1%
Iron and steel and products	4.0%

Exports (1991)

Sector	% of exports
Electro-engineering products	22.4%
Iron and steel and products	15.9%
Chemicals	11.6%
Fuels and power	10.7%
Foodstuffs	10.0%

The most recent budgetary figures available are those for 1990. Privatization was accelerated after 1991, but although Poland made impressive economic reforms, and achieved higher growth rates than other East European countries, living standards have decreased.

Revenue

	Million zlotys	% of revenue
Turnover taxation	39 601 000	29%
Other taxation	156 640 000	71%
Total	196 241 000	100%

Expenditure

	Million zlotys	% of expenditure
National economy	50 105 000	26%
Social welfare, health, etc.	32 621	17%
Social insurance	16 543 000	9%
Defence	13 599 000	7%
Other		41%
Total	193 801	100%

Labour force (1991)

Sector	Number employed
Industry	4 404 000
Agriculture	4 961 000
Construction	1 091 000
Trade	1 459 000
Transport and communications	896 000
Services	425 000
Other	3 242 000
Total	16 477 000

RECENT HISTORY

In the 19th century the greater part of Poland was within Imperial Russia, the remainder ruled by Austria and Prussia. After World War I, Poland was restored to statehood (1919), but the country was unstable. Marshal Józef Pilsudski (1867–1935) staged a coup in 1926, and became a virtual dictator. During the 1930s relations with Hitler's Germany – which made territorial claims on parts of Poland – became strained. An alliance with Britain was not enough to deter Hitler from attacking Poland, and thus precipitating World War II (1939). Poland was partitioned once again, this time between Nazi Germany and the USSR. Occupied Poland lost one sixth of its population, including almost all the Jews, and casualties were high after the ill-fated Warsaw Rising (1944). Poland was liberated by the Red Army (1945), and a Communist state was established. The new Poland lost almost one half its territory in the east to USSR, but was compensated in the north and west at the expense of Germany.

A political crisis in 1956 led to the emergence of a Communist leader who enjoyed a measure of popular support, Wladyslaw Gomulka. In 1980, following the downfall of Gomulka's successor, Edward Gierek, a period of unrest led to the birth of the independent trade union Solidarity (Solidarnośc), led by Lech Walesa (1943–). Martial law was declared by General Wojciech Jaruzelski in 1981 in an attempt to restore Communist authority. Solidarity was banned and its leaders were detained, but public unrest and economic difficulties continued. In 1989 Solidarity was legalized and agreement was reached on political reform. Solidarity won free elections to the new Senate, and with the support of former allies of the Communists won enough seats to gain a majority in the Sejm, and Tadeusz Mazowiecki of Solidarity became PM. Disagreements concerning the speed at which market reforms were advancing and personality clashes during the presidential election split Solidarity. Walesa became president in 1990. Since multi-party elections in 1991 and 1993, several short-lived coalition governments have held office. Nevertheless, Poland made greater economic progress than any of its East European neighbours.

ROMANIA

Official name: Rômania.

Member of: UN, CSCE, Council of Europe (guest).

Area: 237 500 km² (91 699 sq mi).

Population: 22 749 000 (1992 census).

Capital: Bucharest (Bucuresti) 2 325 000 (city 2 064 000) (1992 est.).

Other major cities: Constanta 351 000, Iasi 343 000, Timisoara 334 000, Cluj-Napoca 328 000, Galati 326 000, Brasov 324 000, Craiova 304 000, Ploiesti 252 000, Braila 235 000, Oradea 221 000, Bacau 205 000, Arad 190 000, Pitesti 180 000, Sibiu 170 000, Tirgu Mures 164 000 (1992 est.).

Languages: Romanian (official; 89%), Magyar (Hungarian) (10%), German (1%). See also p. 186.

Religions: Romanian Orthodox (70%), Uniat (Greek Catholic) Church (3%), Roman Catholic (5%), Calvinist (2%). The Romanian Orthodox Church has five metropolitan dioceses, five archbishoprics and nine bishoprics and is headed by a patriach who is based in Bucharest. There are two Roman Catholic Church archdioceses and five Uniat dioceses.

Education: Education is compulsory between the ages of six and 16. There are 15 universities – Bucharest (2), Brasov, Cluj-Napoca (3), Craiova, Galati, Iasi (3), Timisoara (3), Tirgu Mures.

Defence: In 1992 the total armed strength was 201 000 (including 162 000 army personnel, 19 000 in the navy and 20 000 in the air force). Compulsory military service lasts 18 months in the navy and for 12 months in the other two services. In 1992 there were 126 000 conscripts.

Transport: There are 11 127 km (6954 mi) of railway track of which only 2367 km (1479 mi) are electrified. Both passenger and freight systems are operated. There are 72 816 km (45 510 mi) of roads including 113 km (71 mi) of motorway and 14 683 km (9177 mi) of main roads. The Danube is important for inland navigation, and Tulcea, Galati, Braila and Giurgiu are major river ports; Constanta is the only significant Black Sea port. There are four international airports – Otopeni (for Bucharest), Arad, Constanta and Timisoara.

Media: There are 65 main daily newspapers. There is a single (state-owned) radio and television network; regional television broadcasting has begun.

GOVERNMENT

A President is directly elected by universal adult suffrage for a maximum of two five-year terms. A 341-seat National Assembly (lower house) and a 143-seat Senate (upper house) are elected on a system of proportional representation for four years; 13 seats in the Assembly are reserved for ethnic minorities. The main political parties include the Party of Social Democracy of Romania (PSDR), the National Salvation Front (NSF), the (right-wing) Romanian National Unity Party, the Hungarian Democratic Union of Romania, the (right-wing) Greater Romania Party, the (former Communist) Socialist Labour Party, the Agrarian Democratic Party

of Romania and the Democratic Convention of Romania (DCR), an alliance of the Christian Democratic National Peasants' Party, the Party of the Civic Alliance, the New Liberal Party, the Romanian Social Democratic Part and the Romanian Ecology Party. The Assembly electee on 27 September 1992 comprises:

Party	Seat
Party of Social Democracy	11
Christian Democratic National Peasants' Party (DCR)	4
Party of the Civic Alliance (DCR)	1
New Liberal Party (DCR)	1
Romanian Social Democratic Party (DCR)	1
Romanian Ecology Party (DCR)	
National Salvation Front (NSF)	4
Romanian National Unity Party	3
Hungarian Democratic Union of Romania	2
Greater Romania Party	1
Socialist Labour Party	1
Independents (see above)	1
Total	34

Members of the Party of Social Democracy (PSDR) an independents formed a minority government.

President: Ion Iliescu (PDSR).

THE CABINET

Prime Minister: Nicolae Vacaroiou (PSDR).

Deputy Prime Minister and Chairman of the Council fo Economic Strategy and Reform: Misu Negritoiu (ind).

Deputy Prime Minister and Minister of Employment an Social Security: Dan Mircea Popescu (PSDR).

Deputy Prime Minister and Minister of Finance: Flori Georgescu (ind).

Deputy Prime Minister and Minister of Foreign Affairs Teodor Viorel Melescanu (ind).

Minister of Agriculture and Food: Ioan Oancea (PSDR

Minister of Commerce: Constantin Teculescu (PSDR).

Minister of Communications: Andrei Chirica (ind).

Minister of Culture: Mihai Golu (PSDR).

Minister of Education: Liviu Maior (PSDR).

Minister of Employment and Social Security: (see above)

Minister of Finance: (see above).

Minister of Foreign Affairs: (see above).

Minister of Health: Prof. Iulian Micu (PSDR).

Minister of Industry: Dumitru Popescu (PSDR).

Minister of the Interior: Gheorghe Ioan Danescu (ind).

Minister of Justice: Petre Ninosu (PSDR).

Minister of National Defence: Gen. Constantin Nicola Spiroiu (ind).

Minister of Public Works and Planning: Marin Cristea (PSDR).

Minister of Research and Technology: Doru Dumitru Palade (ind).

Minister of Tourism: Matei Agaten Dan (PSDR).

Minister of Transport: Paul Teodoru (ind).

Minister of Waters, Forestry and Environmental Protec tion: Aurel Constantin Ilie (ind).

Minister of Youth and Sports: Gheorghe Anghelesc (PSDR).

GEOGRAPHY

The Carpathian Mountains run through the north, eas and centre of Romania. To the west of the Carpathians i the tableland of Transylvania and the Banat lowland. In the south the Danube Plain ends in a delta on the Black Sea. *Principal rivers*: Danube (Dunăria), Mures, Prut. *Highest point*: Moldoveanu 2544 m (8346 ft).

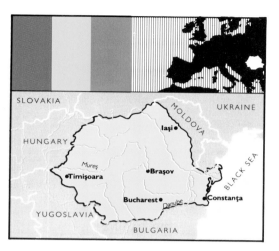

Romania experiences cold snowy winters and hot summers. Rainfall is moderate in the lowlands and heavier in the Carpathians.

ECONOMY

State-owned industry – which employs nearly 40% of the labour force – includes mining, metallurgy, mechanical engineering and chemicals. Natural resources include petroleum and natural gas. Considerable forests support a timber and furniture industry. Major crops include maize, sugar beet, wheat, potatoes and grapes for wine, but agriculture has been neglected, and – because of exports – food supplies have fallen short of the country's needs. By the start of 1993 three-quarters of the country's agricultural land had been privatized.

Labour force (1991)

Sector	Number employed
Industry	3 817 800
Agriculture/forestry	3 133 000
Construction	463 000
Education and culture	468 000
Housing/communal services	706 000
Trade	872 000
Transport and communications	681 000
Science	109 000
Health and social services	298 000
Administration/other	83 000
Total	10 630 000

Economic mismanagement under Ceausescu (see below) decreased already low living standards. Subsequent governments have faced appalling economic problems including high rates of inflation, sharp devaluation of the leu (see below), drastic shortages of raw materials, and falling production and exports.

Imports (1990)

Sector	% of imports
Fuels, minerals, metals	47.6%
Industrial equipment	23.7%
Plant and animal raw materials	15.7%
Chemicals, fertilizer, rubber	6.3%

Exports (1990)

Sector	% of exports
Fuels, minerals	33.7%
Industrial and transport equipment	30.8%
Consumer goods (general)	21.2%

Romania's currency, the leu, is divided into 100 bani; in September 1993 the exchange rate was 812.2 leu to 1US$. The most recent budgetary figures are those for 1991.

Revenue	000 million leu	% of revenue
Tax revenue	724	92%
Other revenue	64	8%
Total	788	100%

Expenditure	000 million leu	% of expenditure
Defence	80	10%
Education and health	150	19%
Social security	207	27%
Other		44%
Total	780	100%

RECENT HISTORY

Romania won territory with large Romanian populations from the Russian and Habsburg Empires at the end of World War I. 'Greater Romania' was beset with deep social and ethnic divisions, which found expression in the rise of the Fascist Iron Guard in the 1930s. King Carol II suppressed the Guard and substituted his own dictatorship, but was forced by Germany to cede lands back to Hungary (1940), while the USSR retook Moldova. Carol fled and Romania, under Marshal Ion Antonescu, joined the Axis powers (1941) fighting the USSR to regain lost territories. King Michael dismissed Antonescu and declared war on Germany as the Red Army invaded (1944), and a Soviet-dominated government was installed (1945). The monarchy was abolished in 1947. From 1952, under Gheorghe Gheorghiu-Dej (1901–65) and then under Nicolae Ceausescu (1918–89), Romania distanced itself from Soviet foreign policy but maintained strict Communist orthodoxy at home. Ceausescu, and his wife Elena, impoverished Romania by their harsh, corrupt, nepotistic rule. When the secret police (Securitate) put down demonstrations in Timisoara (December 1989), a national revolt (backed by the army) broke out. A National Salvation Front (NSF) was formed and a military tribunal executed Nicolae and Elena Ceausescu on charges of genocide and corruption. The Communist Party was dissolved; Ceausescu's oppressive social and economic legislation was annulled. However, opposition groups were initially unable to gain access to the media. In 1990, Ion Iliescu was elected president, and the NSF, of which he was leader, was reelected to power. An international team of monitors judged Romania's first post-war multi-party elections to be 'flawed' but not fraudulent. The NSF was returned in subsequent elections but split in 1992 and the Party of Social Democracy – the larger offshoot – came to power.

RUSSIA

Russia is partly in Europe and partly in Asia; see p. 5. The statistics given below refer to the entire country rather than that part of it which is physically in the continent of Europe.

Official name: Rossiyskaya Federativnaya Respublika (Republic of the Russian Federation) or Rossiya (Russia).

Member of: UN, CIS, CSCE.

Area: 17 075 400 km^2 (6 592 800 sq mi).

Population: 148 543 000 (1991 est).

Capital: Moscow (Moskva) 8 967 000 (city 8 769 000; 1989 census).

Other major cities: St Petersburg (Sankt-Peterburg; formerly Leningrad) 5 020 000 (city 4 456 000), Nizhny Novgorod (formerly Gorky) 1 438 000, Novosibirsk 1 436 000, Yekaterinburg (formerly Sverdlovsk) 1 367 000, Samara (formerly Kuybyshev) 1 257 000, Omsk 1 148 000, Chelyabinsk 1 143 000, Kazan 1 094 000, Perm 1 091 000, Ufa 1 083 000, Rostov 1 020 000, Volgograd 999 000, Krasnoyarsk 912 000, Saratov 905 000, Voronezh 887 000, Vladivostok 648 000, Izhevsk (formerly Ustinov) 635 000, Yaroslavl 633 000, Tol'yatti 630 000, Irkutsk 626 000, Simbirsk (formerly Ulyanovsk) 625 000, Krasnodar 620 000, Barnaul 602 000, Khabarovsk 601 000, Novokuznetsk 600 000, Orenburg 547 000, Penza 543 000, Tula 540 000, Kemerovo 520 000, Ryazan 515 000, Astrakhan 509 000, Tomsk 502 000, Naberezhniye Chelny (formerly Brezhnev) 501 000, Lipetsk 499 000, Tyumen 494 000, Vyatka (formerly Kirov) 491 000, Ivanovo 482 000, Murmansk 473 000, Bryansk 459 000, Tver (formerly Kalinin) 455 000, Cheboksary 449 000, Magnitogorsk 446 000, Nizhny Tagil 439 000, Kursk 433 000, Arkhangelsk 428 000, Kaliningrad 408 000, Grozny 401 000, Chita 377 000, Vladimir 376 000, Kurgan 370 000, Kaluga 366 000, Ulan-Ude 362 000, Saransk 347 000, Oryol 345 000, Sochi 342 000, Tambov 334 000 (all including suburbs; 1989 est).

Languages: Russian (83%), Tatar (4%), Ukrainian (3%), Chuvash (1%), Bashkir (1%), Belarussian (1%), Chechen (1%). Over 0.5% of the population speak one of the following languages as a first language: Mordovian, German, Udmurt, Mari, Kazakh, Avar and Armenian. There are over 100 other languages spoken in Russia; see also p. 186.

Many of the minority languages listed above are the first language of the majority in one of the republics whose borders were defined largely upon linguistic grounds; see below.

Religions: Orthodox (27%), with Sunni Muslim, Jewish, Baptist and other minorities. The Russian Orthodox Church – which is headed by the Patriach of Moscow – has greatly expanded its activities since the collapse of the Soviet Union. Over 600 new churches have been built since 1991. Other Christian denominations include: the Roman Catholic Church (which was reorganized under the Archbishop of Moscow in 1991), the revived Russian 'Greek Catholic' (Uniat) Church,

the Society of Evangelical Christians-Baptists (which is probably the largest of the non-Orthodox Churches), the Armenian Orthodox Church and the Old Believers (also known as the 'Old Faith'; an historic breakaway from the Russian Orthodox Church). Since 1991 there has been a dramatic growth in the number of religious cults and in new religions imported from the West.

Followers of Islam in Russia predominate in the northern Caucasus region (for example, in Dagestan, Chechenya and Kabardino-Balkar) and in the southern regions of Siberia bordering Kazakhstan. The largest Jewish communities are in Moscow and the Jewish Autonomous Region, see below. Buddhism is the majority religion in the republics of Buryatia, Kalmykia and Tuva and is important in other parts of Siberia.

Education: Schooling is compulsory between the ages of seven and 15. There are 42 universities, 32 polytechnics of university status and over 100 other institutes offering courses of degree level.

Defence: Russia has a total armed strength of 2 720 000 (some of whom are part of CIS joint forces).The Russian navy has 1730 vessels including submarines while the Russian air force has 3700 combat aircraft. In 1992 Russia had 2968 nuclear warheads. (The remainder of the former Soviet nuclear arsenal was divided between three republics – Ukraine 176 warheads, Belarus 54 warheads and Kazakhstan 104 warheads. However, these warheads are under joint CIS control and, in theory, cannot be used unilaterally.) All Russian males are subject to military conscription – formerly two years in the army and navy, and two to three years in the navy and CIS border force, but now reduced to 18 months.

Transport: Russia has 87 090 km (54 430 mi) of railways operating both passenger and freight services. Metro and/or rapid light transit systems operate in Moscow, St Petersburg, Nizhny Novgorod, Novosibirsk, Samara and Yekaterinburg.

There are about 855 000 km (534 000 mi) of roads over three quarters of which are hard-surfaced. The number of cars is increasing but Russia still has a low rate of private car ownership.

The most important Russian ports include St Petersburg and Kaliningrad on the Baltic Sea, Murmansk on the Barents Sea, Novorossiysk and Sochi on the Black Sea, and Vladivostok, Magadan, Nakhodka and Petropovlovsk on the Pacific coast. Inland navigation is important on Russia's many major rivers; the Volga handles the greatest amount of inland waterway traffic but the great rivers of Siberia are of growing seasonal importance for shipping.

There are many regional airports. International services only operate from a limited number of centres and are concentrated on Moscow and St Petersburg.

Media: The press in Russia is undergoing drastic restructuring. Some titles are now published intermittently and several new titles, including 'tabloids' have appeared. Nearly 4800 newspapers are published (most of them on a weekly basis) but there are only about one dozen major daily titles. Broadcasting is in the hands of the All-Russian State Television Radio Broadcasting Company.

GOVERNMENT

Russia is federation of 21 republics and 67 other regions which have similar powers under the terms of the new Russian constitution of 1993. (Chechenya has not ratified the new treaty between the republics and has unilaterally declared independence, but has not gained any international recognition of its claims.) An executive President – who appoints a Council of Ministers including a Prime Minister – is directly elected for a maximum of two five-year terms. The new Russian Parliament is the Federal Assembly whose two houses are elected for four years by universal adult suffrage. The lower house, the State Duma, comprises 450 members, 225 of whom are elected by single-member constituencies while the remaining 225 are elected from party lists on a system of proportional representation. The upper house, the Federal Council, comprises two members elected from each of the 21 republics and 67 other regions. The political parties registered for the general election in December 1993 were (liberal reformist) Russia's Choice, the (liberal reformist) Party of Unity and Accord, the (liberal reformist) Yavlinsky-Boldyrev-Lukin bloc, the (liberal reformist) Russian Movement for Democratic Reforms, the (centrist) Democratic Party of Russia, the (centrist) Civic Union, the (centrist) Future of Russia-New Names Party, the (corporatist) Constructive Ecological Movement of Russia, the (corporatist) Women of Russia Movement, the (corporatist) Dignity and Charity Movement, the Communist Party, the (communist and nationalist) Agrarian Party, and the (ultra-nationalist) Liberal Democratic Party. At the general election held on 12 December 1993 these parties gained the following number of seats.

Party	Seats
Russia's Choice	94
Liberal Democratic Party	78
Communist Party	64
Agrarian Party	55
Yavlinsky bloc	28
Russian Unity and Accord	22
Others and independent	109
Total	450

President: Boris Yeltsin (elected 1991).

THE CABINET

(In November 1993).

Prime Minister: Viktor Chernomyrdin.

Deputy Prime Minister and Minister of Economics: Yegor Gaidar.

Deputy Prime Minister and Minister of Finance: Boris Fyodorov.

Deputy Prime Minister and Minister of Press and Information: Vladimir Shumeiko.

Deputy Prime Minister and Chairman of the Committee on Nationalities Policies: Sergei Shakhrai.

Deputy Prime Minister: Anatoly Chubais.

Deputy Prime Minister: Aleksandr Shokhin.

Deputy Prime Minister: Oleg Soskovets.

Deputy Prime Minister: Yuri Yarov.

Deputy Prime Minister: Aleksandr Zavieriukha.

Minister of Agriculture: Victor Khlystun.

Minister of Atomic Energy: Victor Mikhailov.

Minister of Communications: Vladimir Bulgak.

Minister of Culture: Evgeni Sidorov.

Minister of Defence: Pavel Grachev.

Minister of Ecology and Natural Resources: Victor

Danilov-Danilyan.
Minister of Economics: See above.
Minister of Education: Evgeni Tkachenko.
Minister of External Economic Affairs: Yuri Davydov.
Minister of Finance: See above.
Minister of Foreign Affairs: Andrei Kozyrev.
Minister of Health: Eduard Nechayev.
Minister of Justice: Sergei Kalmykov.
Minister of Labour: Gennady Melikyan.
Minister of Oil and Energy: Yuri Shafranik.
Minister of Press and Information: See above.
Minister for Railways: Gennady Fadeyev.
Minister of Science and Technological Policies: Boris Saltykov.
Minister of Security: Nikolai Galushko.
Minister of Social Security: Ella Pamfilova.
Minister of Transport: Victor Erin.
Chairman of the Committee on Antimonopolies Policy: Leonid Bochin.
Chairman of the Committee on Architecture and Construction: Efim Basin.
Chairman of the Committee on Civil Defence and Emergency Situations: Sergei Shoigu.
Chairman of the Committee on Economic Cooperation with Countries of the CIS: Vladimir Mashits.
Chairman of the Committee on Nationalities Policies: See above.
Chairman of the Committee on Social and Economic Development of the Northern Regions: Vladimir Kuramin.
Chairman of the Committee on Social Security and Rehabilitation of Territories Affected During Chernobyl and Other Radioactive Catastrophies: Vassily Vozniak.
Chairman of the Committee on State Customs: Anatoly Kruglov.

REPUBLICS AND REGIONS

(Population figures are 1991 estimates.) Under the former Russian constitution the following republics and regions were divided into five types each enjoying a different amount of self-government. In theory these different categories still exist although, under the terms of the (centralizing) 1993 constitution, all republics and regions have very similar powers. The five types of local government unit are:
- the republic (which had the greatest amount of autonomy within the Russian Federation);
- the autonomous region (autonomous *oblast*);
- the autonomous area (autonomous *okrug*);
- the territory (*krai*); and
- and the region (*oblast*, which had the least amount of local autonomy).

Adygea (formerly **Adygei**) (an autonomous region which has declared itself a republic) *Area:* 7600 km² (2935 sq mi). *Population:* 437 000. *Capital:* Maikop.

Agin-Buryat (an autonomous area) *Area:* 19 000 km² (7300 sq mi). *Population:* 78 000. *Capital:* Aginskoye.

Altay (a territory) *Area:* 261 700 km² (101 050 sq mi). *Population:* 2 906 000. *Capital:* Barnaul.

Amur (a region) *Area:* 363 700 km² (140 430 sq mi). *Population:* 1 080 000. *Capital:* Blagoveshchensk.

Arkhangelsk (a region) *Area:* 587 400 km² (226 800 sq mi). *Population:* 1 610 000. *Capital:* Arkhangelsk.

Astrakhan (a region) *Area:* 44 100 km² (17 027 sq mi). *Population:* 1 008 000. *Capital:* Astrakhan.

Bashkortostan (formerly **Bashkiria**) (a republic) *Area:* 143 600 km² (55 430 sq mi). *Population:* 3 984 000. *Capital:* Ufa.

Belgorod (a region) *Area:* 27 100 km² (10 450 sq mi). *Population:* 1 413 000. *Capital:* Belgorod.

Bryansk (a region) *Area:* 34 900 km² (13 480 sq mi). *Population:* 1 590 000. *Capital:* Bryansk.

Buryatia (a republic) *Area:* 351 500 km² (135 630 sq mi). *Population:* 1 049 000. *Capital:* Ulan-Ude.

Chechenya (a republic; half of the former republic of Checheno-Ingushetia, Chechenya has unilaterally declared its independence from the Russian Federation) *Area:* 10 300 km² (4000 sq mi). *Population:* 700 000. *Capital:* Grozny.

Chelyabinsk (a region) *Area:* 87 900 km² (33 950 sq mi). *Population:* 3 765 000. *Capital:* Chelyabinsk.

Chita (a region) *Area:* 431 500 km² (166 600 sq mi). *Population:* 1 370 000. *Capital:* Chita.

Chuckchi (an autonomous area; formerly known as **Chukot**) *Area:* 737 700 km² (284 800 sq mi). *Population:* 154 000. *Capital:* Anadyr.

Chuvashia (a republic) *Area:* 18 300 km² (7065 sq mi). *Population:* 1 346 000. *Capital:* Cheboksary.

Dagestan (a republic) *Area:* 50 300 km² (19 415 sq mi). *Population:* 1 854 000. *Capital:* Makhachkala.

Evenki (an autonomous area) *Area:* 767 000 km² (296 400 sq mi). *Population:* 25 000. *Capital:* Tura.

Gorno-Altay (an autonomous region which has declared itself a republic) *Area:* 92 600 km² (35 740 sq mi). *Population:* 197 000. *Capital:* Gorno-Altaisk.

Ingushetia (a republic) *Area:* 9000 km² (3500 sq mi). *Population:* 500 000. *Capital:* Nazran.

Irkutsk (a region) *Area:* 767 890 km² (296 485 sq mi). *Population:* 2 868 000. *Capital:* Irkutsk.

Ivanovo (a region) *Area:* 23 900 km² (9225 sq mi). *Population:* 1 410 000. *Capital:* Ivanovo.

Jewish Republic see Yevreysk Republic, below.

Kabardino-Balkaria (a republic) *Area:* 12 500 km² (4825 sq mi). *Population:* 768 000. *Capital:* Nalchik.

Kaliningrad (a region) *Area:* 15 100 km² (5830 sq mi). *Population:* 883 000. *Capital:* Kaliningrad. (This region is a coastal enclave between Poland and Lithuania.)

Kalmykia (a republic) *Area:* 75 900 km² (29 300 sq mi). *Population:* 329 000. *Capital:* Elista.

Kaluga (a region) *Area:* 29 900 km² (11 500 sq mi). *Population:* 307 000. *Capital:* Kaluga.

Kamchatka (a region) *Area:* 472 300 km² (182 355 sq mi). *Population:* 445 000. *Capital:* Petropavlovsk.

Karachay-Cherkessia (formerly Karachevo-Cherkess; an autonomous region which has declared itself a republic) *Area:* 14 100 km² (5440 sq mi). *Population:* 427 000. *Capital:* Cherkessk.

Karelia (a republic) *Area:* 172 400 km² (83 730 sq mi). *Population:* 799 000. *Capital:* Petrozavodsk.

Kemerovo (a region) *Area:* 95 500 km² (36 880 sq mi). *Population:* 3 265 000. *Capital:* Kemerovo.

Khakassia (an autonomous region which has declared itself a republic) *Area:* 61 900 km² (23 900 sq mi). *Population:* 577 000. *Capital:* Abakan.

Khanty-Mansi (an autonomous area) *Area:* 523 100 km² (202 000 sq mi). *Population:* 1 314 000. *Capital:* Khanty-Mansiysk.

Khabarovsk (a territory) *Area:* 824 600 km² (318 380 sq mi). *Population:* 1 782 000. *Capital:* Khabarovsk.

Komi (a region) *Area:* 415 900 km² (160 540 sq mi). *Population:* 1 265 000. *Capital:* Syktyvkar.

Komi-Permyak (an autonomous area) *Area:* 32 900 km² (12 700 sq mi). *Population:* 161 000. *Capital:* Kudymkar.

Koryak (an autonomous area) *Area:* 301 500 km² (116 400 sq mi). *Population:* 40 000. *Capital:* Palana.

Kostroma (a region) *Area:* 60 100 km² (23 200 sq mi). *Population:* 853 000. *Capital:* Kostroma.

Krasnodar (a territory) *Area:* 83 600 km² (32 300 sq mi). *Population:* 5 277 000. *Capital:* Krasnodar.

Krasnoyarsk (a territory) *Area:* 2 401 600 km² (927 300 sq mi). *Population:* 3 550 000. *Capital:* Krasnoyarsk.

Kurgan (a region) *Area:* 71 000 km² (27 400 sq mi). *Population:* 1 044 000. *Capital:* Kurgan.

Kursk (a region) *Area:* 29 800 km² (11 500 sq mi). *Population:* 1 450 000. *Capital:* Kursk.

Lipetsk (a region) *Area:* 24 100 km² (9 300 sq mi). *Population:* 1 306 000. *Capital:* Lipetsk.

Magadan (a region) *Area:* 1 199 100 km² (462 975 sq mi). *Population:* 545 000. *Capital:* Magadan.

Mari El (a republic) *Area:* 23 200 km² (8955 sq mi). *Population:* 758 000. *Capital:* Yoshkar-Ola.

Mordvinia (formerly **Mordovia**) (a republic) *Area:* 26 200 km² (10 110 sq mi). *Population:* 964 000. *Capital:* Saransk.

Moscow (Moskva) (a region) *Area:* 47 000 km² (18 150 sq mi). *Population:* 16 002 000. *Capital:* Moscow.

Murmansk (a region) *Area:* 144 900 km² (55 950 sq mi). *Population:* 1 118 000. *Capital:* Murmansk.

Nenets (an autonomous area) *Area:* 176 400 km² (68 100 sq mi). *Population:* 55 000. *Capital:* Naryan-Mar.

Nizhny Novgorod (a region) *Area:* 74 800 km² (28 900 sq mi). *Population:* 3 945 000. *Capital:* Nizhny Novgorod (formerly Gorky).

North Ossetia (Severo Ossetiya) (a republic) *Area:* 8000 km² (3090 sq mi). *Population:* 643 000. *Capital:*Vladikavkaz.

Novgorod (a region) *Area:* 55 300 km² (21 300 sq mi). *Population:* 788 000. *Capital:* Novgorod.

Novosibirsk (a region) *Area:* 178 200 km² (68 800 sq mi). *Population:* 2 890 000. *Capital:* Novosibirsk.

Omsk (a region) *Area:* 139 700 km² (53 900 sq mi). *Population:* 2 155 000. *Capital:* Omsk.

Oryol (a region) *Area:* 24 700 km² (9 550 sq mi). *Population:* 938 000. *Capital:* Oryol (formerly known as Orel).

Orenburg (a region) *Area:* 124 000 km² (47 900 sq mi). *Population:* 2 278 000. *Capital:* Orenburg.

Penza (a region) *Area:* 43 200 km² (16 680 sq mi). *Population:* 1 603 000. *Capital:* Penza.

Perm (a region) *Area:* 160 600 km² (62 000 sq mi). *Population:* 3 222 000. *Capital:* Perm.

Primorye (a territory which has attempted to declare itself to be a republic) *Area:* 165 900 km² (64 055 sq mi). *Population:* 2 230 000. *Capital* Vladivostok.

Pskov (a region) *Area:* 55 300 km² (21 350 sq mi). *Population:* 900 000. *Capital:* Pskov.

Rostov (a region) *Area:* 100 800 km² (38 900 sq mi). *Population:* 4 890 000. *Capital:* Rostov.

Ryazan (a region) *Area:* 39 600 km² (15 300 sq mi). *Population:* 1 410 000. *Capital:* Ryazan.

St Petersburg (Sankt-Peterburg) (a region) *Area:* 85 900 km² (33 200 sq mi). *Population:* 6 815 000. *Capital:* St Petersburg (formerly Leningrad).

Sakhalin (a region) *Area:* 87 100 km² (33 650 sq mi). *Population:* 728 000. *Capital:* Yuzhno-Sakhalinsk.

Samara (a region) *Area:* 53 600 km² (20 700 sq mi). *Population:* 3 393 000. *Capital:* Samara (formerly Kuybyshev).

Saratov (a region) *Area:* 100 200 km² (38 700 sq mi). *Population:* 2 782 000. *Capital:* Saratov.

Simbirsk (a region) *Area:* 37 300 km² (14 560 sq mi). *Population:* 1 380 000. *Capital:* Simbirsk (formerly Ulyanovsk).

Smolensk (a region) *Area:* 49 800 km² (19 230 sq mi). *Population:* 1 215 000. *Capital:* Smolensk.

Stavropol (a territory) *Area:* 80 600 km² (31 100 sq mi). *Population:* 2 837 000. *Capital:* Stavropol.

Tambov (a region) *Area:* 34 300 km² (13 250 sq mi). *Population:* 1 422 000. *Capital:* Tambov.

Tatarstan (a republic) *Area:* 68 100 km² (26 650 sq mi). *Population:* 3 679 000. *Capital:* Kazan.

Taymyr or **Dolgano-Nenets** (an autonomous area) *Area:* 862 100 km² (332 900 sq mi). *Population:* 54 000. *Capital:* Dudinka.

Tomsk (a region) *Area:* 316 900 (122 350 sq mi). *Population:* 1 006 000. *Capital:* Tomsk.

Tula (a region) *Area:* 25 700 km² (9 930 sq mi). *Population:* 2 0132 000. *Capital:* Tula.

Tuva (a republic) *Area:* 170 500 km² (65 810 sq mi). *Population:* 307 000. *Capital:* Kyzyl-Orda.

Tver (a region) *Area:* 84 100 km² (32 470 sq mi). *Population:*1 760 000. *Capital:* Tver (formerly Kalinin).

Tyumen (a region) *Area:* 1 435 200 km² (554 100 sq mi). *Population:* 2 436 000. *Capital:* Tyumen.

Udmurtia (a republic) *Area:* 42 100 km² (16 250 sq mi). *Population:* 1 628 000. *Capital:* Izhevsk.

Ust-Ordynsky Buryat (an autonomous area) *Area:* 22 400 km² (8600 sq mi). *Population:* 138 000. *Capital:* Ust-Ordynsky.

Vyatka (a region) *Area:* 120 800 km² (46 650 sq mi). *Population:* 1 779 000. *Capital:* Vyatka (formerly Kirov).

Vladimir (a region) *Area:* 29 000 km² (11 200 sq mi). *Population:* 1 718 000. *Capital:* Vladimir.

Volgograd (a region) *Area:* 114 100 km² (44 100 sq mi). *Population:* 2 655 000. *Capital:* Volgograd.

Vologda (a region) *Area:* 145 700 km² (56 250 sq mi). *Population:* 1 421 000. *Capital:* Vologda.

Voronezh (a region) *Area:* 52 400 km² (20 250 sq mi). *Population:* 2 638 000. *Capital:* Voronezh.

Yakut-Sakha (formerly **Yakutia**) (a republic) *Area:* 3 103 200 km² (1 197 760 sq mi). *Population:* 1 109 000. *Capital:* Yakutsk.

Yamalo-Nenets (an autonomous area) *Area:* 750 300 km² (289 700 sq mi). *Population:* 493 000. *Capital:* Salekhard.

Yaroslavl (a region) *Area:* 36 400 km² (14 000 sq mi). *Population:* 1 545 000. *Capital:* Yaroslavl.

Yekaterinburg (a region which has attempted to declare itself the **Urals Republic/Uralsky Respublik**) *Area:* 194 800 km² (75 200 sq mi). *Population:* 4 884 000. *Capital:* Yekaterinburg (formerly Sverdlovsk).

Yevreysk Republic or **Yereyskayaya** (**Jewish Republic**) (an autonomous region which has declared itself a republic) *Area:* 36 000 km² (13 895 sq mi). *Population:* 220 000. *Capital:* Birobijan (Birobidzhan).

GEOGRAPHY

Russia is the largest country in the world and covers over 10% of the total land area of the globe. Most of the land between the Baltic and the Ural Mountains is covered by the North European Plain, south of which the relatively low-lying Central Russian Uplands stretch from the Ukrainian border to north of Moscow. To the east of the Urals is the vast West Siberian Lowland, the greater part of which is occupied by the basin of the River Ob and its tributaries. The Central Siberian Plateau – between the Rivers Yenisey and Lena – rises to around 1700 m (5500 ft). Beyond the Lena are the mountains of east Siberia, including the Chersky Mountains and the Kamchatka Peninsula. Much of the south of Siberia is mountainous. The Yablonovy and Stanovoy Mountains rise inland from the Amur Basin, which drains to the Pacific coast. The Altai Mountains lie south of Lake Baikal and along the border with Mongolia. Between the Black and Caspian Seas are the high Caucasus Mountains on the Georgian border. The Kaliningrad enclave between Poland and Lithuania on the Baltic is a detached part of Russia. *Principal rivers:* Yenisey, Lena, Ob, Amur, Volga, Angara, Irtysh, Dvina, Pechora, Kama. *Highest point:* Elbrus (on the Georgian border) 5642 m (18 510 ft).

Russia has a wide range of climatic types, but most of the country is continental and experiences extremes of temperature. The Arctic north is a severe tundra region in which the subsoil is nearly always frozen. The forested taiga zone – to the south – has long hard winters and short summers. The steppes and the Central Russian Uplands have cold winters, but hot, dry summers. Between the Black and Caspian seas conditions become almost Mediterranean. The Kaliningrad enclave has a more temperate climate than the rest of Russia.

ECONOMY

Russia is one of the largest producers of coal, iron ore,

steel, petroleum and cement. However, its economy is in crisis and Russia's GNP declined by nearly 20% in 1992 and by over 10% in 1993. The economic reforms (1985–91) of Mikhail Gorbachov introduced decentralization to a centrally-planned economy. Since 1991, reform has been accelerated through the introduction of free market prices and the encouragement of private enterprise. However, there have been widespread calls for slower reform as economic chaos has spread and living standards have fallen. (The pace of economic reform was one of the issues of debate between President Yeltsin and the hardliners in the Congress in 1993, see below.)

A lack of motivation in the labour force affects all sectors of the economy and poor distribution has resulted in shortages of many basic goods. Inflation became rampant, reaching 2200% in 1992 but Russia's economic decline slowed in 1993. Russia continues to look for more Western assistance and investment but a combination of political uncertainty and economic problems means that – with the notable exception of the oil and gas industries – Western investment levels have fallen far short of Russian expectations.

Manufacturing involves one third of the labour force and includes the steel, chemical, textile and heavy machinery industries. The production of consumer goods is not highly developed. Russian industry is characterized by a poor infrastructure and out-of-date plant and the country has found very considerable difficulties in competing internationally.

Agriculture is large-scale and organized either into state-owned farms or collective farms, although the right to own and farm land privately has been introduced. Despite mechanization and the world's largest fertilizer industry, Russia cannot produce enough grain for its needs, in part because of poor harvests, and poor storage and transport facilities. Imports from Ukraine and Kazakhstan have assumed added importance. Major Russian crops include wheat, barley, oats, potatoes, sugar beet and fruit.

Natural resources include the world's largest reserves of coal, nearly one third of the world's natural gas reserves, one third of the world's forests, major deposits of manganese, gold, potash, bauxite, nickel, lead, zinc and copper, as well as plentiful sites for hydroelectric power installations. Machinery, petroleum and petroleum products are Russia's major exports and the republic is self sufficient in energy. Russia has a large trade surplus with the other former Soviet republics.

Labour force (1990)

Sector	Number employed
Industry	22 107 800
Agriculture	9 845 000
Construction	7 018 000
Finance	401 000
Trade	5 545 000
Transport and communications	5 778 000
Services and administration	27 106 000
Total	*78 682 000*

The Russian currency is the rouble which, in theory, is divided into 100 kopeks although this smaller unit is no longer in use. Inflation has greatly diminished the value of the rouble and in November 1993 the exchange rate was 1 US$ to 1204 roubles. Russia is now the centre of a 'rouble zone' comprising some of the former Soviet republics whose currencies are linked to the rouble. However, by December 1993 all of the former Soviet republics had adopted their own currencies and the rouble zone was, for most practical purposes, no longer effective. Indeed, as the value of currencies such as the Ukrainian karbovanets and the Belarussian rubel declined the Russian rouble found itself in the unaccustomed role of a 'hard currency'.

There are no recent budgetary figures for the Russian Federation.

RECENT HISTORY

Following the revolution of February 1917 – largely brought about by the catastrophic conduct of World War I – Tsar Nicholas II abdicated and a provisional government was established. On 7 November 1917 the Bolsheviks (Communists) – led by Vladymir Ilich Lenin (1870–1924) – overthrew the provisional government in a bloodless coup. Russia withdrew from the war, ceded Poland to Germany and Austria, and recognized the independence of Estonia, Finland, Georgia, Latvia, Lithuania and the Ukraine. Other parts of the former empire soon declared independence, including Armenia, Azerbaijan and Central Asia. A civil war between the Bolsheviks and the White Russians (led by former Tsarists) lasted until 1922. The Communists gradually reconquered most of the former Russian empire and in December 1922 formed the Union of Soviet Socialist Republics. The economy was reorganized under central control, but shortages and famine were soon experienced. After Lenin's death (1924), a power struggle took place between the supporters of Joseph Stalin (1879–1953) and Leon Trotsky (1879–1940). Stalin expelled Trotsky's supporters from the Communist Party and exiled him. The rapid industrialization of the country began. In 1929–30 Stalin liquidated the kulaks (richer peasants). Severe repression continued until his death – opponents were subjected to 'show trials' and summary execution, and millions died as a result of starvation or political execution.

In World War II – in which up to 20 million Soviet citizens may have died – the USSR at first concluded a pact with Hitler (1939), and invaded Poland, Finland, Romania and the Baltic states, annexing considerable territory. However, in 1941 the Germans invaded the USSR, precipitating the Soviet Union's entry into the war on the Allied side. In victory the Soviet Union was confirmed as a world power, controlling a cordon of satellite states in Eastern Europe and challenging the West in the Cold War. However, the economy stagnated and the country was drained by the burdens of an impoverished and overstretched empire. Leonid Brezhnev (leader 1964–82) reversed the brief thaw that had been experienced under Nikita Khruschev (leader 1956–64), and far-reaching reform had to await the policies of Mikhail Gorbachov (1931–) after 1985.

Faced with severe economic reforms, Gorbachov attempted to introduce reconstruction (*perestroika*) and greater openness (*glasnost*) by implementing social,

economic and industrial reforms. The state of the economy also influenced the desire to reduce military spending by reaching agreements on arms reduction with the West. Dissent was tolerated, a major reform of the constitution led to more open elections, and the Communist Party gave up its leading role. Many hardliners in the Communist Party were defeated by reformers (many of them non-Communists) in elections in 1989. The abandonment of the Brezhnev Doctrine – the right of the USSR to intervene in the affairs of Warsaw Pact countries (as it had done militarily in Hungary in 1956 and Czechoslovakia in 1968) – prompted rapid change in Eastern Europe, where one after another the satellite states renounced Communism and began to implement multi-party rule. From 1989 there were increased nationalistic stirrings within the USSR, particularly in the Baltic republics and the Caucasus.

In August 1991, an attempt by a group of Communist hardliners to depose Gorbachov was defeated by the resistance of Russian President Boris Yeltsin (1931–) and by the refusal of the army to take action against unarmed civilian protestors. The opposition of Yeltsin and the Russian parliament to the coup greatly enhanced the status and powers of Russia and the 14 other Union Republics. Fourteen of the 15 republics declared independence and the secession of the three Baltic republics was recognized internationally. The remaining republics began to renegotiate their relationship. Gorbachov suspended the Communist Party and – with Yeltsin – initiated far-reaching political and economic reforms. However, it was too late to save the Soviet Union, whose fate was sealed by the refusal of Ukraine, the second most important of the republics, to participate in the new looser Union proposed by Gorbachov.

By the end of 1991 the initiative had passed from Gorbachov to Yeltsin, who was instrumental in establishing the Commonwealth of Independent States (CIS), a military and economic grouping of sovereign states that included the majority of the former Union republics. After Gorbachov resigned and the Soviet Union was dissolved (December 1991), Russia took over the international responsibilities of the USSR, including its seat on the UN Security Council. Externally, Russia faced disputes concerning the future of CIS forces and potential territorial claims on other former Soviet republics. Internally, Russia faced a severe economic crisis as the command economy is replaced by a market economy.

These changes were impeded by the activities of former Communist hardliners in the Congress of People's Deputies, who also held up constitutional reform. The contest between Yeltsin and the hardliners came to a head in the autumn of 1993 when a core of hardliners – led by Vice-President Aleksandr Rutskoy and Ruslan Khasbulatov, the speaker of parliament – organized an armed uprising. A two-week siege of the White House (Russia's Parliament) ended when the military intervened on Yeltin's behalf to crush the revolt. Yeltsin has since imposed a new constitution which concentrates power in the hands of the president. At elections in December 1993 Communists and Vladimir Zhirinovsky's extreme right wing 'Liberal Democrats' gained support.

SLOVAKIA

Official name: Republika Slovenská (Slovak Republic).
Member of: UN, CSCE, Council of Europe, CEFTA.
Area: 49 025 km² (18 929 sq mi).
Population: 5 290 000 (1991 census).
Capital: Bratislava 444 000 (including suburbs; 1991 census).
Other major cities: Košice 235 000, Nitra 90 000, Prešov 88 000, Banská Bystrica 85 000, Zilina 84 000, Trnava 72 000, Martin 58 000, Trenčín 57 000, Prievidza 53 000, Poprad 53 000 (1991 census).
Languages: Slovak (87%), Magyar (Hungarian) (12%). See also p. 186.
Religions: Roman Catholic (60%), Evangelical Churches (6%). The Roman Catholic Church is organized into four dioceses under the archbishop of Travna. Roman Catholics following the Slovak rite come under the diocese of Prešov which covers the whole republic. The principal Protestant Churches are the Slovak Evangelical Church of the Augsburg Confession (popularly known as Slovak Lutherans) and the Reformed Christian Church of Slovakia.
Education: Education is compulsory between the ages of six and 15. There are ten universities – Bratislava (3), Košice (3), Zilina, Nitra, Zvolen and Trnava.
Defence: Following the division of the armed forces of the former Czechoslovakia (January 1993), the new Slovak armed forces had a total armed strength of 50 000. Compulsory military service lasts for 12 months.
Transport: There are 17 737 km (11 086 mi) of roads in Slovakia including 191 km (119 mi) of motorway. There are 3661 km (2288 mi) of railway track operating both passenger and freight services. A metro system is under construction in Bratislava. The Danube is an important inland waterway with ports at Bratislava and Komárno. International flights operate from Bratislava and Košice airports.
Media: There are some 700 newspapers (both daily and weekly) including many new titles. About 30 papers are published in minority languages, mainly Magyar (Hungarian). There is a single (state-owned) radio and television network.

GOVERNMENT

The 150-member National Council is elected under a system of proportional representation by universal adult suffrage for four years. The Assembly elects a President for a five-year term. The President, whose role is largely ceremonial, appoints a Prime Minister and a Council of Ministers, responsible to the National Council. The main political parties are the (socialist nationalist) Movement for a Democratic Slovakia (MDS), the (former Communist) Party of the Democratic Left, the (centre) Christian Democratic Movement, the Slovak National Party and Coexistence, an electoral alliance of ethnic Hungarian parties.

The elections held on 5–6 June 1992 resulted in the following representation of parties in the National Council:

Party	Seats
Movement for a Democratic Slovakia	74
Party of the Democratic Left	29
Christian Democratic Movement	18
Slovak National Party	15
Coexistence	14
Total	150

A government of MDS members and independents was formed.
President: Michal Kováč (MDS).

THE CABINET

Prime Minister: Vladimír Mečiar (MDS).
Deputy Prime Minister: Roman Kováč (MDS).
Minister for the Administration and Privatization of National Property: Lubomir Dolgoš (MDS).
Minister of Agriculture: Peter Baco (MDS).
Minister of Culture: Dušan Slobodník (MDS).
Minister of Defence: Imrich Andrejčak (ind).
Minister of the Economy: Jaroslav Kubečka (MDS).
Minister of Education and Science: Matúš Kučera (MDS).
Minister of the Environment: Jozef Zlocha (MDS).
Minister of Finance: Július Tóth (MDS).
Minister of Foreign Affairs: Jozef Moravčík (MDS).
Minister of Health: Viliam Sobona (MDS).
Minister of the Interior: Jozef Tuchnya (ind).
Minister of Justice: Katarína Tóthová (MDS).
Minister of Labour, Social and Family Affairs: Olga Keltošová (MDS).
Minister of Transport, Communications and Public Works: Roman Hofbauer (MDS).

GEOGRAPHY

Slovakia mainly comprises mountain ranges including the Tatra Mountains on the Polish border. The only significant lowlands are in the south adjoining the River Danube and its tributaries. The relief means that the natural routes are mainly north-south, which is incon-

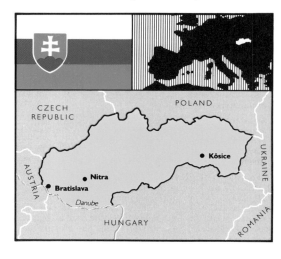

venient in a country where most internal traffic is east to west. *Principal rivers:* Danube, Vah, Hron. *Highest Point:* Gerlachovka 2655 m (8737 ft).

Slovakia has a continental climate characterized by warm summers and cold, snowy winters. There are many local climatic variations. The greatest differences are between the high cold Tatra Mountains and the sheltered Danube lowlands which have lower rainfall and much higher summer temperatures.

ECONOMY

Slovakia has a large agricultural sector. Wheat, maize, potatoes, barley and sheep are important.

Labour force (1992)

Sector	*Number employed*
Industry, mining, utilities	692 000
Agriculture	236 000
Construction	218 000
Education and culture	179 000
Trade	230 000
Transport and communications	156 000
Administration	55 000
Health and social services	129 000
Other (including unemployed)	257 000
Total	*2 152 000*

Heavy industry – particularly steel, chemicals and one of the largest arms industries in Europe – was introduced when the country was part of Communist Czechoslovakia. A drastic fall in international demand for arms has cost about 40 000 jobs in Slovakia and the government has actively sought to revive exports of arms. Other important industries include textiles, clothing, footwear, glass and leather. Varied natural resources include brown coal, copper, zinc and lead. At the dissolution of Czechoslovakia about two-thirds of state-owned enterprises had been privatized but independent Slovakia has slowed the privatization of its uncompetitive out-of-date factories. Slovakia has suffered from the collapse of the former Comecon East European trade bloc. Unemployment has increased, GDP has fallen and the loss of subsidies from Prague has damaged the economy. Slovakia is an associate of the EC.

Imports (1991)

Sector	*% of imports*
Fuels, lubricants	35.2%
Machinery, transport equipment	23.9%
Raw materials (general)	12.9%
Chemicals	8.8%
Manufactures (general)	8.0%

Exports (1990)

Sector	*% of exports*
Manufactures (including arms)	51.9%
Machinery, transport equipment	22.5%
Chemicals	12.2%

In February 1993 Slovakia introduced its own currency, the Slovakian koruna (divided into 100 halierov). Initially the Slovakian and Czech currencies were on a par, but devaluation has decreased the value of the Slovakian koruna. In September 1993 the exchange rate was 32.07 Slovakian koruny to 1US$. The most recent budgetary figures are those for 1991.

Revenue	*Million koruny*	*% of revenue*
Total	*116 881*	*100%*

Expenditure	*Million koruny*	*% of expenditure*
Social services	83 001	65%
Production	23 388	18%
Local government	7 961	6%
Other		11%
Total	*127 109*	*100%*

RECENT HISTORY

What is now Slovakia came under Habsburg rule in 1526. A Slovak national revival intensified during the 19th century when Slovak evolved as a literary language distinct from Czech. Habsburg Hungary, of which Slovakia formed a part, suppressed the use of Slovak in secondary education and did little to develop the region or improve the lot of the rural poor.

On the collapse of the Habsburg Empire (1918), the Slovaks seceded from Habsburg Hungary and joined the Czechs to form Czechoslovakia, a state that proved to be more centralized that the federalist Slovaks had expected. When Hitler's Germany dismembered Czechoslovakia in 1938, Slovakia became an Axis puppet state under the Slovak autonomist leader Jozef Tiso. Slovakia lost its Magyar (Hungarian) south to Hungary (1938). In 1939 Slovakia became nominally independent but allied to Nazi Germany. A popular revolt against German rule (the Slovak Uprising) took place in 1944. Following liberation (1945) Czechoslovakia was re-established and the Magyar lands north of the Danube were returned to Slovakia. After the Communist takeover in 1948, heavy industry was introduced into rural Slovakia.

In 1968, moves by Communist Party Secretary Alexander Dubček (a Slovak) to introduce political reforms met with Soviet disapproval, and invasion by Czechoslovakia's Warsaw Pact allies. In 1969 the Slovak Republic became an equal partner with the Czech Republic under a new federal constitution. The conservative wing of the Communist party regained control until 1989, when student demonstrations developed into a peaceful revolution. The Communist Party renounced its leading role. A new government, in which Communists were in a minority, was appointed. In 1990 free multi-party elections were held, Soviet troops were withdrawn and the foundations of a market economy were laid, but the pace of economic reform brought distress to Slovakia, whose old-fashioned industries were ill-equipped to face competition.

Increased Slovak separatism led to the division of the country in 1993. Independent Slovakia faces severe economic difficulties as well as possible tension concerning the large Hungarian minority in the south. Hungary and Slovakia are also in dispute over the Gabčikovo-Nagymaros hydroelectric dam on the Danube which has agreed by the former Communist governments of both countries. The project – which diverts the Danube – was been abandoned by Hungary on environmental grounds but Slovakia has proceeded with it.

SLOVENIA

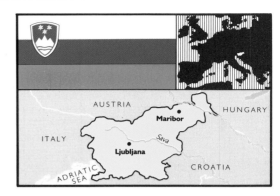

Official name: Republika Slovenija (The Republic of Slovenia).

Member of: UN, CSCE, Council of Europe.

Area: 20 251 km² (7819 sq mi).

Population: 1 966 000 (1992 est).

Capital: Ljubljana 328 000 (city 276 000) (1991 census).

Other major cities: Maribor 189 000 (city 108 000), Celje 41 000, Kranj 37 000, Koper 25 000 (including suburbs; 1991 census).

Languages: Slovene (91%), Serbo-Croat (5%), with small Italian and Magyar (Hungarian) minorities. See also p. 186.

Religions: Roman Catholic (over 90%). The Archbishop of Ljubljana is head of the Catholic Church in Slovenia. Other denominations include the Slovene Old Catholic Church and the Evangelical Lutheran Church of Slovenia.

Education: Education is compulsory between the ages of seven and 15. There are two universities – Ljubljana and Maribor – and a theological institution of university status in Ljubljana.

Defence: In mid-1992 the total strength of the newly-formed Slovene army was 15 000, plus 85 000 reserves. There are plans to increase the size of the standing army to 20 000. A small coastal defence force has been founded. Compulsory military conscription lasts seven months.

Transport: There are 1196 km (748 mi) of railway track, of which 526 km (329 mi) are electrified. Both passenger and freight services are operated. There are 14 552 km (9095 mi) of roads including 81 km (51 mi) of motorway. Koper (once known as Capodistria) is the only major port on Slovenia's short Adriatic coast. There are three international airports – Brnik (for Ljubljana), Maribor and Portoroz, which was developed to cater for tourist charter flights to the Adriatic coast.

Media: There are five principal daily newspapers and nearly 200 other (mainly regional and local) papers. Slovenia has a single radio and television network which broadcasts in Italian and Hungarian (Magyar) as well as in Slovene.

GOVERNMENT

Under a new constitution promulgated in 1991, Slovenia has a bicameral Parliament comprising a 90-member National Assembly (the lower house) and a 40-member National Council (the upper house). The National Assembly serves for four years and comprises 38 members directly elected in constituencies by universal adult suffrage, 50 members indirectly elected by a national 'electoral college' according to a system of proportional representation and two nominated members – one each to represent Slovenia's small Italian and Hungarian minorities. The National Council serves for five years and comprises 20 members directly elected in constituencies by universal adult suffrage and 20 members elected by an electoral college to represent various vocational and other interest groups. The President – whose role is largely a ceremonial one – is directly elected for five years. The Prime Minister (who is appointed by the President) appoints a Council of Ministers who enjoy a majority in the National Assembly.

The main political parties are the (centrist) Liberal Democratic Party (LDP), the Slovenian Christian Democrats (SCD), the (right-wing) Slovenian National Party, the Associated List (AL; an electoral alliance of the Democratic Party of Pensioners, the Social Democratic Reform Party, the Social Democratic Union and the Workers' Party of Slovenia), the (agrarian) Slovenian People's Party, the (centrist) Democratic Party of Slovenia, the Greens of Slovenia, and the Social Democratic Party of Slovenia (SDPS).

The Assembly elected on 6 December 1992 comprises:

Party	Seats
Liberal Democratic Party	22
Slovenian Christian Democrats	15
Associated List	14
Slovenian National Party	12
Slovenian People's Party	10
Social Democratic Party of Slovenia	6
Greens of Slovenia	5
Social Democratic Party of Slovenia	4
Hungarian independent	1
Italian independent	1
Total	90

A coalition of Liberal Democratic Party, Associated List, Slovenian Christian Democrat, Green Party and Social Democratic Party of Slovenia members and independents was formed in December 1992.

President: Milan Kucan.

THE CABINET

Prime Minister: Dr Janez Drnovsek (LDP).
Minister of Agriculture and Forestry: Joze Osterc (SCD).
Minister of Culture: Sergij Pelhan (AL).
Minister of Defence: Janez Jansa (SDPS).
Minister for Economic Affairs: Dr Maks Tajnikar (AL).
Minister of Education and Sport: Dr Slavko Gaber (LDP).

Minister of the Environment and Regional Planning: MIha Jazbinsek (LDP).
Minister of Finance: Mitja Gaspari (ind).
Minister of Foreign Affairs: Lojze Peterle (SCD).
Minister of Health: Dr Bozidar Voljc (Greens).
Minister of Interior Affairs: Ivan Bizjak (SCD).
Minister of Justice: Miha Kozinc (LDP).
Minister of Labour, Family and Social Affairs: Jozica Puhar (AL).
Minister of Science and Technology: Dr Rado Bohinc (AL).
Minister of Transport and Communications: Igor Umek (SCD).

GEOGRAPHY
Most of Slovenia comprises mountains including the Karawanken Alps in the north and the Julian Alps in the centre. In the east, hill country adjoins the Drava valley. In the west, Slovenia has an Adriatic coastline of 30 km (19 mi), wedged between the Italian port of Trieste and the Croatian peninsula of Istria. *Principal rivers:* Drava, Sava, Mura. *Highest point:* Triglav 2864 m (9396 ft).

Western Slovenia has a mild Mediterranean climate; eastern Slovenia tends to be more continental with colder winters. Rainfall is relatively heavy, particularly in the mountains, although the eastern lowlands adjoining the Hungarian border are drier.

ECONOMY
With a standard of living approaching that of West European countries, Slovenia was the most industrialized and economically developed part of the former Yugoslavia. Industries include iron and steel, textiles and coal mining. Agriculture specializes in livestock, fodder crops (particularly maize), potatoes, wheat amd grapes (for wine). About 40% of the republic is wooded and forestry is an important industry.

Before the Yugoslav civil wars Slovenia attracted many summer visitors to its short Adriatic coastline and to inland beauty spots (including Lake Bled and the Lippizaner stud) and winter visitors to Alpine skiing resorts.

The rest of former Yugoslavia was a major trading partner of Slovenia before 1991 and the country's economy has been disrupted by the loss of these markets. German, Austrian and Italian markets now play a much greater role and Slovenia is to join CEFTA.

Imports (1991)
Sector	% of imports
Machinery/transport equipment	34.6%
Manufactures	19.0%
Chemicals	15.7%
Fuels and minerals	8.7%
Other inedible raw materials including wood pulp	8.3%
Food and live animals	5.2%

Exports (1990)
Sector	% of exports
Machinery/transport equipment	38.1%
Steel, metals, metal manufactures	10.2%
Chemicals	8.3%
Food and live animals	4.7%

Slovenia experienced high inflation in the first period of independence but the rate of inflation decreased greatly after the government adopted tough monetarist policies and the republic adopted its own currency – the tolar (which is divided into 100 stotins) – in October 1991. In September 1993 the exchange rate was 114.0 tolars to 1US$.

One of the republic's main economic problems is growing unemployment, but – compared with the other successor states of the former Yugoslavia – Slovenia has not suffered the severe economic decline that has characterized those countries.

Labour force (1991)
Sector	Number employed
Agriculture	121 000
Industry, mining, utilities	314 000
Construction	41 000
Trade/hotel and catering	104 000
Transport and communications	47 000
Finance and allied	49 000
Community, social and personal services	200 000
Other	4 000
Unemployed	67 000
Total	947 000

The most recent budgetary revenue figures available are for 1992, but no recent figures on expenditure are available.

Revenue
	Million tolars	% of revenue
Taxation	437 072	96%
Other receipts	166	4%
Total	453 671	100%

RECENT HISTORY
At the turn of the 20th century, what is now Slovenia had been incorporated within the Habsburg (Austrian) province of Carniola for nearly six centuries. However, the region successfully resisted Germanization and the Slovenes managed to preserve their national identity. Official encouragement of the Slovene language under Napoleonic French rule (1809–14) gave impetus to a Slovene national revival in the 19th century. When the Habsburg Empire collapsed (1918), the Slovenes joined the Serbs, Croats and Montenegrins in the new state that was renamed Yugoslavia in 1929. However, a sizeable Slovene community remained under Italian rule until the border between Italy and Yugoslavia was redrawn after World War II.

When Yugoslavia became a Communist federal state in 1945, the Slovene lands were reorganized as the republic of Slovenia. After the death of Yugoslav President Tito (1980), the federation faltered in nationalist crises. Slovenia, the wealthiest part of Yugoslavia, edged towards democracy. In free elections in 1990, nationalists gained a majority in the Slovene Assembly, which declared independence in June 1991. Following reverses in a short campaign, Yugoslav federal forces were withdrawn from Slovenia. The European Community (EC) recognized Slovenia's independence in January 1992; recognition by the rest of the international community followed.

TURKEY

Only 5% of Turkey – that is the part to the west of the Dardenelles – is physically in Europe (see below), but it is usual to regard Turkey as a European country. Turkey has, for example, joined a number of European organizations and has also applied for membership of the EC/EU.

Official name: Türkiye Cumhuriyeti (Republic of Turkey).

Member of: UN, NATO, OECD, CSCE, Council of Europe.

Area: 779 452 km² (300 948 sq mi).

Population: 59 869 000 (1993 est).

Capital: Ankara 3 022 000 (city 2 560 000; 1990 census).

Other major cities: Istanbul 6 620 000 (city 6 293 000), Izmir 2 665 000 (city 2 319 000), Adana 1 430 000 (city 972 000), Bursa 1 031 000 (city 775 000), Konya 1 015 000 (city 543 000), Gaziantep 760 000 (city 574 000), Mersin (Icel) 701 000 (city 414 000), Kayseri 588 000 (city 461 000), Diyarbakir 560 000 (city 371 000), Manisa 557 000 (city 158 000), Sanliurfa 521 000 (city 240 000), Antalya 514 000 (city 353 000) (1990 census).

Languages: Turkish (86%; official); Kurdish (10% plus). There is no agreement regarding the size of the Kurdish population in Turkey; some sources quote estimates as large as 20% of the total population. Turkish estimates tend to be considerably lower.

Religion: Sunni Islam (67%), Shia Islam (30%), various Christian Churches (3%).

Education: Between the ages of six and 14 all Turkish children must attend six years of schooling. There are 29 universities.

Defence: All male Turks are subject to 18 months conscription at the age of 20. The army has 450 000 personnel, the navy has 52 000 and the air force 58 000. Turkey is the leading regional military power and is an important element within NATO.

Transport: There are over 365 000 km (228 000 mi) of road including 1530 km (957 mi) of motorway. There are 8 439 km (5274 mi) of state-owned railway operating freight and passenger services. The Bosporus is a major shipping route; the main maritime ports are Istanbul and Bandirma, both of which are on the Bosporus route, and Iskenderun. Istanbul, Ankara, Izmir, Adana, Dalaman and Antalya have international airports.

Media: There are five TV channels and four radio networks run by the state-owned company TRT. Turkey has over 50 dailies; the principal titles are printed in separate Istanbul, Ankara and Izmir editions.

GOVERNMENT

The 450-member National Assembly is elected by universal adult suffrage for five years. The President – who is elected by the Assembly for seven years – appoints a Prime Minister and a Cabinet commanding a majority in the Assembly. The main political parties are the (conservative) Motherland Party, the Social Democratic Populist Party (SHP), the True Path Party (DYP), the Welfare Party and the Democratic Left. At the general election held in October 1991 these parties gained the following number of seats. A new coalition government of DYP and SHP members was formed in 1993.

Party	Seats
True Path Party	178
Motherland Party	115
Social Democrats and allies	88
Welfare Party and allies	62
Democratic Left	7
Total	*450*

President: Suleyman Demirel (elected 1993).

THE CABINET

Prime Minister: Prof. Dr. Tansu Ciller (DYP).

Deputy Prime Minister: Murat Karayalçin (SHP).

Minister of Agriculture and Rural Affairs: Refaiddin Sahin.

Minister of Communications: Mehmet Köstepen.

Minister of Culture: D. Fikri Saglar.

Minister of Defence: Mehmet Gölhan.

Minister of Education: Nevzat Ayaz.

Minister of Energy and Natural Resources: Veysel Atasoy.

Minister for the Environment: Riza Akçali.

Minister of Finance and Customs: Ismet Atilla.

Minister of Forestry: Hasan Ekinci.

Minister of Foreign Affairs: Hikmet Cetin.

Minister of Health: Rifat Serdaroglu.

Minister of the Interior: Nahit Mentese.

Minister of Justice: M. Seyfi Oktay.

Minister of Labour and Social Security: Mehmet Mogultay.

Minister of Public Works and Housing: Onur Kumbaracibasi.

Minister of Tourism: Abdulkadir Ates.

Minister of Trade and Industry: M. Tahir Köse.

GEOGRAPHY

Turkey west of the Dardenelles – 5% of the total area – is part of Europe and the city of Istanbul is partly in

Europe and partly in Asia. Asiatic Turkey consists of the central Anatolian Plateau and its basins, bordered to the north by the Pontic Mountains (which adjoin the Black Sea), to the south by the Taurus Mountains (which adjoin the Mediterranean Sea), and to the east in high ranges bordering the Caucasus. Very few of the eastern Aegean islands are included within Turkish boundaries. *Principal rivers:* Euphrates (Firat), Tigris (Dicle), Kizilirmak (Halys), Sakarya. *Highest point*: Büyük Aǧridaǧi (Mount Ararat) 5185 m (17 011 ft). The coastal regions of Turkey have a Mediterranean climate. The interior is continental with hot, dry summers and cold, snowy winters.

ECONOMY

Agriculture involves just under one half of the labour force. Major crops include wheat, rice, tobacco, and cotton. Both tobacco and cotton have given rise to important processing industries, and textiles (including clothing and carpets) account for about one third of Turkey's exports. Manufacturing – in particular the chemical and steel industries – has grown rapidly. Natural resources include copper, coal and chromium. Unemployment is severe. Money sent back by the large number of Turks working in Western Europe – particularly in Germany – is a major source of foreign currency. Tourism is increasingly important and major efforts have been made to promote Turkish Mediterranean resorts. In 1993, however, the future of tourism was overshadowed by attacks by Kurdish terrorists.

Imports (1992)

Sector	% of imports
Machinery	25.7%
Petroleum	11.5%
Cars, lorries, etc.	9.7%
Iron and steel	9.2%
Plastics and rubber	4.3%

Exports (1992)

Sector	% of exports
Cotton, textiles, clothing, etc.	35.0%
Iron and steel and products	10.5%
Dried fruit	5.6%
Leather	3.1%
Tobacco	2.1%

The most recent budgetary figures available are those for 1991.

Revenue	Million TL	% of revenue
Taxation	78 734 000	87%
Other revenue	11 916 000	13%
Total	90 650 000	100%

Expenditure	Million TL	% of expenditure
General public services	34 192 000	26%
Defence	13 783 000	10%
Education	23 294 000	18%
Economic services	33 385 000	25%
Other		21%
Total	10 869	100%

In 1992 Turkey imported goods worth 22 872 million US$ and exported goods worth 14 715 million US$. The

Turkish currency is the lira (TL) which is nominally divided into 100 kurus. In November 1993, the exchange rate was 12 957.8 TL to 1 US$.

Labour force (1991)

Sector	Number employed
Industry	2 722 000
Mining	133 000
Agriculture	9 603 000
Construction	882 000
Public utilities	14 000
Finance, etc.	406 000
Trade	2 104 000
Transport and communications	785 000
Services and administration	2 587 000
Other	1 471 200
Total	20 707 000

RECENT HISTORY

In 1908 the Young Turks revolt attempted to stop the decline of the once-powerful Turkish Ottoman Empire, but defeat in the Balkan Wars (1912–13) virtually expelled Turkey from Europe. Alliance with Germany in World War I ended in defeat and the loss of all non-Turkish areas. The future of Turkey in Asia itself seemed in doubt when Greece took the area around Izmir and the Allies defined zones of influence. General Mustafa Kemal (1881–1938) – later known as Atatürk ('father of the Turks') – led forces of resistance in a civil war and went on to defeat Greece. Turkey's present boundaries were established in 1923 by the Treaty of Lausanne. With the abolition of the sultanate (1922) Turkey became a republic, which Atatürk transformed into a secular Westernized state. Islam was disestablished, Arabic script was replaced by the Latin alphabet, the Turkish language was revived, and women's veils were banned.

Soviet claims on Turkish territory in 1945 encouraged a pro-Western outlook, and in 1952 Turkey joined NATO. PM Adnan Menderes was overthrown by a military coup (1960) and hanged on charges of corruption and unconstitutional rule. Civilian government was restored in 1961, but a pattern of violence and ineffective government led to a further army takeover in 1980. In 1974, after President Makarios was overthrown in Cyprus by a Greek-sponsored coup, Turkey invaded the island and set up a Turkish administration in the north (1975). Differences with Greece over Cyprus have damaged the country's attempts to join the EC, as has the country's record on human rights. In 1983 civilian rule was restored. Since then Turkey has drawn as close as possible to Western Europe. Since the dissolution of the USSR (1991), Turkey has forged economic and cultural links with the former Soviet republics of Central Asia, most of which are Turkic in language and tradition. However, relations with Armenia have been, at best, difficult. Unrest among Turkey's ethnic Kurds – in the southeast – has increased. A Kurdish terrorist movement has been active not only in Turkey, where tourist facilities have been attacked in Kurdish areas, but also in Europe where Turkish diplomatic and other offices have been targets. There has been international criticism of the actions of Turkish forces in containing this violence.

UKRAINE

Official name: Ukraina (The Ukraine).

Member of: UN, CIS, CSCE.

Area: 603 700 km² (233 100 sq mi).

Population: 51 944 000 (1991 est).

Capital: Kiev (Kyiv) 2 616 000 (1990 est).

Other major cities: Kharkov (Kharkiv) 1 618 000, Dnepropetrovsk (Dnipropetrovske) 1 187 000, Donetsk (Donetske) 1 117 000, Odessa (Odesa) 1 106 000, Zaporozhye (Zaporizhia) 891 000, Lvov (Lviv) 798 000, Krivoy Rog (Kryvyi Rih) 717 000, Mariupol 520 000, Mikolaev (formerly Nikolayev) 508 000, Lugansk (Luhansk) 501 000 (1990 est).

Languages: Ukrainian (74%), Russian (22%), Belarussian (2%); see p. 186.

Religions: Orthodox majority – Ukrainian Autocephalous Orthodox (which split from the Russian Orthodox Church after independence) and Russian Orthodox; Ukrainian Uniat (Roman Catholic; thought to be the largest single denomination).

Education: Schooling is compulsory between the ages of seven and 15. There are 10 universities and eight polytechnics.

Defence: Ukraine has a total armed strength of some 230 000 personnel. Russia and Ukraine have still not resolved ownership of the Black Sea fleet. At independence 176 long-range nuclear missiles and 1800 warheads were on Ukrainian soil; Ukraine has not yet ratified the Start-1 nuclear treaty as the country is looking for Western financial aid to dismantle these weapons and for security guarantees against Russian claims on its territory. All Ukrainian males are subject to 18 months conscription.

Transport: There are 247 500 km (154 700 mi) of roads in Ukraine. Ukraine has 22 730 km (14 205 mi) of railway track. The Dnepr is an important inland navigation. The main sea ports are Odessa and Yalta. Kiev, Lvov, Odessa and Chernovtsy have international airports.

Media: There are a dozen major daily papers. A state-run company operates radio and television services.

GOVERNMENT

A 450-member legislature and a President – who appoints a Council of Ministers – are elected for four years by universal adult suffrage. The post of Prime Minister was effectively merged with the presidency in 1993. Unlike the other former Soviet republics, Ukraine has not yet developed party politics on a West European model. The government comprises ex-Communists who have not organized themselves into a new political party although parties in formation include (centre left) New Ukraine, the (nationalist) People's Movement of Ukraine (Rukh), the (conservative) Congress of National Democratic Forces and the Communist Party (reformed in 1993). Crimea is an autonomous republic.

President and Prime Minister: Leonid Kravchuk (elected 1991).

THE CABINET

Deputy Prime Minister and Minister for Agro-Industrial Complexes: Volodymyr Demyanov.

Deputy Prime Minister and Minister for Economic Reform: Viktor Pynzenyk.

Deputy Prime Minister and Minister for Fuel and Energy Complexes: Yuli Ioffe.

Deputy Prime Minister and Minister for Humanitarian Policies: Mykola Zhulynsky.

Deputy Prime Minister and Minister for Industrial Matters: Vasyl Ievtukhov.

Minister for Agro-Industrial Complexes: See above.

Minister of the Cabinet Ministers: Anatoli Lobov.

Minister of Communications: Oleh Prozhyvalsky.

Minister of Culture: Ivan Dzyuba.

Minister of Defence: Col-Gen. Konstantin Morozov.

Minister for Economic Reform: See above.

Minister of Education: Petro Talanchuk.

Minister for the Elimination of the Consequences of the Chernobyl Accident: Heorhi Hotovchits.

Minister for Environmental Protection: Yuri Kostenko.

Minister of Finance: Hrihori Pyatachenko.

Minister of Foreign Affairs: Anatoli Zlenko.

Minister of Foreign Economic Relations: Ivan Herts.

Minister of Forestry: Valeri Samoplavsky.

Minister for Fuel and Energy Complexes: See above.

Minister of Health: Yuri Spizhenko.

Minister for Humanitarian Policies: See above.

Minister for Industrial Matters: See above.

Minister of Industry: Anatoli Holubchenko.

Minister of the Interior: Lieut-Gen. Andrii Vasylyshyn.

Minister of Justice: Vasyl Onopenko.

Minister of Labour: Mykhailo Kaskevych.

Minister for Machine-Building: Viktor Antonov.

Minister of Power and Electrification: Vitali Sklyarov.

Minister of Social Security: Arkadi Yershov.

Minister for Statistics: Mykola Borysenko.

Minister of Transport: Orest Klympush.

Minister of Youth and Sport: Valeri Borzov.

Chairman of the Anti-Monopoly Committee: Oleksandr Zavada.

Chairman of the National Bank: Vadym Hetman.

Chairman of the National Security Service: Col-Gen. Yevhen Marchuk.

Chairman of the State Committee for State Border Defence: Valeri Hubenko.

Chairman of the State Resources Fund: Volodymyr Pryadko.

AUTONOMOUS REPUBLIC

Crimea (Krym) *Area:* 27 000 km² (10 400 sq mi). *Population:* 2 550 000 (1991 est). *Capital:* Simferopol.

GEOGRAPHY

Most of Ukraine – after Russia, the largest country in Europe – comprises plains (steppes), interrupted by low plateaux and basins. The north includes part of the Pripet Marshes; the south is a coastal lowland beside the Black Sea and the Sea of Azov. Central Ukraine comprises the Dnepr Lowland and the Dnepr Plateau, the most extensive upland in the republic. Eastern Ukraine comprises the Don Valley and part of the Central Russian Upland. The most diverse scenery is in the west which includes an extensive lowland and the Carpathian Mountains. The Crimean Peninsula consists of parallel mountain ridges and fertile valleys. *Principal rivers:* Dnepr, Don, Dnestr, Donets, Bug. *Highest point:* Hoverla 2061 m (6762 ft). The Crimean peninsula has a Mediterranean climate. The rest of Ukraine is temperate but becomes more extreme further north and east. Winters are milder and summers are cooler in the west. Rainfall is moderate, usually with a summer maximum.

ECONOMY

Large collectivized farms on the steppes grow cereals, fodder crops and vegetables. Potatoes and flax are important in the north; fruit farming (including grapes and market gardening) is widespread, particularly in the Crimea. Natural resources include iron ore, oil, manganese and rock salt, but the vast Donets coalfield is the principal base of Ukraine's industries. Ukraine has a large iron and steel industry. Other major industries include consumer goods, heavy engineering (railway locomotives, shipbuilding, generators), food processing, and chemicals and chemical equipment. The first steps in privatization have been taken but the economy faces serious difficulties including rampant inflation (80% a month in 1993) and declining industries.

Labour force (1990)

Sector	Number employed
Industry	6 772 000
Agriculture	6 128 000
Construction	1 882 000
Trade	1 753 000
Finace	128 000
Transport and communications	1 732 000
Services and administration	4 401 000
Other	516 000
Total	*24 210 000*

The most recent budgetary figures are 1992 projections.

Revenue	Million roubles	% of revenue
Taxation	270 900	94%
Other receipts	18 400	6%
Total	*289 300*	*100%*

Expenditure	Million roubles	% of expenditure
Defence	17 700	6%
Subsidies	32 621	9%
Government employees	32 600	11%
Education and health	73 300	25%
Social and cultural	33 500	12%
Chernobyl	34 800	12%
Other		25%
Total	*289 300*	*100%*

In 1992 Ukraine replaced the Russian rouble with its own currency, the karbovanets. In November 1993 the exchange rate was 18 230 karbovanetsi to 1 US$. The Ukrainian economy is the least reformed in the former Soviet European bloc. In 1993 large-scale shortages of power, consumer goods and foodstuff were experienced, mainly because of the lack of hard currency to pay for imports from other former Soviet republics. International trade was disrupted and the 1993 trade figures are thought to bear little resemblance to the data given below.

Imports (1990)	
Sector	% of imports
Machines	48.0%
Light industrial goods	30.0%
Chemicals	14.6%
Foodstuffs	10.4%

Exports (1990)	
Sector	% of exports
Machines	39.2%
Iron and steel	16.7%
Foodstuffs	14.6%

RECENT HISTORY

The Ukrainians in Russia took the opportunity afforded by World War I and the Russian Revolution to proclaim independence (January 1918), but a Ukrainian Soviet government was established in Kharkov. Ukraine united with Galicia when the Austro-Hungarian Empire collapsed (November 1918). The new state was invaded by Poland in pursuit of territorial claims and by the Soviet Red Army in support of the Kharkov Soviet. The Red Army prevailed and in 1922 Ukraine became one of the founding republics of the USSR, but the Lvov district of Galicia remained in Polish hands. From 1928, Soviet leader Joseph Stalin instituted purges in Ukraine and a new programme of Russification. After World War II – when Ukraine was occupied by Nazi Germany – Soviet Ukraine was enlarged by the addition of Lvov (from Poland), Bukovina (from Romania), and Ruthenia (from Czechoslovakia), and, finally, Crimea (from Russia) in 1954. Ukrainian nationalism was spurred by the perceived Soviet indifference to Ukraine at the time of the nuclear accident at Chernobyl, N of Kiev, in 1986. Ukrainian politicians responded to the restructuring of the USSR in the late 1980s by seeking increased autonomy. The decision of the republic to declare independence following the abortive coup by Communist hardliners (September 1991) hastened the demise of the USSR. Ukraine gained international recognition in December 1991 when the Soviet Union was dissolved, but tension remained between Moscow and Kiev concerning the status of Crimea, the Black Sea fleet and nuclear weapons based in Ukraine.

YUGOSLAVIA

Official name: Federativna Republika Jugoslavija (The Federal Republic of Yugoslavia).

Member of: UN (suspended), CSCE (suspended).

Area: 102 173 km² (39 449 sq mi).

Population: 10 407 000 (1991 census).

MONTENEGRO (CRNA GORA)

Area: 13 812 km² (5333 sq mi).

Population: 615 000 (1991 census).

Capital: Podgorica (formerly Titograd) 130 000 (city 118 000; 1991 census).

Other main cities: Niksic 75 000, Bar 35 000, Kotor 23 000, Cetinje 15 000 (1991 census).

Languages: Serb (see Serbia, below) (93%), Albanian (7%). The Montenegrin dialect of Serb cannot be regarded as a separate language.

Religions: Orthodox (both Serbian Orthodox and a revived Montenegrin Orthodox Church; nearly 80%), Sunni Islam (19%).

Education: Schooling is compulsory between the ages of seven and 15. There is a university at Podgorica.

Defence: See Serbia (below).

Transport: See Serbia (below).

Media: There are three daily papers. A state-controlled company operates two radio and two TV networks.

Government: A 125-member Assembly and a President are elected by universal adult suffrage. The main political parties are the (former Communist) Democratic Party of Socialists (DPS), the Alliance of Reform Forces and the New Socialist Party of Montenegro.

President: Momir Bulatovic (DPS; elected 1993).

Geography: Ridges of mountains – rising to the Dinaric Alps in the east – occupy most of the country. The few cultivable lowlands include the area around Cetinje and the Zeta lowland. Montenegro's short Adriatic coastline is all that remains of Yugoslavia's coast. *Principal rivers:* Piva, Zeta. *Highest point:* Mt Durmitor 2522 m (8274 ft). Coastal Montenegro has a Mediterranean climate; the interior tends to be more continental with colder winters.

Economy: Agriculture – especially raising livestock – dominates the economy. The land is poor and plots are small and fragmented. Under Yugoslav Communist rule the economy was diversified and iron and steel plants, HEP installations and shipbuilding were developed. The state's economy has been devastated by rampant inflation and international sanctions and Montenegro's lucrative tourist industry no longer exists. See also Economy of Yugoslavia, below.

SERBIA (SRBIJA)

Area: 88 361 km² (34 116 sq mi) including the formerly autonomous provinces of Kosovo (10 817 km² or 4203 sq mi) and Vojvodina (21 508 km² or 8304 sq mi).

Population: 9 791 000 including the formerly autonomous provinces of Kosovo (1 955 000) and Vojvodina (2 013 000) (1991 census). Since 1992, Serb refugees from Bosnia have increased this figure. No reliable figure for the number of refugees is available although most Bosnian Serb refugees in Serbia have resettled in and around Belgrade.

Capital: Belgrade (Beograd) 1 555 000 (city 1 500 000; 1991 census).

Other major cities: Novi Sad 260 000 (city 179 000), Niš 230 000 (city 176 000), Pristina 210 000, Subotica 155 000 (city 100 000), Zrenjanin 81 000, Pancevo 73 000, Smederevo 64 000, Leskovac 62 000 (1991 census).

Languages: Serb – the version of Serbo-Croat written in the Cyrillic alphabet – (73%), Albanian (16%), Hungarian (4%). The number of Hungarian-speakers is diminishing owing to migration.

Religions: Orthodox (over 75%), Sunni Islam (over 12%), small Roman Catholic minority.

Education: Schooling is compulsory between the ages of seven and 15. There are six universities, one of which – in Kosovo – is effectively closed.

Defence: The Yugoslav federal forces have a total armed strength of 135 000. Military service of one year is compulsory.

Transport: There are about 46 020 km (28 595 mi) of roads in Serbia and Montenegro. As not all of the railway lines in the two republics are still operating, no figure for the length of remaining track is available. The Danube in Serbia is a major navigable waterway. Montenegro has a short coastline. Belgrade has an international airport.

Media: There are nearly a dozen principal daily newspapers. A state-controlled company (RTS) broadcasts five radio and three TV networks.

Government: A 250-member National Assembly and a President are elected by universal adult suffrage. Under a new constitution (September 1992), Kosovo and Vojvodina no longer have autonomy. The main political party is the (former Communist) Socialist Party of Serbia (SPS).

President: Slobodan Milosevic (SPS; elected 1992).

Geography: Ridges of mountains occupy the south and centre of the country. In the south the Sar Mountains form a high boundary between Serbia and Macedonia. The north (Vojvodina) is occupied by plains drained by the rivers Danube and Tisa. *Principal rivers:* Danube, Tisa, Morava, Drina. *Highest point:* Titov Vrh 2747 m (9012 ft). Serbia has a continental climate with warm summers and cold snowy winters.

Economy: The economy of Serbia was devastated by international sanctions and rampant inflation in 1992–93. The situation was made worse by the fact that many of Serbia's industrial plants were old and inefficient compared with those in Slovenia and Croatia: before the secession of the latter two republics from Yugoslavia Serbia was effectively subsidized by her northern neighbours. The loss of foreign currency previously earned by the tourist industries of Croatia, Slovenia and Montenegro has also been damaging. See Economy of Yugoslavia, below.

GOVERNMENT OF YUGOSLAVIA

Under the terms of a new federal constitution (April 1992), Yugoslavia consists of two equal republics – Serbia and Montenegro. A Federal Assembly comprises a Chamber of the Republics, which has 40 members (20 elected by each of the two republican parliaments) and a 138-member Chamber of Citizens, which is elected by universal adult suffrage. A Federal President is elected by the Assembly. The President appoints a Prime

Minister and a Council of Ministers but these federal authorities have, in practice, lesser powers than the two republics which have their own legislatures – the Serbian presidency in particular has assumed virtual sovereign powers.

President: Zoran Lilic.
Prime Minister: Radoje Kontic.

ECONOMY OF YUGOSLAVIA

Most of the land is privately owned. Major crops include maize, wheat, sugar beet, grapes, potatoes, citrus fruit and fodder crops for sheep. Industry – which is mainly concentrated around Belgrade – includes food processing, textiles, metallurgy, motor vehicles and consumer goods. The country's economy was severely damaged by the wars in Croatia and Bosnia which began in 1991. The economy was then devastated by rampant inflation – over 20 000% in 1992 rising to 5% an hour in December 1993 – and by international sanctions imposed upon Serbia and Montenegro. The Yugoslav currency is the dinar but no meaningful exchange rate can be given because of rampant inflation. The country's monetary and banking systems and its industrial sector have virtually collapsed. International sanctions have curbed Yugoslavia's trade and living standards have been reduced drastically.

RECENT HISTORY OF YUGOSLAVIA

Both Serbia and Montenegro were recognized as independent in 1878. By the start of the 20th century a Croat national revival within the Habsburg Empire looked increasingly to Serbia to create a South ('Yugo') Slav state. After Serbia gained Macedonia in the Balkan Wars (1912–13), Austria grew wary of Serbian ambitions. The assassination of the Habsburg heir (1914) by a Serb student in Sarajevo provided Austria with an excuse to try to quash Serbian independence. This led directly to World War I and the subsequent dissolution of the Habsburg Empire, whose South Slav peoples united with Serbia and Montenegro in 1918 to form the country known since 1929 as Yugoslavia. Yugoslavia was run as a highly centralized 'Greater Serbia'. The country was wracked by nationalist tensions, and Croat separatists murdered King Alexander in 1934. Attacked and dismembered by Hitler in 1941, Yugoslavs fought the Nazis and each other. The Communist-led partisans of Josip Broz Tito (1892–1980) emerged victorious in 1945, and re-formed Yugoslavia on Soviet lines. Expelled by Stalin from the Soviet bloc in 1948 for failing to toe the Moscow line, the Yugoslav Communists rejected the Soviet model, and pursued policies of decentralization, workers' self-management and non-alignment.

After Tito's death in 1980, the Yugoslav experiment faltered in economic and nationalist crises. The wealthier northern republics of Slovenia and Croatia led the movement towards democracy and Western Europe, while Serbia forcefully resisted the separatist aspirations of Albanian nationalists in Kosovo province. In 1990 the Communists conceded the principle of free elections. By the end of the year, the League of Communists of Yugoslavia had ceased to exist as a national entity, and elections were won by various centre-right, nationalist and regional socialist parties in all the republics except Serbia and Montenegro, where Communist parties won. Serbia exacerbated ethnic Albanian, and (to a much lesser extent) ethnic Hungarian, nationalism by the legal removal of most of the autonomous powers of Kosovo and Vojvodina. In June 1991 Slovenia and Croatia declared independence. Following reverses in a short campaign, Yugoslav federal forces were withdrawn from Slovenia, but Serb insurgents, backed by Yugoslav federal forces, occupied between one third and one quarter of Croatia including Krajina and parts of Slavonia, areas with an ethnic Serb majority.

In 1992 the fierce Serbo-Croat war was halted and a UN peace-keeping force was agreed. The international community recognized the independence of Slovenia and Croatia. When Bosnia-Herzegovina received similar recognition, Bosnian Serbs, encouraged by Serbia, seized 70% of Bosnia, killing or expelling Muslims and Croats in a campaign of 'ethnic cleansing'. Serbia was widely blamed for the continuation of the conflict and – with Montenegro – was subjected to international trade and diplomatic sanctions. The Serb leadership, however, continued to promote the idea of a Greater Serbia which would join the rump Yugoslavia to Serb areas of Croatia (Krajina) and Bosnia-Herzegovina. Serbia and Montenegro formed a new Yugoslav federation but act as virtually independent countries. International peace efforts to end the Bosnian war were attempted in 1993 and tension increased in Kosovo. After the Bosnian Serbs rejected the Owen-Vance peace plan for Bosnia, international pressure upon Serbia to exert influence upon the Bosnian Serbs increased and sanctions upon Yugoslavia were tightened. As the economy collapsed separatism began to grow in Montenegro where the Bosnian conflict was increasingly perceived as a Serbian rather than a Montenegrin concern.

POPULATION

For population statistics of individual Central and East European countries see pp. 143–85. (See also pp. 139–42.)

BIRTH RATE

Country	Birthrate per 1000 population	Year
Czech Republic	12.9	1990
Hungary	12.1	1990
Poland	14.3	1990
Slovakia	13.9	1990
Estonia	14.1	1990
Latvia	14.1	1990
Lithuania	15.3	1990
Belarus	13.9	1990
Moldova	17.7	1990
Russia	13.4	1990
Ukraine	12.7	1990
Albania	24.7	1989
Bulgaria	10.7	1991
Romania	13.6	1990
Turkey	28.0	1991
Bosnia	14.1	1990
Croatia	11.9	1990
Macedonia	16.9	1990
Slovenia	12.5	1990
Yugoslavia	14.6	1990

DEATH RATE

Country	Death rate per 1000 population	Year
Czech Republic	11.7	1990
Hungary	14.0	1990
Poland	10.2	1990
Slovakia	11.7	1990
Estonia	12.3	1990
Latvia	13.0	1990
Lithuania	10.7	1990
Belarus	10.7	1990
Moldova	9.7	1990
Russia	11.2	1990
Ukraine	12.1	1990
Albania	5.7	1989
Bulgaria	12.2	1991
Romania	10.7	1990
Turkey	6.0	1991
Bosnia	n/a	
Croatia	11.4	1990
Macedonia	7.0	1990
Slovenia	9.9	1990
Yugoslavia	9.3	1990

LIFE EXPECTATION (at birth)

Country	Male (years)	Female (years)
Czech Republic	69.9	76.1
Hungary	65.1	73.7
Poland	66.8	75.5
Slovakia	67.9	74.1
Estonia	65.8	75.0
Latvia	64.2	74.6
Lithuania	66.9	76.3
Belarus	63.9	74.7
Moldova	65.2	72.0
Russia	63.9	74.3
Ukraine	66.0	75.0
Albania	72.0	79.0
Bulgaria	68.0	74.7
Romania	66.5	72.4
Turkey	68.0	72.0
Bosnia	n/a	n/a
Croatia	67.0	74.0
Macedonia	68.0	72.0
Slovenia	67.0	75.0
Yugoslavia	68.2	73.2

URBAN AND RURAL POPULATION

Country	Urban	Rural
Czech Republic	68.5%	31.5%
Hungary	61.8%	38.2%
Poland	61.2%	38.8%
Slovakia	62.5%	37.5%
Estonia	71.6%	28.4%
Latvia	71.1%	28.9%
Lithuania	68.0%	32.0%
Belarus	65.5%	34.5%
Moldova	46.9%	53.1%
Russia	73.6%	26.4%
Ukraine	66.9%	33.1%
Albania	35.5%	64.5%
Bulgaria	64.8%	35.2%
Romania	54.4%	45.6%
Turkey	45.9%	54.1%
Bosnia *	36.2%	63.8%
Croatia	50.8%	49.2%
Macedonia	53.9%	46.1%
Slovenia	48.9%	51.1%
Yugoslavia	46.8%	53.2%

* pre-civil war

POPULATION GROWTH

Country	% annual growth
Czech Republic	0.2%
Hungary	- 0.3%
Poland	0.4%
Slovakia	0.4%
Estonia	0.5%
Latvia	0.2%
Lithuania	0.9%
Belarus	0.4%
Moldova	0.6%
Russia	0.5%
Ukraine	0.3%
Albania	1.8%
Bulgaria	0.0%
Romania	0.3%
Turkey	2.2%
Bosnia (pre-civil war)	0.6%
Croatia	0.4%
Macedonia	0.6%
Slovenia	0.4%
Yugoslavia	0.4%

FAMILY SIZE

Country	Average number of children per family
Czech Republic	0.9
Hungary	0.8
Poland	0.9
Slovakia	0.9
Estonia	0.8
Latvia	0.8
Lithuania	0.8
Belarus	0.8
Moldova	1.1
Russia	0.8
Ukraine	0.8
Albania	1.3
Bulgaria	0.7
Romania	n/a
Turkey	2.0
Bosnia	n/a
Croatia	0.7
Macedonia	1.3
Slovenia	0.7
Yugoslavia	0.9

LARGEST CITIES OF CENTRAL AND EASTERN EUROPE

City	Country	Date of census estimate	Details	Population
Moscow	Russia	1989	with suburbs	8 967 000
Istanbul	Turkey	1990	with suburbs	6 620 000
St Petersburg	Russia	1989	with suburbs	5 020 000
Kiev	Ukraine	1990	with suburbs	2 616 000
Bucharest	Romania	1992	(city 2 064 000)	2 325 000
Budapest	Hungary	1992	with suburbs	1 992 000
Warsaw	Poland	1990	with suburbs	1 656 000
Minsk	Belarus	1989	with suburbs	1 618 000
Kharkov	Ukraine	1990	with suburbs	1 611 000
Katowice	Poland	1990	(city 367 000)	1 604 000
Belgrade	Yugoslavia	1991	(city 1 500 000)	1 555 000
Nizhny Novgorod	Russia	1989	formerly Gorky; with suburbs	1 438 000
Samara	Russia	1989	formerly Kuybyshev; with suburbs	1 257 000
Sofia	Bulgaria	1990	with suburbs	1 221 000
Prague	Czech Republic	1991	with suburbs	1 212 000
Dnepropetrovsk	Ukraine	1990	with suburbs	1 187 000
Donetsk	Ukraine	1990	with suburbs	1 117 000
Odessa	Ukraine	1990	with suburbs	1 106 000
Kazan	Russia	1989	with suburbs	1 094 000
Perm	Russia	1989	with suburbs	1 091 000
Ufa	Russia	1989	with suburbs	1 083 000
Rostov	Russia	1989	with suburbs	1 020 000
Volgograd	Russia	1989	with suburbs	999 000
Zagreb	Croatia	1991	(city 707 000)	934 000

LINGUISTIC COMPOSITION OF THE POPULATION

Czech Republic
Czech 94%
Slovak 4% German 1% Polish 1%

Hungary
Magyar 97%
German 2% Slovak 1%

Poland
Polish 99%
Ukrainian 0.5% German 0.5% (or others 1%)

Slovakia
Slovak 87%
Magyar 12% Czech 1%

Estonia
Estonian 63%
Russian 31% Ukrainian 3% Belarussian 2% Finnish 1%

Latvia
Lettish 53%
Russian 34% Belarussian 5% Ukrainian 4% Polish 2% Lithuanian 1% German 1%

Lithuania
Lithuanian 81%
Russian 10% Polish 7% Belarussian 2%

Belarus
Belarussian 80%
Russian 13% Polish 4% Ukrainian 3%

Moldova
Romanian 67%
Ukrainian 13% Russian 13% Gagauz 4% Bulgarian 2% others 1%

Russia
Russian 83%
Tatar 4% Ukrainian 3% Chuvash 1% Bashkir 1% Belarussian 1% Chechen 1% others 6%

Ukraine
Ukrainian 74%
Russian 22% Belarussian 2% Romanian 1% Polish 1%

Albania
Albanian 98%
Greek 2%

Bulgaria
Bulgarian 89%
Turkish 9% Macedonian 2%

Romania
Romanian 89%
Magyar 10% German 1%

Turkey
Turkish 86%
Kurdish 10% Arabic 2% others 2%

Bosnia
Serbo-Croat 96%
(divided into Bosnian Muslim 44%, Serb 33%, Croat 17%)   others 4%

Croatia
Croat 75%
Serb 23% Magyar 1% others 1%

Macedonia
Macedonian 67%
Albanian 20% Turkish 5% Serb 6% others 2%

Slovenia
Slovene 91%
Croat 3% Serb 3% Magyar 1% others 2%

Yugoslavia
Serb 80% (including Montenegrin)
Albanian 13% Magyar 4% Croat 2% others 1%

ECONOMY

For information on the economies of individual countries of Central and East Europe see pp. 143–83. (See also pp. 140–42.)

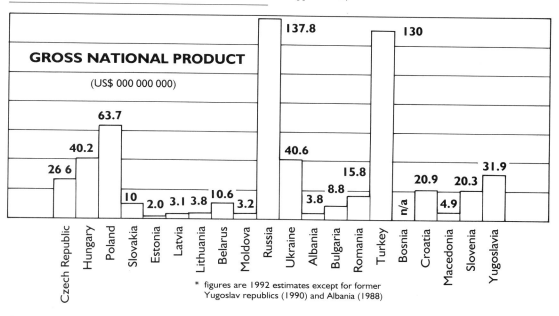

GROSS NATIONAL PRODUCT

(US$ 000 000 000)

Czech Republic	26 6
Hungary	40.2
Poland	63.7
Slovakia	10
Estonia	2.0
Latvia	3.1
Lithuania	3.8
Belarus	10.6
Moldova	3.2
Russia	137.8
Ukraine	40.6
Albania	3.8
Bulgaria	8.8
Romania	15.8
Turkey	130
Bosnia	n/a
Croatia	20.9
Macedonia	4.9
Slovenia	20.3
Yugoslavia	31.9

* figures are 1992 estimates except for former Yugoslav republics (1990) and Albania (1988)

IMPORTS AND EXPORTS				
Country	Imports US$ million	Exports US$ million	Year	Major trading partners
Czech Republic	6 970	7 600	1990	Germany, Austria, Slovakia
Hungary	11 532	10 301	1991	Germany, Austria, Italy
Poland	14 261	14 460	1991	Germany, Russia, UK
Slovakia	2 990	3 260	1990	Czech Rep., Ukraine, Germany
Estonia	380	310	1991*	Russia, Germany, Finland
Latvia	635	560	1991*	Russia, Belarus, Germany
Lithuania	870	1230	1991*	Russia, Poland, Germany
Belarus	4 000	3 820	1991*	Russia, Ukraine, Germany
Moldova	645	610	1991*	Russia, Ukraine, Romania
Russia	4 780	4 160	1991*	Germany, Ukraine, Kazakhstan
Ukraine	6 310	5 100	1991*	Russia, Germany, Spain
Albania	446	267	1990	Italy, Germany, Czech Rep.
Bulgaria	12 893	13 347	1990	Russia, Germany, Italy
Romania	5 600	4 124	1991	Germany, Russia, Italy
Turkey	20 019	13 603	1991	Germany, USA, Italy
Bosnia	n/a			
Croatia	4 430	2 910	1990	Germany, Italy, Austria
Macedonia	1 120	580	1990	Bulgaria, Turkey, Yugoslavia¹
Slovenia	4 720	4 150	1990	Germany, Italy, France
Yugoslavia	in May 1992 UN sanctions on Yugoslavia restricted trade to food and medicines			

* estimates   ¹ before UN sanctions were imposed upon Yugoslavia (Serbia and Montenegro) in May 1992 over 60% of Macedonia's trade was with Yugoslavia.

AGRICULTURE

BARLEY

Country	Tonnes p.a.
Russia	28 000 000
Ukraine	14 000 000
Turkey	8 000 000
Poland	4 100 000
Romania	3 100 000

MAIZE

Country	Tonnes p.a.
Romania	9 200 000
Hungary	4 500 000
Ukraine	4 000 000
Turkey	2 000 000

POTATOES

Country	Tonnes p.a.
Russia	38 000 000
Poland	36 300 000
Ukraine	16 700 000
Belarus	11 100 000
Romania	7 600 000
Turkey	4 100 000

SUGAR BEET

Country	Tonnes p.a.
Ukraine	44 000 000
Russia	33 900 000
Poland	15 200 000
Turkey	12 500 000
Romania	7 000 000
Hungary	5 000 000

WHEAT

Country	Tonnes p.a.
Russia	47 500 000
Ukraine	27 000 000
Turkey	20 000 000
Poland	8 600 000
Romania	8 000 000
Hungary	6 200 000

CATTLE

Country	Number
Russia	60 000 000
Ukraine	25 200 000
Turkey	11 600 000
Poland	10 600 000
Belarus	7 200 000
Romania	7 200 000

SHEEP

Country	Number
Russia	62 000 000
Turkey	31 500 000
Romania	19 000 000
Ukraine	9 000 000
Bulgaria	8 000 000
Poland	4 300 000

PIGS

Country	Number
Russia	39 200 000
Ukraine	20 000 000
Turkey	19 800 000
Romania	15 500 000
Hungary	7 700 000
Belarus	5 200 000
Czech Republic	4 400 000

AGRICULTURAL LAND USE

Country	Land under crops	Pasture	Woods and other
Czech Republic	90%	9%	1%
Hungary	61%	14%	25%
Poland	78%	21%	1%
Slovakia	60%	39%	1%
Estonia	78%	21%	1%
Latvia	68%	32%	-
Lithuania	67%	32%	1%
Belarus	65%	33%	2%
Moldova	68%	12%	20%
Russia	61%	37%	2%
Ukraine	80%	16%	4%
Albania	64%	35%	1%
Bulgaria	75%	26%	1%
Romania	77%	22%	1%
Turkey	85%	7%	5%
Bosnia	44%	55%	1%
Croatia	50%	48%	2%
Macedonia	46%	53%	1%
Slovenia	35%	64%	1%
Yugoslavia	65%	34%	1%

INDUSTRY, ENERGY AND MINERALS

CEMENT

Country	Tonnes p.a.
Russia	84 500 000
Turkey	24 000 000
Ukraine	23 400 000
Romania	13 200 000
Poland	12 600 000

CARS

Country	Number p.a.
Poland	265 000
Czech Republic	180 000
Russia	135 000
Turkey	120 000

CRUDE STEEL

Country	Tonnes p.a.
Russia	94 000 000
Ukraine	57 000 000
Poland	13 600 000
Romania	13 000 000
Turkey	7 500 000
Czech Republic	6 000 000

TELEVISION SETS

Country	Numbers p.a.
Russia	6 000 000
Belarus	1 100 000
Poland	650 000
Romania	480 000
Hungary	450 000

BAUXITE

Country	Tonnes p.a.
Russia	5 800 000
Yugoslavia	2 500 000
Hungary	2 400 000
Croatia	310 000
Romania	270 000

IRON ORE

Country	Tonnes p.a.
Ukraine	66 300 000
Russia	60 500 000
Turkey	3 000 000

The minerals that are exploited to provide energy are among the most important. Coal, natural gas and oil dominate, although lignite (brown coal) assumes local importance. Russia is by far the greatest producer of energy sources in Eastern and Central Europe, although Ukraine and Poland are also major producers of coal. *Note:* The totals given below for Russia include production east of the Urals, that is in Asia.

COAL

Country	Tonnes p.a.
Russia	415 000 000
Ukraine	155 000 000
Poland	148 000 000
Czech Republic	22 000 000
Turkey	6 000 000

The principal coal fields of Eastern and Central Europe are the Donets coalfield of Ukraine and the Silesia-Ostrava coalfield which straddles the border between Poland and the Czech Republic.

NATURAL GAS

Country	Terajoules
Russia	21 700 000
Ukraine	3 000 000
Romania	1 200 000
Hungary	200 000

The Ukrainian natural gasfield is one of the most important in Eastern Europe. The bulk of Russia's production comes from Asiatic Russia beyond the Urals although there are important fields near Samara and in the lower Volga valley.

OIL

Country	Tonnes p.a.
Russia	569 000 000
Romania	8 000 000 000
Turkey	4 000 000
Ukraine	3 000 000
Hungary	2 000 000
Croatia	2 000 000
Yugoslavia	1 100 000

The Russian oilfield near Perm is the largest in Eastern Europe. Other major fields are to be found in northern European Russia, near Samara (Russia) and the Ploiesti fields of Romania.

ELECTRICITY

Country	kwh
Russia	1 300 000 000 000
Ukraine	298 000 000 000
Poland	136 000 000 000
Romania	64 300 000 000
Turkey	60 500 000 000
Czech Republic	51 000 000 000
Belarus	39 500 000 000
Yugoslavia	39 400 000 000
Bulgaria	38 900 000 000
Hungary	29 700 000 000
Lithuania	29 200 000 000
Slovakia	24 000 000 000
Estonia	17 600 000 000
Moldova	15 700 000 000
Bosnia-Herzegovina*	14 600 000 000
Slovenia	12 400 000 000
Croatia	8 700 000 000
Macedonia	5 800 000 000
Latvia	5 800 000 000
Albania	4 000 000 000

* much of Bosnia's capacity has been destroyed since 1992.

INDEX